- Includes a website with **online quizzes, assessment of key concepts, Video Skillbuilders,** and **news feeds** so you aren't always stuck in the book

- Has a design that is sleek, friendly, and easy to use. Think BMW, but in paper form. OK, bad analogy. Really though, it looks nice.

And that's only the beginning. To help get the material across and make it easier for you, each chapter includes Check Point Questions, a Marginal Glossary that gives you definitions right when you need them, Terms to Know at the beginning of chapters, Marginal Icons that link you to web content, and a Learning Objectives Review so you know what's going to be covered.

Oh yeah, and the website is very cool.
It's got **Video Skillbuilders, online quizzes, assessment of key concepts,** and **news feeds.** Get a better handle on concepts like taking notes, reading textbooks, and taking tests, by watching real students in the Video Skillbuilders. If you're like me and learn better from visual information, you'll love this website . . . . !!!

website:
www.college.
cengage.com
/pic/WongESS6e

Some Last Things
--> -> Before the Fun Begins

So what you end up with is a text that is well organized, easy to read, and maybe, just maybe, even enjoyable to use. It's been tailor-made to include the type of things you want so that studying (and your grade) come easier. When students were asked to compare a chapter from this book to another, they responded overwhelmingly in favor of this one.

So that's it. You can quit reading this and start using a book that's easier and more enjoyable. Yes, you still have to read it, but hey, at least students like you helped design it.

Greg

Essential Study Skills

Essential Study Skills
Sixth Edition

Linda Wong

WADSWORTH
CENGAGE Learning™

Australia • Brazil • Japan • Korea • Mexico • Singapore • Spain • United Kingdom • United States

Essential Study Skills, Sixth Edition
Linda Wong

Executive Publisher: Pat Coryell

Sponsoring Editor: Shani B. Fisher

Marketing Manager: Edwin Hill

Discipline Product Manager: Giuseppina Daniel

Development Editor: Julia Giannotti

Senior Project Editor: Nancy Blodget

Senior Media Producer: Philip Lanza

Content Manager: Janet Edmonds

Art and Design Manager: Jill Haber

Cover Design Director: Tony Saizon

Senior Photo Editor: Jennifer Meyer Dare

Senior Composition Buyer: Chuck Dutton

New Title Project Manager: Patricia O'Neill

Editorial Assistant: Amanda Nietzel

Marketing Assistant: Bettina Chiu

Editorial Assistant: Jill Clark

Cover Image Credits

Headphones: ©Johan Ramberg/iStockphoto

Young Man Carrying File Folders: ©Ant Strack/ CORBIS

Index Card: ©Christine Balderas/iStockphoto

Desk Image: ©Izvorinka Rankovic/iStockphoto

Student Choice Logo: Trevor Hunt/iStockphoto

Pages 147–149: Excerpt from "Stand and Deliver" by Maia Szalavitz, *Psychology Today*, August 2003, pp. 50–54. Reprinted with permission from *Psychology Today* magazine, Copyright © 2003 Sussex Publishers, LLC.

For product information and technology assistance, contact us at
Cengage Learning Customer & Sales Support, 1-800-354-9706

For permission to use material from this text or product, submit all requests online at **www.cengage.com/permissions**
Further permissions questions can be emailed to
permissionrequest@cengage.com

Library of Congress Control Number: 2007938676

ISBN-13: 978-0-547-04871-0

ISBN-10: 0-547-04871-8

Wadsworth
20 Channel Center Street
Boston, MA 02210
USA

Cengage Learning is a leading provider of customized learning solutions with office locations around the globe, including Singapore, the United Kingdom, Australia, Mexico, Brazil, and Japan. Locate your local office at **international.cengage.com/region**

Cengage Learning products are represented in Canada by Nelson Education, Ltd.

To learn more about Wadsworth, visit **www.cengage.com/wadsworth**

Purchase any of our products at your local college store or at our preferred online store **www.ichapters.com**

Printed in the United States of America
5 6 7 11 10 09

Brief Contents

Contents

CHAPTER 8

LEARNING FROM COLLEGE TEXTBOOKS   210

CHAPTER 9

DEVELOPING NOTETAKING SKILLS   250

CHAPTER 10

LISTENING AND TAKING LECTURE NOTES   282

Preface

Essential Study Skills, 6e, is a redesigned study skills textbook that is both instructor-friendly and student-friendly in its approach to presenting learning theories and strategies that enhance classroom instruction and student performance. As you examine the Sixth Edition, you will discover a sharper focus and emphasis on *essential* study skills, which resulted in a reduced page count for the textbook. You will also notice many exciting features that reinforce objective-based learning. The process of redesigning *Essential Study Skills,* 6e, began by redefining essential topics for chapters and then identifying specific learning objectives for each chapter. The challenge then turned to identifying major headings that linked directly to each learning objective and matching all subheadings and chapter features to the major heading and the learning objective. The redesigning of *Essential Study Skills* resulted in a powerful new textbook format that includes the following:

- A direct, step-by-step approach based on metacognitive learning strategies
- Sets of learning objectives and strategies that enable students to assume responsibility for their own learning and emphasize students' roles in monitoring, adjusting, strengthening, and tailoring their study strategies to improve academic performance
- A concise, to-the-point, succinct student-friendly format that uses easy-to-grasp bulleted points, marginal notes to highlight key concepts and terminology, and self-assessment tools to monitor understanding and reinforce learning
- A wealth of resources for students to master the textbook content
- Extensive resources for instructors to use to create a dynamic, engaging, and highly effective study skills course
- An instructional approach that instructors can modify and implement in a manner best suited to their instructional styles, students' needs and skill levels, and instructor course schedules

▶ OVERVIEW

Essential Study Skills, 6e, is a textbook appropriate for all post-secondary students interested in learning powerful study strategies to increase academic performance. This textbook empowers students with versatile, practical, and powerful strategies to use, as well as with support materials to reinforce essential study skills. Before beginning your adventure teaching your course with this textbook, familiarize yourself with the following materials and resources:

- The textbook chapters and topics
- The textbook features used in each chapter
- Appendices A, B, and C in the back of the textbook
- The Digital Instructor Resource Manual (IRM) available online
- The Instructor Website for this textbook

▌ The Student Website for this textbook

▌ The Eduspace course materials available for online or hybrid courses

▌ The Diploma Testing CD-ROM to create quizzes, tests, midterm and final exams

▶ Transitioning from the Fifth Edition to the Sixth Edition

The new format adds an exciting new dimension to teaching the essential study skills included in the Fifth Edition. Instructors who use the Fifth Edition of *Essential Study Skills* will find an easy transition to the Sixth Edition as the familiar course content has been preserved even though it may be reorganized under new chapter titles or headings. For a comprehensive explanation of changes in chapters and content, go to the Instructor Website and click on *Transitioning from the Fifth Edition to the Sixth Edition*. Following are highlights of changes for the Sixth Edition:

▌ One easy-to-understand, updated, contemporary Information Processing Model is presented as the foundation for essential study skills strategies used throughout the textbook. (Chapter 2)

▌ A new chapter is dedicated solely to understanding the Twelve Principles of Memory and their applications. (Chapter 3)

▌ Time management and goal setting, two sets of skills that go hand-in-hand, now appear together in one chapter. (Chapter 4)

▌ A new chapter on self-management skills covers four essential sets of skills: concentration, motivation, procrastination, and stress. (Chapter 5)

▌ Reading skills have been revised and regrouped into two chapters. Chapter 7 focuses on strengthening reading skills by surveying, understanding paragraph elements, and developing vocabulary strategies. Chapter 8 presents two new reading strategies in addition to the SQ4R reading system.

▌ New reading skills include learning from graphic materials and reading in the content areas. (Chapter 8)

▌ Annotating textbooks appears with four additional textbook notetaking systems. (Chapter 9)

▌ Index card notes appears with three additional forms of visual notetaking systems students can use to take notes or create study tools. (Chapter 10)

▌ Appendix A provides students with answer keys for all Chapter Profiles, Check Points, and Chapter Review Questions.

▌ Appendix B provides new ready-to-use inventories and assessment checklists for students.

▌ Appendix C includes the longer excerpts used for chapter exercises and excerpts that can be used to practice or reinforce other textbook skills.

▌ Instructors will also encounter new exercises, new student-oriented features, new instructional transparencies and PowerPoint slides, and detailed step-by-step instructions in the Digital Instructor Resource Manual to facilitate the process of transitioning to the Sixth Edition.

▶ CHAPTER FEATURES

STUDENT-ORIENTED FEATURES CONTINUE IN THE SIXTH EDITION

Instructors who have used previous editions of *Essential Study Skills* will find many familiar features continue to be an essential part of this student-oriented textbook:

▌ *Terms to Know* listed at the beginning of each chapter identify the key terms to learn.

▌ *Chapter Profiles* provide students with a self-correcting series of ten questions to assess their current attitudes and behaviors. Before beginning to work with a new chapter, students complete the profiles and record their responses on the Master Profile Chart in Appendix A. To show progress and changes made through the course of the term, students complete the profiles again at the end of the term. Students may also complete and receive their Profile scores online at the Student Website. Profile questions link to chapter objectives.

▌ *Essential Strategies Charts* appear throughout each chapter to highlight essential strategies presented in the chapter. The Essential Strategies Charts provide students with an overview of essential skills and a quick reference tool for reinforcing skills.

▌ *Case Studies* appear in every chapter. Two textbook case studies and four online case studies present students with real-life student situations to analyze. Students then suggest strategies from the chapter to use to solve the case-study problems or increase student performance. Students may respond on paper or online with the option to print or e-mail their responses directly to their instructors.

▌ *Reflective Writing Assignments* provide students with opportunities to personalize the chapter content, discuss their current skills and attitudes, and integrate the chapter's skills with other study skills and personal experiences. Students can respond to the two Reflective Writing Assignments on paper, in journals, or online with the option to print or e-mail their responses directly to their instructors.

▌ *Group Processing: A Collaborative Learning Activity* in each chapter provides a small-group activity that enhances student interest; creates a forum for student interaction through brainstorming, discussion, and cooperative work; and promotes critical thinking skills.

▌ *Student Exercises* to practice and reinforce skills appear throughout each chapter. These exercises may be used as homework assignments, for class discussions, or for small-group activities in the classroom. Exercises include excerpts from multiple disciplines, including social science and science. Instead of using or assigning all of the exercises in each chapter, instructors may select the exercises that are best suited for their students.

▌ *Links Exercises* connect content in the chapter to skills, concepts, and excerpts presented in previous chapters. These exercises promote the integration of key concepts and strategies that lay the foundation for effective learning.

▌ *Online Practices* refer students to the Student Website for interactive, self-correcting exercises that reinforce the strategies and the concepts in the chapter and provide students with valuable feedback for each question. The Online Practices are nongraded, enrichment exercises that help students hone their test-taking skills.

▌ ***Online ACE Practice Tests*** refer students to the Student Website. Four Online Practice tests are available for each chapter. Practice Test 1 consists of ten fill-in-the-blank questions to review chapter terminology. Practice Test 2 consists of ten true-false questions. Practice Test 3 consists of ten multiple-choice questions. Practice Tests 1, 2, and 3 are scored online. Practice Test 4 provides students with response boxes to write answers to two short-answer questions. Students may print or e-mail their responses to their instructor.

▌ ***Chapter Review Questions*** at the end of each chapter provide students with a tool to assess their understanding and recall of essential concepts, skills, and strategies discussed in the chapter. *New for the Sixth Edition:* Answer keys for the Chapter Review Questions now appear in Appendix A.

NEW CHAPTER FEATURES

Refer to the section "To the Student" for information about new chapter features.

▶ NEW INSTRUCTOR RESOURCES FOR THE SIXTH EDITION

▌ ***Chapter Tests*** are available online on the Instructor Website in a password-protected file. Chapter tests consist of fifteen true-false questions (15 points), five fill-in-the-blank questions (5 points), ten multiple-choice questions (10 points), and four short-answer questions (20 points). Each test is ready to print for immediate classroom use. Instructors may use the Diploma Testing CD-ROM Test Bank to modify or create new tests.

▌ ***Diploma Testing CD-ROM*** provides fifty additional true-false questions, fifteen additional fill-in-the-blank questions, twenty-five additional multiple-choice questions, and five additional short-answer questions to use to modify existing tests or to create new chapter tests, midterms, and final exams.

▌ ***Eduspace***, Cengage Learning's online learning tool powered by Blackboard, provides text-specific online course content. In addition to a handy gradebook and other course-management tools, the *Essential Study Skills* Eduspace course includes interactive components developed specifically for the Eduspace course: Threaded Discussions, Chapter Exercises, Homework Assignments, Reflective Writing Assignments, Case Studies, Chapter Tests, a Master Profile Inventory, and other materials. Contact your sales rep for more information.

THE ONLINE INSTRUCTOR'S RESOURCE MANUAL

Offered online, the Instructor's Resource Manual includes the following content:

▌ Part 1 of the Instructor's Resource Manual provides you with suggestions for planning your course, selecting instructional materials to use, assessing student performance, recording student progress, and incorporating website materials into your instructional approach.

▌ Part 2 of this IRM is organized chapter by chapter. For each chapter you will find chapter objectives, an expanded chapter outline, a list of suggested reading assignments, a list of textbook activities and exercises, a list of student website activities, two lists of available transparency masters, a list of resources on the instructor website, and step-by-step teaching tips and answer keys.

THE INSTRUCTOR WEBSITE

The *Essential Study Skills,* 6e, Instructor Website is password protected. All of the instructor materials (with the exception of the Diploma Testing CD) are available online for quick downloading. Following are materials located on the Instructor Website:

▮ The Instructor Resource Manual

▮ A complete list of Concept Checks with teaching suggestions

▮ Expanded chapter outlines

▮ Transparency masters and PowerPoint slides

▮ Enrichment and Learning Option activities

▮ Rubrics for grading

▮ Ready-to-use chapter tests, a midterm exam, and a final exam

 When you see this icon, check out the accompanying website for additional material and resources relating to a chapter topic.

To access the Instructor Website, go to the following website and click on INSTRUCTORS:

http://college.cengage.com/pic/wongESS6e

► DEDICATION

The Sixth Edition of *Essential Study Skills* is dedicated to my son, Kailee Wong, who continuously pursues new learning opportunities and who exemplifies the characteristics of a life-long learner. This edition is also dedicated to Daniel L. Hodges, Ph.D., former director of assessment and testing at Lane Community College in Eugene, Oregon, for his insightful contributions, valuable feedback, and expertise in the areas of educational psychology and research-based learning strategies. He exemplifies the characteristics of a true educator whose interest in student success does not cease upon retirement.

► ACKNOWLEDGMENTS

My appreciation is extended to the following reviewers who contributed valuable ideas to further strengthen the effectiveness of this textbook and create a textbook that is instructor-friendly and student-friendly. Thank you all for your contributions.

Karen Becker, Youngstown State University, OH
Jacqueline T. Cohen, Augusta State University, GA
Karen Fenske, Kishwaukee College, IL
Marie Gore, University of Maryland
Phyllis Guthrie, Tarleton State University, TX

Leslie King, SUNY Oswego
Patricia Malinowski, Finger Lakes Community College, NY
Joel McGee, Texas A&M University
Jaseon Outlaw, Arizona State University
Allison Parry, Capilano College, Canada
Anna Shiplee, University of West Florida
Holly Smith, Lake City Community College, FL
Kathleen Wagner, Purdue University, IN
Susan Wickman, Des Moines Area Community College, IA
Craig Winchell, Louisiana State University

I stand up and loudly applaud the outstanding editorial and production staff that has worked diligently with me through all the phases of redesigning Essential Study Skills into its new format and creating the wealth of resource materials that are now available for both instructors and students. All the attention to details, coordination, and teamwork happened because of their dedication and commitment to quality. Thank you!

To the Student

Essential Study Skills, Sixth Edition, is designed to provide you with an array of study skills strategies that will unlock your learning potential and empower you with the essential skills to monitor and modify your learning strategies and improve your academic performance. Reading the following section carefully provides you with valuable information that explains how to get the most out of *Essential Study Skills,* 6e.

 ## STARTING THE TERM

As soon as you purchase this book, begin familiarizing yourself with the textbook. Read through this introductory section carefully and examine the contents that appear at the end of the textbook: Appendix A, B, and C, and the index.

Essential Study Skills, 6e, has a comprehensive Student Website to enhance your learning experience and strengthen your understanding of course materials. Go to the Student Website to familiarize yourself with the resources available to assist you throughout the term. Read and complete the optional Quick Start Checklist, which is a step-by-step process to organize the beginning of the term and prepare you for your many upcoming successes.

 When you see this icon, check out the accompanying website for additional material and resources relating to a chapter topic.

To access the Student Website, go to the following website and click on STUDENTS:

http://college.cengage.com/pic/wongESS6e

As you explore the Student Website, familiarize yourself with the following materials:

- The Quick Start Checklist
- Interactive Visual Mapping of key chapter topics
- Studying from the Expanded Chapter Outline
- Studying the "Terms to Know"
- Using the Concept Checks
- The online flashcards and the online glossary
- The chapter profile, Reflective Writing assignments, textbook and online case studies, and chapter exercises under Improve Your Grade
- The self-correcting Online Practices (immediately scored online)
- Online Topic In-Depth materials
- Four online ACE Practice Tests

▶ STARTING EACH CHAPTER

Surveying is an effective study strategy that provides you with an overview of a chapter before you begin the process of careful reading. Surveying familiarizes you with the topic, creates a mindset for studying, and prepares your memory to receive new information. Use the following steps for surveying a new chapter:

1. Read the ***Chapter Objectives*** that list learning goals or objectives for the chapter. The chapter objectives clearly indicate the skills you will learn and will be able to demonstrate when you finish studying the chapter.

2. Read through the ***Chapter Outline*** for an overview of the organization and content of the chapter.

3. Read through the ***Terms to Know*** that lists the course-specific terminology that you will learn to define.

4. Complete the ***Chapter Profile*** before continuing to survey the chapter. This is not a graded assignment; answer the questions honestly. The profiles are designed to examine your current attitude and habits in specific skill areas. These scores will be compared to end-of-the-term scores to show your progress and growth. You can complete the profile and have it scored online on the Student Website.

5. Survey or skim through the chapter by reading all of the bold ***headings*** and ***subheadings***. Notice the kind of information that appears in the margins next to the paragraphs.

6. Read the ***Learning Objectives Review*** at the end of the chapter. Key points for each of the objectives provide you with additional insights about the content of the chapter.

7. Read through, but do not answer, the ***Chapter Review Questions***. Plan to answer these questions after you have read the chapter carefully. For immediate feedback, you will be able to check your answers with the answer keys in Appendix A.

▶ USING CHAPTER FEATURES

In addition to the chapter features previously mentioned, the following chapter features are designed to increase your comprehension and reinforce key concepts and skills in each chapter. Using these features consistently facilitates the process of mastering the concepts and skills in the chapter.

▐ ***Definitions*** in the margins provide a quick view of key terminology and definitions to learn. Review these definitions when you study for tests.

▐ ***Concept Checks*** in the margins provide you with study questions to assess your comprehension and promote critical thinking skills. For each Concept Check, answer the questions on paper, mentally, or out loud to yourself. At times, your instructor may ask you to use written responses. Return to these questions when you prepare for tests.

▐ ***Check Points*** in each chapter provide you with a short assessment tool to check your comprehension of information presented under each main heading in the chapter. Answer keys in Appendix A provide you with immediate feedback.

▌ *Exercises* appear throughout each chapter. Your instructor will assign some, but usually not all, of the exercises in the chapter. You will notice that the shorter exercises appear within the textbook chapter, and the longer exercises appear in Appendix B or Appendix C. For practice and enrichment, you may complete any of the exercises that your instructor does not assign as homework or use as a class activity.

▌ *Case Studies* are exercises that describe student situations or problems. After reading a case study, identify the key issues or problems that are presented in the case study. Answer the question at the end of each case study by providing specific answers or suggestions that deal with the problem. Use specific strategies and terminology from the chapter in your answers. Case studies use open-ended questions, meaning there are many possible answers. They can be completed on paper or online at the Student Website for this textbook.

▌ *Online Exercises* are textbook exercises that you may also complete online at the Student Website. You will have the option of printing your responses or e-mailing them to your instructor.

▌ *Online Practices* consist of interactive, self-correcting exercises that provide you with additional practice and reinforcement of the skills in the chapter. You can complete these practices as many times as you wish. You will receive feedback and brief explanations with each answer.

▌ *Essential Strategy Charts* appear in every chapter. These charts highlight key strategies to use to improve the way you study, process information, and master course content. Applying the essential strategies in these charts will increase your performance and academic success. Refer to these charts when you want to brush up on essential study skills or review for tests.

▌ *Chapter Review Questions* provide you with practice test questions to assess your memory or recall of chapter concepts and key terms. Complete the Chapter Review Questions without referring to your textbook pages or your notes. Check your answers with the answer keys in Appendix A.

▌ *Online ACE Practice Tests* provide you with the opportunity to review chapter concepts and prepare for tests. ACE Tests 1, 2, and 3 are interactive and self-correcting. ACE Test 4 with two short-answer questions requires a written response that you can print or e-mail to your instructor.

▶ A Note to You from the Author

Your goal is not to learn *about* study skills, but to learn *to use* powerful study skills to consistently achieve your goals and experience success. Learning is a lifelong process. Each time you are faced with a new learning situation—whether at school, at home, or at work—you can draw upon the skills you have learned in this textbook. By applying the skills of time management, goal setting, concentration, processing information, strengthening memory, reading comprehension, test-taking, and an array of additional strategies in this textbook, you will be prepared to experience the rewards of success . . . again and again and again. May my commitment to you, belief in you, and support of you in the learning process be reflected in the pages of this textbook.

—*Linda Wong*

Essential Study Skills

1 Discovering and Using Your Learning Styles

LEARNING OBJECTIVES

1 ▶ *Identify your preferred cognitive learning style and describe learning strategies you can use to utilize your preferred learning style and strengthen your other modalities.*

2 ▶ *Identify your linear- or global-learner tendency and discuss how it affects the way you process information.*

Chapter Outline

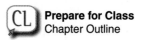 **Prepare for Class**
Chapter Outline

3 ▶ *Define the term* intelligences *and describe the common characteristics of each of Howard Gardner's eight intelligences.*

Understanding your individual style of learning can help you become a more effective learner. In this chapter, you will examine your preference for using your visual, auditory, or kinesthetic cognitive learning style (modality) for learning new information. You will learn to use multisensory study and learning strategies that are compatible with your learning preferences. You will gain additional insights about your learning preferences as you identify yourself as a global or linear learner. Finally, you will learn about the eight intelligences that you already possess. Through this process of understanding more about yourself as a learner, you will quickly discover that you already have many skills and abilities that will contribute to your college success.

CHAPTER 1 PROFILE

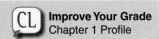

Improve Your Grade
Chapter 1 Profile

Discovering and Using Your Learning Styles

ANSWER each profile question honestly. Your answers should reflect what you do, not what you wish to do. Check YES if you do the statement always or most of the time. Check NO if you do the statement seldom or never.

SCORE the profile. To get your score, give yourself one point for every answer that matches the answer key on page A2 in the back of your book. If you complete the profile online, the profile will be scored for you.

RECORD your score on the Master Profile Chart on page A1 in the column that shows the chapter number.

ONLINE: You can complete the profile and get your score online at this textbook's website.

		YES	NO
1.	I am aware of my learning style preference as a visual, auditory, or kinesthetic learner.	_____	_____
2.	I can describe four or more effective learning strategies for each learning preference: visual, auditory, and kinesthetic.	_____	_____
3.	When I study, I use a variety of learning strategies that capitalize on my learning style and preferences.	_____	_____
4.	I usually study new information in a straightforward manner without spending time making creative study or review tools.	_____	_____
5.	I know whether my thinking patterns reflect global (right-brain) or linear (left-brain) learning patterns.	_____	_____
6.	When I initially begin processing new information, I am aware of my tendency to focus first on the "big picture" or focus first on the details.	_____	_____
7.	I tend to use the same study methods for all of my classes even when my learning preferences differ from my instructor's style of presentation.	_____	_____
8.	I recognize which of Howard Gardner's eight intelligences are strongest in me.	_____	_____
9.	I have the potential to acquire new skills that will increase my abilities in the eight different intelligences.	_____	_____
10.	I am confident that I can adjust my learning strategies to meet the demands of new learning situations or tasks.	_____	_____

QUESTIONS LINKED TO THE CHAPTER LEARNING OBJECTIVES:

Questions 1–4:	objective 1	Questions 8, 9:	objective 3
Questions 5–7:	objective 2	Question 10:	all objectives

Three Cognitive Learning Styles

 Identify your preferred cognitive learning style and describe learning strategies you can use to utilize your preferred learning style and strengthen your other modalities.

Learning is an individualized process; different educational and background experiences, personality traits, levels of motivation, and numerous other variables affect the way you learn. The term *cognitive* refers to thinking and reasoning processes, so **cognitive learning styles** refers to the general way people *prefer* to have information presented in order to problem-solve, process, learn, and remember new information. **Figure 1.1** shows the three main cognitive learning styles. Understanding your cognitive learning style helps you select learning strategies that capitalize on your strengths, and it helps you understand why learning in certain situations that are contrary to your learning style may be more difficult than anticipated.

Learning Style Preferences

Three commonly recognized cognitive learning styles, or **learning modalities**, are *visual, auditory,* and *kinesthetic.* Most people have a **learning style preference**, which is a tendency to use a *visual, auditory,* or *kinesthetic* modality when there is a choice of ways to learn and process new information. For example, a *visual learner* may prefer to read the manual or learn from pictures, charts, or graphs. An *auditory learner* may prefer to be told how the new process or equipment works. A *kinesthetic learner* may prefer to be shown how the process or piece of equipment works and then be given an opportunity to try each step during the training session.

Your learning style preference started in your childhood. If you are a visual learner, you may have been fascinated by books, pictures, colors, shapes, and animation. If you are an auditory learner, you may have been perceived as a nonstop talker who frequently asked questions, sang, or recited nursery rhymes. If you are a kinesthetic learner, you very likely were a bundle of energy and actively explored your surroundings—running, jumping, rolling around, taking things apart, and building things out of whatever objects were available. As you matured, entered into the educational system, and were exposed to new learning situations, you

---

FIGURE 1.1

Cognitive Learning Styles

1. **Visual learners** learn and remember best by *seeing* and *visualizing* information.

2. **Auditory learners** learn and remember best by *hearing* and *discussing* information.

3. **Kinesthetic learners** learn and remember best by using large and small body *movements* and *hands-on experiences.*

CONCEPT CHECK 1.1

In general terms, how do you go about learning something new? What study or learning techniques generally work best for you?

Cognitive learning styles refers to the general way people *prefer* to have information presented in order to problem-solve, process, learn, and remember new information.

Learning modalities refers to learning styles such as visual, auditory, or kinesthetic.

Learning style preference indicates a tendency to use a visual, auditory, or kinesthetic modality when there is a choice of ways to learn and process new information.

CONCEPT CHECK 1.2

Which one of the three learning modalities were strongest in you as a child? Which characteristics have you observed recently in a child you know to indicate what might be his or her learning style preference?

learned to use, strengthen, and integrate all of your modalities. The modality preference still exists, but you have broadened your skills so that you are able, in most situations, to learn even when information is presented in a form that is not based on your preferred method of learning.

Understanding your learning style preference helps you select effective learning strategies that will boost your memory and your ability to recall information. As you take in and process information, your brain uses visual, auditory, and kinesthetic (motor) codes to accept and move the information into different locations in your memory system. The following points are important to understand:

▌ When you use your strongest modality or your preferred learning style to take in and process information, learning can occur more efficiently and recalling information at a later time may occur more smoothly.

▌ Many learning strategies involve the use of more than one modality. In other words, more than one kind of coding into memory occurs.

▌ When you use more than one sensory channel to process information, you create a stronger impression of the information in your memory, so recalling information often occurs more rapidly.

EXERCISE 1.1

Learning Styles Inventory

PURPOSE: Identify your learning style preference and strength of your modalities. Understanding your learning style preference can guide your selection of study and learning strategies to use to be more effective and successful.

DIRECTIONS: Complete the following Learning Styles Inventory by reading each statement carefully. Check YES if the statement relates to you all or most of the time. Check NO if the statement seldom or never relates to you. There is no in-between option, so you must check YES or NO. Your first, quick response to a question is usually the best response to use.

	YES	NO
1. I like to listen and discuss information with another person.	_____	_____
2. I could likely learn or review information effectively by hearing my own voice on tape.	_____	_____
3. I prefer to learn something new by reading about it.	_____	_____
4. I often write down directions someone gives me so I do not forget them.	_____	_____
5. I enjoy physical sports and exercise.	_____	_____
6. I learn best when I can see new information in picture or diagram form.	_____	_____
7. I am easily able to visualize or picture things in my mind.	_____	_____
8. I learn best when someone talks or explains something to me.	_____	_____

9. I usually write things down so that I can look back at them later.

10. I pay attention to the rhythm and patterns of notes I hear in music.

11. I have a good memory for the words and melodies of old songs.

12. I like to participate in small-group discussions.

13. I often remember the sizes, shapes, and colors of objects when they are no longer in sight.

14. I often repeat out loud verbal directions that someone gives me.

15. I enjoy working with my hands.

16. I can remember the faces of actors, settings, and other visual details of movies I have seen.

17. I often use my hands and body movements when explaining something to someone else.

18. I prefer standing up and working on a chalkboard or flip chart to sitting down and working on paper.

19. I often seem to learn better if I can get up and move around while I study.

20. I prefer pictures or diagrams instead of paragraph explanations to assemble something, such as a bike.

21. I remember objects better when I have touched them or worked with them.

22. I learn best by watching someone else first.

23. I tend to doodle when I think about a problem or situation.

24. I speak a foreign language.

25. I am comfortable building or constructing things.

26. I can follow the plot of a story when I listen to a book on tape.

27. I often repair things at home.

28. I can understand information when I hear it on tape.

29. I am good at using machines or tools.

30. I enjoy role-playing or participating in skits.

31. I enjoy acting or doing pantomimes.

32. I can easily see patterns in designs.

33. I work best when I can move around freely.

34. I like to recite or write poetry.

35. I can usually understand people with foreign accents or dialects.

36. I can hear many different pitches or melodies in music.

37. I like to dance and create new movements or steps.

38. I participate in activities that require physical coordination.

39. I follow written directions better than oral ones.

40. I can easily recognize differences between similar sounds.

41. I like to create or use jingles/rhymes to learn things.

42. I prefer classes with hands-on experiences.

43. I can quickly tell if two geometric shapes are identical.

44. The things I remember best are the things I have seen in print or pictures.

45. I follow oral directions better than written ones.

46. I could learn the names of fifteen medical instruments more easily if I could touch and examine them.

47. I remember details better when I say them aloud.

48. I can look at a shape and copy it correctly on paper.

49. I can usually read a map without difficulty.

50. I can "hear" a person's exact words and tone of voice days after he or she has spoken to me.

51. I remember directions best when someone gives me landmarks, such as specific buildings and trees.

52. I have a good eye for colors and color combinations.

53. I like to paint, draw, sculpt, or be creative with my hands.

54. I can vividly picture the details of a meaningful past experience.

SCORING YOUR PROFILE:

1. Ignore the NO answers. Work only with the questions that have a YES answer.

2. For every YES answer, look at the number of the question. Find the number in the following chart and circle that number.

3. When you finish, not all the numbers in the following boxes will be circled. Your answers will very likely not match anyone else's.

4. Count the number of circles for the Visual box and write the total on the line. Do the same for the Auditory box and Kinesthetic box.

Visual					Auditory					Kinesthetic				
3	4	6	7	9	1	2	8	10	11	5	15	17	18	19
13	16	20	22	32	12	14	24	26	28	21	23	25	27	29
39	43	44	48	49	34	35	36	40	41	30	31	33	37	38
51	52	54			45	47	50			42	46	53		
Total: _____					Total: _____					Total: _____				

ANALYZING YOUR SCORES:

Highest Score = Preferred learning style

Lowest Score = Weakest or least developed modality

Scores >10 = Frequently used modality

Scores <10 = Less frequently used modality

Your highest score is your preferred way to receive and process new information. If your two highest scores are the same, you can work equally well in each of the modalities. You may find yourself alternating between these two modalities, depending on the learning situation. Your lowest score is your least frequently used or your weakest modality. Scores higher than 10 indicate that you use the modality frequently, even if it is not your preferred modality. Scores lower than 10 indicate modalities that you do not use frequently. Your weakest modality and any modalities with scores lower than 10 may be the result of little or no training in techniques to strengthen these modalities, or they may be due to a physical or neurological impairment (such as a learning disability) that makes using the modality difficult. In such cases, students can learn to capitalize on their strengths and to use alternative learning strategies to process information.

Characteristics and Essential Strategies

As you read through the following common characteristics for each of the three types of learners or learning styles, relate this information to what you learned about yourself in the Learning Styles Inventory. Do you have the same or similar characteristics? Note that a person does not necessarily possess abilities or strengths in all of the characteristics but may instead "specialize" in some of the characteristics. Some of this may be due to a person's educational or personal background. For example, an auditory learner may be strong in the area of language skills but may not have had the experience or the opportunity to develop skills with a foreign language or music. Finally, pay close attention to the variety of essential learning strategies that you can incorporate into your approach to learning.

CONCEPT CHECK 1.3

What factors contribute to the development of a learning style preference? Is your learning style preference always the same for all learning situations?

Visual Learners

Visual learners prefer to process and learn information in visual forms such as pictures, charts, or other printed information, such as lists or paragraphs. They learn and remember best by *seeing* and *visualizing* information. The following are additional characteristics of visual learners:

Visual learners prefer to process and learn information in visual forms such as pictures, charts, or printed information.

▌ Can easily recall information in the form of numbers, words, phrases, or sentences

▌ Can easily understand and recall information presented in pictures, charts, or diagrams

▌ Have strong visualization or visual memory skills and can look up (often up to the left) and "see" information

▌ Make "movies in their minds" of information they are reading

▌ Have strong visual-spatial skills that involve sizes, shapes, textures, angles, and dimensions

▌ Have a good eye for colors, design, visual balance, and visual appeal

▌ Pay close attention and learn to interpret body language (facial expressions, eyes, stance)

▌ Have a keen awareness of aesthetics, the beauty of the physical environment, and visual media

Visual learners often favor creating and using visual strategies when they study. Having something that they can *see*, examine for details, and even possibly memorize as a mental image is important and effective for visual learners. **Figure 1.2** shows ten Essential Strategies for Visual Learners.

FIGURE 1.2

Essential Strategies for Visual Learners

Strategies	Explanations
Highlight important information.	When you read, use colored highlighter pens to highlight important facts, definitions, formulas, and steps. Colors often stand out better and create stronger visual images in your memory.
Create movies in your mind.	Use your visual memory as a television screen with the information that you read or hear moving across the screen "as a movie" with cameras rolling.
Visualize graphic materials and short sections of printed information.	Examine and visually memorize pictures, charts, graphs, or small sections of printed information. Practice looking away and visualizing the information. Then look back at the material to check your accuracy.
Create visual study tools.	Create visual mappings, hierarchies, and comparison charts with several levels of detail to represent information that you are studying. Use colors and pictures.
Expand chapter mappings.	Add details, colors, shapes, or pictures next to each heading that appears in the chapter mappings. Practice visualizing and reciting the information.
Use colors and pictures.	Enhance your notes, flashcards, or any other study tools by adding colors and pictures so that the information stands out more clearly in your memory.
Copy information in your own handwriting.	Copy printed text. Creating a visual memory of information you personally write tends to be easier than visualizing printed text. Practice looking away, visualizing, and checking your accuracy.
Create a visual memory of answers.	Write questions in the margins of your textbook. Highlight words and phrases in the text that answer your question. Cover the text. Read the questions and visualize the highlighted answers.
Use your keen observational skills.	Pay attention to physical details of objects and people. Interpret other people's body language for signs that reveal their attitudes, feelings, or important points they present as they speak.
Carry a pen and notepad with you.	Visual learners often want to write down information or directions, so be ready.

Auditory Learners

Auditory learners prefer to process and learn by hearing and discussing information. They prefer to have information presented to them verbally instead of, or in addition to writing. They learn by listening to others explain, debate, summarize, or discuss information about topics they are studying. Auditory learners, however, are not passive. Auditory learners like to *talk* and *listen* as they learn. They often get involved with discussions and learn by explaining information in their own words, expressing their understanding or opinions, and providing comments and feedback to other speakers. The following are additional characteristics of auditory learners:

▌ Can accurately remember details of information heard in conversations or lectures

▌ Have strong language skills, well-developed vocabularies, and an appreciation of words

▌ Have strong oral communication skills and are articulate

▌ Have "finely tuned ears" and may find learning a foreign language relatively easy

▌ Hear tones, rhythms, and notes of music, and often excel in areas of music

▌ Have keen auditory memories

Auditory learners often select learning strategies that code or process information through their auditory channel into memory. **Figure 1.3** shows ten Essential Strategies for Auditory Learners.

Kinesthetic Learners

Kinesthetic learners prefer to process and learn information through large and small muscle movements and hands-on experiences. They learn best by using their hands in "hands-on" learning or by using full body movement. They are able to remember and recall information more readily if they have the opportunity to feel, handle, use, manipulate, sort, assemble, or experiment with concrete objects. Large and small muscles hold memory, so involving movement in the learning process creates muscle memory. The following are additional characteristics of kinesthetic learners:

▌ Learn best by doing or manipulating physical objects and engaging in "hands-on" learning

▌ Learn well through movement, such as working at large charts, role-playing, or dancing

▌ Learn well in activities that involve performing (athletes, actors, dancers)

▌ Work well with their hands in areas such as repair work, sculpting, or art

▌ Are well coordinated, with a strong sense of timing and body movements

▌ Often wiggle, tap their feet, or move their legs when they sit

Kinesthetic learners often prefer to use strategies that engage their small and large muscles in the learning process. **Figure 1.4** shows ten Essential Strategies for Kinesthetic Learners.

Auditory learners prefer to process and learn by hearing and discussing information.

Kinesthetic learners prefer to process and learn information through large and small muscle movements and hands-on experiences.

CONCEPT CHECK 1.4

Define the terms *visual learner, auditory learner,* and *kinesthetic learner.* Describe the characteristics of each type of learner.

FIGURE 1.3

Essential Strategies for Auditory Learners

Strategies	Explanations
Participate in discussions.	Engage in group activities. Express your ideas, paraphrase speakers, and summarize lectures, conversations, or discussions.
Read out loud (verbalize).	Reading out loud (verbalizing), with a normal voice or with exaggerated expression uses the natural rhythm and patterns of language to automatically group information into units of meaning. Reading out loud activates auditory channels and clarifies meanings.
Ask questions.	Asking questions shows your interest and provides an opportunity to interact with the speaker. Answers clarify information and are often easier to recall later.
Work with others.	Use your verbal skills by working with a study buddy, participating in a study group, or working with tutors.
Recite frequently.	Reciting involves stating information out loud, without referring to printed materials, and speaking in complete sentences. Reciting provides immediate feedback about your level of understanding. Practice reciting your notes and answers to questions.
Tape lectures.	For lectures in difficult classes, request permission to tape the lectures. Continue to take notes, but back up your notes with the tapes. After class, review only the sections of the tapes that cover the confusing or difficult information.
Make your own study tapes.	Read or recite main ideas, facts, and important details into a tape recorder. Studying tapes with your own voice may strengthen auditory memory and recall.
Explain information.	Explain information you are learning to another person or even to an imaginary person. You receive immediate feedback that shows what you know and what you do not yet understand clearly.
Create rhymes, jingles, or songs.	Use your language and musical abilities to create easy-to-remember tunes.
Use technology.	Check your learning labs, library, and Internet resources for audio or video-audio materials to reinforce learning. Use voice-activated technology that is available on computers and personal products.

Strategic Learners

CONCEPT CHECK 1.5

Which strategies from Figures 1.2, 1.3, and 1.4 will you try using? How will you benefit from trying new strategies to learn new information?

Now that you are aware of your learning style and learning preference, you can begin the process of becoming a strategic learner. Strategic learners explore using new learning strategies, selecting some that utilize their strengths and some that will help them "stretch" and strengthen their other modalities. Using a variety of learning strategies has many benefits:

▌ It adds motivation and interest to the learning process.

▌ It creates stronger sensory paths into your memory system.

FIGURE 1.4

Essential Strategies for Kinesthetic Learners

Strategies	Explanations
Use hands-on learning.	Handle objects, tools, or machinery that you are studying. For processes such as computer applications, repeat the hands-on learning application several times.
Create manipulatives.	Manipulatives are study tools that you can move around with your hands. For example, create flashcards that you can shuffle, spread out, sort, or categorize.
Cut apart charts or diagrams.	Copy charts or diagrams. Practice re-assembling the pieces in their correct order.
Use exaggerated movements and hand gestures when you study.	Use large muscle movement by engaging in drama, dance, pantomime, and role-playing. Use small muscle movement by moving and using hand gestures as you study.
Use your muscle memory.	Redo hands-on tasks multiple times. Your muscles retain memory of hand and body movements.
Use a computer.	Type information and create notes, tables, and charts. Keyboard strokes help create muscle memory that you can use to simulate the actions and recall information.
Walk as you recite or practice information.	Pacing or walking with study materials in hand helps some people learn without being distracted by the discomfort of sitting too long.
Stand up as you work.	Work at a chalkboard, flip chart, or large poster paper to create study tools. List, draw, practice, or write while you stand up and work on a large surface.
Use creative movement and action-based activities.	For example, if you are studying perimeters in math, tape off an area of a room and walk the perimeter.
Create action games.	Convert the information you are studying into a game, such as Twenty-One Questions, Jeopardy, or Concentration. Review the information by playing the game with another student or group.

▮ It helps you recognize that there is always more than one way to process information.

▮ It helps you gain confidence in your ability to handle information regardless of the form or the learning situation in which it is presented.

Find Alternative Strategies

The following examples show alternative strategies students can use to deal with difficulties they encountered with specific kinds of learning tasks.

Student 1: Patrice had a low score in the visual category of the Learning Styles Inventory. She has difficulty reading maps or interpreting information presented in diagrams or charts.

Alternative Strategies: Participate in discussion groups or work with a tutor to receive verbal explanations of the graphic material. After discussing the material, make lists of the important points or write a summary to explain the information.

Student 2: Mandy had a low score in the auditory category of the Learning Styles Inventory. She has problems following sequences of ideas and comprehending lectures. Mandy does not have a hearing loss, but she does have difficulty with auditory processing.

Alternative Strategies: Try taping lectures and reviewing the tapes at a slower pace outside of class. Continue to try taking notes, but ask a classmate to share his or her lecture notes with you. Meet with the instructor to explore the possibility of getting copies of overheads used in the lectures, study guides, or lecture outlines.

Student 3: Ralph had a low score in the kinesthetic category. Due to some coordination problems, he finds detailed work that requires the use of his hands difficult to complete to his satisfaction. He has poor—sometimes almost illegible—handwriting. In his science lab, he feels as though he is "all thumbs" and that his finished products look immature and incomplete.

Alternative Strategies: Use a computer for written assignments. Ask a tutor or another student to help identify the steps that need to be done to complete a lab project. Allocate more time to work through each step carefully and slowly.

Use Multisensory Strategies

As you experiment with the various essential learning strategies, strive to design **multisensory strategies**, strategies that combine two or more modalities. Explore combinations that help you *see* the information in new ways, *say* the information you are learning, and *do* some type of movement or hands-on activity. By incorporating strategies that use two or all three of your modalities, you boost your memory. With visual, auditory, and kinesthetic coding of information into your memory system, you create multiple ways to access and recall information at later times.

For example, to learn a process to solve a difficult math problem, you could: 1) **verbalize** (read out loud) the steps for a solution, 2) copy the steps into your notes, 3) color-code each step, and 4) **recite** (talk out loud as you recall information from memory). As a second example, assume you have a complex project for your computer class that must be done in the computer lab. To utilize a multisensory approach to the project, you: 1) discuss the lab project with another student, 2) take notes on important points or steps, 3) reread the notes out loud to check their clarity, 4) highlight key points or steps, and 5) perform the operation on the computer at least twice. In this example, you *see* your color-coded notes, *say* things about the process, and *do* by writing and performing hands-on tasks.

Multisensory strategies are learning strategies that combine two or more modalities.

Verbalizing involves speaking or reading out loud to activate your auditory channel and build auditory memory.

Reciting involves explaining information out loud, in complete sentences, and in your own words without looking at printed information.

CONCEPT CHECK 1.6

Why are multisensory strategies so effective?

GROUP PROCESSING:
A COLLABORATIVE LEARNING ACTIVITY

Form groups of three or four students. Then complete the following directions.

Create a chart with three columns. Label the columns *Visual, Auditory,* and *Kinesthetic.* As a group, brainstorm different learning strategies or "things you can do when you study" that capitalize on each of the learning modalities. Use your own experiences and ideas for study strategies as well as ideas presented in this textbook. You may use the following examples to begin your chart.

GROUP SCORES:

Visual	Auditory	Kinesthetic
Use colored pens to highlight.	Talk out loud to study.	Make wall charts to review.

EXERCISE 1.2

Using Cognitive Modalities

DIRECTIONS: Go to Exercise 1.2 in Appendix C, page A24, to identify modalities used in various student activities and to use a multisensory approach to solve a problem.

CHECK POINT 1.1

ANSWERS APPEAR ON PAGE A4

True or False?

_____ 1. The term *cognitive* refers to people's awareness of their surroundings.

_____ 2. To be considered a "visual learner," one must show strong signs of possessing all the characteristics of a visual learner.

_____ 3. To some degree, a person's learning style preference reflects his or her personal background and educational experiences.

_____ 4. Having a learning style preference means that a person is strong in only one of the three cognitive learning styles.

_____ 5. Multisensory learning strategies include some form of learning that involves two or all three learning modalities.

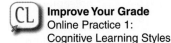
Improve Your Grade
Online Practice 1:
Cognitive Learning Styles

LINEAR AND GLOBAL LEARNERS

 Identify your linear- or global-learner tendency and discuss how it affects the way you process information.

How can the results of the various learning style inventories benefit you?

How humans process information and the factors that affect learning are areas of study that continue to expand. A multitude of theories, models, and inventories exist to assess and analyze thinking styles and emotional intelligence as well as behavioral, personality, and psychological styles. Learning style inventories are mere indicators of the way you prefer to learn. The main goal behind these inventories is for you to understand yourself and the ways in which you process information, deal with people, and handle situations most effectively. Regardless of the model or inventory you use, keep in mind that no one learning style is better than another; each style is simply a distinctive way of learning, interacting, or responding.

Research beginning in the late 1960s discovered that the human brain consists of two hemispheres or cortices that are connected by a complex network of nerve fibers called the *corpus callosum*. Though the two hemispheres are linked together neurologically, each hemisphere dominates specific kinds of mental activities and learning patterns. This research resulted in the Brain Dominance Theory. The **Brain Dominance Theory** is a cognitive model that identifies specific functions of the left hemisphere and the right hemisphere of the brain.

The **Brain Dominance Theory** is a cognitive model that identifies specific functions of the left hemisphere and the right hemisphere of the brain.

This theory suggests that people tend to have a preference for initially processing information through the left hemisphere (also referred to as the left brain) or the right hemisphere (the right brain). However, once they receive and start processing information from one side of the brain, the information is then shared with the other side of the brain for total processing. **Figure 1.5** summarizes the functions of the right and the left hemispheres.

Left-Brain or Linear Learners

A **linear learner** is a person who initially processes information through the left hemisphere of the brain, which deals with logic, structured, and verbal information.

A **linear learner** is a person who initially processes information through the left hemisphere of the brain, which deals with logic, structured, and verbal information. The left hemisphere of the brain processes mental activities that involve logical sequencing, such as lists or steps, predictable patterns, verbal language (words), numbers, and analytical thinking. People who begin the initial learning or intake process by activating the left hemisphere first are referred to as left-brain or linear learners. Figure 1.5 summarizes the mental activities of left-brain and right-brain learners. The following are additional characteristics of linear learners:

▌ They prefer information that provides them with specific details, clearly defined steps, words, numbers, and logical arguments.

▌ Their initial focus is on the details followed by understanding the "big pictures" these details form.

▌ They tend to master information in the structured sequence in which it is presented.

▌ They tend to do well in straightforward, detail-oriented lectures and with textbooks that present information in a sequential, structured, and clear manner.

FIGURE 1.5

Brain Dominance Theory

Brain Dominance Theory

Left Hemisphere		Right Hemisphere
Linear or Left-Brain Learners	L R	*Global or Right-Brain Learners*
Logic		Generalized
Structured		Spatial
Sequences		Colors
Lists		Visualization
Specific details		Imagination/Creativity
Verbal language		Pictures, Graphs, Charts
Words and numbers		Intuition
Analytical		Interactive
Predictable		Rhythm

Source: Bernstein/Nash. *Essentials of Psychology,* Houghton Mifflin, c. 2008, p. 70.

▌ They tend to prefer learning situations in which concepts, terminology, facts, details, applications, uses, and conclusions are clearly presented. In courses that require problem solving, such as science or mathematics, linear learners learn the fundamentals, such as problem-solving steps, and then proceed to apply the steps to solve problems or answer questions.

▌ They tend to do well in science, mathematics, social science, and computer technology.

Linear learners may experience some initial difficulty in courses that tend to be more right-brain oriented than left-brain or linear-learner oriented. For example, open-ended learning approaches, loosely structured learning environments, learning communities, or courses in which students acquire new information through discussions or group processes may be challenging for the linear learner and require the linear learner to make adjustments in his or her learning processes. Linear learners may also be challenged by classroom lectures that require the learner to interpret passages, attach meanings to symbols, or find creative solutions, such as is often the case in literature, poetry, performing arts, career development, or personal development courses. Unstructured use of textbooks, multiple readings or sources of information, and lectures focusing more on anecdotal experiences than specific facts, data, or technical information may also cause initial frustration for the linear learner. **Figure 1.6** shows strategies a linear learner can use to impose more structure and organization to courses and course materials that tend to be more global-learner oriented.

CONCEPT CHECK 1.8

What kinds of adjustments or learning strategies can a linear learner use in learning environments or with learning materials that tend to be more global-learner oriented?

FIGURE 1.6

Essential Strategies for Linear Learners in Global-Learning Situations

1. Ask for a summary of important points at the end of an open-ended or discussion-oriented class. List the significant points and the conclusions. After class, organize the information into a more meaningful format or structure.

2. During discussions, jot down the various points or opinions expressed. After class, organize the information into more meaningful lists or into charts.

3. When working with multiple sources of information, take notes from each source. Then use your organizational skills to integrate the information logically.

4. Add your own headings or subheadings to textbooks and lecture notes that lack the detailed organizational structure that works effectively for you.

Right-Brain or Global Learners

A **global learner** is a person who initially processes information through the right hemisphere of the brain, which deals with colors, visualization, creativity, and visual information.

A **global learner** is a person who initially processes information through the right hemisphere of the brain, which deals with colors, visualization, creativity, and visual information. The right hemisphere of the brain processes mental activities that involve spatial skills, pictures, colors, visual memories (visualizations), imagination, creativity, intuition, and rhythm. Because the right hemisphere deals with information in more generalized or big-picture patterns, people who begin the initial learning or intake process by activating the right hemisphere first are referred to as right-brain or global learners. (See Figure 1.5.) The following are additional characteristics of global learners:

▌ They tend to first see "the big picture," and then focus their learning on the details.

▌ They enjoy learning details through discovery, experiment, exploration, discussion, brainstorming, or group processes. As a result, they tend to learn details in random order; they may not understand the details clearly until the *light bulb turns on,* and all the details come together and form the "big picture."

▌ They prefer information in the form of pictures, charts, diagrams, and colorful visual stimuli.

▌ They enjoy using their creativity and intuition to process information, its meaning, and its applications. In problem-solving situations, they tend to take intuitive leaps to find solutions, sometimes creating their own problem-solving steps. They may be unable to explain to others how they arrive at their solutions.

▌ They do well in classes that involve learning communities, informal structured environments, discussions, group or cooperative learning activities, creative problem solving, and creative interpretation such as in literature, poetry, creative writing, performing arts, or personal development classes.

▌ To learn from textbooks, global learners often benefit from reading a chapter introduction, skimming through the entire chapter, and reading the summary. This helps them create a big picture before they begin learning specific details.

Global learners may experience some initial difficulty in courses that tend to be more left-brain oriented than right-brain or global-learner oriented. Teacher-

FIGURE 1.7

Essential Strategies for Global Learners in Linear-Learning Situations

1. When appropriate during a lecture, ask for specific examples or anecdotes to clarify factual information that is presented in a straightforward manner.

2. Ask instructors and other students questions about connections, relationships, trends, or themes when the details seem detached from the whole or the "big picture."

3. Find a "study buddy," form a study group or an online chat group, or participate in tutoring or dis-

cussion sessions so you can discuss course topics and interact with other students.

4. Add creativity to your lecture notes or course materials by adding colors, pictures, or diagrams to emphasize important points.

5. Rearrange information into charts or visual notes to show the "big picture" and the significant details.

6. Preview (survey) an entire chapter to get the "big picture" before reading the chapter for details.

directed or traditional lecture-based classrooms that focus on specific details, facts, steps, or processes without sufficient attention to the "big picture" can be challenging. Classroom environments with little opportunity to interact, use leadership skills, actively participate, or use hands-on learning may also be challenging for the global learner. In such classes, global learners may feel less engaged, and the learning process may feel impersonal or lack in creativity. **Figure 1.7** shows strategies a global learner can use to create a greater sense of involvement and interaction in a learning situation that tends to be more linear-learner oriented.

CONCEPT CHECK 1.9

What kinds of adjustments or learning strategies can a global learner use in learning environments or with learning materials that tend to be more linear-learner oriented?

EXERCISE 1.3

Brain Dominance Inventory—Left/Right, Linear/Global Dominance

PURPOSE: The Brain Dominance Theory suggests that people tend to have a preference for initially processing information through the left hemisphere or the right hemisphere of the brain. Use this inventory as one way to identify yourself as a linear or a global learner.

DIRECTIONS: Answer all of these questions quickly; do not stop to analyze them. When you have no clear preference, choose the one that most closely represents your attitudes or behaviors.

_____ 1. When I buy a new product, I
   a. usually read the directions and carefully follow them.
   b. refer to the directions, but really try and figure out how the thing operates or is put together on my own.

_____ 2. Which of these words best describes the way I perceive myself in dealing with others?
   a. Structured/Rigid
   b. Flexible/Open-minded

_____ 3. Concerning hunches:
   a. I generally would not rely on hunches to help me make decisions.
   b. I have hunches and follow many of them.

_____ 4. I make decisions mainly based on
   a. what experts say will work.
   b. a willingness to try things that I think might work.

_____ 5. In travelling or going to a destination, I prefer
   a. to read and follow a map.
   b. to get directions and map things out "my" way.

_____ 6. In school, I preferred
   a. geometry.
   b. algebra.

_____ 7. When I read a play or novel, I
   a. see the play or novel in my head as if it were a movie or TV drama.
   b. read the words to obtain information.

_____ 8. When I want to remember directions, a name, or a news item, I
   a. visualize the information or write notes that help me create a picture or maybe even draw the directions.
   b. write structured and detailed notes.

_____ 9. I prefer to be in the class of a teacher who
   a. has the class do activities and encourages class participation and discussions.
   b. primarily lectures.

_____ 10. In writing, speaking, and problem solving, I am
   a. usually creative, preferring to try new things.
   b. seldom creative, preferring traditional solutions.

Source: Berko/Wolvin/Wolvin, _Communicating: A Social and Career Focus,_ © 2007, Allyn and Bacon, pp. 108–109.

SCORING:

For items 1 through 5, give yourself one point for each **b** answer: _____

For items 6 through 10, give yourself one point for each **a** answer: _____

Total Score: _____

Circle your total points on the following scale.

Left   1   2   3   4   5   6   7   8   9   10   Right

INTERPRETATION:

Scores of 1 or 2:	Left-brain tendency; highly linear
Scores of 3 and possibly 4:	Left-brain or linear tendency
Scores of 4 through 7:	Possibly no dominance; flexible in learning style
Scores of 8 and possibly 7:	Right-brain or global tendency
Scores of 9 and 10:	Right-brain tendency; highly global

Source: Scoring modified from: Berko/Wolvin/Wolvin, _Communicating: A Social and Career Focus,_ © 2007, Allyn and Bacon, p. 109.

Whole-Brain Learning

As previously mentioned, one hemisphere is *dominant* and begins the mental processing activity. The information is then shared with the other hemisphere, so both sides work to process information—but in different ways. For example, consider the mental activities involved in the process of composing music. Initially, you might assume that the composer is a global learner (right-brain dominance) because composing involves rhythm, creativity, intuitive feelings, and imagination. After the initial process begins, however, the left-brain or linear learner skills are activated in order to apply specific musical conventions such as writing the music in a logical, recognizable format. Could a composer be a linear learner? Yes. The composer could begin by identifying a specific style or format for the composition and by analyzing the required elements—linear-type thinking. With a logical structure in mind, the composer could then activate the right hemisphere to bring creativity and imagination to the work.

To think of yourself as only a linear learner or only as a global learner limits your perception of yourself and your mental processing skills. Instead, think of yourself as a *whole-brain learner,* a person who has a brain-hemisphere dominance for the initial intake of information, but who then combines learning activities that activate both brain hemispheres. Making a conscious effort to use a wide variety of study strategies, some linear and some global, will strengthen you as a whole-brain learner and enhance your ability to learn new information.

CONCEPT CHECK 1.10

As with multisensory learning, is it beneficial to also use both linear- and global-learning strategies? Why or why not?

Diverse Learners in the Classroom

As you sit in your classrooms, you can be assured that you are a member of a diverse group of learners. Students with visual-, auditory-, kinesthetic-, linear-, and global-learning style preferences sit side by side, taking in and processing information differently. You undoubtedly have experienced these differences in the classroom as some students seem to grasp information more readily while other students struggle with making sense of the new information.

The teaching styles instructors use to organize and present information often reflect the instructors' own learning styles and preferences. Historically, the American approach to education favored the visual and linear learners. However, by implementing new teaching methods that address the needs of a diverse group of learners, many instructors now use instructional approaches that are compatible with a greater variety of learning style preferences. Even with such changes, you will inevitably find yourself in a classroom with an instructor whose teaching style does not match your learning styles or preferences. If you are flexible and know how to modify your approaches to the class and the materials, you can still do well in classes that do not match your learning style preferences. Your goal as an adult learner is to increase your ability to perform well in a wide range of learning situations.

When you have the option, consider the following suggestions for identifying courses and instructors that are compatible with your learning style preferences.

1. Before enrolling in a course that offers several sections with different instructors, talk to other students, instructors, and counselors to learn more about the teaching and classroom styles of each instructor. *If you have a choice,* enroll in the section with the instructor who seems most compatible with your learning styles and preferences.

2. Find out what support services are available for the course, Are there study guides, study groups, supplemental computer instruction, or tutors available? If so, use them.

3. Find out what forms of assessment are used in the course. Are grades based solely on tests, or do grades include group or individual projects, assignments, or portfolios?

EXERCISE 1.4

Textbook Case Studies

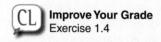 **Improve Your Grade**
Exercise 1.4

 **Improve Your Grade**
Online Case Studies

DIRECTIONS:

1. Read each case study carefully. Respond to the question at the end of each case study by using *specific* strategies discussed in this chapter. Answer in complete sentences.

2. Write your responses on paper or online at the Student Website, Exercise 1.4. You will be able to print your online response or e-mail it to your instructor.

CASE STUDY 1: Elaine is an outgoing person who started college in the middle of the year and does not know anyone on campus. After she received her midterm grades, she became concerned because she knew her work did not reflect her abilities. She knows that she is an auditory and global learner. She studies three or four hours every day alone in the library. She turns in her assignments on time but has difficulty retaining information. She also has trouble motivating herself and getting interested in her classes. What learning

strategies can Elaine use to combat the problems she has encountered in the first half of this term?

CASE STUDY 2: Conor is enrolled in a poetry class to complete one of his program requirements. He has never enjoyed or really understood poetry. He had hoped that this class would provide him with specific methods, steps, and guidelines to analyze, interpret, and respond to poetry. However, the class time consists of open-ended discussions that seem to be nothing more than a lot of different opinions. He is frustrated with the instructor and the lack of structure, clear directions, and specific answers. He is not comfortable talking to other students about this because they seem excited about the class, the instructor, and the content. He is doing well in all of his other classes, which include math and advanced physics. What are Conor's learning styles, and how do they contribute to the problems and frustrations he is experiencing in the poetry class?

EXERCISE 1.5

Analyzing a Learning Environment

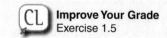 **Improve Your Grade**
Exercise 1.5

PURPOSE: Learning environments vary within each classroom. Some are compatible with your learning style preferences, and some require you to adjust your strategies to manage the classroom environment effectively. This exercise provides you with an opportunity to analyze the learning environment for any one of your classes.

DIRECTIONS:

1. Select any class you are enrolled in this term. Write the course name on the following chart.

2. Think about the various strategies used in the classroom. Identify approaches or activities that are compatible with each learning style preference.

COURSE:	
Learning Style Preference	**Compatible Approaches or Activities**
Visual Learners	
Auditory Learners	
Kinesthetic Learners	
Linear Learners	
Global Learners	

REFLECTIVE WRITING 1.1

CL **Improve Your Grade**
Reflective Writing 1.1

On separate paper, in a journal, or online at this textbook's website, complete the following directions.

1. Make a chart with two columns. In the first column, list the strategies from the charts in Figures 1.2–1.4, 1.6, and 1.7 that you currently use.

2. In the second column, list new strategies that you will strive to learn to use this term to utilize your learning style preferences, strengthen your other modalities, and adjust to different learning environments.

Currently Use	**Goals to Learn to Use**

3. In paragraph form, discuss what you see as the value of learning to use a variety of learning strategies. How will this help you adjust to the learning environment in your various courses?

CHECK POINT 1.2

ANSWERS APPEAR ON PAGE A4

True or False?

_____ 1. The three cognitive learning styles are hands-on, visual, and kinesthetic.

_____ 2. Visual learners have strong memories for printed material and visualization; auditory learners have strong auditory memories for information they hear and discuss.

_____ 3. A study strategy that uses a multisensory approach incorporates more than one cognitive learning style or modality.

_____ 4. Linear learners often prefer using intuition, visually graphic materials, interactive approaches, and structured, predictable formats to learn new information.

_____ 5. The Brain Dominance Theory states that people first take information into the left hemisphere of their brain and then integrate it with the right hemisphere.

CL **Improve Your Grade**
Online Practice 2:
Linear/Global Learners

You possess interests, abilities, and learning styles unique to you. Learning to use your strengths and apply your abilities increases your academic performance. How do you use your talents, interests, and learning styles in your courses?

MULTIPLE INTELLIGENCES

3 *Define the term* intelligences *and describe the common characteristics of each of Howard Gardner's eight intelligences.*

In 1983, Howard Gardner, a noted Harvard University psychologist, presented a new theory of cognitive development in his book, *Frames of Mind: The Theory of Multiple Intelligences.* Gardner's **Theory of Multiple Intelligences** (MI) is a cognitive theory that proposes that individuals have at least eight different kinds of intelligences. Gardner established specific scientific criteria that aptitudes, core capabilities, or sets of skills must fulfill in order to be recognized as an intelligence. Initially, Gardner proposed that individuals have seven different kinds of intelligences. In 1996, Gardner added an eighth intelligence, the *naturalist,* and he contends that very likely additional intelligences that fulfill his scientific criteria will be identified in the future. **Figure 1.8** shows the eight intelligences Gardner has identified.

Gardner's theory challenged the traditional theory of an intelligence, which is based on intelligence quotient (IQ), and IQ tests that measure intellectual abilities in the areas of verbal, visual-spatial, and logical mathematics. In addition to recognizing more intellectual abilities than the traditional IQ, Gardner defines intelligence as more than problem-solving skills; his definition includes the ability *to create* products as an important component of intelligence. Unlike traditional definitions of intelligence, Gardner's definition also recognizes the significance of cultural settings and the fact that abilities may not be valued equally in all cultures.

Howard Gardner's Theory of Multiple Intelligences has opened a new door to understanding individual differences, skills, abilities, and interests. This theory recognizes that most people have some degree of each of the intelligences, but that some intelligences are more developed than others in the individual. The MI Theory also recognizes that people have the *potential* to activate and strengthen all eight intelligences.

Theory of Multiple Intelligences is a cognitive theory that proposes that individuals have at least eight different kinds of intelligences.

 **Topic In-Depth**
Scientific Criteria

FIGURE 1.8

The Eight Intelligences in Howard Gardner's MI Theory

Linguistic

Logical-Mathematical

Musical

Bodily-Kinesthetic

Spatial

Interpersonal

Intrapersonal

Naturalist

Intelligences Defined

In 1983, Gardner defined *an intelligence* as "the ability to solve problems or to create products that are valued within one or more cultural settings." In 1999, Gardner's definition of intelligences broadened. Gardner stated:

> I now conceptualize **an intelligence** as *biopsychological potential to process information that can be activated in a cultural setting to solve problems or create products that are of value in a culture.*

Gardner continued, "This modest change in wording is important because it suggests that intelligences are not things that can be seen or counted. Instead, they are potentials . . . that will or will not be activated, depending upon the values of a particular culture, the opportunities available in that culture, and the personal decisions made by individuals and/or their families, schoolteachers, and others." [From Howard Gardner, *Intelligence Reframed: Multiple Perspectives for The 21st Century*, 1999, pp. 33–34. Copyright © 1999 Howard Gardner. Reprinted by permission of Basic Books, a member of Perseus Books, L.L.C.]

The Theory of Multiple Intelligences serves as a reminder that we are all "evolving beings." Through effective training, experience, and conducive environments, we have the potential to expand our abilities and intelligences to reach greater levels of performance and fulfillment. We can also consciously make choices to capitalize on our abilities and intelligences and strive for ways to cultivate and enhance them. Not surprisingly, many people seek and find success in careers that emphasize their stronger intelligences.

> **An intelligence** is the potential to process information that can be activated in a cultural setting to solve problems or create products that are of value in a culture.

> **CONCEPT CHECK 1.11**
>
> How does Gardner's theory of intelligences (MI) differ from the traditional theory of intelligence (IQ)? What abilities does MI add to the traditional IQ theory?

> **CONCEPT CHECK 1.12**
>
> How can you increase or strengthen your eight intelligences?

Subintelligences

Gardner states that **subintelligences** are core abilities that are part of a larger individual intelligence. Each of the eight intelligences has subintelligences. For example, people can exhibit many different talents and abilities under the category of musical intelligence. Due to lack of opportunity, experiences, or training, a person with a high musical intelligence may not have all of the subintelligences of music well developed. Singing, playing different instruments, composing, conducting, critiquing, and appreciating a variety of music require different skills, abilities, and processes. The level of accomplishment or degree of mastery will vary within an individual among the subintelligences, but the *potential exists* to process information that can be activated to solve problems or create products that are valued. Subintelligences or core abilities are described in the following sections for each of the eight intelligences.

> **Subintelligences** are core abilities that are part of a larger individual intelligence.

> **CONCEPT CHECK 1.13**
>
> Do individuals tend to demonstrate all of the subintelligences that belong to a specific intelligence? Do they have the *potential* to demonstrate all of the core abilities?

Linguistic Intelligence

Linguistic intelligence is the ability to use verbal and written language effectively. Common subintelligences or core abilities of this intelligence include:

- A love of language—a curiosity and fascination with words and meanings (semantics), and structure (syntax)—and sensitivities to how words are used, how they sound (phonology), and how they evoke feelings

- Sharp, detailed, vivid memories about written or spoken language

- The ability to excel in word games such as crossword puzzles or Scrabble

- The ability to create, recite, and remember puns, jingles, or poetry

- An ability to learn languages

> **Linguistic intelligence** is the ability to use verbal and written language effectively.

▌ An ability to express ideas well in public presentations, storytelling, or debates and express ideas well in writing, whether in journals, prose, or poetry

Following are common career options for people with strong linguistic intelligence:

> author, journalist, editor, poet, newscaster, television announcer, motivational speaker, playwright, politician, consultant, lawyer

Logical-Mathematical Intelligence

Logical-mathematical intelligence is the ability to use logic, problem solving, analysis, and mathematical calculations effectively.

Logical-mathematical intelligence is the ability to use logic, problem solving, analysis, and mathematical calculations effectively. Other subintelligences or core abilities include the ability to:

▌ Use sound reasoning, identification of patterns, and sequential thinking

▌ Think both concretely and abstractly

▌ Understand and apply abstract numerical symbols and operations, and perform complex calculations

▌ Use systematic, logic-based, sequential problem-solving techniques and scientific methods to measure, hypothesize, test, research, and confirm results

Following are common career options for people with strong logical-mathematical intelligence:

> mathematician, math or business teacher, scientist, computer programmer, accountant, tax expert, banker, researcher

Musical Intelligence

Musical intelligence is the ability to show an acute sensitivity and appreciation of musical patterns and elements.

Musical intelligence is the ability to show an acute sensitivity and appreciation of musical patterns and elements, such as pitch, timbre, and harmony. People with these developed abilities may use vocal or instrumental music to express creativity, imagination, and the gamut of human emotions. Other subintelligences, or core abilities include:

▌ Skills in reading and writing (composing) music

▌ An understanding of music theory and symbols

▌ A passion for different types and structures of music

▌ An enjoyment of singing, chanting, humming, or drumming

▌ Strong auditory memories for verbal and musical information

Following are common career options for people with strong musical intelligence:

> music teacher, composer, conductor, performer, sound engineer, filmmaker, television crew or director, marketing or advertising personnel

Bodily-Kinesthetic Intelligence

Bodily-kinesthetic intelligence is the ability to use precise body rhythms and movements, motor coordination skills, and other skills such as timing, balance, and flexibility. People with high bodily-kinesthetic intelligence often prefer "hands-on" or activity-oriented tasks. Other subintelligences, or core abilities, include:

▌ Dexterity and possibly strength and speed

▌ Well-developed gross (large) motor skills, an ability to judge how their bodies will respond to certain situations, and an ability to fine-tune and train their bodies to perform at higher levels

▌ Well-developed fine (small) motor skills and an ability to work well with their hands to create or modify the objects they work with

▌ An acute sensitivity "through their hands." For example, a mechanic unable to see inside an engine may be able to locate and fix a problem using only his or her hands

▌ An enjoyment of physical exercise, sports, dancing, drama, role-playing, inventing, building, and repairing things

Following are common career options for people with strong bodily-kinesthetic intelligence:

> dancer, athlete, actor, musician/instrumentalist (guitarist, drummer, pianist), dance teacher, choreographer, photographer, mime artist, painter, sculptor, surgeon, inventor, craftsperson

Bodily-kinesthetic intelligence is the ability to use precise body rhythms and movements, motor coordination skills, and other skills such as timing, balance, and flexibility.

Spatial Intelligence

Spatial intelligence is the ability to use keen perceptions of patterns, shapes, textures, and visual skills. People with developed spatial intelligence often possess strong visual imagery or visualization skills, creativity, and active imaginations. Other subintelligences include:

▌ An ability to accurately perceive sizes, geometric forms, lines, curves, and angles in the physical world

▌ An ability to present their ideas graphically; for example, a gifted chess player can play a challenging game of chess blindfolded, or an architect can picture the floor plans of a building before drawing them

▌ Interest and abilities in the areas of fine arts, such as painting, sculpting, drawing, drafting, or photography

Following are common career options for people with strong spatial intelligence:

> architect, designer, interior decorator, artist, painter, sculptor, fashion designer, landscaper, carpenter, contractor, graphic artist, advertiser, cartographer, inventor, pilot, surgeon

Spatial intelligence is the ability to use keen perceptions of patterns, shapes, textures, and visual skills.

Interpersonal Intelligence

Interpersonal intelligence is the ability to use effective communication, social, leadership and cooperative teamwork skills.

Interpersonal intelligence is the ability to use effective communication, social, leadership, and cooperative teamwork skills. Individuals with strong interpersonal intelligence participate actively in groups, create bonds with diverse groups of people, and feel a sense of global responsibility toward others. Other subintelligences include:

▌ The ability to interpret nonverbal clues that appear in the form of facial expressions, gestures, or general body language

▌ The ability to interpret the behavior, motivation, and intentions of others

▌ Enjoyment of socializing, helping others, sharing their skills, tutoring or teaching others

▌ The ability to contribute to the development of positive group dynamics

Following are common career options for people with strong interpersonal intelligence:

> parent, tutor, teacher, therapist, counselor, healer, social activist, motivational speaker, workshop leader, religious leader, sociologist, actor, political organizer, salesperson

Intrapersonal Intelligence

Intrapersonal intelligence is the ability to use skills related to personal growth, self-understanding, and self-motivation and to use intuition and spirituality.

Intrapersonal intelligence is the ability to use skills related to personal growth, self-understanding, and self-motivation and to use intuition and spirituality. Individuals with strong intrapersonal intelligence use personal reflection and self-motivation to achieve personal potential. Other core abilities include:

▌ Enjoyment of exploring their feelings, values, goals, strengths, weaknesses, and personal history

▌ The ability to interpret life experiences as lessons and guides to change aspects of their lives and to give their lives meaning

▌ An ability to project a sense of pride, self-esteem, confidence, self-responsibility, control, and empowerment

▌ An ability to be self-regulating, self-motivated, and goal-oriented

▌ An ability to adapt well to a wide variety of situations and circumstances

Following are common career options for people with strong intrapersonal intelligence:

> psychiatrist, spiritual or personal counselor, self-help or motivational writer or speaker, philosopher, biographer

Naturalist Intelligence

The **naturalist intelligence** is the ability to show a sensitivity to the physical world, which includes the balance of plants, animals, and the environment. People with strong naturalist intelligence are keen observers of nature's elements—such as daily, seasonal, and cyclical changes—and of the relationships in nature. Subintelligences also include:

▌ An ability to demonstrate detailed knowledge and expertise in recognizing and classifying plants and animals

▌ An ability to organize, classify, arrange, or group items and ideas into logical units or categories

▌ An ability to apply strong pattern-recognition talents to areas outside of the plant-animal world, such as with artists, poets, laboratory scientists, and social scientists

Following are common career options for people with strong naturalist intelligence:

> meteorologist, geologist, botanist, herbalogist, biologist, naturopath, holistic healer, medicine man, gardener, environmentalist

Naturalist intelligence is the ability to show a sensitivity to the physical world, which includes the balance of plants, animals, and the environment.

Tests for Multiple Intelligences

No scientific tests exist at this time to assess people's intellectual levels in the eight intelligences. However, there are informal Multiple Intelligences inventories that use a linguistic or logical paper-pencil test to identify people's *preferences* for using *existing* abilities, but they do not actually assess the intelligences themselves. Since intelligence is defined as "the potential to process information that can be activated in a cultural setting to solve problems or create products that are of value in a culture," valid assessment procedures require that testers place individuals in settings where the individuals are required to activate specific intelligences.

As Gardner explains in *Intelligence Reframed*, "If one wants to assess spatial intelligence, one should allow people to explore a terrain for a while and see whether they can find their way around it reliably, perhaps even when they have to enter or exit at an unfamiliar point. Or, if one wants to examine musical intelligence, one should expose people to a new melody in a reasonably familiar idiom and determine how readily they can learn to sing it, recognize it, transform it, and so on." [From Howard Gardner, *Intelligence Reframed: Multiple Perspectives for the 21st Century.* Copyright © 1999 Howard Gardner, pages 80–81. Reprinted by permission of Basic Books, a member of Perseus Books, L.L.C.]

Gardner adds, "I would recommend that any intelligence be assessed by a number of complementary approaches that consider the several core components [subintelligences] of an intelligence. Thus, for example, spatial intelligence might be assessed by asking people to find their way around an unfamiliar terrain, to solve an abstract jigsaw puzzle, and to construct a three-dimensional model of their home." [From Howard Gardner, *Intelligence Reframed: Multiple Perspectives for the 21st Century.* Copyright © 1999 Howard Gardner, page 82. Reprinted by permission of Basic Books, a member of Perseus Books, L.L.C.]

EXERCISE 1.6

Recognizing Intelligences

PURPOSE: Various activities activate specific intelligences by utilizing core abilities or subintelligences in the process. By analyzing specific tasks, you can more readily identify the intelligences that individuals activate and utilize.

DIRECTIONS:

1. Work with a partner, in a small group, or by yourself.

2. Each intelligence is numbered below. Use these numbers to identify the intelligence or intelligences that are most activated by the activities described. Write your responses on the lines.

1	=	Linguistic	5 =	Spatial
2	=	Logical-Mathematical	6 =	Interpersonal
3	=	Musical	7 =	Intrapersonal
4	=	Bodily-Kinesthetic	8 =	Naturalist

_____ **1.** Work as a group to create a student handbook for incoming freshmen.

_____ **2.** Perform a scene from a book in a literature class.

_____ **3.** Interview four people who work in the career field of interest to you and then compile the results of the four interviews you conducted.

_____ **4.** Select appropriate plants to use for experiments in an existing greenhouse on campus.

_____ **5.** Collect and organize samples of music from five different cultural or ethnic groups.

_____ **6.** Use a computer graphics program to create an eye-catching presentation about your heritage or cultural ties.

_____ **7.** Construct a 3-D model that shows your idea for making better use of an existing space on campus.

_____ **8.** Keep a daily journal or log to record your progress in reaching a specific goal.

_____ **9.** Role-play a conflict resolution strategy.

_____ **10.** Organize a small group of students to tutor elementary school students.

Additional Intelligences

In Gardner's book *Intelligence Reframed,* Gardner discusses spiritual and existential capabilities and whether or not they qualify as new intelligences. Gardner concludes that neither spiritual nor existential capabilities meet all eight scientific criteria used to categorize a set of abilities as an intelligence; therefore, neither can at this time be classified as a ninth intelligence. Gardner states:

> Despite the attractiveness of a ninth intelligence, however, I am not adding existential intelligence to the list. I find the phenomenon perplexing enough and the distance from other intelligences vast enough to dictate prudence—at least for now. At most, I am willing . . . to joke about "8½ intelligences" [p. 66].

EXERCISE 1.7

Your Multiple Intelligences Strengths

PURPOSE: For each of the eight intelligences, identify subintelligences or core abilities you already possess and currently demonstrate as you process new information and work in various learning environments. Note, however, that identifying the subintelligences that you currently use does not indicate your *potential* for each intelligence.

DIRECTIONS:

1. Refer to the subintelligences described for the eight intelligences on pages 25–29. For each intelligence, highlight the subintelligences or core abilities you currently demonstrate an ability to use effectively.

2. Create a chart with two columns to show your results. In the first column, list the eight intelligences. In the second column across from each intelligence, list the core abilities that are strong in you.

Improve Your Grade
Reflective Writing 1.2

REFLECTIVE WRITING 1.2

On separate paper, in a journal, or online at this text-book's website, respond to the following questions.

1. What academic major or career path interests you? How does your choice of careers reflect or not reflect your abilities or perceived intelligences as defined by Gardner?

2. What would be an ideal classroom environment and instructional approach for you that would allow you to capitalize on your various learning styles and preferences? Use specific details to describe the classroom and the instructional approach.

EXERCISE 1.8

Links

PURPOSE: Three theories provide different perspectives on how people learn and process information: Cognitive Learning Styles, Brain Dominance, and Multiple Intelligences. In this exercise, explore the relationships among the three different theories.

DIRECTIONS:

Work with a partner or in a small group to complete this exercise. Complete the following directions to explore how these three perspectives are interrelated. Write your answers on separate paper. Your answers may be in the form of a list, a paragraph, or a chart.

1. Which cognitive learning styles are actively used for each intelligence?

2. Which intelligences do you think would be strongest for global learners?

3. Which intelligences do you think would be strongest for linear learners?

4. What kind of relationship can you suggest that might exist between global and linear learners and the three cognitive learning styles?

CHECK POINT 1.3

True or False?

_____ 1. Howard Gardner has identified eight intelligences; each intelligence consists of different core abilities called subintelligences.

_____ 2. To be considered intellectually strong in any one of the intelligences, a person must exhibit developed abilities in all of the core abilities for that intelligence.

_____ 3. Just as there are tests to determine intelligence quotient (IQ) scores, there are tests to determine intellectual scores for each of Gardner's eight intelligences.

_____ 4. Having a well-developed interpersonal intelligence indicates the ability to demonstrate leadership skills and work well with others.

Improve Your Grade
Online Practice 3:
Multiple Intelligences

LEARNING OBJECTIVES REVIEW

1 *Identify your preferred cognitive learning style and describe learning strategies you can use to utilize your preferred learning style and strengthen your other modalities.*

• Three main cognitive learning styles or learning modalities (visual, auditory, and kinesthetic) determine how individuals prefer to have information presented in order to problem solve, process, learn and remember new information. Most adults have a learning style preference but are able to function using all three modalities.

• Effective study strategies for each modality preference as well as multisensory activities that involve *seeing, saying,* and *doing* activities are available to use during the learning process.

2 *Identify your linear- or global-learner tendency and discuss how it affects the way you process information.*

• The Brain Dominance Theory groups thinking patterns into right-hemisphere and left-hemisphere thinking. Though the two hemispheres are linked together neurologically, each dominates specific kinds of mental activities and learning patterns.

• Linear learners are left-brain learners. Global learners are right-brain learners. Common characteristics explain the differences between the two kinds of learners.

• Since both hemispheres share and process information, using a variety of strategies promotes *whole-brain* learning.

3 *Define the term* intelligences *and describe the common characteristics of each of Howard Gardner's eight intelligences.*

• Gardner identifies eight intelligences that people possess: linguistic, logical-mathematical, musical, bodily-kinesthetic, spatial, interpersonal, intrapersonal, and naturalist. Each intelligence meets the scientific criteria Gardner has established to qualify as an intelligence.

• Gardner's definition of intelligence differs from other definitions of intelligence. He defines intelligence as "biopsychological potential to process information that can be activated in a cultural setting to solve problems or create products that are of value in a culture."

• Each of the eight intelligences has core abilities called subintelligences. A person may not exhibit developed abilities in all of the subintelligences.

CHAPTER 1 REVIEW QUESTIONS

True or False?

_____ 1. Cognitive learning styles refer to the way people interact in group settings.

_____ 2. Learning styles indicate people's preferred ways of learning and processing new information, but they may not always be in learning situations that utilize their preferred modality.

_____ 3. Global learners tend to prefer creative, interactive, and intuitive approaches to learning new information.

_____ 4. Howard Gardner's Multiple Intelligences Theory claims that the eight intelligences reflect potential abilities that individuals can develop and strengthen.

_____ 5. The skills or abilities exhibited by a person with a well-developed logical-mathematical intelligence reflect characteristics of linear learners.

Multiple Choice

_____ 1. Which statement is *not* true about the Brain Dominance Theory?
   a. The human brain consists of two hemispheres that are linked together neurologically.
   b. Each hemisphere of the brain dominates specific kinds of mental activities.
   c. The majority of students are global learners.
   d. Both hemispheres share information to achieve total processing.

_____ 2. Linear learners
   a. are also referred to as left-brain learners.
   b. prefer information presented in logical, structured, and predictable ways.
   c. can learn to function effectively in "right-brain" oriented learning environments.
   d. exhibit all of the above.

_____ 3. Which of the following is *not* true about multi-sensory learning?
   a. It involves selecting strategies that utilize two or more modalities.
   b. It always requires verbalizing and reciting to process information.
   c. It provides multiple ways to access and recall information later.
   d. It focuses on strategies that use a combination of *see*, *say*, and *do* processes.

_____ 4. A person with a well-developed *naturalist intelligence* may exhibit
   a. strong pattern-recognition skills.
   b. the ability to organize and classify objects in the plant and animal world.
   c. a sensitivity to the cycles and balances in nature.
   d. all of the above.

Definitions

On separate paper, define each of the following terms.

1. Multisensory strategies
2. Reciting
3. Subintelligence
4. Intrapersonal intelligence

Short-Answer Question

Use complete sentences to answer the following question. Use information and terminology from this chapter. Write your answer on separate paper.

Question: The Theory of Multiple Intelligences contends that the traditional IQ tests are too limiting. What intelligences did Howard Gardner add to expand the concept of traditional intelligence and include a wider range of talents and abilities?

 **ACE the Test**
Four Online Practice Tests

Online Resources

2 Processing Information into Your Memory

LEARNING OBJECTIVES

1 *Explain how the three memory systems (sensory memory, working memory, and long-term memory) work to process information.*

2 *Identify study skills strategies that strengthen working memory.*

Chapter Outline

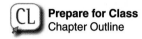

Prepare for Class
Chapter Outline

For centuries people have been fascinated by the workings of the human mind. Researchers and cognitive psychologists are now able to use sophisticated technology to study the human brain, its processing functions, and its complex structure. In this chapter, you will learn about a contemporary Information Processing Model that consists of three memory systems. Working memory, one of the three memory systems, is the part of your mind that is conscious and aware of all cognitive processes. You will learn strategies to strengthen and use your working memory more effectively. By understanding *how* your mind processes information and *how* your memory works, you can use this information to increase your learning potential and to tailor or personalize your approach to learning different kinds of information.

CHAPTER 2 PROFILE

Information Processing

ANSWER, **SCORE**, and **RECORD** your profile before you read this chapter. If you need to review the process, refer to the complete directions given in the profile for Chapter 1 on page 4.

ONLINE: You can complete the profile and get your score online at this textbook's website.

	YES	NO
1. I have a general understanding of the kinds of mental activities and connections that take place when I learn new information.	_____	_____
2. I pay attention to the different kinds of information I receive on a regular basis from my senses: sight, sound, smell, taste, and touch.	_____	_____
3. I code all new information in a visual form so it is easy to remember or recall at a later time.	_____	_____
4. I monitor the speed that I take in information and the quantity of information that I try to learn at one time.	_____	_____
5. I am aware of my thought patterns and the way I connect ideas when I begin learning new information.	_____	_____
6. When I try to recall information from my memory, I use words, pictures, or other cues to find the information.	_____	_____
7. I take time to relate or associate new information to information that I already know.	_____	_____
8. When I do not immediately know an answer to a question, I realize that I do not have that information in memory, so I move on to something else.	_____	_____
9. When I study, I usually do a variety of activities to help me process new information into my memory.	_____	_____
10. I am confident in my ability to use effective strategies to boost my ability to process information without overloading working memory.	_____	_____

QUESTIONS LINKED TO THE CHAPTER LEARNING OBJECTIVES:
Questions 1–5:   objective 1   Question 10:   both objectives
Questions 6–9:   objective 2

THE INFORMATION PROCESSING MODEL

1 ► *Explain how the three memory systems (sensory memory, working memory, and long-term memory) work to process information.*

Understanding memory and information processing lays a strong foundation for many study skills strategies in later chapters. Brain research and learning theories are more complex than the information that you will encounter in this chapter. However, the technical information in this chapter will equip you with basic knowledge about *how* your mind processes information, *how* your memory works, and *how* you can use this information to increase your learning potential and to tailor or personalize your approach to learning different kinds of information.

Understanding how your mind processes and how your memory works is the first step to using the powerful process of metacognition. **Metacognition** is the process of understanding *how* you learn, *what* you need to learn, and finally, *which* strategies or techniques would be the most effective or the best matched to the learning task. Throughout this textbook, you will learn how to identify what it is that you need to understand, learn, and apply when you read textbooks, take lecture notes, and prepare for tests. You will learn strategies that are supported by learning theories and research. Your role as an effective learner is to have familiarity with a wide range of learning strategies so that you can select the most appropriate strategies to match the learning task. Your ability to use metacognition effectively will increase as you acquire new study skills and strategies.

The **Information Processing Model** is a cognitive model that consists of three memory centers: sensory memory, working memory, and long-term memory. The Information Processing Model provides a foundation for understanding the kinds of mental activities and connections that are necessary for learning to take place. The model shown in **Figure 2.1** is the result of extensive research and learning theories that explain how sensory stimuli from the physical world move back and forth through the three memory systems when information is processed.

Metacognition is the process of understanding *how* you learn, *what* you need to learn, and finally, *which* strategies or techniques would be the most effective or the best matched to the learning task.

The **Information Processing Model** is a cognitive model that consists of three memory centers: sensory memory, working memory, and long-term memory.

FIGURE 2.1

The Information Processing Model

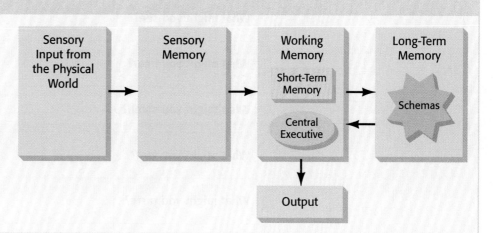

Sensory memory is the first memory center; it holds stimuli for one or two seconds. Working memory, *the second memory center, has two parts:* short-term memory *and the* central executive. Long-term memory, *the third memory center, contains schemas, or clusters of related information stored in long-term memory.*

Each part of the Information Processing Model plays an important role in the learning process. In the following sections, you will learn about each part of the Information Processing Model. You will also become familiar with strategies that you can use to strengthen your memory and your ability to learn new information. In Chapter 3, "Using Twelve Principles of Memory," you will learn additional strategies that you can apply to any learning situation to increase your level of performance and improve your memory.

Input from the Physical World

The Information Processing Model begins with sensory input from the physical world. **Sensory input** refers to all the sensory stimuli from the physical world that we receive through our five senses— sight, sound, touch, taste, and smell. Sensory input comes in many forms: letters, numbers, words, visual images, sounds, smells, or tactile sensations, such as textures or the hardness or softness of objects. At this very second, you are receiving sensory input from your environment. You see, hear, feel, and smell things; you taste things even when you are not putting items in your mouth.

CONCEPT CHECK 2.1

What do you see as your greatest memory strengths? What are your memory problem areas? Overall, do you feel your memory is vivid and accurate, or does it tend to be unclear and inaccurate?

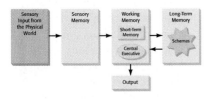

Sensory input refers to all the sensory stimuli from the physical world that we receive through our five senses.

CONCEPT CHECK 2.2

What are the five forms of sensory input that you receive from your physical world? Are you keenly aware of the sensory information that you receive on a regular basis?

EXERCISE 2.1

Sensory Input

PURPOSE: Recognize that a multitude of sensory information bombards our senses on a continuous and regular basis.

DIRECTIONS: Imagine yourself sitting on a bench near a busy street in your city or town. In the following chart, jot down the kinds of sensory input that would most likely bombard your senses.

Sensory Input	Kinds of Sensory Information You Might Receive
What might you see?	
What might you hear?	
What might you smell?	
What might you feel?	
What might you taste?	

Sensory Memory

When you receive sensory input from the physical world, it enters into your sensory memory. **Sensory memory** is a temporary storage center that receives and holds sensory input for one or two seconds before beginning to *encode* the information for further processing. Information that you do not attend to or that you ignore fades or becomes discarded quickly. To see how quickly sensory memory receives and holds on to sensory input, look briefly across the room you are in. Shut your eyes and move your head to the right. Open your eyes for a second and shut them again. Notice how the images you received remain for only a second or two and then fade.

This function of sensory memory holding sensory input for only one or two seconds works as a filter for the rest of your memory system. Our memory system would overload if we attempted to use mental activity to process every piece of sensory information we receive. For example, as you drove or rode the bus to school today, your senses took in large amounts of sensory information. Some of it you processed, but much of it you ignored or dumped from memory. Answering the following questions indicates the information you processed further and the information you dumped: How many red cars did you pass? What was the license number of the car in front of you? What music did you listen to on your iPod, radio, or CD? What smells did you experience?

Codes and Encoding

As soon as you receive information from your senses, your brain begins to prepare the information for your memory systems by encoding the information. **Encoding** is the process of attaching codes to stimuli so your long-term memory can accept, understand, use, and store the sensory information. Encoding translates the stimuli into meaningful forms for long-term memory. The following are three important points about encoding information:

▌ The type of encoding that initially takes place depends on the type of sensory information that you receive. For example, visual stimuli are automatically encoded into horizontal and vertical lines, curves, moving lines, colors, or brightness.

▌ Even though some encoding occurs automatically without conscious effort, you can *intentionally encode information specific ways* so you can process it more effectively.

▌ Encoding occurs more than once. More in-depth encoding occurs later in *working* memory.

For example, assume your geology instructor introduces the term *stalagmite* (a conical deposit of minerals that projects upward from the floor of a cavern or a cave). You hear the new information (linguistic coding). You instantly think about a time you saw or went inside a cave and saw a stalagmite (semantic coding). You repeat the word to yourself and draw a picture of a stalagmite and practice picturing it in your mind (visual coding). With you finger, you trace the shape in the air (kinesthetic coding). Within a matter of a few short seconds, you have moved the information into working memory and have encoded it multiple ways.

Figure 2.2 shows the four common kinds of codes that may be used to prepare sensory information for processing. Note that the first three kinds of codes reflect the three main modalities you learned about in Chapter 1.

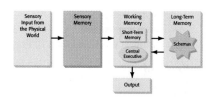

Sensory memory is a temporary storage center that receives and holds sensory input for one or two seconds before beginning to *encode* the information for further processing.

CONCEPT CHECK 2.3

How long does sensory memory hold sensory input? What is the value of the limited ability of sensory memory?

Encoding is the process of attaching codes to stimuli so your long-term memory can accept, understand, use, and store the sensory information.

CONCEPT CHECK 2.4

What are the four ways you encode information for further processing? What kinds of information does each code process?

FIGURE 2.2

Four Common Kinds of Codes to Prepare Stimuli for Processing

Kinds of Coding	Also Called . . .	Type of Information Encoded	Ways to Encode
Linguistic Coding	Acoustical coding or auditory coding	Language information; sounds: ▌ Letters, words, phrases, sentences ▌ Syntax, meanings ▌ Sounds, volume, pitch, rhythms	▌ Talk to yourself about the meaning of information. ▌ Read aloud and listen to your voice. ▌ Imagine hearing the voice of an instructor. ▌ Imagine the sounds of events.
Visual Coding	Imaginal coding	Visual information: ▌ Brightness, color, shapes, location ▌ Pictures, diagrams ▌ Images of objects or people ▌ Written symbols	▌ Make mental images of information. ▌ Notice color, shape, location. ▌ Practice visualizing or recreating images.
Motor Coding	Physical coding or kinesthetic coding	Muscle- and physical-movement information: ▌ Large muscle actions performed by full body movement ▌ Small muscle actions performed by hands or feet movement	▌ Make movements that illustrate the information. ▌ Explain with hand movements. ▌ Retrace shapes or objects. ▌ Manipulate parts of an object.
Semantic Coding	Conceptual or abstract coding	General meaning of an event or personal experience: ▌ Categories, concepts ▌ Abstract generalizations ▌ Descriptions of things and events ▌ Emotions or emotional response to an event or personal experience ▌ Stored as one chunk or unit of memory (episodic memory), not as individual details	▌ Identify and think about concepts and generalizations—the "big pictures". ▌ Arrange information into categories of related concepts. ▌ Recall the chronological sequence of events. ▌ Recall or replay the experience in your mind.

Understanding the different kinds of encoding can help you when you study. For example, if you see a diagram, a passage, or watch a demonstration, you can take the sensory stimuli from that learning experience and remind yourself that there are other ways to think about the information. As soon as your mind turns toward other ways to encode, for example, recalling the sounds you heard during the demonstration, or thinking of doing something similar to what was presented in a passage, you encode the stimuli in new ways.

EXERCISE 2.2

Encoding Information

PURPOSE: Sensory information you receive can be translated into different codes: visual, linguistic (auditory), motor (kinesthetic), and semantic (experiences of events). Your instructors use a variety of approaches to present information in ways that promote the use of different kinds of encoding.

DIRECTIONS: Work by yourself, with a partner, or in a small group to answer the following questions.

1. What was a main topic discussed in the previous class? _____

_____

2. Complete the following chart to show the different kinds of codes you used for new information on the topic.

Visual Codes	
Linguistic Codes	
Motor Codes	
Semantic Codes	

Selective Attention

Sensory input can appear and fade or be discarded from your memory within one or two seconds. However, by using selective attention, you can hold the information in your sensory memory for a few seconds longer and prevent the information from fading away. This **selective attention** is the process of focusing on or attending to specific sensory input that is important to process further. Selective attention also involves ignoring stimuli from the physical world that are not important to process further. For example, if you are in a room filled with talking people, you cannot take in and process all the conversations or all the visual stimuli. Instead, you focus your selective attention on a specific conversation or on a smaller group of people, and you ignore the other stimuli.

Selective attention works when you study as well. Assume that you are reading your textbook. The letters and words in a sentence enter your sensory memory. When you are using selective attention, you recognize that a sentence is important, select it for further mental processing and encoding, and immediately begin attaching meaning to the words. However, if you shift your focus from your book to a television screen, the sensory input of the printed sentence fades and quickly is replaced by the television image. Consciously using selective attention will help you control and limit the sensory stimuli that you allow to enter into your memory systems.

Selective attention is the process of focusing on or attending to specific sensory input that is important to process further.

CONCEPT CHECK 2.5

What is selective attention? What kinds of activities can disrupt your selective attention?

EXERCISE 2.3

Labeling the Information Processing Model

PURPOSE: Familiarity with the skeleton or the structure of a model lays a foundation to which you can add or attach details. Thinking about the structure of the Information Processing Model "refreshes your memory" and prepares you for adding more details to the model.

DIRECTIONS:

1. Without referring to Figure 2.1, label the following chart to show *Sensory Input, Sensory Memory, Working Memory, Short-Term Memory, Central Executive, Long-Term Memory, Schemas,* and *Output.*

2. Add the arrows to the chart to show the direction of the flow of stimuli and information.

3. Check the accuracy of your work by comparing it to Figure 2.1.

Information Processing Model

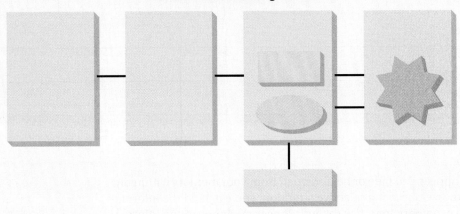

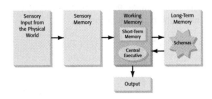

Working memory (WM) refers to all cognitive processes or activities that occur in our conscious mind.

CONCEPT CHECK 2.6

What kinds of cognitive activities occur in working memory?

Working Memory

Working memory (WM) refers to all cognitive processes or activities that occur in our conscious mind. In other words, *anything that you are aware of doing or thinking occurs in working memory.* Each time you pay attention to new information, rehearse, practice, recall, make connections, link information, retrieve concepts or details, get feedback, and achieve some form of output, you are in working memory. The following points help explain the variety of cognitive activities that occur in working memory:

▌ To understand new information, working memory searches for related information in long-term memory, activates it, and brings that information back into your working memory or your awareness.

▌ Working memory integrates the retrieved information with the new information to form a larger, stronger, or more comprehensive unit of meaning. Working memory then returns this expanded unit of meaning to long-term memory until it is needed and retrieved at a later time.

▌ As you work in new ways with new information, you encode the information on deeper levels using the same four kinds of coding as shown in Figure 2.2 (page 40). The effectiveness of your strategies to encode information on deeper levels directly affects your ability to retrieve or recall information at later times from long-term memory.

▌ As you work with information, your working memory rapidly moves encoded information both into and out of long-term memory. All in-depth learning and processing take place in working memory as you think about the material.

▌ When you work with *familiar* information (not new information), there is a large "cloud of activated information" being held in working memory. For example, if you are skilled at troubleshooting and correcting computer problems, as you work with computers, large amounts of related information about computers is activated and present in your working memory.

▌ Working memory manages all cognitive functions. Two parts of working memory are essential for working memory to function effectively:

   ▌ A smaller, temporary storage center called *short-term memory*

   ▌ The *central executive,* the administrator or the "C.E.O." (chief executive officer) of all working memory's operations

Short-Term Memory

Coded information from sensory memory that has been "tagged" for further processing moves into short-term memory. **Short-Term Memory (STM)** is a temporary storage center in working memory that receives and briefly holds sensory memory for further processing. Information in short-term memory becomes discarded if further attention and encoding of the information do not occur. To keep *new* information active and to move it farther into memory for processing, you need to consciously work with the information. The following are important points about the limitations of short-term memory:

▌ *STM is limited in duration.* New information stays in short-term memory for up to thirty seconds. If there is no attempt to work further with the information, it fades and drops out of memory. For example, if you ask someone for a phone number or directions, unless you rehearse (practice) the information, encode it in a new way, or work with it, within thirty seconds you most likely will not recall accurately the phone number or the directions.

▌ *STM is limited in capacity.* Short-term memory, on the average, holds fewer than nine items or "chunks" of new information at one time. The **Magic 7 ± 2 Theory** states that immediate memory span is 7 items, plus 2 (total 9 items) or minus 2 (total 5 items). Other studies show an average memory span of *new* information is three to five items or chunks of information. In either case, the number of items is limited. (See **Figure 2.3.**)

▌ If too much new information enters short-term memory at one time, short-term memory becomes overloaded and some or all of the information is discarded. For example, if you are given twelve new items to learn at one time, short-term memory becomes overloaded and cannot begin to process all

Short-Term Memory (STM) is a temporary storage center in working memory that receives and briefly holds sensory memory for further processing.

CONCEPT CHECK 2.7

What are the limitations of short-term memory? What happens to information in this memory system?

The **Magic 7 ± 2 Theory** states that immediate memory span is 7 items plus 2 (total 9 items) or minus 2 (total 5 items).

FIGURE 2.3

The Capacity of Short-Term Memory

LEARN BY DOING: Here is a test of your immediate memory span. Ask someone to read to you the numbers in the top row at the rate of about one per second; then try to repeat them back in the same order. Then try the next row, and the one after that, until you make a mistake. Your immediate memory span is the maximum number of items you can repeat back perfectly.

```
9 2 5
8 6 4 2
3 7 6 5 4
6 2 7 4 1 8
0 4 0 1 4 7 3
1 9 2 2 3 5 3 0
4 8 6 8 5 4 3 3 2
2 5 3 1 9 7 1 7 6 8
8 5 1 2 9 6 1 9 4 5 0
9 1 8 5 4 6 9 4 2 9 3 7
```

Source: from Bernstein/Nash, *Essentials of Psychology,* © 2008, Houghton Mifflin, page 215, Figure 6.3.

twelve items. However, if you break the list of items into three groups with four items each, your short-term memory can begin processing the first four items, then the second four items, and finally the last four items in your list.

❚ Selective attention increases the size of your immediate memory span.

The Central Executive

After learning about the functions and activities that occur in working memory, you may be wondering how our brains manage all these activities. Alan Baddeley, a British researcher and psychologist, introduced the concept that a specific part of the brain, referred to as the central executive, serves as the coordinator of brain activity. The **central executive** is the part of working memory that manages and coordinates the cognitive functions and the flow of information throughout the processing system. One analogy to use to grasp the functions of the central executive is to think of an executive of a large firm. He or she continually searches for relevant data needed to run the firm efficiently, activates information, sends out directives, initiates changes, and integrates all the operations of the firm. **Figure 2.4** shows the multiple functions of the central executive.

The **central executive** is the part of working memory that manages and coordinates the cognitive functions and the flow of information throughout the processing system.

CONCEPT CHECK 2.8

What is the central executive of your brain? What essential functions does it perform?

CONCEPT CHECK 2.9

How does working memory become overloaded? What strategies can you use to avoid overloading your working memory when you study?

Overload in Working Memory

Due to the many mental or cognitive activities that occur in working memory, working memory can become overloaded and can operate less efficiently when too many demands are placed on it at one time. To avoid overloading your working memory, do not attempt to take in too much new information too quickly. Cramming for tests or reading complex textbooks quickly, for example, are ineffective strategies that may overload working memory. Avoid placing excessive demands at one time on your central executive (and working memory) by following these tips:

❚ *Monitor the speed you take in new information.* Work slowly enough to allow working memory sufficient time to retrieve meanings and related information

---

FIGURE 2.4

The Multiple Functions of the Central Executive

The **central executive** in working memory:

▌ Receives, organizes, and coordinates the flow of information throughout the memory system

▌ Integrates data from the sensory centers and long-term memory

▌ Initiates and controls deliberate actions and goal-directed behavior

▌ Initiates and manages attention and planning

▌ Activates decision-making functions of the conscious mind

---

from long-term memory and return them to working memory— a process that occurs each time you attempt to comprehend or attach meaning to new information. For example, read a short section of information, pause to think and make connections, and then read a little more, pause, and make new connections or associations.

▌ *Work with three to five chunks of new information at one time.* A "chunk" of new information may be as small as new words or phrases, or it may involve larger images or steps, as in a process. The size of chunks of information will vary from one person to another and depend on familiarity with the material. For example, if you have a limited background in chemistry, you may need to break some sentences in a chemistry book into word-sized chunks; however, a person with a strong chemistry background may be able to make phrases or whole sentences into unified chunks. Trying to learn or memorize too many chunks of information moves beyond the capacity of working memory, resulting in incomplete or partial learning.

▌ *Break larger pieces of information into smaller units.* Focus your attention on one unit at a time. For example, when reviewing your lecture notes, do not read an entire set of notes from start to finish without stopping. Instead, read a small section, pause to make associations, and check comprehension before moving to the next section of your notes.

▌ *Free up working memory by ignoring intrusive thoughts.* Intrusive thoughts, such as daydreaming, stress, general anxiety, or distractions (television, radio, stereo, or iPods) can occupy working memory space. By removing intrusive thoughts and distractions, you increase the amount of working memory available for thinking processes.

Long-Term Memory

As you have learned, through a complex series of interactions, working memory sends information back and forth to the final memory center, long-term memory. **Long-term memory (LTM)** is a permanent storage center that holds chunks of information received from working memory. Unlike working memory that involves everything you are aware of thinking (your conscious mind), long-term memory simply exists as a storage center. You become aware of long-term memory only when your working memory activates parts of long-term memory to locate

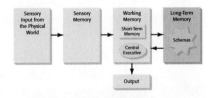

Long-term memory (LTM) is a permanent storage center that holds chunks of information received from working memory.

previously learned information or to imprint new information. The following are key points about long-term memory:

▌ Long-term memory has unlimited capacity; it never runs out of storage space.

▌ Long-term memory is your enormous mental filing cabinet or data center that permanently "files away" coded information received from working memory.

▌ Information that you have rehearsed, coded clearly, linked to other related information, and have filed in a logical manner will be easier to locate than information that is disorganized, not linked to other ideas, or has not been processed effectively.

▌ Permanently stored information can be pulled back into working memory to be expanded, strengthened, or modified.

▌ Even though coded information is believed to be permanently imprinted in long-term memory, the information may not always be accessible. Lack of use of the information may "bury" it deep into long-term memory or create "rusty doors" that make access to the information difficult or impossible.

CONCEPT CHECK 2.10

How does long-term memory storage in terms of duration and capacity differ from short-term memory's duration and capacity?

CONCEPT CHECK 2.11

How does the information about the three memory systems compare to Figure 8.14, page 238?

GROUP PROCESSING:
A COLLABORATIVE LEARNING ACTIVITY

Form groups of three or four students. Then complete the following directions.

1. On large paper, create the two charts shown below.

2. Brainstorm *specific topics* or kinds of information that members of your group have encountered in any of their classes within the last two weeks that were *easy* for them to understand and learn. Record all the responses on the chart.

3. As a group, brainstorm all the reasons each topic may have been easy for the group member to learn. Record the reasons in the right column of the chart.

4. Repeat this process for *specific topics* or kinds of information that were difficult for group members to understand and learn. Brainstorm and record the reasons those topics may have been difficult to understand and learn.

5. Examine and summarize the results.

Easy to Learn	Why

Difficult to Learn	Why

Schemas in Long-Term Memory

As coded information enters long-term memory, it is categorized, *imprinted,* and stored with related clusters of information called schemas. **Schemas** are sets of memories (clusters of related information) that form large concepts or frameworks in which other related ideas, facts, and details can be attached. The following are important points about schemas:

Schemas are sets of memories (clusters of related information) that store large concepts or frameworks in which other related ideas, facts, and details can be attached.

▌ The number of schemas in a person's memory system is unlimited. For example, you already have schemas for concepts such as shelter, fast foods, pets, multiplication, cancer, global warming, taxes, loyalty, and football.

▌ The information in your schemas affects how you understand and process new information. For example, any new information you take in about football gets interpreted or understood based on what information about football you already have in your football schema. If you are an avid football fan, your football schema will include more information than the football schema of a person who seldom watches a game.

▌ When you do memory searches for information, your central executive scans long-term memory seeking to locate schemas with information that is relevant to the topic. For example, if you are trying to recall the Spanish word for "administration," through a series of associations and connections, you might scan the schemas related to Spanish, administration, and perhaps English-Spanish language patterns until you locate the answer, *administración*.

▌ If you encoded the information carefully, through memory searches, you will locate the sought-after information or answer to a question.

Forming and Expanding Schemas

Understanding the concept of schemas provides one explanation as to why learning new information sometimes is difficult and other times is relatively easy. When you start to learn something new or unfamiliar, the learning process at first may feel challenging, frustrating, or impossible because you lack schemas or a foundation for the new information. Once you begin learning basic concepts and related details for a new subject, you create a schema in long-term memory. Learning new information about the familiar topic becomes easier and more rewarding.

For example, assume that you enroll in a French class, and this is your first experience studying a foreign language. At first, you may feel confused and struggle with the course until you begin to form a schema for French. As the course progresses, you will acquire skills that enable you to compare information, make connections, and establish a stronger schema. If your friend who already speaks Spanish enrolls in the same course, he or she already has foreign language schemas in long-term memory. Even though French is new to both of you, your friend most likely will feel fewer frustrations and will learn more quickly than you mainly because of the existence of schemas.

Throughout this textbook, you will be encouraged to think about schemas, and you will learn strategies for building schemas and connecting or associating new information to information you already know. As your knowledge expands, the learning experience becomes even more enjoyable, exciting, and rewarding.

Output

When you successfully move information through your information processing system, you will be able to show some form of *output* that demonstrates that memory and learning have taken place. This *output* may include *recognition tasks* that show that you recognize correct information or details when some kind of clue is provided, or it may include *recall tasks* that show that you can retrieve specific information or details from your memory system. Output that involves *recall*

CONCEPT CHECK 2.12

How many schemas do you have in your long-term memory? Explain.

CONCEPT CHECK 2.13

What feelings did you experience the first time you sat down to use a computer? How do you feel now about working on a computer? What caused the change in your feelings?

CONCEPT CHECK 2.14

How do you know if learning has taken place?

tasks from memory is usually more difficult than output that involves recognition tasks. The following are examples of two forms of output:

Recognition Tasks

▌ Recognize the correct answer from a list of options, such as on a multiple-choice question or a quiz-show format.

▌ Recognize parts of an object when the labels for the parts are provided.

▌ Recognize familiar faces, pictures, sounds, or tunes.

Recall Tasks

▌ Respond with a correct answer when no clues are provided.

▌ Use specific steps to solve a math problem or perform a process or a procedure.

▌ Recall and explain information with accurate details.

▌ Use critical thinking skills to evaluate, draw a conclusion, or debate a point.

▌ Write an effective essay or report without referring to printed sources of information.

▌ Apply information to create or construct a product.

EXERCISE 2.4

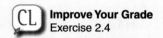

Improve Your Grade
Exercise 2.4

Using Schemas

PURPOSE: Information that already exists in your long-term memory schemas affects your ability and speed for understanding new information. Taking the time to compare new information to what you already know facilitates the process of learning.

DIRECTIONS:

1. Read the excerpt from Bernstein and Nash's *Essentials of Psychology* (Houghton Mifflin, © 2008) that appears at the top of the next page.

2. After reading the excerpt, answer the following questions. Write your answer on separate paper or online at Exercise 2.4.

   a. As you read the excerpt, were you aware of your working memory tapping into an existing schema for hemispheres of the brain? What concepts or pictures were captured from your long-term memory?

   b. Does the information in the excerpt support what you already have in your schema?

   c. What new information does this excerpt add to your existing schema?

   d. Was it easy or difficult for you to grasp this new information? Why?

   e. Return to Figure 1.5 in Chapter 1 (page 17). What details could you add to Figure 1.5 to expand your knowledge of the two hemispheres?

The Divided Brain: Lateralization

A striking suggestion emerged from observations of people with damage to the language centers of the brain. Researchers noticed that damage to specific areas of the left hemisphere interfered with the ability to use or understand language. Damage to those same areas in the right hemisphere usually did not cause such problems. Could it be that the right and left hemispheres of the brain serve different functions?

This idea was not entirely new. It had long been understood that most sensory and motor pathways cross over from one hemisphere to the other as they enter or leave the brain. As a result, the left hemisphere receives information from, and controls movement of, the right side of the body. The right hemisphere receives input from and controls the left side of the body. The image [at the right] shows the two hemispheres. The fact that the language centers . . . almost always occur on the left side of the brain suggests that each hemisphere might be specialized to perform some functions almost independently of the other hemisphere. Having these two somewhat specialized hemispheres allows the normal brain to perform some tasks more efficiently, particularly difficult ones. But the differences between the hemispheres should not be exaggerated. Remember, the corpus callosum usually integrates the functions of the "two brains." As a result the hemispheres work closely together, each making up well for whatever lack of ability the other may have.

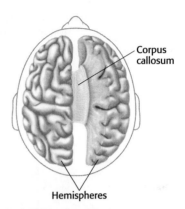

Corpus callosum

Hemispheres

The Brain's Left and Right Hemispheres

The brain's two hemispheres are joined by the bundle of fibers knows as the corpus callosum. In this figure the hemispheres are separated so that the corpus callosum can be seen. The two cerebral hemispheres look nearly the same but perform somewhat different tasks. For one thing, the left hemisphere receives sensory input from, and controls movement on, the right side of the body. The right hemisphere senses and controls the left side of the body.

REFLECTIVE WRITING 2.1

CL **Improve Your Grade**
Reflective Writing 2.1

On separate paper, in a journal, or online at this textbook's website, respond to the following questions.

1. What current study practices can you change to avoid overloading your working memory?

2. What are the most interesting and valuable points you learned so far in Chapter 2 about the way your mind processes information?

ANSWERS APPEAR ON PAGE A4

CHECK POINT 2.1

True or False?

_____ 1. Recognition tasks involve more complex mental processes than recall tasks.

_____ 2. Stimuli remain in sensory memory longer than they remain in short-term memory.

_____ 3. All sensory memory is first encoded linguistically.

_____ 4. Using selective attention is one way to hold information longer in your sensory memory and in your working memory.

_____ 5. Working memory and long-term memory have unlimited capacities to store information.

Improve Your Grade
Online Practice 1:
Information Processing

YOUR CONSCIOUS MIND: WORKING MEMORY

2   *Identify study skills strategies that strengthen working memory.*

The majority of cognitive activities that are a part of learning occur in working memory. *What* you do in working memory and *how* you encode information in working memory have a major impact on how well you are able to locate information in long-term memory and show some form of *output*. Conducting memory searches, using retrieval cues, tracking your thought patterns, and using effective study strategies are activities that you can do to use your working memory effectively.

Conducting Memory Searches

As you have learned, working memory involves rapid and complex interactions with information you have stored in your long-term memory schemas. Working memory frequently uses memory searches to locate, activate, and bring learned information back into your conscious mind (working memory). A **memory search** involves linking together a series of facts, concepts, or previously learned associations in order to locate information stored in your long-term memory.

Sometimes a memory search is quick and the answer to a question immediately comes to mind; other times, more extensive searches are required to retrieve information. As an example, if someone asks you where you were born, for most people the answer is immediate. Other questions, such as where your mother was born, or where your maternal grandmother was born, may require a more in-depth search and the use of retrieval cues to locate the answer.

Creating and Using Retrieval Cues

Retrieval cues are words, phrases, pictures, graphics, or memory tricks (mnemonics) associated with units of information sent to long-term memory. Retrieval cues link one piece of information to another. Using a retrieval cue triggers memory of the information and its meaning. For example, to identify the birth location of your maternal grandmother, you might need to "chat your way" to the answer by using associations:

> *"My mother was born in Detroit, Michigan, but her family had moved there right before she was born. I remember visiting Michigan. We drove up to the*

A **memory search** involves linking together a series of facts, concepts, or previously learned associations in order to locate information stored in your long-term memory.

CONCEPT CHECK 2.15

What factors determine the time it takes for a memory search to locate information?

Retrieval cues are words, phrases, pictures, graphics, or memory tricks (mnemonics) associated with units of information sent to long-term memory.

northern peninsula for a family gathering. We drove by the house in Copper Harbor where she grew up. I can still picture the little brown house at the end of the rocky road. I remember Grandma saying that she was born in that house."

If you are pressed for the exact address, perhaps no amount of memory searching will produce the answer, for it is likely that you never attached a retrieval cue to the address and the information was never registered in your memory.

Retrieval cues are an essential element of the learning process. Assume that you are learning new information about labor unions. To attach or associate this new information to your existing schemas, your working memory first uses retrieval cues to seek and locate information in long-term memory that relates to labor, unions, and perhaps specific unions, such as the Teamsters or the United Auto Workers. It may also seek information in long-term memory about personal experiences you have had with unions. With your previously learned knowledge pulled back into working memory, you can integrate the new information with information you already know, thus strengthening your schemas.

Tracking Your Thought Patterns

Paying attention to the way you think and tracking your thought patterns increase your awareness of the complexity of thinking and learning. It also helps you realize the importance of creating strong retrieval cues and making strong associations to link chunks of information. Jackson, a student like you, reads this test question: *What are three of Gardner's intelligences that rely heavily on physical movement and activity? Explain your answer.* This is how Jackson recorded his thought patterns:

> *Gardner . . . eight intelligences . . . To answer this, I need to look at all eight intelligences. What were they? The first . . . language . . . oh yeah, we talked about the word* lingua *. . . Right, linguistic is what it's called. The visual one is called . . . What the heck is that word? Architects have it . . . They work with space . . . oh right . . . spatial. Two people ones . . . I remember seeing the group of people I drew in my notes . . . interpersonal. The other is about me . . . intrapersonal. What was that chart I copied in my notes? Come on, think! I remember trees. The last one is about nature . . . the naturalist. Okay only three more to go. Oh yeah, the two M's . . . musical and mathematical . . . What's the last one? What did we talk about in the group when we listed people for each intelligence? Oh yeah, the other was Lance Armstrong and Michael Jordon . . . athletes. That's right, bodily-kinesthetic. Now I can use this to answer the question* (His thoughts continued.)

Thought processes, schemas created, and memory searches vary from person to person. Heather approached the question from a different angle by recalling a memory tool (a mnemonic) that she created for the eight intelligences. She wrote the eight intelligences on a piece of paper and selected an initial letter for each intelligence: L, L, M, K, S, I, I, and N. She rearranged the letters to form two words: *SLIM LINK.* In order to use *SLIM LINK* to name the eight intelligences, she had to practice converting the letters to the original words to keep the information fresh and active. Following is how Heather recorded her thought processes:

> *Easy. I just need to write out the intelligences and then find the three that deal with physical movement and activity. SLIM LINK!*

CONCEPT CHECK 2.16

Why are retrieval cues important in the process of conducting memory searches? How would a lack of clear retrieval cues affect your working memory?

CONCEPT CHECK 2.17

After reading a passage, how could you use this technique of tracking your thought patterns to check how well you understood the passage?

Tracking your thought patterns as you conduct memory searches, use retrieval cues, and recall associations increases your awareness of the ways you organize and store information. When you attempt to recall learned information, do you give yourself sufficient time to activate these processes?

S = spatial; L = linguistic; I = interpersonal; M = musical; L = logical-mathe-matical; I = intrapersonal; N = naturalist; and K = kinesthetic . . . I mean bodily-kinesthetic. Okay . . . let's see. Bodily-kinesthetic is one for sure. Inter-personal involves interacting with people, so that has movement and activity. Musical . . . that will be my third choice. Okay, now I just need to explain my reasoning . . . (Her thoughts continued.)

EXERCISE 2.5

Retrieval Cues

PURPOSE: When you try to recall answers to questions, often you need to "chat to yourself" about the information, or use retrieval cues to conduct memory searches for the answer. Sometimes you cannot find answers; perhaps the infor-mation was never learned, or if learned, it was not practiced on a regular enough basis to be accessible.

DIRECTIONS: In the following chart, read the questions and write the answer to as many of the questions as possible. Pay attention to your thinking processes. Check one of the last three columns to show how you responded to the question.

Question	Answer	Immediately Knew the Answer	Needed to Do a Memory Search	I Do Not Know
1. How many states are in the United States?				
2. Which state was the 49th state to join the Union?				
3. What is the capital city of New Mexico?				
4. What is the value of the Roman numeral XL?				
5. There are two cups in one pint. How many cups are in one gallon?				
6. Which fraction is smaller: $6/7$ or $2/3$?				
7. What is the name of your third grade teacher?				
8. What is *photosynthesis*?				

Rehearsing Learned Information

Even when you have effectively learned and imprinted information in long-term schemas, failure to rehearse the information may make it difficult or impossible to recall. Speaking a foreign language is a good example of the necessity to practice frequently. Imagine that you learned to speak a foreign language as a child, but you have not practiced it for many years. You can still understand a few basic words in that language and you remember the general sentence structure used, but you have forgotten the vocabulary and can no longer speak the language fluently. The knowledge you have for speaking that language still exists in your schemas, but it is no longer accessible. However, by reviewing language lessons and materials and socializing with speakers of that language, you can reactivate the information stored in your schemas. You will be able to "relearn" the language in less time than you needed for the initial learning because of the schemas you previously formed.

CONCEPT CHECK 2.18

Why is rehearsal important to do? What might happen to information in long-term memory that you do not practice frequently?

EXERCISE 2.6

Working Memory Inventory

DIRECTIONS: Go to the Working Memory Inventory in Appendix B, page A6, to assess the effectiveness of the study skills strategies you currently use. You can retake this inventory at different times throughout the term.

Using Effective Strategies for Working Memory

Understanding how you process information lays the foundation for learning how to use working memory effectively to become a more powerful learner. **Figure 2.5** summarizes ten Essential Strategies for Strengthening Working Memory. Details about each strategy are below.

CONCEPT CHECK 2.19

What strategies can you use to strengthen your working memory?

Limited Intake

Limit the number of items and the speed at which you take in stimuli. Your working memory needs time to work, integrate, and process stimuli. Avoid overloading working memory or placing unreasonable demands on your processing system. Pay attention to and monitor your thinking processes. Reduce the number or sizes of chunks of information or slow down your "in-take speed" as soon as you realize you have overloaded your working memory.

Interest and Excitement

Create an interest and excitement in new information. You can create an interest in a subject by discussing it with other students, sharing the newly learned information with friends or family members, or finding meaningful ways to apply the new information in your life. Creating an interest adds an emotional charge to the learning process; working memory responds to emotional charges. Your interest level reflects your attitude toward a subject; your attitude affects the quality of a learning experience.

FIGURE 2.5

Essential Strategies for Strengthening Working Memory

▌ Limit the number of items and the speed at which you take in stimuli.

▌ Create an interest and excitement in new information.

▌ Set learning goals when you study.

▌ Create and use associations to link together chunks of information.

▌ Make a strong impression of new information, and practice retrieving that impression.

▌ Work with information to encode it in new ways.

▌ Give additional rehearsal attention to items in the middle of lists.

▌ Use self-quizzing and other techniques that provide feedback.

▌ Spread learning over several time periods.

▌ Rehearse frequently.

▌ If you have a *positive attitude* and are excited and motivated to learn about a subject, your mind is more alert and working memory becomes receptive to incoming stimuli.

▌ If you harbor *negative attitudes* toward the subject or the learning process, your short-term memory tends to "tag" the information as unimportant and ignores the incoming stimuli; it never moves into working memory for further processing.

Learning Goals

Set learning goals when you study. Goal-oriented behavior activates working memory. When you have an *intention* to learn, you create a purpose with desired outcomes. This builds motivation and momentum and engages your working memory in the learning process. You will learn more about setting learning goals and motivation in Chapters 4 and 5.

Associations

CONCEPT CHECK 2.20

What associations have you recently created to learn new information?

Create and use associations to link together chunks of information. Intentionally seek ways to relate the new information to information you already know. Take the time to create associations using words, pictures, symbols, or mnemonics (memory tools). Actively use your background knowledge to create associations. Ask yourself questions such as: How is this similar to something I already know? Where have I seen or experienced something like this? How can I use this information? Associations form retrieval cues that can help you locate and retrieve information stored in long-term memory.

Strong Impressions

Make a strong impression of new information, and practice retrieving that impression. Creating strong impressions involves focusing your attention on the information so you can "take it in" as a vivid unit of information. Include important details, such as shape, size, colors as well as auditory impressions such as tone of voice, intensity, and specific words in your impressions. Revisiting information, such as rereading sections of a textbook or sections of notes over several different periods, helps solidify an impression. To work effectively, practice recalling or retrieving the impressions from your long-term memory.

New Encoding

Work with information to encode it in new ways. Use multisensory learning strategies to learn new information and to encode it using the three main modalities. Using a variety of modalities strengthens the memory paths in and out of long-term memory and creates multiple retrieval cues to use at later times. Rearranging information in new ways, reorganizing information into meaningful groups or categories, and adding details such as colors or pictures help you personalize new information and create solid retrieval cues to use to recall information from long-term memory.

CONCEPT CHECK 2.21

What are the benefits of encoding information more than one way?

Items in Lists

Give additional rehearsal attention to items in the middle of lists. When you study and memorize items in a list, frequently you will remember items at the beginning of the list when your rehearsal or "memory work" began. This is called the *primacy effect*—the first items are easier to recall or remember. You will also have good recall of the last few items in a list. Remembering the last few items in a list is called the *recency effect*, which states that you will remember the items most recently practiced. The items in the middle of a list of items are the most difficult items to recall accurately. Therefore, when you study, give additional attention to rehearsing and recalling the most difficult items— the items in the middle of a list.

CONCEPT CHECK 2.22

In a list of twelve items, which items will be the most difficult to recall accurately? Why is this so?

Self-Quizzing and Feedback

Use self-quizzing and other techniques that provide feedback. Self-quizzing involves a form of activity in which you test your accuracy and completeness of understanding. Asking questions, reciting information without looking at printed materials, reworking math problems, and writing or recreating visual materials from memory are forms of self-quizzing.

Spaced Practice

Spread learning over several time periods. Allowing time between study blocks and spreading contact with materials and tasks over several different time periods give working memory time to consolidate and integrate the new information into your long-term memory schemas. You will learn about *spaced practice* in Chapters 3 and 4.

Rehearsal

Rehearse frequently. Include time when you study to review new information and previously learned information from your textbooks, lecture notes, and homework assignments. Each time you review, you practice locating and retrieving chunks of information from your long-term memory schemas. Frequent review keeps the information active and accessible.

CONCEPT CHECK 2.23

How does rehearsing help working memory function smoothly?

EXERCISE 2.7

Textbook Case Studies

Improve Your Grade
Exercise 2.7

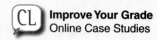
Improve Your Grade
Online Case Studies

DIRECTIONS:

1. Read each case study carefully. Respond to the question at the end of each case study by using strategies from Chapter 2 to answer each question. Answer in complete sentences.

2. Write your responses on paper or online at the Student Website, Exercise 2.7. You will be able to print your online response or e-mail it to your instructor.

CASE STUDY 1: By the end of the week, Curtis needs to read a thirty-page chapter and be prepared to discuss it in class. Curtis does not enjoy this textbook or course, so he tends to procrastinate. The night before class he reads quickly through the chapter to get an overview. He jots down a few words, phrases, and main ideas and shoves the list in his book so he will be prepared for the class discussion the next day. Instead of a class discussion, however, the instructor gives a short quiz. Curtis answers only two out of ten questions. What strategies should Curtis have used to achieve better results?

CASE STUDY 2: Mary, normally a very confident student, needs to take a science class this term to fulfill a degree requirement. Before the class even began, she worried about her ability to handle the course. She has never enjoyed science, and she knows that her background in science is weak. After the first week of class, Mary was frantic. She could not understand why she felt lost, confused, and defeated, and she did not know what to do to get on track. What strategies could you suggest Mary begin using to deal with her frustrations and get herself back on track?

EXERCISE 2.8

Links

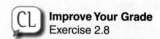
Improve Your Grade
Exercise 2.8

DIRECTIONS: Work with a partner or in a small group. Discuss answers for the following questions. Be prepared to share your answers with the class.

1. What types of encoding occur when you use multisensory study strategies?

2. Are schemas stored in both hemispheres of the brain? Explain your answer.

3. The Multiple Intelligence Theory recognizes the potential people have to activate and strengthen the eight intelligences. What relationships do you see between schemas in long-term memory and strengthening multiple intelligences?

REFLECTIVE WRITING 2.2

Improve Your Grade
Reflective Writing 2.2

On separate paper, in a journal, or online at this textbook's website, respond to the following questions.

1. What have you learned from the Information Processing Model that will help you strengthen your ability to learn and improve your memory?

2. What schemas in your long-term memory do you believe are well developed due to special interests or a degree of expertise? How do you feel about learning new information related to these schemas?

CHECK POINT 2.2

ANSWERS APPEAR ON PAGE A4

Multiple Choice

_____ 1. Encoding information using more than one sensory channel
    a. impacts your ability to show output.
    b. creates multiple retrieval cues.
    c. facilitates the process of conducting memory searches.
    d. does all of the above.

_____ 2. Which of the following is *not* true about memory searches?
    a. They produce immediate results.
    b. They involve using associations to connect related items.
    c. They scan schemas for relevant information.
    d. They activate previously learned information.

_____ 3. You can make a strong impression of new information by
    a. thinking or pondering the new information.
    b. focusing your attention on details.
    c. rereading the information several times over several different days.
    d. doing all of the above.

_____ 4. Which of the following is *not* true about retrieval cues?
    a. They may involve words, pictures, or memory tools.
    b. They are created in sensory memory and reinforced in short-term memory.
    c. They link together chunks of information.
    d. They may include semantic encoding.

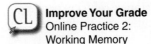
Improve Your Grade
Online Practice 2:
Working Memory

LEARNING OBJECTIVES REVIEW

▶ *Explain how the three memory systems (sensory memory, working memory, and long-term memory) work to process information.*

- Metacognition is the process of understanding *how* you learn, *what* you need to learn, and *which* strategies or techniques would be the most effective or the best matched to the learning task. Understanding the Information Processing Model is the first step in learning to use the powerful process of metacognition.

- The Information Processing Model consists of three memory centers: sensory memory, working memory, and long-term memory. Each performs specific functions.

- Output, which may include *recognition tasks* and *recall tasks,* demonstrates that memory and learning have taken place.

- Four kinds of codes are used to encode information:
  - Linguistic codes, also called acoustical or auditory codes
  - Visual codes, also called imaginal codes
  - Motor codes, also called physical or kinesthetic codes
  - Semantic codes, also called conceptual or abstract codes

- Encoding translates stimuli into meaningful forms that long-term memory can recognize and use. You can use strategies to encode information in new ways.

- Selective attention holds stimuli in sensory memory, and later in short-term memory and working memory, for further processing.

- Working memory refers to all cognitive processes or activities that occur in your conscious mind. Short-term memory (STM), a temporary storage center in working memory, and the central executive are two parts of working memory.

- Long-term memory (LTM) is a permanent storage center that consists of schemas, which are sets or clusters of memory that store large concepts of related information.

▶ *Identify study skills strategies that strengthen working memory.*

- Memory searches and retrieval cues help locate, activate, and retrieve information from LTM. Tracking your thought patterns helps you increase your awareness of the way you think and process information.

- Ten essential strategies can help you strengthen your working memory and become a more powerful learner.
  - Limit the number of items and the speed at which you take in stimuli.
  - Create and interest and an excitement in new information.
  - Set learning goals when you study.
  - Create and use associations.
  - Make a strong impression of new information, and practice retrieving that impression.
  - Work with information to encode it in new ways.
  - Give additional rehearsal attention to items in the middle of lists.
  - Use self-quizzing and other techniques that provide feedback.
  - Spread learning over several time periods.
  - Rehearse frequently.

Matching

Match the terms below with the descriptions at the right. On the line, write the letter from the list at the right to show your answer.

_____ 1. Schemas

_____ 2. Long-term memory

_____ 3. Output

_____ 4. Selective attention

_____ 5. Sensory input

_____ 6. Semantic coding

_____ 7. Working memory

_____ 8. Sensory memory

_____ 9. Short-term memory

_____ 10. Central executive

a. Stimuli received by our five senses from the physical world

b. A memory with generalized meaning of a personal experience or event

c. A temporary storage center that holds stimuli for only a few seconds

d. Conscious memory that includes all mental activities that you are aware of performing

e. The part of working memory that coordinates brain activity

f. Includes recognition tasks and recall tasks

g. Clusters of related information in long-term memory

h. Permanent memory with unlimited capacity

i. The process of focusing on specific input or stimuli

j. A temporary storage center in working memory

True or False?

_____ 1. Short-term memory and working memory hold all sensory stimuli until all of the information is thoroughly learned.

_____ 2. Long-term memory can recognize and process linguistic, motor, visual, and semantic codes.

_____ 3. Most sensory input that you ignore in sensory memory fades or gets discarded from memory.

_____ 4. When you conduct a memory search for information, associations often work as retrieval cues to locate information.

_____ 5. Selective attention can delay or prevent stimuli from fading or being discarded.

_____ 6. People can control and direct what goes into long-term memory, but they cannot control or direct what goes into and out of the other memory systems.

_____ 7. The central executive of working memory coordinates many cognitive processes, responds to goal-oriented behavior, and makes decisions.

_____ 8. Creating an interest, setting learning goals, creating and using associations, and self-quizzing are some strategies to use to strengthen working memory.

Recall Question

On separate paper, draw and label the parts of the Information Processing Model.

CL **ACE the Test**
Four Online Practice Tests

**Online
Resources**

3 Using Twelve Principles of Memory

LEARNING OBJECTIVES

1 ▶ Use the mnemonic SAVE CRIB FOTO to identify the Twelve Principles of Memory.

2 ▶ Explain how to use the Memory Principles of Selectivity, Association, Visualization, and Elaboration.

3 ▶ Explain how to use the Memory Principles of Concentration, Recitation, Intention, and Big and Little Pictures.

60

Chapter Outline

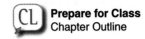

Prepare for Class
Chapter Outline

4 ▶ *Explain how to use the Memory
Principles of Feedback, Organization,
Time on Task, and Ongoing Review.*

The Twelve Principles of Memory discussed in this chapter lay a strong foundation for many study skills strategies you will learn in later chapters. The mnemonic (memory tool) SAVE CRIB FOTO helps you quickly recall these twelve principles. The first four principles, represented by SAVE, include Selectivity, Association, Visualization, and Elaboration. The middle four principles, represented by CRIB, include Concentration, Recitation, Intention, and Big and Little Pictures. The last four principles, represented by FOTO, include Feedback, Organization, Time on Task, and Ongoing Review. These Principles of Memory are memory tools that you can use to strengthen your memory and refine your study methods.

CHAPTER 3 PROFILE

Using Twelve Principles of Memory

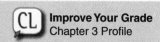

Improve Your Grade
Chapter 3 Profile

ANSWER, **SCORE**, and **RECORD** your profile before you read this chapter. If you need to review the process, refer to the complete directions given in the profile for Chapter 1 on page 4.

ONLINE: You can complete the profile and get your score online at this textbook's website.

	YES	NO
1. I have a method for assessing the effectiveness of my study skills strategies and modifying or changing my approaches to learning.	_____	_____
2. I have problems identifying what textbook and lecture material is important to learn.	_____	_____
3. I take time to associate new information with familiar information and to visualize the associations.	_____	_____
4. I frequently use rote memory by memorizing specific details exactly as they are presented in a textbook.	_____	_____
5. I set goals and plan a course of action before I begin a learning task.	_____	_____
6. I recognize different levels of information in the materials I study.	_____	_____
7. I use self-quizzing and reciting to check my understanding and my memory.	_____	_____
8. I rearrange information into meaningful units or clusters so it is easier to learn and to remember.	_____	_____
9. I wait until close to test time before I practice the information that I previously read or studied.	_____	_____
10. I am confident in my ability to monitor, evaluate, and modify strategies I use to study.	_____	_____

QUESTIONS LINKED TO THE CHAPTER LEARNING OBJECTIVES:

Question 1:	objective 1	Questions 7–9:	objective 4
Questions 2–4:	objective 2	Question 10:	all objectives
Questions 5, 6:	objective 3		

MEMORY TOOLS

 Use the mnemonic SAVE CRIB FOTO *to identify the Twelve Principles of Memory.*

You use memory tools on a regular basis every day to boost your memory and your ability to process information. All of the working memory strategies you learned in Chapter 2 are memory tools. The Twelve Principles of Memory in this chapter are memory tools that can help you assess the effectiveness of your learning strategies, and they provide you with new strategies to use in any learning situation to become a powerful learner.

In this chapter, the mnemonic SAVE CRIB FOTO will help you recall quickly the Twelve Principles of Memory. A **mnemonic** is a memory technique or a memory tool that serves as a bridge to help you recall information from long-term memory. In the mnemonic SAVE CRIB FOTO, each letter in these three words represents one of the Memory Principles. Each Principle of Memory focuses on a *cognitive process* that research shows builds memory and improves cognitive performance. **Figure 3.1** summarizes the twelve Memory Principles represented by each of the letters.

Mnemonics, such as SAVE CRIB FOTO, provide you with a retrieval cue to trigger your memory so you can recall information more quickly. For mnemonics to work effectively, however, you must practice translating the mnemonic back into the original items it represents. For example, if you are asked to name the Twelve Principles of Memory, responding with the answer "SAVE CRIB FOTO" will not suffice.

 Improve Your Grade
Online Flashcards
Glossary

FIGURE 3.1

The Twelve Principles of Memory (SAVE CRIB FOTO)

1. **Selectivity:** Select what is important to learn.
2. **Association:** Associate or link together chunks of information.
3. **Visualization:** Picture in your mind the information you are learning.
4. **Elaboration:** Work with information and encode information in new ways.
5. **Concentration:** Stay focused and attend to specific stimuli.
6. **Recitation:** Repeat information verbally in your own words.
7. **Intention:** Create a learning goal with clearly defined desired outcomes.
8. **Big and Little Pictures:** Recognize different levels of information.
9. **Feedback:** Check the accuracy of your learning and use forms of self-quizzing.
10. **Organization:** Reorganize information in meaningful, logical ways.
11. **Time on Task:** Dedicate and schedule ample time to learn.
12. **Ongoing Review:** Practice retrieving information from long-term memory.

A **mnemonic** is a memory technique or a memory tool that serves as a bridge to help you recall information from long-term memory.

CONCEPT CHECK 3.1

What memory tools do you already use to help your working memory work efficiently? Do you have a system you use to assess the effectiveness of your learning strategies?

CHECK POINT 3.1

True or False?

_____ 1. Mnemonics are memory techniques that work as retrieval cues to trigger the recall of information in long-term memory.

_____ 2. SAVE CRIB FOTO uses the technique of chunking information into meaningful units.

_____ 3. Knowing a mnemonic for a list of items guarantees that you will be able to name all the items in a list without hesitancy or mistakes.

EXERCISE 3.1

Memory Principles Inventory

PURPOSE: The following inventory helps you identify which Principles of Memory you currently use effectively and which you need to strengthen. Understanding how you process information is the first step in the powerful process of using metacognition.

DIRECTIONS: Complete the following inventory by answering YES or NO to each question. Be honest with your answers so they reflect your *current* use of the principles.

SELECTIVITY	YES	NO
1. Do you spend a lot of time studying but seem to study the "wrong information" for tests?	_____	_____
2. Do you get frustrated when you read because everything seems important?	_____	_____
3. Do you tend to highlight too much when you read textbooks?	_____	_____
4. Do your notes seem excessively long and overly detailed?	_____	_____
5. Do you avoid making study tools such as flashcards because you are not sure what information to put on the study tools?	_____	_____

ASSOCIATION	YES	NO
1. Do you tend to memorize facts or ideas in isolation?	_____	_____
2. When you try to recall information you have studied, do you sometimes feel "lost" because there is no direct way to access the information in your memory?	_____	_____
3. Do you feel that you are memorizing numerous lists of information but not really understanding what they mean or how they are connected?	_____	_____
4. Do you "go blank" on tests when a question asks for information in a form or context different from the way you studied it?	_____	_____
5. Do you lack sufficient time to link difficult information to familiar words or pictures?	_____	_____

VISUALIZATION	**YES**	**NO**
1. When you finish reading, do you have difficulty remembering what paragraphs were even about?	_____	_____
2. Do you have difficulty remembering information that appeared in a chart your instructor presented on the chalkboard or on a screen?	_____	_____
3. Do you find it difficult to recall a visual image of printed information?	_____	_____
4. When you try to recall information, do you rely mainly on words rather than pictures?	_____	_____
5. When your instructor explains a new concept by giving a detailed example or anecdote (story), do you have difficulty recalling the example or anecdote after you leave class?	_____	_____

ELABORATION	**YES**	**NO**
1. Do you learn individual facts or details without thinking about the schema in which they belong?	_____	_____
2. Do you frequently attempt to use rote memory to memorize facts, definitions, or rules?	_____	_____
3. Do you complete a math problem and immediately move on to the next problem?	_____	_____
4. Do you study information in the same order and in the same form in which it was presented?	_____	_____
5. Do you avoid creating new study tools that involve reorganizing information?	_____	_____

CONCENTRATION	**YES**	**NO**
1. Do you often experience divided attention because too many unrelated thoughts disrupt your thinking?	_____	_____
2. Do you have so many interruptions when you study that you are not quite sure what you have accomplished at the end of a study block?	_____	_____
3. Do you miss important information during a lecture because your mind tends to wander or daydream?	_____	_____
4. When you are reading, do you find it difficult to keep your mind focused on the information in the textbook?	_____	_____
5. Do you study with the television, radio, or stereo turned on?	_____	_____

RECITATION	**YES**	**NO**
1. When you review for a test, do you do all or most of your review work silently?	_____	_____
2. Do you have difficulty defining new terminology out loud?	_____	_____
3. Do you have difficulty clearly explaining textbook information to another person?	_____	_____

4. When you rehearse information out loud, do you often feel that your explanations are "fuzzy," unclear, or incomplete? _____ _____

5. Do you feel awkward or uncomfortable talking out loud to yourself? _____ _____

INTENTION   YES   NO

1. When you sit down to study, do you set a goal to complete the assignment as quickly as possible? _____ _____

2. Do you always have the same purpose in mind when you sit down to study? _____ _____

3. Do you lack curiosity, interest, or enthusiasm in the course content for one or more of your classes? _____ _____

4. When you begin learning new information, do you find setting a specific learning goal difficult to do? _____ _____

5. Do you study facts, details, concepts in the same way that you study steps or processes for a procedure? _____ _____

BIG AND LITTLE PICTURES   YES   NO

1. Do you have problems distinguishing between main ideas and individual details in textbook passages? _____ _____

2. Do you understand general concepts but oftentimes have difficulty giving details that relate to the concept? _____ _____

3. Do you grasp specific details but oftentimes have difficulty connecting them together to form a larger picture or a concept? _____ _____

4. Do your lecture notes capture main ideas but lack details? _____ _____

5. Do your notes include running lists of details without a clear method of showing main ideas? _____ _____

FEEDBACK   YES   NO

1. Do you use tests as your main means of getting feedback about what you have learned? _____ _____

2. Do you keep taking in new information without stopping to see whether you are trying to learn too much too fast? _____ _____

3. When you are rehearsing, do you "keep on going" even if you sense that you have not clearly understood something? _____ _____

4. Do you tend to use self-quizzing only when you are preparing for a test? _____ _____

5. If you get feedback that you did not complete a math problem correctly, do you ignore your original answer and try working the problem again? _____ _____

ORGANIZATION   YES   NO

1. Does information from lectures often seem to be one continuous stream of information without any apparent organization or structure? _____ _____

2. Do you have difficulty remembering the sequence of important events or the steps of a process?

3. When you try to do a "memory search" to locate information in your memory, are you usually unable to find the information?

4. Do you spend most of your time trying to learn information in the exact order in which it is presented?

5. Do you feel unsure about rearranging, reorganizing, or regrouping information so that it is easier to learn and recall?

TIME ON TASK

YES   NO

1. When your assignment is to read and study a specific chapter, do you spend a lot of time on the assignment so that you will not need to make contact with it again for several weeks?

2. When you are studying, do you often feel as though you are trying to study too much information too quickly?

3. When you study, do you change to a second subject as soon as you complete the assignments for the first subject?

4. Are some of your study blocks more than three hours long?

5. In at least one of your courses, do you spend less time studying that subject than most other students in class do?

ONGOING REVIEW

YES   NO

1. Once you have completed an assignment, do you put it aside until close to the time of the next test?

2. Do you have problems remembering or recalling information that you know you learned several weeks earlier?

3. Do you need to add more review time to your weekly study schedule?

4. Do you study fewer than two hours per week for every one hour in class?

5. Do you sit down to study and feel that you are all caught up and have nothing to study?

ASSESSING YOUR CURRENT USE OF THE PRINCIPLES OF MEMORY

1. A NO answer indicates you are already using the Principle of Memory when you study. If you gave NO answers to all the questions within one Memory Principle box, you are using the Principle of Memory consistently and effectively.

2. A YES answer indicates that you will benefit by learning to use this Principle of Memory more effectively when you study. The more YES answers you have, the greater the need to add this Principle of Memory to your learning strategies or study techniques.

CONCEPT CHECK 3.2

Which Principles of Memory do you use effectively on a consistent basis? Which Principles of Memory do you need to improve using when you study?

THE FIRST FOUR PRINCIPLES OF MEMORY

2 ▸ *Explain how to use the Memory Principles of Selectivity, Association, Visualization, and Elaboration.*

The following sections introduce you to the first four Principles of Memory: Selectivity, Association, Visualization, and Elaboration. Carefully read the explanations, definitions, learning goals, and the essential strategies for each principle, for they lay the foundation for many study skills strategies discussed in later chapters. These principles, when used consistently throughout the learning process, result in a stronger, more efficient memory.

Selectivity

Trying to learn everything—every detail, every example, every word you read—is not possible, certainly not reasonable, and would result in overloading your working memory. By using Selectivity, you can identify what is important to attend to and learn, and what you can ignore for further processing. **Selectivity** is the process of identifying and separating main ideas and important details from a larger body of information. Without Selectivity, you risk the chance of processing insignificant information along with important information. The result could lead to cluttered, disorganized, and ineffective schemas of information in your long-term memory.

Selectivity helps you decide what to survey in a chapter, what to highlight in your textbook, what information to put in your notes or to include in study tools that you create, and what to study for a test. Each time you use Selectivity, you will be honing your skills in identifying and pulling out main ideas and supporting details. **Figure 3.2** shows four Essential Strategies for Using Selectivity.

Principles

SAVE

CRIB

FOTO

Selectivity is the process of identifying and separating main ideas and important details from a larger body of information.

CL **Improve Your Grade**
Exercise 3.2

Identifying Concepts, Main Ideas, and Important Details

PURPOSE: This "student-friendly" textbook incorporates a variety of features to help you identify overall concepts, main ideas, and important details. Through this exercise, you will be able to identify textbook and chapter features that promote the use of Selectivity.

DIRECTIONS:

Work with a partner or by yourself to answer the following questions. Write your answers on separate paper or online at the Student Website, Exercise 3.2.

1. What is the overall concept or topic for this chapter? How do you know this?

2. What features in this textbook help you identify the main ideas, the "big ideas," or the main categories of information in the chapter?

3. What features used throughout each textbook chapter help you identify the important details that you are expected to understand and learn?

FIGURE 3.2

Essential Strategies for Using Selectivity

Learning Goal: To identify the information for further processing and to discard the information that is not relevant or important to process into memory.

▌ **Identify main ideas, concepts, or themes.** Use your course syllabus, the introduction in your textbook, and your lecture notes to help you identify the main ideas, concepts, or themes that receive frequent or repeated emphasis.

▌ **Identify important details by using chapter features.** Use lists of terminology, definitions, marginal notes, boxed features, steps or formulas to use to solve problems, chapter summaries, and chapter review questions to help you identify important details.

▌ **Use examples to grasp concepts, but do not focus on them as details to memorize.** Examples in textbooks and in lectures provide you with background information, capture your attention, and clarify concepts, but often they are not the details that you need to memorize or learn thoroughly.

▌ **Create study tools that show main ideas and important details.** In Chapters 7–11, you will learn about visual mappings, index cards, forms of notetaking, and other study tools that use Selectivity to identify main ideas and important details.

Association

Association is the process of forming visual or auditory cues to link together two or more items or chunks of information to process in memory. The associations that you form may consist of words, phrases, verbal expressions, pictures, familiar objects, numbers, tunes, personal experiences, familiar situations, or mnemonics. The following are important points about associations:

▌ As soon as you recall previously learned information from memory and use it to understand new information, you are using the Principle of Association.

▌ When you create associations, you hold the new information longer in your working memory and begin encoding the information in new ways or link items together to form a stronger impression.

▌ Associations become *retrieval cues* to use when you conduct *memory searches* to locate and retrieve information at a later time.

▌ Effective associations are ones that are easy to remember and to use. Often they involve connecting one new item or chunk of information to a second item that is familiar or involves previously learned information.

▌ **Paired associations** are two items that are linked together in working memory so that recall of one item triggers recall of the second item. Each time you study a word and its definition, link an event to a specific person or date, or do matching questions on a test, you use paired associations. In Chapter 2, you read

Principles

s**A**VE

CRIB

FOTO

Association is the process of forming visual or auditory cues to link together two or more items or chunks of information to process in memory.

Paired associations are two items that are linked together in working memory so that recall of one item triggers recall of the second item.

CONCEPT CHECK 3.4

What other paired associations do you recall from Chapter 2?

CONCEPT CHECK 3.5

How are paired associations used in a chain of associations? What chain of associations can you recall using recently?

CONCEPT CHECK 3.6

How can you incorporate associations into your study methods?

many examples of paired associations: pairing kinds of sensory input with the experience of sitting on a bench near a busy street; pairing selective attention with conversations in a room filled with people; and pairing previous knowledge about labor unions to new information about labor unions.

▌ Retrieving information from long-term memory often involves thinking through a series or a chain of associations. Your thoughts leap from one association to another to another and so on until you locate the desired information in memory. The examples in Chapter 2 about recalling the birthplace of a grandmother or tracking thought processes to answer a question about three of Gardner's intelligences demonstrate how chains of associations unlock stored memories.

▌ Mnemonics, memory tools such as SAVE CRIB FOTO for the Twelve Principles of Memory, involve creating a paired association. The mnemonic is paired with the original information to assist recall. You will learn more about mnemonics in Chapter 6.

Associations are an essential component of cognitive processing. Working memory creates associations on a regular basis; access into long-term memory often occurs through the use of associations. As you progress through this textbook, you will become more and more aware of the use of associations in most study skills strategies. **Figure 3.3** summarizes six Essential Strategies for Using the Memory Principle of Association.

FIGURE 3.3

Essential Strategies for Using Association

Learning Goal: To create a strong, vivid association between two or more items so one can serve as a memory cue to recall the other.

▌ **Create associations between new information and previously learned information.** Ask yourself: What do I already know about this? What schemas does this belong in? What is familiar and what is new?

▌ **Make associations vivid and detailed.** Identify the key parts of the information that you need to learn and then create clear associations with those details.

▌ **Visually link two items together into one image.** Instead of separating two items into two different images, form one picture that contains both images. To strengthen the image, add colors, sounds, and/or action.

▌ **Create and rehearse frequently paired associations and chains of associations.** Associations activate working memory and create ways to access long-term memory.

▌ **Associate the information you learned with the setting in which you learned it.** Ask yourself: Did I learn this from the textbook, from a lab project, in class, or from a homework assignment? Linking information to learning settings can be an effective association to use later as a retrieval cue.

▌ **Pay attention to your thought processes and associations.** Watch for ways associations are used in your textbook and as you process new information.

Visualization

Visualization is a powerful memory tool that involves visual encoding. For many students, and especially for visual learners, information presented in a visual or graphic form, such as a picture or a diagram, is often easier to process than information presented in printed form such as paragraphs. The ability to recall visual information is strengthened by the fact that many visualization strategies include verbalizing or explaining the information out loud, which results in the use of a second form of encoding.

Visualization is the process of making pictures or "movies" in your mind. Even though you may begin by looking at or drawing a specific picture and associating it with information you are learning, visualization involves "seeing" the picture in your mind *without looking at the visual form itself*. To visualize, close your eyes and strive to "see" the picture, the graphic, or the movie "on the inside of your eyelids." Or you may prefer to look up, *to the left*, toward the ceiling to visualize. Looking up and to the left can be interpreted as a signal that you are accessing visual information from the right hemisphere of your brain. Once you have pulled your visualization back into your working memory, check the accuracy of the image by referring back to the original visual form.

You can use the following four methods for practicing the Principle of Visualization:

▮ Examine, stare at, and create a strong visual impression of objects that you need to know, such as medical instruments, a skeleton, rock samples, an electronic component, or a work of art. Also think about the function or uses of the object. Then, use the essential strategies in Figure 3.4.

▮ Draw a picture of information you read in a passage to clarify the information, or encode the information in a visual form, to create a picture to use for visualizing. For example, the picture at the right was drawn after reading a textbook passage about kinds of radiation. The strategies in Figure 3.4 can be used to visualize this picture.

▮ Create *movies in your mind* as you read. To increase reading comprehension and your ability to recall details from passages, visualize the characters, the setting, important details, and the unfolding action or sequence of events as soon as you begin reading. If the process of *making movies in your mind* does not occur automatically, slow down your reading rate and make a concerted effort to activate your visual skills to "get the camera rolling" to create a movie in your mind.

▮ Use visualizations to picture yourself achieving specific goals, creating a mindset to concentrate on a task, studying productively for a test, or performing well in a specific area, such as competing in a sport or interviewing for a job. You will learn more about visualizing in Chapter 5 and Chapter 6.

Throughout this textbook, you will encounter many study skills strategies that use the process and the power of visualization. **Figure 3.4** highlights five Essential Strategies for Using the Memory Principle of Visualization.

Principles

SA**V**E

CRIB

FOTO

Visualization is the process of making pictures or "movies" in your mind.

CONCEPT CHECK 3.7

What examples can you give to show ways you use visualization during a typical day?

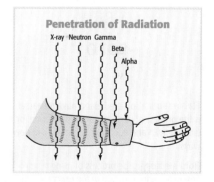

FIGURE 3.4

Essential Strategies for Using Visualization

Learning Goal: To create a strong visual image of important information that can be recalled as needed from long-term memory.

▌ **Create a strong visual impression of the information.** As you encode and form a visual image, include details such as size, shape, color, brightness, and texture.

▌ **Attach additional meaning to the impression.** Think about its purpose, its uses, personal experiences related to the item, and similarities it has with other objects.

▌ **Practice or rehearse the information without looking at the physical form.** Visualizing occurs *in your mind,* so practice "seeing" objects or sequences of events in your imagination.

▌ **Check your accuracy.** Refer back to the physical object or printed passage. Compare the information in your visualization with the original information. Check for accuracy and the completeness of the details.

▌ **Rehearse frequently.** Keep the visualization active, accurate, and accessible by recalling the image frequently.

Principles

SAV **E**

CRIB

FOTO

Elaboration, also called elaborative rehearsal, is the process of thinking about, pondering, or working with and encoding information in new ways.

Rote memory is the process of using repetition to learn information *in the exact form* in which it was presented.

CONCEPT CHECK 3.8

How do elaborative rehearsal and rote memory differ?

Elaboration

Elaboration, also called *elaborative rehearsal,* is the process of thinking about, pondering, or working with and encoding information in new ways. Elaboration provides you with the opportunity to personalize information during the encoding and rehearsal processes of learning. Encoding, as you have learned, helps working memory prepare information into meaningful, logically organized chunks of information that can be transferred to and accepted by long-term memory.

Elaboration involves working with the information, clarifying meanings, attending to details, and focusing on steps or processes. Elaboration forces you to move beyond rote memory. **Rote memory** is the process of using repetition to learn information *in the exact form* in which it was presented. Rote memory works for tasks such as memorizing a telephone number, the spelling of a word, or memorizing a direct quotation, but it is ineffective for learning factual information from textbooks because sufficient attention is not given to comprehending the information or learning ways to manipulate or use the information. When you use rote memory for recalling textbook information, such as a series of steps or a formula for a math equation, you may find yourself unable to respond to questions that present the information in a form other than the exact form you memorized. However, by elaborating on the information and encoding and using it in a variety of ways, you move beyond the limitations of rote memory. **Figure 3.5** provides you with six Essential Strategies for Using Elaboration.

FIGURE 3.5

Essential Strategies for Using Elaboration

Learning Goal: To work with, encode, and practice information in new ways to increase comprehension and application of information.

▌ **Encode and rehearse information in new ways.** For example, if the information initially was encoded visually, encode it linguistically: read the information out loud, recite it, or talk about it with someone else. If the initial encoding was visual from reading, use another form of visual coding to elaborate: copy it, condense it, group it into related categories, convert it to a picture, or create a visual study tool, such as a visual mapping.

▌ **Use repetition but attach meaning and applications.** For steps and processes, such as in math problems, use repetitive practice, but explain each step to yourself, and think of applications for the steps and processes. Rework the same problem several times, explain why each step is important, mentally summarize the steps, and notice the key elements of the problem so that you can recognize those same elements in new problems.

▌ **Use elaborative questioning by asking *why* questions.** *Why does this work this way? Why is this important?* The responses show the use of critical thinking and lead to deeper comprehension.

▌ **Use elaborative questions by asking *how* questions.** *How can I use this? How can this apply to other situations? How does this work?* The responses help you generalize the information, see cause-effect relationships, recognize applications, and make stronger connections to other schemas.

▌ **Notice similarities and differences between chunks of information.** Pay attention to and work with the details.

▌ **Weave big ideas or concepts together with their related details.** Creating visual mappings is ideal for connecting different levels of information. (Go to the Student Website for this textbook to see the interactive visual mappings for each textbook chapter.)

CHECK POINT 3.2

ANSWERS APPEAR ON PAGE A4

True or False?

_____ 1. Attempting to memorize large sections of information word by word shows effective use of the Memory Principles of Selectivity, Rote Memory, and Elaboration.

_____ 2. When you identify main ideas and important supporting details and then work to encode the information in new ways, you are using the Memory Principles of Selectivity and Elaboration.

_____ 3. Elaborative rehearsal may involve the use of creating multisensory study tools.

_____ 4. Asking *why* and *how* questions are important strategies for Elaboration.

_____ 5. The Memory Principle of Visualization involves creating strong visual impressions that work as retrieval cues for long-term memory.

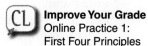 **Improve Your Grade**
Online Practice 1:
First Four Principles

> **REFLECTIVE WRITING 3.1**
>
> On separate paper, in a journal, or online at this textbook's website, respond to the following questions:
>
> 1. Which of the first four Principles of Memory do you use effectively? Give examples to show how you currently use them when you study.
> 2. How do each of the first four Memory Principles (Selectivity, Association, Visualization, and Elaboration) help strengthen your working memory?

THE MIDDLE FOUR PRINCIPLES OF MEMORY

> **3** *Explain how to use the Memory Principles of Concentration, Recitation, Intention, and Big and Little Pictures.*

The four middle Principles of Memory, *Concentration, Recitation, Intention,* and *Big and Little Pictures,* provide you with four more sets of strategies to use to strengthen your memory. Read this information carefully, for it lays the foundation for many study skills strategies discussed in later chapters.

Concentration

Concentration is the ability to block out distractions in order to stay focused on one specific item or task. Concentration involves monitoring incoming stimuli and blocking distractions that could interrupt your thought process or divide your attention. Concentration is one of four *self-management skills* that you will learn about in Chapter 5.

You can strengthen your ability to concentrate by being an active learner. **Active learning** is the process of using a variety of strategies that actively involve or engage you in the learning process. Studying with a pen in your hand, taking notes, making diagrams, creating flashcards, writing questions and notes in the margins of your textbooks, and highlighting important information as you read keep you from shifting into *automatic pilot,* which is a state of mind in which you mechanically go through the motions without registering information into your memory. Active learning activates working memory and holds stimuli for further processing. It also keeps your mind focused on one specific learning task.

Learning to use the Memory Principle of Concentration results in a disciplined and attentive mind that is receptive to the learning process. **Figure 3.6** shows five Essential Strategies for Using the Memory Principle of Concentration.

Principles

SAVE

CRIB

FOTO

Concentration is the ability to block out distractions in order to stay focused on one specific item or task.

Active learning is the process of using a variety of strategies that actively involve or engage you in the learning process.

CONCEPT CHECK 3.9

What actions or behaviors are often exhibited by active learners?

FIGURE 3.6

Essential Strategies for Using Concentration

Learning Goal: To have a focused mind and undivided attention by blocking out disruptive thoughts and distractions.

▌ **Select a conducive learning environment that has limited distractions.**

▌ **Ask yourself a question about what you are studying.** As soon as you ask a question and begin to respond, you stimulate or activate working memory. Your answer gives you a purpose and focuses your attention.

▌ **Limit your activities to one task.** Avoid disrupting your thought patterns by trying to multitask or by attending to other kinds of stimuli.

▌ **Use active learning strategies to stay engaged in the learning process.**

▌ **Use concentration strategies in Figure 5.2, page 126, to increase concentration when you study.**

Recitation

Recitation is a powerful Memory Principle that encodes information linguistically and uses an auditory channel into your long-term memory. **Recitation** is the process of explaining information clearly, out loud in your own words, and in complete sentences without referring to printed materials. Reading information out loud encodes the information linguistically, but reciting information out loud goes further: it requires you to pull the information out of your long-term memory and it becomes a form of self-quizzing with feedback.

Using flashcards is one excellent way to use recitation. Place the terms you need to learn on the fronts of the cards and the definitions on the backs of the cards. Look at the term on the front and explain the definition out loud without looking at the definition. After reciting, turn the card over to check your accuracy. You can use flashcards in the same way to write questions on the fronts of the cards and answers on the back. Using this method is much more effective than simply reading the information on each card.

Throughout this textbook, you will learn that recitation is an integral part of many study skills strategies. You will use recitation as you study notes, process textbook passages, use study tools such as flashcards or visual mappings, and as you prepare for tests. Recitation is a powerful way to boost your memory for the following reasons:

▌ It actively engages you in the learning process. It holds information longer in working memory for processing.

▌ It provides a way to practice or rehearse new information and retrieve previously learned information from long-term memory.

▌ It helps you personalize and express information in your own words.

▌ It provides a form of self-quizzing with feedback to check your level of accuracy and understanding.

If initially you are uncomfortable talking out loud to yourself, remind yourself of the many benefits of reciting and the importance of being willing to try new

Principles

SAVE

c**R**IB

FOTO

Recitation is the process of explaining information clearly, out loud in your own words, and in complete sentences without referring to printed materials.

CONCEPT CHECK 3.10

What do reading out loud and reciting have in common? Why is reciting a more effective process for testing comprehension?

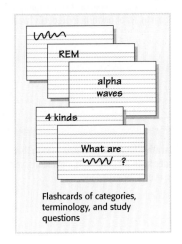

Flashcards of categories, terminology, and study questions

FIGURE 3.7

Essential Strategies for Using Recitation

Learning Goal: To explain information clearly and in an organized, knowledgeable manner without looking at printed information.

▌ **Use a *Look-Away Technique* to recite information immediately.** (See page 83.) After you read a passage, examine a graph, or read your notes, immediately look away and recite the information while it is fresh in your mind.

▌ **Use reciting to rehearse and retrieve information learned at an earlier time.** Reciting information hours, or even days, after the initial learning process provides you with practice locating and retrieving information from memory.

▌ **Explain information out loud to yourself or to someone else.** Finding ways to express and explain information in your own words improves comprehension and provides practice putting ideas together coherently.

▌ **Create associations between visual and verbal information.** Reciting information that first appeared in printed form creates an association and a retrieval cue for information encoded two different ways.

▌ **Use recitation to prepare for tests.** In testing situations, it is imperative that you can retrieve information quickly from long-term memory. Ongoing use of recitation helps you locate and practice retrieving information quickly.

▌ **Use the feedback you get from reciting.** Pay attention to your ability to recite accurately. If you cannot express the information, or you recite inaccurate or incomplete information, return to the original material for further processing.

Principles
SAVE
CR▌B
FOTO

Intention is the process of creating a purpose or a goal to act or perform in a specific way.

Declarative knowledge is information that includes facts, sets of details, definitions, concepts, events, or experiences.

approaches to learning. The more frequently you recite, the more comfortable you will become with this powerful Principle of Memory. **Figure 3.7** shows six Essential Strategies for Using the Memory Principle of Recitation.

Intention

Metacognition involves understanding *how* you learn, *what* you need to learn, and *which* strategies would be best matched for a specific learning task. Intention focuses on *what you need to learn.* Action-oriented and goal-oriented behavior activates working memory. Intention involves setting learning goals as you work with and process information.

Intention is the process of creating a purpose or a goal to act or perform in a specific way. Intention involves setting a *learning goal* that clearly states what you plan to accomplish and a *plan of action* that shows *how* you intend to achieve your goal. An underlying requirement for using the Principle of Intention is that you plan ample time to achieve your goal. You do not merely read material without thinking about it, nor do you race through the material to finish as quickly as possible. **Figure 3.8** shows different kinds of learning goals (intentions) with possible plans of action.

The learning goals you set as a part of the Principle of Intention will vary depending on the kind of information you are learning or rehearsing. **Declarative knowledge** is information that includes facts, sets of details, definitions, concepts, events, or experiences. Learning a specific fact (one meter equals 100 centimeters), a set of details (three kinds of cognitive learning styles), a definition (a chronic stressor is a stress-producing event that continues over a long period of time), a concept (the Theory of Multiple Intelligences), an event (the 9-11 terrorist attack), or an experience (a first job interview) all involve declarative knowledge in your working memory. Learning goals and plans of action for declarative knowledge often involve the following strategies:

▌ Activities that promote working with the information in new ways

▌ Elaborative rehearsal

▌ Creating associations and retrieval cues

▌ Reciting out loud without looking at printed materials

▌ Using a variety of activities for ongoing review

The second kind of information you may be working with is procedural knowledge. **Procedural knowledge** is information that involves steps or processes to use to solve problems or create specific products with accuracy and speed. Every time you perform a series of steps (balance your checkbook), apply a sequence of rules (subtract a double-digit number from a triple-digit number), unconsciously perform a procedure (ride a bike or rollerblade), or repeat a habit without having to consciously think about the individual steps (conduct Internet searches), you are working with procedural knowledge in working memory.

Strategies used to study declarative (factual) knowledge differ from strategies used to study procedural knowledge. Repetition of steps for procedural knowledge moves beyond using rote memory. How can working with other students help strengthen procedural knowledge?

Procedural knowledge is information that involves steps or processes to use to solve problems or create specific products with accuracy and speed.

FIGURE 3.8	
Learning Goals and Plans of Action for Different Intentions	
Learning Goal	**Possible Plans of Action**
Become familiar with new information	▌ Survey a chapter to get an overview before reading the chapter in-depth. Read introductory materials, look at a list of terms for the chapter, and read a chapter summary to begin setting up schemas for later details.
Understand new information	▌ Use strategies to identify main ideas and important supporting details, highlight passages, identify relationships, and understand the information. ▌ Create associations, visualizations, notes, other study tools, and retrieval cues for the new information. ▌ Use elaborative rehearsal, recitation, and self-quizzing techniques to check accuracy and understanding.
Review learned information	▌ Use retrieval cues to practice retrieving information. ▌ Review sets of notes, sections of a chapter, or answer textbook review questions. Check your accuracy. ▌ Rework previous math problems for solutions. Increase speed and accuracy when reworking math problems. ▌ Recite definitions, concepts, answers to questions, and steps in a process without referring to printed information.

CONCEPT CHECK 3.11

Why is it helpful to know if information you are working with is declarative or procedural knowledge?

Learning goals and plans of action for procedural knowledge often involve the following strategies:

▌ Emphasis on repeating the original process *multiple times* over a period of several days and often over several months until it becomes automatic

▌ Performing the steps with increased speed and accuracy

▌ Explaining each step and understanding the processes to avoid rote memory

Figure 3.9 highlights three Essential Strategies for Using Intention. You will learn more about these strategies plus learn additional goal-oriented strategies in Chapter 4.

FIGURE 3.9

Essential Strategies for Using Intention

Learning Goal: To put yourself in a learning mode that identifies a purpose (a goal) and a plan of action for achieving your learning goal.

▌ **Identify a specific learning goal before you begin a learning activity.** Take the time to figure out and state clearly what you want to accomplish. Know your purpose.

▌ **Create a plan of action.** After identifying your goal, choose a set of activities that will produce the results that you desire. An organized plan of action motivates you to fulfill your intention to perform a specific task.

▌ **Determine if you are working with information that involves declarative knowledge or procedural knowledge.** Knowing the kind of information you are working with will help you select learning activities that involve working with the information in new ways, or working with the information through repetition.

GROUP PROCESSING: A COLLABORATIVE LEARNING ACTIVITY

1. Form groups of three or four students. Complete the following directions.
2. Copy the chart below on large chart or poster paper.
3. Brainstorm specific examples of declarative knowledge and procedural knowledge that you would need to learn for each type of course. List your ideas in the appropriate boxes in the chart.
4. In the final column, list activities you could do to receive feedback when you study both declarative and procedural knowledge for each kind of course.

Course	Declarative	Procedural	Feedback
Writing			
Science			
Computer			
Math			

Big and Little Pictures

The Memory Principle of Big and Little Pictures is sometimes referred to as seeing "the forest and the trees." If you focus only on the forest, you miss the meaning and beauty of individual trees. If you focus only on a few individual trees, you miss seeing how all the trees together make the forest. The Memory Principle of **Big and Little Pictures** is a process of identifying different levels of information. The "big pictures" are the schemas, themes, concepts, and main ideas. The "little pictures" are the supporting details, such as facts, definitions, examples, or parts or components of a larger concept. Both higher and lower levels of information are important in the learning process.

Principles
SAVE
CRI**B**
FOTO

Big and Little Pictures is a process of identifying different levels of information.

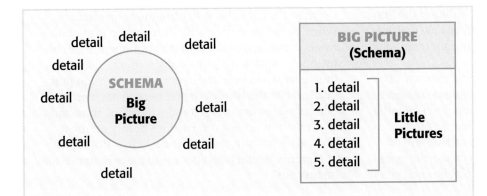

The structure of long-term memory validates the need to identify the big and little pictures of information. Schemas are clusters or sets of memories that form the "big pictures." The details organized in the schemas are the "little pictures." Each time you use associations, conduct memory searches, or activate retrieval cues, you access your memory bank by retrieving both concepts and details. **Figure 3.10** shows three Essential Strategies for Using Big and Little Pictures.

CONCEPT CHECK 3.12

What kinds of problems might you encounter if you do not identify different levels of information in materials that you are studying?

FIGURE 3.10

Essential Strategies for Using Big and Little Pictures

Learning Goal: To identify the different levels of information in the materials you are studying: themes, concepts, and main ideas as well as the important supporting details, such as facts, definitions, functions, causes, effects, or steps in a process.

▌ **Convert textbook and lecture materials into diagrams, visual mappings, or lists to show the different levels of information.**

▌ **Ask yourself questions that focus your attention on the level of the information.** Is this a main idea? Was this a chapter heading? Is this a recurring theme? Is this a schema? Under what category does this detail belong? What are other related details? What big picture do these details support?

▌ **Use textbook marking and notetaking techniques that clearly show different levels of information.** (See Chapters 7–11.)

EXERCISE 3.3

Textbook Case Studies

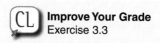 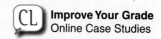

Improve Your Grade
Exercise 3.3

Improve Your Grade
Online Case Studies

DIRECTIONS:

1. Read each case study carefully. Respond to the question at the end of each case study by using *specific* strategies discussed in this chapter. Answer in complete sentences.

2. Write your responses on paper or online at the Student Website, Exercise 3.3. You will be able to print your online response or e-mail it to your instructor.

CASE STUDY 1: Leia is having problems in many of her classes. She feels it is because no one ever taught her how to study or how to learn college level material. Leia is a global learner who quickly sees and grasps large concepts or big pictures. She is artistic and creative, but she does not see ways she can use those talents and interests when she studies. She is bored when she studies and feels like a lazy learner. What strategies from the first eight Principles of Memory could Leia learn to use to be a more active, enthusiastic, and successful learner?

CASE STUDY 2: Eduardo spends far more time studying than do any of his other friends or classmates. When he sits down to study, his intention is to memorize everything that he highlights or underlines in his textbook—which is almost every sentence. He repeats the information over and over and over. He can practically recite the whole chapter back to his friends. Eduardo does not understand why all his time and effort are not paying off. He does poorly on most tests. Which strategies for the first eight Principles of Memory would help Eduardo achieve better results on his tests?

CHECK POINT 3.3

ANSWERS APPEAR ON PAGE A4

Multiple Choice

_____ 1. Which of the following is *not* true about the Memory Principle of Recitation? Recitation
   a. involves adding linguistic or auditory codes to information.
   b. when used correctly, provides you with immediate feedback.
   c. is one way to use active learning when you study.
   d. relies on rote memory to be effective.

_____ 2. Using the Memory Principle of Intention
   a. provides a purpose for learning, which increases concentration.
   b. involves goal-oriented behavior that activates working memory.
   c. works with both declarative and procedural knowledge.
   d. does all of the above.

_____ 3. The four Memory Principles represented by the mnemonic CRIB are
   a. Clarification, Recitation, Intention, and Big and Little Pictures.
   b. processes that involve thinking patterns and active learning behaviors.
   c. memory processes that are unrelated to the first four Memory Principles of Selectivity, Association, Visualization, and Elaboration.
   d. involved in all of the above.

Improve Your Grade
Online Practice 2:
CRIB Principles

THE LAST FOUR PRINCIPLES OF MEMORY

 Explain how to use the Memory Principles of Feedback, Organization, Time on Task, and Ongoing Review.

As you have noticed by now, none of the Twelve Principles of Memory works solely by itself. For example, to use Selectivity, you need to know how to use Big and Little Pictures; to use Visualization, you need to know how to form and use Associations. Before learning details about the last four Principles of Memory, complete Exercise 3.4.

EXERCISE 3.4

Recalling the Twelve Principles of Memory

DIRECTIONS: In the following chart, write the names of the Twelve Principles of Memory. A short retrieval cue appears under the lines for each of the principles.

S _____   **C** _____   **F** _____
 (Picking and choosing)   (Focusing)   (Self-quizzing)

A _____   **R** _____   **O** _____
 (Linking ideas)   (Explaining out loud)   (Structuring logically)

V _____   **I** _____   **T** _____
 (Seeing it in your mind)   (Identifying a purpose or goal) (Using minutes and hours)

E _____   **B** _____   **O** _____
 (Working with information)   (Concepts and details)   (Repeated practice)

Feedback

Whether you are learning factual or procedural information, a successful *outcome*, such as a correct answer to a factual question or a solution to a math problem, demonstrates that learning has taken place. Monitoring your learning progress and the effectiveness of your learning strategies should occur at the beginning stages of learning new information, during rehearsal stages of learning, and during review stages of learning. Waiting for a grade on a test to indicate your learning progress is too late to modify learning strategies.

Principles
SAVE
CRIB
FOTO

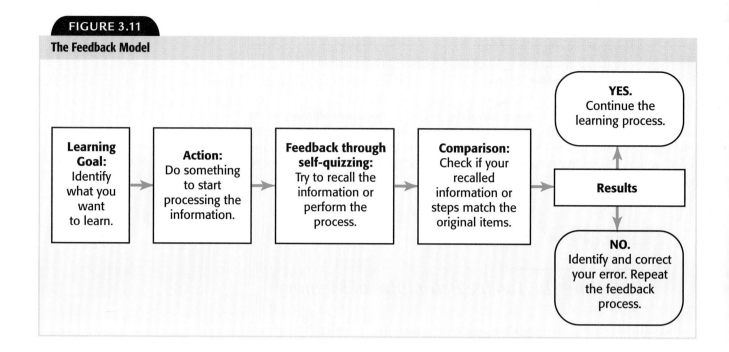

FIGURE 3.11

The Feedback Model

Learning Goal: Identify what you want to learn. → **Action:** Do something to start processing the information. → **Feedback through self-quizzing:** Try to recall the information or perform the process. → **Comparison:** Check if your recalled information or steps match the original items. → **Results** → **YES.** Continue the learning process. / **NO.** Identify and correct your error. Repeat the feedback process.

Feedback is the process of verifying how accurately and thoroughly you have or have not learned specific information.

You can monitor your learning progress by using feedback. **Feedback** is the process of verifying how accurately and thoroughly you have or have not learned specific information. Feedback involves a sequence of steps: goal—action—feedback—comparison—results. **Figure 3.11** shows the Feedback Model.

The following example demonstrates the steps in the Feedback Model for working math problems.

Learning Goal:	Learn how to calculate compound interest rates.
Action:	Read the textbook directions and examples.
Feedback:	Self-quiz: look away from your textbook and try to recall the process.
Comparison:	Compare your memory of the process with the textbook explanation.
Results:	If the result is YES, your recall matches the textbook information. If the result is NO, reread the information, and use another technique for learning the process. Repeat the steps to check your new understanding.

CONCEPT CHECK 3.13

How can you benefit from both positive feedback and negative feedback?

Both positive feedback and negative feedback are beneficial to you and your cognitive processes.

Positive Feedback:

▎ Shows you that your memory of the information is accurate and thorough

▎ Reinforces and strengthens the mental impression of the information

▎ Creates new associations between questions and correct answers

▎ Motivates you and provides you with rewards for learning

Negative Feedback:

❚ Makes you aware of faulty or incomplete memory of information

❚ Provides you with the opportunity to modify your learning strategies or select completely different strategies to encode the new information in other ways

❚ Signals to you that you are not ready to move on to learning new information

❚ Motivates you to find new ways to clarify, understand, and process the information

The Memory Principle of Feedback often involves using self-quizzing. **Self-quizzing** is the process of testing yourself so you can receive feedback about the accuracy and completeness of your understanding. **Figure 3.12** shows you six Essential Strategies for Using Feedback when you study. Notice the importance of using self-quizzing in these strategies.

Self-quizzing is the process of testing yourself so you can receive feedback about the accuracy and completeness of your understanding.

FIGURE 3.12

Essential Strategies for Using Feedback

Learning Goal: To check your accuracy of remembering facts or processes and to correct any inaccuracies by modifying your approach or using new strategies to learn.

❚ **Recite often.** Expressing information out loud, in complete sentences, and using your own words without looking at printed material is one of the most powerful forms of feedback.

❚ **Use Look-Away Techniques.** Read a short passage, pause, and look away. As you look away, *mentally rehearse and review, visualize an image of the material,* or *recite the information without looking.* Look-Away Techniques keep information active in your working memory and provide time for the information to gel or integrate with other information.

❚ **Write summaries without referring to printed materials.** Writing summaries gives you practice expressing main ideas and important details, listing items that belong together, or writing steps of a process from memory. Always check your accuracy by comparing your work to your textbook or your notes.

❚ **Rework math problems in the textbook and on homework assignments.** Procedural knowledge needs to be practiced multiple times. Feedback includes not only accurate answers, but also improved problem-solving speed.

❚ **Work with a partner to quiz each other.** Create sets of study questions, words to define, or problems to solve. Quiz a partner and have your partner quiz you.

❚ **Use self-quizzing strategies.** Use flashcards for definitions, study questions, or lists in a process for self-quizzing. Use the self-quizzing steps that are a part of notetaking and textbook reading strategies.

Principles

SAVE

CRIB

F**O**TO

Organization is the process of creating a meaningful, logical structure or arrangement of *ideas* and information.

CONCEPT CHECK 3.14

What other Principles of Memory are activated when you use the Principle of Organization?

Organization

The Memory Principle of **Organization** is the process of creating a meaningful, logical structure or arrangement of *ideas* and information. It does *not* refer to organizing your workspace or your materials. One way to use this principle is to imitate the way authors and instructors organize information. Identifying their patterns of organization can help you follow their logic and understand the material more quickly.

Another way to use this principle is to organize information in new, meaningful ways. Reorganizing, regrouping, or rearranging information in new ways helps you:

▌ Examine information carefully and identify main ideas, concepts, or themes

▌ Connect important details to those "big ideas"

▌ Personalize the information and express your creativity

▌ Hold information longer in your working memory

▌ Transfer the information into your long-term memory as chunks of related information to add to existing schemas

▌ Increases comprehension, concentration, interest, and motivation

Figure 3.13 shows three Essential Strategies for Using the Memory Principle of Organization. You will learn an array of reading, notetaking, and study strategies in Chapters 7–11 that are based on the Principle of Organization.

FIGURE 3.13

Essential Strategies for Using Organization

Learning Goal: To organize information into meaningful chunks, to work with information in new ways to personalize and clarify it, and to create associations that connect levels of information.

▌ **Categorize information by making lists.** To avoid working with isolated details, group related details together under one category using the subject, main idea, theme, or concept as the heading for your category.

▌ **Organize the information chronologically, or by time sequence.** Create time lines for a series of events (such as in history or social science courses), the development of a product (such as in business or marketing courses), or a process involving steps (such as in math, science, or writing courses).

▌ **Present information in new ways.** Use index cards, visual mappings, hierarchies, formal outlines, Cornell notes, two- and three-column notes, mnemonics, and other ways to reorganize and create a new representation of the information.

Time on Task

Time on Task is the process of allocating sufficient time and spacing contact time effectively to learn, rehearse, and retrieve information in memory. How you use time and how much time you spend on a learning task affect the quality of your learning experience. The following are two important points about the Time on Task Principle:

▌ If you overload your memory system by trying to study too much information at one time (cramming), or for a period of time that is too long (three or more continuous hours), the ability to comprehend and remember what you have studied decreases.

▌ Researchers also have found a high correlation between the amount of time spent studying and the grades earned in courses. Students who dedicate sufficient time to studying, which includes rehearsing, creating associations, and using retrieval cues efficiently, show greater success. Students who spend too little quality time studying, students who plot and plan ways to spend the minimal amount of time studying, and students who knowingly spend just enough time to hopefully "get by" tend to have lower levels of performance.

In Chapter 4, you will learn an array of time-management strategies that will help you monitor and use time effectively. **Figure 3.14** shows four Essential Strategies for Using Time on Task.

Principles
SAVE
CRIB
FO**T**O

Time on Task is the process of allocating sufficient time and spacing contact time effectively to learn, rehearse, and retrieve information in memory.

CONCEPT CHECK 3.15

Do you see yourself at this time as a student who uses Time on Task effectively? Why or why not?

FIGURE 3.14

Essential Strategies for Using Time on Task

Learning Goal: To use time to your advantage by allocating sufficient time to the learning process and spacing practices effectively.

▌ **Do not rush the learning process.** The learning process and its many cognitive functions take time. When you read or study materials, take the time to pause, think about, and process the information.

▌ **Plan sufficient study time for each course.** Use the 2:1 ratio (two hours of studying for every one hour in class) so you will have ample time to learn, practice, and review course information. (See Chapter 4.)

▌ **Use fifty-minute study blocks to study one subject.** Work with only one subject for fifty minutes to keep your working memory active and your mind focused. After a fifty-minute period, take a short break to give your working memory time to process further and to free up working memory space for new information. After your break, return to the same subject, or move to a new subject.

▌ **Use spaced practice.** Spaced practice involves making multiple contacts with information and spreading those contacts over several different time periods. To avoid the fading of new information from memory, in early stages of learning, use spaced practice within the first day or two to review the information. Later, when you have learned material more solidly, you can use longer time periods between review sessions.

Principles

SAVE

CRIB

FOT**O**

Ongoing Review is the process of practicing previously learned information.

Ongoing Review

Ongoing Review is the process of practicing previously learned information. Even though information in long-term memory is considered to be permanent, without ongoing review, information can fade, become confused with other memories, or be difficult to locate and retrieve. To access previously learned information, you need to reactivate the paths to that information, practice using retrieval cues and associations, and revisit the information frequently to keep it active in your working memory.

Ongoing Review is such a crucial step in the learning process that you will find it as the final step of most reading, notetaking, and study skills strategies. In addition to the strategies you will learn in later chapters, **Figure 3.15** shows four Essential Strategies for Using the Principle of Ongoing Review.

CONCEPT CHECK 3.16

What are some consequences that might occur if you do not use Ongoing Review in one of your courses?

FIGURE 3.15

Essential Strategies for Using Ongoing Review

Learning Goal: To use time and effort on a regular basis to review previously learned information.

▌ **Include time each week to review previously learned information.** At the beginning of a study block, review information you studied the previous day. Also, allow some time each week to review notes, textbook information, homework assignments, or study tools created at earlier times.

▌ **Conduct memory searches frequently.** Practice locating and retrieving information quickly from your long-term memory. Track your thought processes, practice associations, recall where you learned specific information, and connect details to schemas when you review.

▌ **Use frequent repetition of steps and solutions for procedural knowledge.** Rework math or science problems to increase your accuracy and your problem-solving speed. Ongoing review leads to performing the steps more automatically.

▌ **Conduct a final review right before you know you will need to use the information.** Recently studied information is freshest in working memory (recency effect). Do a final review right before a test, a class discussion, a speech, or a performance task. This brings the information back into working memory.

EXERCISE 3.5

Working with the Twelve Principles of Memory

PURPOSE: Working with new information shortly after the initial learning process helps form a stronger impression, increases understanding, creates stronger associations, and personalizes the information.

DIRECTIONS: Go to Exercise 3.5 in Appendix C, page A25, for the directions to expand a visual mapping for the Twelve Principles of Memory.

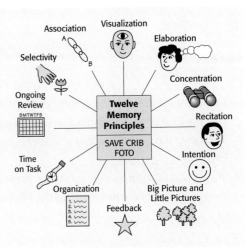

REFLECTIVE WRITING 3.2

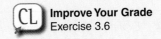
Improve Your Grade
Reflective Writing 3.2

On separate paper, in a journal, or online at this textbook's website, respond to the following questions:

1. Which Principles of Memory would bring about the greatest changes in your study methods if you used them on a regular basis? Explain with details, including strategies you would add to your study methods.

2. What plan of action will you use to incorporate these Memory Principles into your study methods on a more regular basis?

EXERCISE 3.6

Links

Improve Your Grade
Exercise 3.6

PURPOSE: Strategies and skills you learned in previous chapters integrate well with information in this chapter. Seeing relationships and associations between previously learned information and new information strengthens understanding and schemas in long-term memory.

DIRECTIONS: Work with a partner or a small group. Discuss answers for the following questions. Be prepared to share your answers with the class.

1. Are the Twelve Principles of Memory more applicable to specific kinds of learning styles? Explain your answer with specific details.

2. We have three memory centers: sensory, working, and long-term. In which memory center are the Memory Principles used most actively? Explain your answer.

3. As mentioned on page 81, "None of the twelve Principles of Memory works solely by itself. For example, to use Selectivity, you need to know how to use Big and Little Pictures." On paper, list all Twelve Principles of Memory. Across from each principle, list other principles that are activated when a specific principle is used effectively.

CHECK POINT 3.4

ANSWERS APPEAR ON PAGE A4

Fill-in-the-Blank

Write one word (key term) per blank to complete each sentence.

1. _____, which can often be the result of recitation, is the process of verifying whether or not you understand and remember information.
2. The first step of the Feedback Model is to identify a learning _____.
3. When you rearrange, categorize, or present information in new ways, you are using the Memory Principle of _____.
4. The Principle of Time on Task promotes the use of _____ practice so you spread contact time with materials over different periods of time.
5. When you practice retrieving information from long-term memory on a regular basis to keep the information fresh in your mind, you are using the Memory Principle of Ongoing _____.

CL Improve Your Grade
Online Practice 3:
FOTO Principles

LEARNING OBJECTIVES REVIEW

▶ 1 *Use the mnemonic* SAVE CRIB FOTO *to identify the Twelve Principles of Memory.*

- Mnemonics are memory tools that serve as bridges to help you recall information from long-term memory. SAVE CRIB FOTO is a mnemonic for the Twelve Principles of Memory.
- To work effectively, you must practice translating each letter of the mnemonic into its original word.

▶ 2 *Explain how to use the Memory Principles of Selectivity, Association, Visualization, and Elaboration.*

- Selectivity is the process of identifying and separating main ideas and important details from a larger body of information. Four essential strategies provide you with ways to use this Memory Principle.
- Association is the process of using visual or auditory cues to link together two or more items or chunks of information to process into memory. It involves memory searches, retrieval cues, paired associations, chains of associations, and using six essential strategies for Associations.
- Visualization is the process of making pictures or movies in your mind. Four methods for creating visualizations and five essential strategies can help you use this Principle of Memory effectively.

- Elaboration, also called *elaborative rehearsal,* is the process of working with and encoding information in new ways. Six essential strategies are available to help you use the Principle of Elaboration.

▶ 3 *Explain how to use the Memory Principles of Concentration, Recitation, Intention, and Big and Little Pictures.*

- Concentration is the ability to block out distractions in order to stay focused on one specific item or task. Five essential strategies, including one for active learning, can help you increase your level of concentration.
- Recitation is the process of explaining information clearly, out loud and in your own words, and in complete sentences without referring to printed materials. Six essential strategies, including Look-Away Techniques, show ways to use the Principle of Recitation.
- Intention is the process of creating a purpose or a goal to act or perform in a specific way. Goals and plans of action will vary depending on the stage of learning and the kind of information: declarative knowledge or procedural knowledge. Three essential strategies show how to use the Principle of Intention.
- Big and Little Pictures is the process of identifying different levels of information: concepts and details. Three essential strategies can help you work with the Principle of Big and Little Pictures.

4▸ *Explain how to use the Memory Principles of Feedback, Organization, Time on Task, and Ongoing Review.*

- Feedback is the process of verifying how accurately and thoroughly you have, or have not, learned specific information. Key concepts include understanding the Feedback Model, the use of both positive and negative feedback, and the essential strategies for using the Principle of Feedback.

- Organization is the process of creating a meaningful, logical structure or arrangement of ideas or information. Three essential strategies provide ways to use the Principle of Organization.

- Time on Task is the process of allocating sufficient time and spacing contact time effectively to learn, rehearse, and retrieve information. Four essential strategies show you how to begin using this Principle of Memory.

- Ongoing Review is the process of practicing previously learned information. Four essential strategies promote the use of using Ongoing Review on a regular basis.

CHAPTER 3 REVIEW QUESTIONS

ANSWERS APPEAR ON PAGE A4

Matching

Match the terms below with the descriptions at the right. On the line, write the letter from the list at the right to show your answer.

_____ 1. Paired associations
_____ 2. Active learning
_____ 3. Self-quizzing
_____ 4. Declarative knowledge
_____ 5. Procedural knowledge
_____ 6. Goal—action—feedback—comparison—results
_____ 7. Look-Away-Techniques
_____ 8. Rote memory
_____ 9. SAVE CRIB FOTO
_____ 10. Elaborative rehearsal

a. Factual information, such as facts and definitions
b. Any technique that tests your understanding
c. Techniques to immediately check recall ability
d. A mnemonic for twelve cognitive processes that build and improve memory
e. Knowledge of steps to use for a procedure or process
f. Memorizing information in its exact form without emphasizing understanding
g. Two items linked together for processing
h. Using strategies to engage you in the learning process
i. Thinking about and practicing information in new ways
j. Steps in the Feedback Model

True or False?

_____ 1. The Memory Principle of Selectivity relies on the use of the Principles of Time on Task and Ongoing Review to work effectively.
_____ 2. You are using the Memory Principle of Visualization effectively when you examine pictures, photographs, or charts.
_____ 3. The Memory Principles of Association, Intention, and Organization are usually used in elaborative rehearsal techniques.
_____ 4. Self-quizzing, reciting, and Look-Away Techniques are ways to get feedback about how well you are learning information.
_____ 5. More repetition and practice are often required for declarative knowledge than are required for procedural knowledge.

Short-Answer Question

On separate paper, answer the following question. Use complete sentences and use terminology from this chapter.

Question: What five Principles of Memory could you use to break the habit of using rote memory to learn and practice information? Explain your reasoning for choosing these five Principles of Memory.

CL **ACE the Test**
Four Online Practice Tests

 **Online Resources**

Becoming a Time Manager and a Goal Setter

LEARNING OBJECTIVES

1 Analyze your use of time; identify ways to create balance in your life.

2 Create and use effective term, weekly, and daily schedules to manage your time.

3 Describe the four kinds of goals defined by time required to achieve goals; describe and use the four steps for writing goals.

Chapter Outline

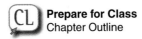

Prepare for Class
Chapter Outline

4 ▶ *Demonstrate understanding and use of essential goal-setting strategies that include task schedules, goal organizers, managing and monitoring your goals, and setting goals for long-term projects.*

Time management paired with goal setting is perhaps the most essential of all study skills, for it lays the foundation for you to have adequate time and structure to utilize all other study skills. Learning to use time management to balance your academic, work, and leisure time leads to greater productivity, more successes, and less stress. Learning to set goals provides you with well-defined plans of action to achieve specific results. Time management and goal-setting skills form a powerful partnership of lifelong skills that will benefit you in your academic, professional, and personal life.

Becoming a Time Manager and a Goal Setter

CL **Improve Your Grade**
Chapter 4 Profile

ANSWER, **SCORE**, and **RECORD** your profile before you read this chapter. If you need to review the process, refer to the complete directions given in the profile for Chapter 1 on page 4.

ONLINE: You can complete the profile and get your score online at this textbook's website.

	YES	NO
1. I use strategies to create a comfortable balance in my school, work, and leisure life.	_____	_____
2. I use a weekly schedule to organize my studying, work, and leisure time.	_____	_____
3. I try to make each scheduled day different so I do not get bored.	_____	_____
4. I often study for three hours or more in a row so I can stay current with my reading and homework assignments.	_____	_____
5. I usually study two hours during the week for every one hour in class.	_____	_____
6. I use a systematic four-step process for planning and setting goals.	_____	_____
7. I use task schedules to organize my short-term and study-block goals.	_____	_____
8. When faced with a list of short-term goals, I work to complete high-priority goals before working on goals with lower levels of importance.	_____	_____
9. I tend to have difficulty completing long-term projects on time.	_____	_____
10. I am confident that I have the skills necessary to manage my time effectively and to stay motivated to complete goals that I set.	_____	_____

QUESTIONS LINKED TO THE CHAPTER LEARNING OBJECTIVES:

Question 1:	objective 1	Questions 7–9:	objective 4
Questions 2–5:	objective 2	Question 10:	all objectives
Question 6:	objective 3		

BALANCE IN YOUR LIFE

> **1** ▷ *Analyze your use of time; identify ways to create balance in your life.*

As a student, you will need to continually balance three main areas in your life: school, work, and leisure. How you spend your time in these three main areas will vary term by term and be influenced by your personal goals, needs, and interests. Imbalances in these three areas of life can lead to an array of negative consequences, including frequent frustration, low productivity, resentment, confusion, or a lack of motivation. By identifying the areas of your life that are not receiving sufficient time to flourish, you can begin to manage your time in new ways to achieve the goals you set for each area and to create a more productive and rewarding balance in your life.

The Pie of Life

The **Pie of Life** is a graphic representation that shows how much time you dedicate to each of the three main areas of your life: *school, work,* and *leisure*. **Figure 4.1** shows the activities, responsibilities, and commitments that are a part of each section of the Pie of Life. The dotted lines within each of the areas of Figure 4.1 indicate subcategories of activities for that area.

FIGURE 4.1

Three Main Areas of the Pie of Life

School	Work	Leisure
Attend classes	Job (employment)	Family time
Do homework	Work at home (self-employed; home business)	. . . .
Study and review		Socialize with friends
Work with tutors	. . . .	Do recreational activities
Study with partner or group	Spend time parenting; tend to children's needs	Attend sporting events
Prepare for tests		Play sports: golf, baseball . . .
Do lab projects	. . . .	
. . . .	Do household chores: laundry, cleaning, cooking	. . . .
Attend meetings		Take personal "alone" time
Participate in student organizations	Work in the yard or on home maintenance	Exercise: walk, jog, swim . . .
. . . .	. . . .	Work on hobbies
Attend team practices/ games	Do volunteer work	Watch television/ movies
	Do committee work	Listen to music
		Use Internet; do e-mail

TERMS TO KNOW

Pie of Life   *p. 93*
Increase-Decrease Method
   p. 95
term schedule   *p. 97*
weekly schedule   *p. 98*
fixed study block   *p. 100*
flex study block   *p. 100*
2:1 ratio   *p. 101*
spaced practice   *p. 102*
marathon studying   *p. 102*
daily schedule   *p. 105*
trading time   *p. 106*
goals   *p. 108*
immediate goal   *p. 108*
short-term goal   *p. 108*
intermediary goal   *p. 108*
long-term goal   *p. 108*
Four-Step Approach for
   Achieving Goals   *p. 110*
extrinsic reward   *p. 111*
intrinsic reward   *p. 111*
task schedule   *p. 113*
goal organizer   *p. 114*
ABC Method   *p. 115*

 Improve Your Grade
Online Flashcards
Glossary

The **Pie of Life** is a graphic representation that shows how much time you dedicate to the three main areas of your life: *school, work,* and *leisure*.

CONCEPT CHECK 4.1

Are you already an effective time manager? If yes, what strategies are successful for you? If no, what time-management issues do you frequently encounter? What are the major obstacles that prevent you and other people from becoming time managers?

Improve Your Grade
Pie of Life

A balanced Pie of Life is not necessarily divided into three equal parts; the amounts of time dedicated to school, work, and leisure vary according to an individual's circumstances, goals, and values. A student who is not employed while attending school will have a different Pie of Life than a student who works a graveyard shift and attends college full-time. Likewise, a student who lives at home and attends school full-time on an athletic scholarship will have a different Pie of Life than a single parent who is enrolled in college part-time.

The first circle in **Figure 4.2** shows a Pie of Life divided into three equal parts. Divide the second circle into a pie that shows the *estimated amount of time* you currently spend per week in each of the three areas. In the last circle, adjust the lines to show your *ideal* Pie of Life that reflects the balance that you wish to obtain. If you wish, use dotted lines to divide the *school, work,* and *leisure* sections of the pie into subcategories, such as classes/studying, student meetings, team practice, job, parenting, household chores, family, friends, or personal time.

Achieving your ideal Pie of Life requires a willingness to examine the ways you currently use time and to commit to exploring new strategies that will improve your time-management and goal-setting skills. Change is not always easy, but the benefits of having a more balanced life make the process rewarding and worthwhile.

CONCEPT CHECK 4.2

Would one person's ideal Pie of Life be appropriate or suitable for another person who is the same age? Why or why not?

EXERCISE 4.1

How You Use Time

Topic In-Depth
7-Day Time Log

PURPOSE: Creating a more effective balance of time in your life begins with an awareness of your daily patterns, habits, and priorities for using time. Keep a log of how you spend your time for three complete days. After analyzing the results of your three-day time log, you can begin applying time-management strategies to create a more effective balance in your life. (A form for a 7-day time log is available on this textbook's Student Website.)

DIRECTIONS: Go to Exercise 4.1 in Appendix B, pages A7–A8. Complete the following steps:

1. **Step 1:** On the chart, record all your activities for three days. *Be specific.* For example, you might

write: in class, met with tutor, lab work, team practice, job, laundry, television, gym, hobby, e-mail, talked on phone, commuted, napped, or ate dinner.

2. **Step 2:** After completing your three-day log, count the number of hours spent each day in the areas shown on the final chart. Some activities may fit into more than one category; however, count them only once in the most appropriate category.

3. **Step 3: Class Discussion:** How do the results of your three-day log match your ideal Pie of Life as shown in Figure 4.2 on page 95? Explain.

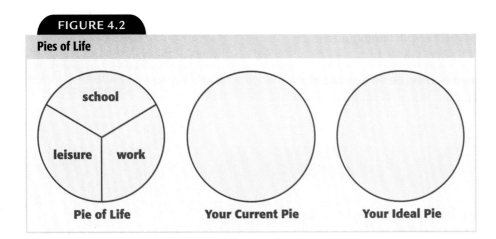

FIGURE 4.2

Pies of Life

Pie of Life | Your Current Pie | Your Ideal Pie

The Increase-Decrease Method

You only have so many hours in a week. If your Pie of Life is unbalanced, you have two choices. First, you can learn more efficient ways to study, do household chores, or finish projects at home or at work. In other words, the time you have set aside for each piece of your Pie of Life becomes more focused and more productive with less time wasted.

Second, you can use the Increase-Decrease Method to change the boundaries in your Pie of Life. The **Increase-Decrease Method** involves increasing or decreasing time used in one area of life in order to make more time for another area of life. Begin by identifying the section of your Pie of Life that needs more time in order to create a better balance in your life. As you increase time in this section, you will need to decrease time allocated to one or both of the remaining sections of your pie. For example, if your goal is to increase the amount of time allocated to *school*, you will need to decrease the time you spend in the area of *work* and/or *leisure*. Using the Increase-Decrease Method to bring you closer to achieving an ideal balance involves learning new skills that can help you change or modify your old behaviors and routines.

CONCEPT CHECK 4.3

How does the use of the Increase-Decrease Method for one main area of your life affect the other two areas of your Pie of Life? Explain with specific examples.

The **Increase-Decrease Method** involves increasing or decreasing time used in one area of life in order to make more time for another area of life.

EXERCISE 4.2

Using the Increase-Decrease Method to Find Time

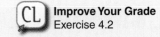
Improve Your Grade
Exercise 4.2

PURPOSE: Identifying ways to use the Increase-Decrease Method to increase or "find" time for one area of your life by decreasing time spent in one or both of the other areas leads to a more effective balance in life.

INSTRUCTIONS:

1. Work with a partner. The three students described on the next page want suggestions that will help them

increase a specific area of their Pie of Life. Several suggestions appear for each student.

2. Brainstorm with your partner. Write additional suggestions for each student. Include ways to reduce the other two areas of their Pie of Life. You may also refer to and include the suggestions available on the Student Website for Exercise 4.2.

Student 1: I want to increase my *leisure* time with family and friends. Suggestions include:

1. Reduce time spent on leisure activities that you do by yourself.
2. Reduce time spent on chores by learning to do them more efficiently.
3.
4.
5.

Student 2: I want to increase my *school* time so I can earn better grades. Suggestions include:

1. Schedule "quality" social time; decrease "spur of the moment" socializing.
2. Make better use of time between classes to study or review.
3.
4.
5.

Student 3: I want to increase my *work* (employment) time so I will have fewer financial stresses. Suggestions include:

1. Talk to employer about adding a few extra hours on the weekend.
2. Seek new strategies for budgeting and managing existing income.
3.
4.
5.

CHECK POINT 4.1

ANSWERS APPEAR ON PAGE A4

True or False?

_____ 1. Balance in the areas of school, work, and leisure often results in less stress, greater productivity, and a more positive lifestyle.

_____ 2. For realistic balance in one's daily life, a person should allocate equal time to school, work, and leisure activities.

_____ 3. The majority of *school* time in the Pie of Life occurs within the classroom.

_____ 4. The main goal of the Increase-Decrease Method is to encourage students to increase their school and study time by decreasing their social and leisure time.

_____ 5. The concept of *work* includes more than an income-earning job.

Improve Your Grade
Online Practice 1: Balance

KINDS OF SCHEDULES

Topic In-Depth
Quick Start Forms

2 ▶ *Create and use effective term, weekly, and daily schedules to manage your time.*

Well-designed schedules serve as road maps to guide you through the months of a term, through the week, and through each day. Rather than being at the mercy of time, schedules empower you and give you the ability to take control of time. With schedules, *you* create goals and plans for how you wish to spend your time. Your skills as a time manager become lifelong skills that benefit you well in school, at home, and in your chosen career.

Term Schedules

A **term schedule** is a month-by-month calendar that shows important events and deadlines for the entire term. You can use a regular calendar, a monthly planner, a PDA (personal digital assistant, also called a pocket computer), an electronic organizer, or a computer calendar program for each month in your current academic term. At the beginning of each term, create your term schedule by adding the items to your calendar that appear in **Figure 4.3**.

> **FIGURE 4.3**
>
> **Items to Include on Your Term Schedule**
>
> 1. Important deadlines for special projects, reports, and writing or lab assignments that appear on your course syllabi
> 2. Scheduled tests, midterms, and final exams
> 3. Special events, meetings, workshops, or conferences
> 4. Holidays
> 5. Scheduled times for tutors, study groups, or other support services
> 6. Personal appointments on or off campus

> **CONCEPT CHECK 4.4**
>
> What kinds of schedules do you currently maintain? Do you use a daily planner, a PDA (pocket computer), or computer software to create schedules?

> A **term schedule** is a month-by-month calendar that shows important events and deadlines for the entire term.

> **CONCEPT CHECK 4.5**
>
> What potential problems can you avoid by using a term schedule? Why is it important for you to have a "big picture" of the term?

> **EXERCISE 4.3**

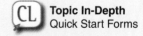
Topic In-Depth
Quick Start Forms

Create a Term Schedule

PURPOSE: Create a term schedule that provides you with an overview of the term and serves as a guide when you create your weekly schedule.

DIRECTIONS: Gather together your campus calendar, the syllabus from each of your courses, and your personal calendar of events to create a term schedule.

1. Use a month-by-month planner, a computer calendar program, an electronic organizer, a PDA, or the monthly calendars available online. On these calendars, write the dates for the items shown in Figure 4.3. (Always download PDA calendars to your computer to avoid losing data or in case you lose your PDA device.)

2. Place your month-by-month calendars in the front of your notebook, or if you are using an electronic calendar program, refer to the monthly calendar at the beginning of each week when you create your weekly schedule.

3. Update your term calendar throughout the term with deadlines for new assignments or significant events.

Weekly Schedules

While term schedules provide you with an overview of important events and deadlines on a month-to-month basis, weekly schedules focus your attention on details and requirements for the upcoming week. A **weekly schedule** is a detailed plan that serves as a guide for creating a manageable, daily routine for each day of the week. Using a weekly schedule helps you maintain a focus and helps you organize, monitor, and regulate your use of time.

Unlike a time log made *after* you complete activities or tasks, a weekly time-management schedule is made *before* you engage in the activities. The weekly schedule becomes your *plan,* your guide, and your structure for the week. **Figure 4.4** shows seven Essential Elements of a Well-Planned Weekly Schedule.

Each Sunday spend a few minutes planning your schedule for the upcoming week. Keep this schedule in the front of your notebook or in your electronic organizer. Refer to your weekly schedule whenever you wish to make new plans or set up appointments. By using the five steps on pages 100–101 to create your weekly schedule, you can feel confident that you will have a more balanced weekly routine. **Figure 4.5** shows a weekly schedule that includes the essential elements of a well-planned schedule.

> A **weekly schedule** is a detailed plan that serves as a guide for creating a manageable, daily routine for each day of the week.

CONCEPT CHECK 4.6

If you were to analyze another student's weekly schedule, what criteria would you use to evaluate its effectiveness?

FIGURE 4.4

Essential Elements of a Well-Planned Weekly Schedule

▌ **It reflects a realistic, balanced Pie of Life.**

▌ **It shows adequate time for study blocks.** Study blocks are scheduled throughout the week so you study on a regular basis, not just when you have assignments due or a test the following day.

▌ **It makes good use of all blocks of time.** You "tighten up" your schedule to avoid wasted blocks of time, such as an hour between classes or an hour or two after dinner.

▌ **It includes hours of employment.** If your work hours change weekly, your weekly schedule reflects these changes.

▌ **It shows specific time blocks for work and leisure activities.** Time blocks are set aside for household chores, errands, exercise, recreation, social and family time, and daily routines, such as getting ready in the morning, commuting, or preparing and eating meals.

▌ **It shows strong, consistent patterns.** Patterns, such as specific times for studying specific classes, eating meals, doing chores, or engaging in recreation help you live your schedule to the point that it becomes routine and habitual.

▌ **It allocates time to work on personal goals.** For example, if you want to jog three times a week or spend time in the park with your children twice a week, your schedule shows time aside for those goals.

▌ **It establishes a routine time to go to sleep each night.** Going to bed about the same time each night helps stabilize your internal clock and your sleep-awake patterns. Short nights occasionally followed by long nights of sleep disrupt your normal rhythm and a more natural flow of energy.

FIGURE 4.5

Example of a Weekly Time-Management Schedule

WEEKLY TIME-MANAGEMENT SCHEDULE

For the week of _____

Time	Monday	Tuesday	Wednesday	Thursday	Friday	Saturday	Sunday
12–6 AM	SLEEP ——————————————————————→						
6–7:00	SLEEP ——————————————————————→						
7–8:00	Get up, get ready, eat breakfast ————————→					SLEEP	SLEEP
8–9:00	Commute to school ——————————————→					Get up	Get up
9–10:00	PE Class	Study Math	PE Class	Study Math	PE Class	Breakfast	Breakfast
10–11:00	Math Class	Math Class	Math Class	Math Class	Study Math	Career Class	Get ready
11–12 NOON	Study Math	LUNCH	Study Math	LUNCH	with TUTOR	Study Career	CHURCH
12–1:00	LUNCH	Computer Class	LUNCH	Computer Class	LUNCH	ERRANDS	CHURCH
1–2:00	Reading Class	Computer Class	Reading Class	Computer Class	Reading Class	LUNCH	LUNCH
2–3:00	Study Reading	Lab-Study Computer	Study Reading	Lab-Study Computer	Study Reading	CHORES	LEISURE
3–4:00	Study Reading	Lab-Study Computer	FLEX	Lab-Study Computer	FLEX	CHORES	LEISURE
4–5:00	Commute home ————————————————→					CHORES	LEISURE
5–6:00	DINNER ——————————————————————→						LEISURE
6–7:00	LEISURE	LEISURE	LEISURE	LEISURE	WORK	WORK	DINNER
7–8:00	Study Reading	WORKOUT	Study Math	WORKOUT	WORK	WORK	Study Math
8–9:00	Study Reading		Study Computer		WORK	WORK	Study Computer
9–10:00	LEISURE		LEISURE		WORK	WORK	FLEX
10–11:00	LEISURE		LEISURE		WORK	WORK	PLAN WEEK
11–12 AM	SLEEP ——————————————————————→				WORK	WORK	SLEEP

FIGURE 4.6

Five Steps for Creating a Weekly Time-Management Schedule

1. Write in all your fixed activities.
2. Write in your fixed study times for each class.
3. Add two or three flexible study blocks.
4. Add time for personal goals and personal responsibilities.
5. Schedule leisure, family, and social time.

Topic In-Depth
Quick Start Forms

Use Five Steps for Creating a Weekly Time-Management Schedule

Using a systematic approach to create your weekly time-management schedule helps you plan sufficient time for important areas of your daily life. Once you create an effective schedule, you can continue to use that schedule for the remainder of the term. On occasion, you may need to make minor modifications in your schedule to accommodate special events or work schedules. If you use a PDA (pocket or palm computer) or an electronic organizer, you may want to plan your weekly schedule first on paper and then transfer the information into your PDA. **Figure 4.6** shows the five steps for creating a weekly time-management schedule.

Step 1: Write your fixed activities. Fixed activities are those activities that do not vary much from week to week. Fixed activities for a specific week may also include special appointments. On your weekly schedule, write the following fixed activities in the appropriate time blocks:

1. Class times
2. Work schedule (employment)
3. Getting ready in the morning; commuting
4. Breakfast, lunch, and dinner
5. Special appointments
6. Sleep

Step 2: Write your fixed study times. After learning about the importance of the Memory Principles of Time on Task and Ongoing Review, you understand the importance of making study blocks a high priority on your weekly schedule. **Fixed study blocks** are well-planned blocks of time set aside to study specific subjects during the course of the week. With effective fixed study blocks, you will have sufficient time to complete your reading and homework assignments, create study tools, use elaborative rehearsal, and practice retrieving information through ongoing review. Figure 4.7 and Figure 4.8 on pages 101 and 103 show Essential Strategies for Scheduling Fixed Study Blocks.

Fixed study blocks are well-planned blocks of time set aside to study specific subjects during the course of the week.

Step 3: Add several flexible study blocks. **Flex study blocks** are flexible blocks of time on a weekly schedule that you use only when you need them. Flex blocks are safety nets for extra study time. Identify two or three hours each week that you can hold in reserve in case you need additional time to study for a specific class, prepare for a test, or complete a special project. On your weekly schedule, write *FLEX* for these time blocks. Unlike fixed study blocks, which you should use each time they appear on your schedule, if you do not need to use the flex blocks, *convert them to free time.*

Flex study blocks are flexible blocks of time on a weekly schedule that you use only when you need them.

Step 4: Add time for personal goals and responsibilities. Schedule time blocks to work specifically on important goals or personal responsibilities. If you do not set aside time specifically for these important goals, tasks, or responsibilities, you may find yourself postponing them or procrastinating about them.

Step 5: Schedule leisure, family, and social time. Label the remaining time on your schedule as *family, social,* or *leisure.* For the upcoming week, you can specify specific plans for time blocks, such as "swimming" "movie," or "entertaining," or you can leave the time blocks open and flexible to do whatever you decide on that day. Having family, social, and leisure time is important for mental and physical health and strong relationships. If you do not have adequate time on your schedule for these activities, explore ways to use the Increase-Decrease Method to find more social and leisure time.

CONCEPT CHECK 4.7

What are the five steps to create a weekly schedule? Why are the first three steps focused on school?

Six Essential Strategies for Scheduling Fixed Study Blocks

Your fixed study blocks on your weekly schedule help you organize your time and your academic commitments. **Figure 4.7** summarizes six Essential Strategies for Scheduling Fixed Study Blocks. Details about each strategy follow.

Use the 2:1 ratio to schedule fixed study blocks. The **2:1 ratio** is a time-management technique that involves studying two hours for every one hour in class. This ratio applies to the majority of college courses that require reading and homework assignments. For example, if your writing class meets for three hours each week, schedule six hours of studying *for the writing class* each week. The following are important points about the 2:1 ratio:

2:1 ratio is a time-management technique that involves studying two hours for every one hour in class.

▌ Studying in college means more than just doing homework. The 2:1 ratio provides you, in most cases, with sufficient time not only to take notes, memorize, and elaborate on course work, but to rehearse or review to keep information "fresh" and accessible.

▌ In some cases, however, fewer fixed study hours may be acceptable; perhaps a 1:1 ratio is sufficient.

▌ For the most demanding classes, such as science or math courses, you may need to use a 3:1 ratio to schedule more fixed study hours in order to master the course content.

FIGURE 4.7

Summary of Six Essential Strategies for Scheduling Fixed Study Blocks

▌ Use the 2:1 ratio to schedule fixed study blocks.
▌ Label each study block with the name of the subject you will study.
▌ Plan to use the entire study block for one subject.
▌ Use spaced practice.
▌ Avoid marathon studying.
▌ Schedule at least one study block every day of the week.

Label each study block with the name of the subject you will study. Show specifically the course you intend to study during each time block. Labeling a block "study" does not provide you with a specific study plan and tends to promote an ineffective habit of studying whatever feels to be of the greatest urgency. Use specific labels such as *Study English, Study Math,* or *Study Psychology.*

Plan to use the entire study block for one subject. Jumping from one subject to another within an hour block disrupts the process of creating a "mindset" for the subject matter. Use the entire fifty-minute study block to review previous work, complete the current assignment, make notes or other study tools, and review. At the end of fifty minutes, give yourself a *ten-minute break* before moving into the next hour of studying.

Spaced practice, also known as *distributed practice,* involves making multiple contacts with new information and spreading this contact over several days or weeks.

Use spaced practice. **Spaced practice,** also known as *distributed practice,* is a time-management and learning technique that involves making multiple contacts with new information and spreading this contact over several days or weeks. Spaced practice limits the length of a study block and spreads study blocks out over time. You will understand and recall information better for a subject if you study it for one hour six times a week, or two hours three times a week, rather than study it for six hours on the same day. Spaced practice has additional benefits:

▌ Comprehension and retention (ability to recall) increase.

▌ Motivation, concentration, and productivity increase.

▌ Less time is spent rereading or relearning information.

Topic In-Depth
Spaced Practice

The breaks or rest intervals between every fifty-minute study block give your memory system time to sort, process, and connect information. The Topic In-Depth: Spaced Practice on the Student Website discusses the impact study breaks have on comprehension and retention. After studying two or three hours (with short breaks between each fifty-minute study block), change to a different kind of activity, such as a leisure or social activity. Your thinking processes do not shut down when you step away from the books for a few hours. When you return to studying, you will be more alert and receptive to new information.

Marathon studying, also known as *massed practice,* occurs when you study more than three hours in a row.

Avoid marathon studying. **Marathon studying,** also known as *massed practice,* occurs when you study more than three hours in a row. Three or more continuous hours of studying without a break leads to problems with productivity, concentration, and retention.

Marathon studying *is* acceptable in some learning situations that involve a creative flow of ideas or energy. Learning tasks such as painting, sculpting, constructing a model, or writing a research paper may benefit from marathon studying because tapping into the same channel of creativity and thought patterns at a later time may be more difficult to achieve. In such situations, scheduling longer study blocks is acceptable.

CONCEPT CHECK 4.8

What are the major differences between spaced practice and massed practice? When is spaced practice preferred over massed practice?

Schedule at least one study block every day of the week. By spreading your study times throughout the entire week, you will be using spaced practice, and you will create a better balance in your Pie of Life with less stress and frustration. Studying long hours during the weekdays and then engaging mainly in leisure or social activities on the weekend is ineffective.

FIGURE 4.8

Six More Essential Strategies for Scheduling Fixed Study Blocks

- Study during your most alert times of the day.
- Schedule a math study block every day.
- Schedule your hardest or least-liked subject early in the day.
- Schedule a study block right *before* a class that involves discussions or student participation.
- Schedule a study block right *after* a lecture class.
- Use the 3:1 ratio for independent study or online courses.

Six More Essential Strategies for Scheduling Fixed Study Blocks

The fact that there are six additional strategies for scheduling fixed study blocks stresses the importance of putting some thought into organizing your study blocks effectively. **Figure 4.8** summarizes six more Essential Strategies for Scheduling Fixed Study Blocks. Details about each strategy are discussed below.

Study during your most alert times of the day. Study when you feel the most mentally sharp, alert, and focused, not when you know your body and eyes are physically fatigued. Mornings, mid-afternoons, and early evenings are often the most productive times to study. Studying late at night or right after a meal is often the least productive. Use "low energy or low attention times" for tasks that do not require high cognitive functioning.

Schedule a math study block every day. Math involves working with steps and processes, the kind of knowledge that is best learned through repetition, repetition, and more repetition. Studying math on a daily basis provides essential time for ongoing review and application of math problem-solving skills. When possible, schedule a math study block right after your math class; on the days of the week that you do not have a math class, schedule your math study block during your alert times of the day.

Schedule your hardest or least-liked subjects early in the day. By placing the hardest or least-liked subjects first on your study priorities, you are able to use a more alert mind and focused attention to tackle the assignments and process new information.

Schedule a study block right before a class that involves discussion or student participation. This puts you in the mindset for the course, refreshes your memory of key concepts, and provides you with time to rehearse as needed.

Schedule a study block right after a lecture class. During lecture classes, your main task is to take lecture notes. By scheduling a study time right *after* the class, you can review your notes, compare them with other students' notes, fill in missing details, and reorganize your notes in more meaningful ways while the information is still fresh in your mind.

CONCEPT CHECK 4.9

The Memory Principle of Time on Task applies to the "Essential Strategies for Scheduling Fixed Study Blocks." What other Memory Principles do you actively use when you implement the essential strategies in Figures 4.7 and 4.8?

Use the 3:1 ratio for independent study or online courses. Even though you may find independent study and online courses appealing because of their flexibility, they often require a higher level of self-discipline, dedication, and time commitment to complete successfully. For independent study or online courses that have few or no in-class hours, you need to schedule a minimum of *nine hours* per week for coursework. Use the course syllabus to create a term schedule and a week-by-week schedule that commits you to covering specific course materials in a timely manner.

EXERCISE 4.4

Topic In-Depth
Peer/Teacher Assessment Checklists

Creating Your Weekly Schedule

PURPOSE: A well-planned weekly schedule helps you make the very best use of your time, increases your opportunity to create a balanced Pie of Life, and guides you through each day with sufficient time to accomplish your school, work, and personal goals.

DIRECTIONS: Go to Exercise 4.4 in Appendix B, pages A9–A10 for a weekly time-management form and a Time-Management Self-Assessment Checklist. Photocopy the weekly schedule form to use for this exercise or download the form from online Chapter 4 in the Topic-In-Depth: Quick Start Forms. Complete the following directions.

Step 1: Use the steps diagrammed below to create a weekly time-management schedule. Use a pencil at first so you can rearrange time blocks and make adjustments as needed to create a manageable and realistic schedule.

Step 2: Mentally walk through each day on your schedule to determine whether it is realistic.

Step 3: Complete the Time-Management Self-Assessment Checklist on page A10 in Appendix B.

Use that information to make any necessary adjustments on your schedule.

Step 4: Color-code your schedule so it is easier to see at a glance. Use one color for your classes; another for study times; and a third for leisure, family, and social time. Use a fourth color for work or leave the spaces without color coding.

Step 5: Make a copy of your schedule to keep in the front of your notebook if your instructor asks you to turn in your original schedule and the Self-Assessment Checklist (page A10).

Step 6: Begin following your schedule as soon as possible. Several times during the day, indicate on your schedule how often you followed it as planned. Create a code system such as using stars for blocks that worked as planned and checks for blocks that you did not follow according to the plan.

Step 7: Use your schedule for a full seven days. After you have used your schedule for a full week, your instructor may ask you to turn in your first schedule and the Time-Management Self-Assessment Checklist.

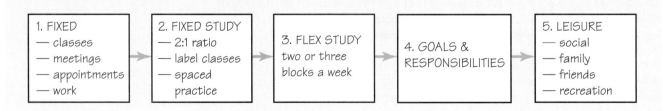

Daily Schedules

A **daily schedule** is a specific list of tasks that you plan to achieve over the course of a day. It is your "To-Do List" that helps you move through the day efficiently. Use an index card, a daily planner, or an electronic organizer for your daily schedule. Each night before you go to bed, take a few minutes to prepare your daily schedule for the next day's activities. Keep the schedule in a convenient place for quick reference. In **Figure 4.9**, after examining the example of the daily schedule on the left, make a daily schedule for yourself in the box on the right.

A **daily schedule** is a specific list of tasks that you plan to achieve over the course of a day.

FIGURE 4.9

Example of a To-Do List

TO DO WEDNESDAY:

8–9:00 AM   Study Psy.
             Read & notes for
             pages 95–116

CLASSES   Regular schedule

1–3:00 PM   Study Algebra
             —Redo Ex. 6 #2–5
             —Do Ex. 7 odd numbers
             —Make study flash cards

3–5:00 PM   —Start laundry
             —Grocery shop
             —Read mail
             —Finish laundry

MY DAILY SCHEDULE FOR TOMORROW:

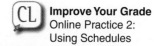

Improve Your Grade
Online Practice 2:
Using Schedules

GROUP PROCESSING:
A COLLABORATIVE LEARNING ACTIVITY

Form groups of three or four students. You will need to have a chart to record information. Select one member of your group to be the group recorder. Complete the following directions.

1. Divide a large chart into two columns. In the left column write all the problems the members of your group have encountered with managing time. List as many different ideas or problems as possible.

2. After you have a list of common problems, brainstorm possible solutions. Write the possible solutions in the right column. You may provide more than one possible solution for each problem. Be prepared to share your list of problems and possible solutions with the class.

Improve Your Grade
Online Practice 3:
Adjusting to Change

Adjusting to Change

Change is not always an easy process. Flexibility on your part can make the process of change easier. Use the following tips to adjust behaviors, attitudes, and use of your time:

▌ **Be ready for change.** Be willing to: relax your old patterns or ways of doing things, try new approaches, and give something new a chance to succeed.

▌ **Be patient with yourself.** As soon as you recognize that you are wandering from your time-management plan, do not be hard on yourself or discard the schedule. Instead, return to the schedule and start getting back on track from that point in time.

▌ **Apply effort.** Give your very best effort to use your weekly schedules for three weeks.

▌ **Monitor your behavior and success.** Learning to observe, understand, and monitor your choices is part of learning to use time management (and metacognition) successfully. During the first three weeks of using your schedule, examine the times and the reasons why parts of your schedule did not work. Analyze each situation and identify ways you could have handled the situation differently.

> **CONCEPT CHECK 4.10**
>
> What would you suggest to a student who resists time-management schedules in order to live spontaneously?

▌ **Seek help and support from friends and family members.** Inform them about your goals to organize your time more effectively. Include them in the process of planning your weekly schedule. Post your schedule so they are aware of your plans and your available time.

▌ **Use trading time, but sparingly.** Use the time-management technique of trading time when you need flexibility in your schedule to adjust to a special event. **Trading time** is a time-management technique that allows you to trade or exchange time blocks for two activities within the same day. For example, if you want to participate in an unexpected social activity that will occur during your 7:00–9:00 pm study block, trade the study block with a 2:00–4:00 block of time you had set aside to spend with friends. Use trading time sparingly. If you trade time blocks too frequently, you will lose the sense of routine, and your self-discipline to follow your schedule may decline.

Trading time is a time-management technique that allows you to trade or exchange time blocks for two activities within the same day.

▌ **Consider changing your sleep patterns.** Early morning hours can be productive and conducive to high concentration, so try getting up earlier in the morning before children or other members in your household are awake.

▌ **Find study time—even when you have children.** If you have children who attend childcare, consider extending the childcare an hour or two and stay on campus to study during that time. Use all available time between classes to complete as much studying on campus as possible so that more of your time at home can be devoted to your children's needs.

▌ **Be on campus five days a week.** If you scheduled classes to be on campus only two or three days of the week with good intentions to study at home the remaining days, consider coming to campus five days a week so you can have access to tutors, labs, instructors, and other students. Your study time on campus away from the distractions at home may be more productive and effective.

Learning to become a time manager involves a willingness to adjust behaviors, attitudes, and ways you use time. As a successful time manager, you will experience greater successes achieving your goals, increasing productivity, and balancing your Pie of Life. The time-management skills you learn now and in the future are highly prized skills recognized and admired in both the work force and the academic world.

CONCEPT CHECK 4.11

Do you see time management as rigid, flexible, or a combination of both? Explain your answer.

REFLECTIVE WRITING 4.1

 **Improve Your Grade**
Reflective Writing 4.1

On separate paper, in a journal, or on this textbook's website, respond to the following questions.

1. What are the major adjustments you have had to make in your attitude, behavior, or use of time as you learn to become a more effective time manager? How has your Pie of Life changed since you began using time management? Be specific.

2. What are the most difficult times of the day for you to "stay on schedule"? What areas of time management are most difficult for you to implement? How can you use time-management strategies to overcome these difficulties?

CHECK POINT 4.2

ANSWERS APPEAR ON PAGE A4

Matching

Match the terms on the left with the shortened definitions or descriptions on the right. Write the letter of the definition next to the word in the left column.

_____ 1. flex blocks		a. often require more than the hours associated with the 2:1 ratio
_____ 2. 2:1 ratio		b. occurs with marathon studying
_____ 3. spaced practice		c. best to schedule study block right before class
_____ 4. massed practice		d. distributed practice
_____ 5. trading time		e. study blocks set to study specific courses
_____ 6. online courses		f. set of monthly calendars with deadlines and events
_____ 7. lecture classes		g. two or three blocks of time set aside as "safety nets"
_____ 8. speech classes		h. best to schedule study block after class
_____ 9. fixed study blocks		i. a formula for allocating sufficient time to study in most courses
_____ 10. term schedule		j. an exchange of two blocks of time within the same day

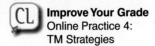 **Improve Your Grade**
Online Practice 4:
TM Strategies

GOAL SETTING

3 *Describe the four kinds of goals defined by time required to achieve goals; describe and use the four steps for writing goals.*

Goals are well-defined plans aimed at achieving specific results. Goals are your road map to become the person you want to be and to create the life you want to live. They reflect your values and priorities about what is truly important to you.

Time management and goal setting go hand in hand. Effective time management requires effective goal setting. You can use your blocks of time more effectively when you have a clear goal of what you want to accomplish during specific times and you have ample time allocated to work on the goals. You will be rewarded with a sense of pride and accomplishment, and you will feel more in control of your time, your choices, and your personal life.

Different Kinds of Goals

Goals can be defined and organized in a variety of ways, such as educational goals, financial goals, or organizational goals. Another way to define goals is according to the length of time established to reach the desired outcome. **Figure 4.10** shows four kinds of goals defined according to the length of time involved to achieve a specific result.

Your educational plan is an example of a long-term goal comprised of one or more intermediary goals. For example, if you plan to complete a four-year degree, graduation from a university is your *long-term goal.* To reach that long-term goal, you may need to accomplish *intermediary goals,* such as complete a two-year degree, or you may need to complete a series of general requirement courses. To achieve your intermediary goals, you would need to complete a series of *short-term goals* such as completing specific courses, earning a specific number of credits, and establishing an acceptable grade-point average. Throughout your college years, you will face an abundance of *immediate goals,* tasks or assignments that must be done within a short time frame.

Goals are well-defined plans aimed at achieving specific results.

CONCEPT CHECK 4.12

Are you already an effective goal setter? If yes, in what areas of your life have setting goals been effective? If no, what problems do you encounter in setting or achieving goals?

Goals can be defined based on the length of time required to achieve the desired results: **immediate goal** (hours/day); **short-term goal** (week, month, or one term); **intermediary goal** (one year or more); **long-term goal** (years).

CONCEPT CHECK 4.13

How are intermediary goals related to long-term goals? How are short-term goals related to intermediary goals?

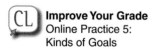

Improve Your Grade
Online Practice 5:
Kinds of Goals

FIGURE 4.10

Kinds of Goals

1. An **immediate goal** is achievable within the range of a few hours to a few days.

2. A **short-term goal** is achievable within the range of a week to the length of an academic term. A short-term goal may be broken into smaller steps or goals.

3. An **intermediary goal** is achievable over a time period of a year or more. It is achieved after the completion of a series of short-term goals that serve as benchmarks, motivators, and links to a long-term goal.

4. A **long-term goal** is achievable after a longer period of time, usually measured in years. Most long-term goals are achieved after the completion of a series of intermediary goals.

FIGURE 4.11

A Flow Chart for a Long-Term Goal

The diagram shows how the long-term goal is the "big picture" to achieve. The intermediary, short-term, and immediate goals are "the smaller pictures," each a subgoal for a higher level accomplishment.

long-term goal — Acquire a 4-year degree

intermediary goal — Acquire a 2-year transfer degree

short-term goal — Complete each course this term with a B grade or higher

immediate goals — Pass the math test on Friday | Complete essay draft by 8:00 PM Wednesday

Immediate and short-term goals need not be directly linked to a long-term goal. For example, you may want to create a goal to organize an effective study area, sort your boxes of photographs, change the oil in your car, or plant a vegetable garden. You can plan, implement, and achieve immediate or short-term goals such as these within a relatively short period of time without the goals being part of a larger intermediary or long-term goal.

EXERCISE 4.5

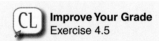
Improve Your Grade
Exercise 4.5

Your Long-Term Educational Goal Flow Chart

PURPOSE: Achieving your long-term educational goal requires the completion of several intermediary goals, such as completion of specific degree requirements, courses, or tests. Creating a flow chart shows your understanding of where you are and where you want to go.

DIRECTIONS:

1. Use **Figure 4.11** as a model for this exercise, or use the form online in the Online Study Center, Exercise 4.5. On your paper, make boxes in your flow chart for "long-term educational goal," "intermediary goals," "short-term goals," and "immediate goals."

2. Write you long-term educational goal in the box on the top of your flow chart.

3. Locate a printed page of a catalog or brochure that shows the classes and requirements you need to complete your program or degree. List those in the box for "intermediary goals."

4. Complete your flow chart by adding items in the boxes for "short-term goals" for this term, and "immediate goals" for the next few days.

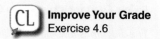

> ### EXERCISE 4.6
>
> ## *Initial Thoughts about Personal Goals*
>
> **Improve Your Grade**
> Exercise 4.6
>
> **DIRECTIONS:** Go to the Online Study Center, Exercise 4.6, to complete the Initial Thoughts about Personal Goals chart for this term, the next two years, and the next five years. This exercise is designed to encourage you to begin thinking about where you are and where you want to go or be during different time periods of your life.

The **Four Step Approach for Achieving Goals** is a process to set and achieve goals by using these steps: Specific, Target, Steps, and Rewards.

A Four-Step Approach for Achieving Goals

Many people have good intentions and a strong desire or motivation to succeed by achieving their goals; however, many of these same people fall short of making their goals reality. Frequently the inability to achieve goals begins with the lack of a sound process or strategy to write effective goals. The **Four-Step Approach for Achieving Goals** is a process to set and achieve goals by using these steps: Specific, Target, Steps, and Rewards. **Figure 4.12** shows these four steps.

Step 1: Set Specific Goals

Take the time to do a personal inventory to identify what it is that you wish to achieve. When your goal is clear, specific, and realistic, you have an exact picture or vision of the desired outcome. To simply say, "I will do better" or "I want something new" results in vague and immeasurable goals. To say, "I will be a millionaire tomorrow" is not realistic for most people. Before you commit to a goal, evaluate whether the goal is clear, specific, and realistic for you.

Some people shy away from setting specific goals. Attitudes such as the following hinder their success with goal setting:

▮ I have a fear of failure, or I have a fear of success.

▮ It's better not to try than to try and not succeed.

▮ I'll just get discouraged, frustrated, or embarrassed, so why bother?

▮ I've never been a goal setter and I'm doing okay.

▮ I have never learned how to set goals and don't know where to start.

FIGURE 4.12

Four Steps for Achieving Goals [STSR]

1. Set **S**pecific, clear, and realistic goals.
2. Set a specific **T**arget date and time to complete each goal.
3. Identify the individual **S**teps involved in reaching the goal.
4. Plan a **R**eward for yourself when you reach the goal.

Fortunately, by learning to write effective goals and to use strategies to achieve goals, you will find that many of your fears and reasons for avoiding goal setting vanish. Begin by identifying a *specific,* realistic *immediate goal* that you can achieve within a few hours. Select strategies to complete the goal. One success at completing a goal leads the way to more successes and combats reasons for shying away from goal setting.

Step 2: Set a Specific Target Date and Time

Procrastinators (people who put off doing something) seldom achieve goals. You can reduce or eliminate procrastination by setting a *specific target date* (deadline) and even *a specific time* to finish the steps involved in reaching your goal. The target date and time work as a form of motivation to keep you moving forward and on time. (Chapter 5 discusses motivation and procrastination.)

Step 3: Identify Steps

On paper, list the individual steps you will need to do to achieve the goal. For goals with multiple steps, list specific target dates and times for completing each step. Schedule time on your weekly schedule to complete each step. When you use this method of breaking one large goal into several smaller ones, you gain momentum each time you achieve a smaller goal by its targeted time.

Step 4: Plan a Reward

You can celebrate the completion of a goal with a reward. You can use that reward as an incentive—a motivation—to achieve your goal. You can use two kinds of rewards in your goal-setting plan: extrinsic rewards and intrinsic rewards.

Extrinsic rewards are material things or activities that are awarded when a goal is achieved. Buying a CD, going to a movie, going out to dinner, or planning a short trip are examples of extrinsic rewards. An extrinsic reward is a strong motivator only if you use it *after* you achieve the goal. You must also withhold the reward if you do not achieve the goal.

Intrinsic rewards are emotions or feelings that a person experiences when a goal is achieved. An increased self-esteem, pride, relief, joy, more confidence, or immense satisfaction are examples of intrinsic rewards. For any rewards to work as motivators, select rewards that truly represent what you *want* and can look forward to receiving.

A Plan of Action

The four steps for writing and achieving goals become your *plan of action.* Creating a plan of action for any immediate goal increases the likelihood that you will achieve the goal. Each of the four steps for writing and achieving goals activates your working memory and helps you build momentum to achieve your goals:

Step 1 helps you clarify what you wish to achieve.

Step 2 increases your awareness of time and activates your time-management skills.

Step 3 motivates you to identify and organize the tasks involved.

Step 4 builds a motivation for you to follow through with your plan of action.

Long-term goals are the result of the accomplishment of multiple intermediary, short-term, and immediate goals. Do you have a clear vision for your long-term educational goal? What intermediary goals must you complete to reach your long-term goal?

Extrinsic rewards are material things or activities that are awarded when a goal is achieved.

Intrinsic rewards are emotions or feelings that a person experiences when a goal is achieved.

CONCEPT CHECK 4.15

Why is each step of the four-step goal-setting process important? What would happen if you left out any one of the steps?

You can use these four powerful steps for a plan of action to tackle high-priority tasks that need to be done immediately at work, to organize and complete household chores, to achieve personal goals, or to organize a study block or a project for school. **Figure 4.13** shows an example of using the steps to organize an efficient study area for yourself at home.

FIGURE 4.13

Example of the Four Steps in Goal Setting

Step 1—Specific goal: Organize my desk to create an ideal study area.

Step 2—Target date and time: Have it done by this Sunday at 4:00.

Step 3—Individual steps:

1. Sort/organize paperwork stacked on my desk (bills, mail, class notes, and homework).

2. For each class, put current assignments and notes into my notebooks in chronological order. Put all others into file folders. Label and file each folder.

3. Organize my work surface: textbooks, dictionary, supplies . . .

4. Get rid of any remaining clutter. Empty wastepaper basket.

Step 4—Reward: Extrinsic: Go out for pizza and a movie with friends.

EXERCISE 4.7

Improve Your Grade
Exercise 4.7

Achieving an Immediate Goal

PURPOSE: Select an immediate goal that you can complete within the next day or two. Use the four goal-setting steps to tackle a small task that you would like to accomplish but keep putting off doing.

DIRECTIONS:

1. Use all four steps for planning your goal. On a separate piece of paper or online under Exercise 4.7, answer the following questions.

   Step 1: What is your *specific* goal?

   Step 2: What are the *target date* and *time* to complete this goal?

   Step 3: What are the individual *steps* you must complete to achieve the goal? List each step.

   Step 4: What is your planned reward?

2. Implement your plan of action. Begin working to complete each step as soon as possible.

3. After your target date and time pass, respond to the following question: Did you achieve your goal by the target date and time? If yes, explain what contributed to your success. If no, describe the obstacles that interfered with the process.

True or False?

_____ 1. Setting a specific target date to complete a goal can help reduce or eliminate procrastination.

_____ 2. Extrinsic rewards involve positive feelings, a sense of pride, and renewed motivation to tackle new goals.

_____ 3. Effective time managers are usually also effective goal setters.

_____ 4. All immediate and short-term goals are sub-goals of long-term goals that require years to achieve.

_____ 5. Lack of a specific goal-setting strategy, lack of a vision or desired direction, and lack of fears related to setting goals are the three main reasons some people have limited success with goal setting.

CL **Improve Your Grade**
Online Practice 6:
Setting Goals

GOAL-SETTING STRATEGIES

4 *Demonstrate understanding and use of essential goal-setting strategies that include task schedules, goal organizers, prioritizing your goals, managing and monitoring your goals, and setting goals for long-term projects.*

The *Four Steps for Achieving Goals* is the starting point for becoming an effective goal setter. **Figure 4.14** shows six Essential Strategies for Goal Setting. Explanations of each strategy follow.

CONCEPT CHECK 4.16

What strategies do you use that help you achieve the goals you set? What do you do if you find yourself unmotivated or if you fall short of completing a goal?

FIGURE 4.14

Essential Strategies for Goal Setting

▐ Use the four steps for achieving goals.
▐ Use task schedules to plan specific tasks for specific blocks of time.
▐ Use goal organizers to think about and carefully plan a course of action.
▐ Use the ABC Method to prioritize your goals.
▐ Manage and monitor your goals.
▐ Set goals for long-term projects.

Task Schedules

A **task schedule** is a step-by-step plan for completing a specific task in a specific block of time. Task schedules provide structure for a block of time so you waste less time trying to decide what to do or where to start. You can use task schedules to set goals for study blocks, organize household chores efficiently, or complete job-related tasks at work in an organized, logical manner. **Figure 4.15** shows how to incorporate the four goal-setting steps into task schedules.

A **task schedule** is a step-by-step plan for a completing a specific task in a specific block of time.

CONCEPT CHECK 4.17

How could you use a task schedule *today*? How can a task schedule assist you with effective use of your time?

FIGURE 4.15

Example of a Task Schedule for a Study Block

Step 1—Specific goal: Review math class and do math homework pp. 26–33.

Step 2—Target date and time: Wednesday, 10:00–11:00 am

Step 3—Individual steps:

1. Review class notes and rework class problem sets.
2. Read pages 26–32. Highlight key points. Study examples.
3. Do even-numbered problems on p. 33.
4. Check answers with answer key. Study/rework any incorrect problems.

Step 4—Reward: Extrinsic: Watch my favorite show on television.

EXERCISE 4.8

Create Task Schedules

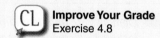

Improve Your Grade
Exercise 4.8

PURPOSE: Developing task schedules for study blocks helps you think about, organize, and plan how to use blocks of time without wasting time trying to decide what to do or where to start.

DIRECTIONS: Use the four steps for setting goals to create task schedules for any three of your study blocks. Then use the task schedules for those blocks of time. Below each task schedule, briefly discuss its value and effectiveness.

Goal Organizers

A **goal organizer** is a chart that consists of six questions to help you plan a course of action to achieve a specific goal.

A **goal organizer** is a chart that consists of six questions to help you plan a course of action to achieve a specific goal. Using a goal organizer helps you think seriously about the benefits, consequences, obstacles, and resources related to a specific goal. **Figure 4.16** shows the six important questions that assist you in organizing your goals and planning a course of action.

Topic In-Depth
Quick Start Forms

FIGURE 4.16

The Goal Organizer

1. What is your goal?
2. What benefits will you gain by achieving this goal?
3. What consequences will you experience by *not* achieving this goal?
4. What obstacles might you encounter while working on this goal?
5. How can you deal with the obstacles effectively if they occur?
6. What people or resources could help you with achieving this goal?

The ABC Method

If you try to achieve too many goals at one time, you may feel overwhelmed and frustrated. Use the ABC Method. The **ABC Method** is a goal-setting strategy to prioritize your goals according to rank of importance. Use the following steps for the ABC Method:

1. **List all the goals you want to achieve.** Limit your list to a specific time period.
2. **Assign a priority letter A, B, or C** to the goals on your list.
   "A" Goals: the most important to you or the ones you want or need to achieve first.
   "B" Goals: not as high a priority as the "A" goals.
   "C" Goals: not of such immediate importance.
3. **Begin working on the "A" goals.** After achieving the "A" high-priority goals, move on to the "B" goals. Once those are achieved, work on achieving the lower-priority goals.

The **ABC Method** is a goal-setting strategy to prioritize your goals according to rank of importance.

CONCEPT CHECK 4.18

Assume that you start getting nervous or frustrated about four short-term goals you have set for yourself. How can you convert your negative feelings to positive ones and get yourself back on track with your goals?

Self-Management

Self-management involves managing and monitoring your progress for achieving your goals. Goal setting is an art that requires practice and refinement. Strive to strengthen your goal-setting skills by using the following strategies to increase your success with each goal that you set.

Break Larger Goals into Smaller Goals

If you break a large task or goal into smaller steps or a series of steps (subgoals), achieving your goal feels more possible, realistic, and manageable. Completion of each of the smaller steps brings you closer to achieving the larger goal. By using this "chunking down technique," you will also experience less stress and avoid the feeling of being overwhelmed.

Evaluate the Importance of a Goal

Goals, especially long-term goals, can become outdated. Life circumstances and your personal values change. If a goal is no longer of value to you, abandon it; replace it with a new, more significant goal or a goal that is higher on your priority list. Do not, however, abandon a goal because it is more difficult to achieve or requires more from you than you had originally anticipated.

Analyze Your Goal-Setting Strategies

Learning to set and achieve goals is a process that improves with practice. On occasion, if you do not achieve a goal by a specific target date, or you do not achieve the desired outcome, you can turn such situations into learning experiences that can provide you with valuable insights about yourself and the processes you used. Use the following questions to analyze each situation and adjust your approach the next time you create a similar goal.

▮ Was the goal that I set unrealistically high? Did I really believe I could achieve the goal?

▮ Was the goal I set too low? Did I feel a lack of purpose or unchallenged?

▌ Was the goal high on my priority list of importance?

▌ Did I think through the steps carefully when I planned the goal?

▌ Did I allot sufficient time on my weekly schedule to work on the goal?

▌ Was I motivated? Did I really apply effort and follow my plan of action?

▌ What would I do differently if I were to set this goal again?

CONCEPT CHECK 4.19

If goal setting is an art, then what strategies or tools does a goal setter need to refine to master the art? What are primary characteristics of an effective goal setter?

Monitor Your Progress

Choose an easy-to-use system that you can refer to quickly to confirm that you are meeting your target dates and completing the steps required to achieve your goal. A calendar, a detailed checklist, or a daily or a weekly journal can all help you monitor your progress and add motivation.

Keep Your Goals in the Forefront

If on occasion you find yourself struggling with your goal-setting plans, your motivation dwindles, your momentum temporarily stalls, or you find yourself ignoring your goals, try writing your goals on index cards that you can place around your house and in your notebook as a constant reminder to spend time each day working toward the outcome. By moving your goals back into the forefront, they serve as motivators. In Chapter 5, pages 136–137, you will learn about visualizing, positive self-talk, affirmations, and other strategies for building and maintaining motivation.

EXERCISE 4.9

Textbook Case Studies

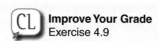 **Improve Your Grade**
Exercise 4.9

 **Improve Your Grade**
Online Case Studies

DIRECTIONS:

1. Read each case study carefully. Respond to the question at the end of each case study by using *specific* strategies discussed in this chapter. Answer in complete sentences.

2. Write your responses on paper or online at the Student Website, Exercise 4.9. You will be able to print your online response or e-mail it to your instructor.

CASE STUDY 1: Julian always seems to be caught off-guard. He is surprised when he arrives in class and hears that a specific assignment is due that day. He seldom has his assignments done on time. Sometimes he does not remember them, and other times he runs out of time. He prefers to do all his studying on the weekends, so when something is due in the middle of or at the end of the week, he never has it completed. What suggestions would you give to Julian so he might modify his approach to his assignments?

CASE STUDY 2: Ronnie is an "overachiever" and a "supermom" who can't say no to friends or family members. Ronnie is an avid, organized goal setter. Every Sunday she writes a new list of goals for the week. Throughout each day, she adds more goals to her lists and then works on whichever goals seem most pressing until something or someone sidetracks her. By the end of a typical day, she has accomplished few goals, and she finds herself shuffling the unfinished goals into the list of goals for the next day. By Saturday, she feels defeated; she has multiple lists of goals that she failed to achieve during the week. How can Ronnie become a more successful goal setter?

Goals for Long-Term Projects

Preparing for a major test, such as a midterm or a final exam, is one kind of long-term project that you will face as a student. In Chapter 6, pages 161–163, you will learn about the five-day study plan, which is a goal-oriented approach for organizing and managing your time and your review materials for major tests. The steps used in the five-day study plan are similar to the steps used to plan and achieve a long-term project.

Another kind of long-term project occurs when early in the term instructors assign a project that is not due until the middle or the end of the term. Many students have a false sense of time; rather than start immediately, they procrastinate and begin to work on the project too close to its due date, often neglecting their other study times and classes in order to meet the deadline. This pattern of running short or running out of time adds unnecessary stress and lowers the quality of the work. To avoid the many problems that result from poor planning for long-term projects, begin the project as soon as you receive the assignment. **Figure 4.17** guides you through the process of setting goals for long-term projects. On page 118, **Figure 4.18** provides you with an example of using the steps to plan a long-term project in a literature class.

Do not waste time procrastinating. If you finish a task ahead of schedule, it is because you did not need the "doubled time" you allocated. Begin the next task immediately. If you finish your project ahead of schedule, you will have time to revise it again if you wish, and you will be able to breathe a sigh of relief!

CONCEPT CHECK 4.20

Look ahead to the five-day study plan on pages 161–163. What goal-setting steps are used to plan your study time for a major exam?

 **Topic In-Depth**
Quick Start Forms

CONCEPT CHECK 4.21

What kinds of long-term projects have you been assigned as a college student? How would these steps have affected the quality of your work and the timeliness for completing the project?

FIGURE 4.17

Setting Goals for a Long-Term Project

1. **Break the assignment into specific tasks.** Analyze the project carefully until you can identify the individual tasks involved for the entire project. List these tasks or steps on paper.

2. **Estimate the time needed for each task.** Estimate the number of hours you think you will need to complete each task. Base this estimate on your past experiences with similar projects.

3. **Double the estimated time needed for each task.** To avoid running short on time or to counteract underestimating the time you will need, double your estimate. This gives you extra time in case you run into unforeseen problems or find that you have to change directions.

4. **Record target dates on your term calendar for each task.** Plan target dates and times to complete each step. Identify time each week on your weekly schedule to work on specific steps for the long-term project.

5. **Begin immediately.** The sooner you start, the sooner you will finish!

FIGURE 4.18

Example of the Steps in Planning a Long-Term Project

STEP 1: List the Tasks	STEP 2: Estimated Time	STEP 3: Doubled Time
1. Review lists of American poets. Select one I like.	1 hr.	2 hrs.
2. Do library or Internet research on his or her life.	3 hrs.	6 hrs.
3. Read several of the author's poems. Find some that reflect events that influenced the author's life.	2 hrs.	4 hrs.
4. Write a draft of the summary of the author's life.	1 hr.	2 hrs.
5. Select two specific poems.	½ hr.	1 hr.
6. Write about the structure and the meaning of poem 1 (draft).	2 hrs.	4 hrs.
7. Write about the structure and the meaning of poem 2 (draft).	2 hrs.	4 hrs.
8. Revise the drafts and integrate into the final paper.	4 hrs.	8 hrs.
9. Proofread. Revise as needed.	1 hr.	2 hrs.
10. Assemble the final project. Include the poems, the research notes, and a bibliography.	½ hr.	1 hr.
Time to plan for project:		34 hrs.

STEP 4: Write These Tasks on the Term Schedule.

Week 3: Do Tasks 1 and 2 (8 hours).

Week 4: Do Tasks 3 and 4 (6 hours).

Week 5: Do Tasks 5 and 6 (5 hours).

Week 6: Do Task 7 (4 hours).

Week 7: Do Task 8 (8 hours).

Week 8: Do Tasks 9 and 10 (3 hours).

Week 9: I completed the project last week!

EXERCISE 4.10

Links

PURPOSE: The term *study skills* refers to a variety of skills and concepts integrated or linked together. As you begin to use one type of study skill or concept, you activate others. Use your critical thinking skills to explore the relationships between the following paired items.

DIRECTIONS: Follow your instructor's directions. You may be asked to discuss the relationships between the following paired items with a partner or in a group, or

to respond in writing on separate paper. Explain the relationship between each of the following paired items:

1. goal setting and weekly schedules
2. goal setting and intrapersonal intelligence
3. 2:1 ratio and elaborative rehearsal
4. goal setting and Principle of Time on Task
5. goal setting and the Principle of Intention
6. spaced practice and working memory

REFLECTIVE WRITING 4.2

 Improve Your Grade
Reflective Writing 4.2

On separate paper, in a journal, or online at this textbook's website, respond to the following questions.

1. Which time-management and goal-setting strategies in this chapter are potentially the most valuable or beneficial for you? Explain with specific details.
2. What is your plan of action to implement these strategies in your daily and weekly routines?

CHECK POINT 4.4

ANSWERS APPEAR ON PAGE A4

True or False?

_____ 1. Immediate and short-term goals are the only goals that are well-defined plans of action designed to achieve specific results.

_____ 2. If a goal seems too overwhelming, you should discard it and write only immediate goals that you can achieve in one day.

_____ 3. A person who sets too many goals and tries to achieve them all simultaneously would benefit from using the ABC Method.

_____ 4. A goal organizer helps a person identify the importance of a goal, plan ways to deal with obstacles, and use resources that can help achieve success.

_____ 5. When you plan a long-term project, you should double the estimated time to complete each step to compensate for underestimating the time the task may require.

 Improve Your Grade
Online Practice 7:
Goal-Setting Strategies

LEARNING OBJECTIVES REVIEW

1 ▷ *Analyze your use of time; identify ways to create balance in your life.*

- Analyzing the way you spend time in the three main areas of your Pie of Life helps you find a healthy, fulfilling balance in your school, work, and leisure life.
- The Increase-Decrease Method helps you adjust the boundaries of your Pie of Life in order to achieve greater balance.

2 ▷ *Create and use effective term, weekly, and daily schedules to manage your time.*

- Term schedules provide you with an overview or a "big picture" of all the deadlines and special events for the term, weekly schedules provide you with a seven-day plan to balance your activities, and daily schedules provide you with organized lists of goals and tasks to complete on a specific day.
- You can use a five-step plan for organizing an effective weekly schedule: show fixed activities, fixed study blocks, flex blocks, time for personal goals, and family, social, and leisure time.
- Twelve essential strategies for effective study blocks guide you in planning fixed study blocks on your weekly schedule. The Time-Management Self-Assessment Checklist helps you evaluate your schedule.
- Using time management involves adjusting to change. Trading time, when used sparingly, can add flexibility to your schedule. You can use a variety of other techniques to help yourself adjust to change.

3 ▷ *Describe the four kinds of goals defined by time required to achieve goals; describe and use the four steps for writing goals.*

- Goals are well-defined plans aimed at achieving a specific result. Immediate, short-term, intermediary, and long-term are four kinds of goals based on the length of time required to complete and achieve the goal.
- Using a four-step approach for achieving goals (STSR) enhances your performance and success in achieving your desired outcomes. S = specific, clear, realistic goals; T = target date; S = steps involved; and R = intrinsic or extrinsic reward.

4 ▷ *Demonstrate understanding and use of essential goal-setting strategies that include task schedules, goal organizers, prioritizing your goals, managing and monitoring your goals, and setting goals for long-term projects.*

- Task schedules help you create a plan of action for a specific block of time. *Goal organizers* encourage you to think carefully about a goal and your plan of action.
- The ABC Method is one strategy that helps you prioritize your goals and focus your attention on the high-priority goals.
- A variety of strategies are available to help you self-manage your strategies and success.
- A five-step process can help you to complete long-term projects successfully and punctually.

CHAPTER 4 REVIEW QUESTIONS

ANSWERS APPEAR ON PAGE A4

True or False?

_____ 1. Time management is a plan for organizing your time, and goal setting is a plan for using your time constructively to achieve desired outcomes.

_____ 2. A weekly schedule reflects some of the tasks and target dates shown on a term schedule.

_____ 3. An effective weekly schedule helps you avoid wasted time, tighten up your available time, and plan for tasks or activities that are meaningful and important to you.

_____ 4. Extrinsic and intrinsic rewards should be awarded only after a person completes a specific goal.

Multiple Choice

_____ 1. A well-planned term schedule
   a. shows only midterm and final exams.
   b. reflects academic and personal time lines and commitments.
   c. states your weekly goals and shows your daily homework assignments.
   d. accomplishes all of the above.

_____ 2. When you use a fifty-minute study block effectively, you should

    a. spend time reviewing each of your courses.

    b. create a mindset that focuses on only one subject.

    c. cover as many textbook pages as possible by reading fast.

    d. begin by identifying which class has an assignment due the next day.

_____ 3. An effective weekly time-management schedule includes

    a. eight hours of studying on weekends.

    b. adequate time to use the 2:1 ratio, elaborative rehearsal, and spaced practice.

    c. three or more flex blocks and three times set aside for trading time.

    d. all study blocks completed by 9:00 PM.

_____ 4. A goal organizer

    a. is a four-step approach for writing short-term goals.

    b. shows that you have thought about benefits, consequences, and strategies to face obstacles related to a specific goal.

    c. is used every time you plan a task in a daily organizer.

    d. does all of the above.

_____ 5. If you feel overwhelmed because you have too many goals, you can

    a. use the ABC Method to prioritize your goals.

    b. evaluate the importance of each goal and then discard the most difficult ones.

    c. write all your goals on index cards and post them around your house.

    d. visualize yourself completing all the goals ahead of schedule.

_____ 6. Setting goals for a long-term project

    a. begins by listing all the tasks required to finish the project.

    b. includes doubling the amount of time you estimate you need for each task.

    c. involves writing target dates on your term calendar and your weekly schedule.

    d. involves all of the above.

_____ 7. Which of the following is _not_ a recommended goal-setting strategy to keep yourself motivated?

    a. Visualize yourself achieving your goal.

    b. Use a checklist or a journal to track your progress.

    c. Select meaningful intrinsic or extrinsic rewards that motivate you.

    d. Write your goals in a safe place so other people cannot see them and possibly discourage you from achieving your goals.

_____ 8. The primary purpose of the Increase-Decrease Method is to

    a. help you find ways to increase your social time each week.

    b. find a more satisfying and productive balance in your Pie of Life.

    c. move you toward having a Pie of Life that shows an equal amount of time each week for school, work, and leisure.

    d. decrease the amount of time you need to study each day.

Short-Answer Questions

On separate paper, answer the following questions. Use complete sentences and terminology from this chapter in your answers.

1. Define _spaced practice_ and explain how using spaced practice assists information processing in working memory.

2. In your opinion, what are the five most important strategies to use to become an effective goal setter?

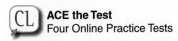
ACE the Test
Four Online Practice Tests

Online Resources

5 Developing Self-Management Skills

LEARNING OBJECTIVES

1 ▸ *Define concentration and identify strategies to block out distractions and maintain a focused, disciplined mind.*

2 ▸ *Define motivation and discuss factors that affect motivation and strategies to strengthen motivation.*

3 ▸ *Define stress and identify strategies and techniques for effective stress management.*

Chapter Outline

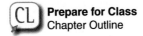 **Prepare for Class**
Chapter Outline

4 ▶ *Define procrastination and identify strategies and techniques for effective procrastination management.*

Self-management refers to the ability to use strategies to deal constructively and effectively with variables that affect the quality of your personal life. Self-management consists of six different sets of skills; you have already learned to use the first two: time management and goal setting. In this chapter you will learn four more sets of self-management skills. You will learn strategies for managing and strengthening your *concentration* and *motivation*. You will also learn strategies for managing, reducing, and eliminating *stress* and *procrastination*. These self-management skills will empower you and put you in greater control of your life.

CHAPTER 5 PROFILE

Self-Management Skills

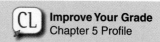

Improve Your Grade
Chapter 5 Profile

ANSWER, **SCORE**, and **RECORD** your profile before you read this chapter. If you need to review the process, refer to the complete directions given in the profile for Chapter 1 on page 4.

ONLINE: You can complete the profile and get your score online at this textbook's website.

	YES	NO
1. I have little control over the people or things that break my concentration when I am studying.		
2. I often study with the radio, stereo, or television turned on.		
3. I use effective strategies to block out internal and external distractors when I study.		
4. I use effective strategies, such as visualizations, positive self-talk, and affirmations to boost my motivation and keep my momentum going.		
5. I am motivated when I study and believe in my ability to do well.		
6. I use a variety of relaxation techniques to manage my stress.		
7. My level of stress often reduces my performance or ability to concentrate.		
8. I recognize when and why I procrastinate, and then I take action to combat the sources of my procrastination.		
9. I tend to procrastinate when faced with unpleasant or uninteresting tasks.		
10. I am confident that I have adequate self-management skills to monitor and manage my concentration, motivation, stress, and procrastination.		

QUESTIONS LINKED TO THE CHAPTER LEARNING OBJECTIVES:

Questions 1–3:   objective 1   Questions 8, 9:   objective 4
Questions 4, 5:   objective 2   Question 10:   all objectives
Questions 6, 7:   objective 3

TERMS TO KNOW

self-management   *p. 125*
concentration   *p. 125*
external distractors   *p. 126*
internal distractors   *p. 126*
motivation   *p. 132*
Incentive Theory of Motivation   *p. 133*
intrinsic motivation   *p. 133*
extrinsic motivation   *p. 133*
Expectancy Theory of Motivation   *p. 134*
self-esteem   *p. 134*
positive self-talk   *p. 136*
affirmations   *p. 136*
self-efficacy   *p. 138*

stress   *p. 139*
stressors   *p. 140*
procrastination   *p. 145*

SPECIFIC TECHNIQUES

study ritual   *p. 127*
warm-ups   *p. 127*
mental rehearsal   *p. 127*
take-charge   *p. 128*
say no   *p. 130*
no need   *p. 130*
red bow   *p. 130*
check mark   *p. 131*

mental storage box   *p. 131*
tunnel vision   *p. 131*
emotional *e* words   *p. 131*
perfect place   *p. 143*
soothing mask   *p. 143*
relaxation blanket   *p. 143*
breathing by threes   *p. 144*
deep breathing   *p. 144*
deep muscle relaxation   *p. 144*

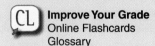 **Improve Your Grade**
Online Flashcards
Glossary

CONCENTRATION

1 ► *Define concentration and identify strategies to block out distractions and maintain a focused, disciplined mind.*

The term **self-management** refers to the ability to use strategies to deal constructively and effectively with variables that affect the quality of your personal life. A successful self-manager uses his or her skills to monitor, orchestrate, and adjust or redirect thinking or behavior patterns in order to increase personal satisfaction and performance of regular daily functions. You have already learned about the first two sets of self-management skills: time management and goal setting. *Concentration* is the third set of self-management skills you can learn to master to increase your performance. **Figure 5.1** show the six common sets of self-management skills.

Concentration is the ability to block out *external* and *internal distractors* in order to stay focused on one specific item or task. Concentration is a flighty process; you can concentrate one minute and then easily become distracted and lose that concentration the very next. The following are important points about concentration:

▍ Concentration requires a concerted effort on your part to train or discipline your mind.

▍ Concentration involves monitoring not only your thoughts and emotions, but also your environment.

▍ External and internal distractors consume space in working memory, disturb your brainwave patterns, and affect the flow of stimuli throughout your memory system.

Self-management is the ability to use strategies to deal constructively and effectively with variables that affect the quality of your personal life.

CONCEPT CHECK 5.1

What is the relationship between self-management skills and intrapersonal intelligence?

Concentration is the ability to block out *external* and *internal distractors* in order to stay focused on one specific item or task.

FIGURE 5.1

The Six Common Sets of Self-Management Skills

▍ Time Management
▍ Motivation
▍ Goal Setting
▍ Stress Management
▍ Concentration
▍ Procrastination Management

External distractors are disruptions caused by things in your physical environment.

Internal distractors are disruptions that occur inside you physically or emotionally.

CONCEPT CHECK 5.2

What are common internal and external distractors you encounter when you study? Which strategies in Figure 5.2 could you use to deal with your distractors?

▌ **External distractors** are disruptions caused by things in your physical environment, such as noises, people, television, enticing or harsh weather, clutter, and lighting. You can use strategies to train your mind and your attention not to respond to external distractors—unless of course they involve an emergency or potential danger.

▌ **Internal distractors** are disruptions that occur inside you physically or emotionally. Worries, stress, anxiety, depression, sickness, hunger, pain, daydreams, and anticipation of upcoming events are examples of internal distractors that reduce your level of concentration.

Concentrating When You Study

All of the Essential Strategies for Strengthening Working Memory (Chapter 2, Figure 2.5, page 54) and Essential Strategies for Using Concentration (Chapter 3, Figure 3.6, page 75) engage your working memory and strengthen your ability to concentrate. **Figure 5.2** summarizes seven strategies to increase your concentration when you study. These strategies free up working memory for cognitive processes. Explanations of each strategy follow.

Set Learning Goals

Knowing *what* you plan to do and *how* you plan to achieve your goals gives you a purpose, a motivation to stay focused, and a "mission" to achieve. At the beginning of a study block, identify your specific intentions for your time. Setting learning goals activates your working memory. Setting goals also involves creating a plan of action to achieve the goals.

Be an Active Learner

Active learning discourages you from reading or working in a detached, mechanical way. Active learning engages you in the learning process, increases concentration, and helps you avoid internal distractors, such as sleepiness, boredom, or disinterest. As you recall from Chapter 3, page 74, active learners study with a pen in hand, take notes, highlight textbooks, write questions, and create study tools, such as diagrams, flashcards, and visual notes.

FIGURE 5.2

Essential Strategies to Increase Concentration When You Study

▌ **Set learning goals.** Learning goals include a plan of action.
▌ **Be an active learner.** Choose strategies that engage you in the learning process.
▌ **Chunk information.** Break large assignments into smaller units to study.
▌ **Create a study ritual.** Create your personal routine for study blocks.
▌ **Begin with a warm-up activity.** Choose an activity that creates a mindset to study.
▌ **Use mental rehearsal.** Mentally see yourself studying with success.
▌ **Control your physical environment.** Create an ideal study area.

Chunk Information

Chunking involves breaking larger assignments or pieces of information into more meaningful units that working memory can manage. Trying to take in too much information too rapidly overloads working memory and results in loss of concentration and ineffective learning.

Create a Study Ritual

A **study ritual** is a series of steps or a consistent routine that helps you to get started quickly on a task. Instead of wasting time trying to decide what to do or where to begin, a study ritual moves you directly into the mindset of studying. For example, your study ritual might be to use a quick relaxation or visualization technique, create a task schedule, and do a *warm-up activity.*

A **study ritual** is a series of steps or a consistent routine that allows you to get started quickly on a task.

Begin with a Warm-Up Activity

Warm-ups are activities at the beginning of a study block that shift thoughts and create a mindset for studying and concentrating. Warm-ups activate working memory and long-term memory. They also set up frameworks, schemas, or big pictures for new information. *Previewing* (skimming through a new chapter or assignment to get an overview) and *reviewing* previous work are effective warm-up activities.

Warm-ups are activities at the beginning of a study block that shift thoughts and create a mindset for studying and concentrating.

Use Mental Rehearsal

The image that you hold of yourself as a learner and a person with a high concentration level often affects the behaviors you exhibit. **Mental rehearsal** is the process of creating a picture or a movie in your mind that shows you performing effectively. Mental rehearsal replaces negative images with positive images of success. For example, picture yourself beginning an assignment working with ease, writing answers on a test with confidence, or studying without distractions.

Mental rehearsal is the process of creating a picture or a movie in your mind that shows you performing effectively.

Control Your Physical Environment

Create an ideal study area at school or at home that is conducive to learning. Use techniques to eliminate internal and external distractors.

An Ideal Study Area

To increase your ability to concentrate, give careful attention to three elements in your physical environment: the noise level, the lighting, and the workspace. Depending on the noise, lighting, and workspace, the location where you study may be highly conducive to learning, or it may be filled with distractors that reduce your ability to concentrate. Studying in an ideal study area not only improves concentration, but it also increases motivation and reduces the tendency to procrastinate (postpone or delay work).

The Noise Level

People have different tolerance levels to noise. Some students need a silent environment in order to concentrate; others can tolerate minor sounds or noises without becoming distracted. Contrary to some students' beliefs that they can study in noisy environments, research shows that noisy environments, music with lyrics and frequent variations in rhythm, and the auditory and visual stimuli

CONCEPT CHECK 5.3

How does a room's noise level affect working memory processes? What is your noise tolerance level for effective concentration?

from television interrupt thought processes and brainwave patterns, causing concentration to turn on and off and on and off in split-second intervals. Auditory stimuli take up space in working memory, thus reducing the amount of working memory available to process information efficiently. However, research shows that soft, classical, and instrumental music (especially baroque music) does not cause the on-and-off pattern and may enhance learning by helping the mind be more receptive to new information. Monitor the effects of the noise level in your study environment and be willing to change your study location and environment until you find one that increases rather than decreases your level of concentration.

The Lighting

Proper lighting is important in any study area. If you have too little light, your eyes can easily become strained and tired. Some lighting can create shadows or glare on your books. To avoid many of the problems created by poor lighting, have *two* sources of light in your study area. This may include an overhead light and a desk lamp or two lamps in different locations. Two sources of lighting may seem like a minor detail, but sometimes ignoring small details leads to vision and concentration problems.

The Workspace

Trying to study in an area that lacks sufficient space to spread out your textbooks, open your notebooks, take notes as you read, or use other study materials and supplies creates distractions. A work surface cluttered with items not related to studying also creates distractions. To be conducive to studying, select a workspace that is clutter-free, provides ample work space, and has minimal visual stimuli, such as photographs or memorabilia. If necessary, use your goal-setting skills to write a goal to create your ideal study space. Your ideal study space should also be equipped with a comfortable chair that is an appropriate height for the table and for your legs. Avoid trying to study on the floor, in a recliner, on a couch, or on a bed.

The Take-Charge Technique

Do not waste your valuable time trying to study in an environment filled with distractions. *Take charge* of your environment. The **Take-Charge Technique** involves taking responsibility for your environment by seeking an alternative place to study or by modifying the existing environment so it has few or no distractions. Your goal is to choose a study location that has an acceptable noise level, appropriate lighting, sufficient workspace, and few or no distractions. **Figure 5.3** shows decisions students made to take charge of their physical environments. In each case, students displayed a willingness to let go of old habits, and rather than blame other people or other things for their distractions, they took charge.

CONCEPT CHECK 5.4

What is the ideal lighting for the room where you plan to study?

CONCEPT CHECK 5.5

Is your study space an ideal workspace? Explain why or why not.

The **Take-Charge Technique** involves taking responsibility for your environment by seeking an alternative place to study or by modifying the existing environment so it has few or no distractions.

CONCEPT CHECK 5.6

How does using the Take-Charge Technique shift responsibility to the student?

FIGURE 5.3

Using the Take-Charge Technique

Description of the Student Situation	The Student's Solution
Robert has a short attention span and is easily distracted. He tries studying in the library, but ordinary library noises and the movement around him are too distracting.	▌ Work in a quiet environment with less movement, such as an empty office or a conference room. ▌ Move to the back of the library away from foot traffic.
Joel grew up in a house with a large family, so studying in a noisy environment seems normal. Joel usually studies in the cafeteria, but he is not pleased with how little he accomplishes while studying there.	▌ Avoid trying to study in the cafeteria, which is designed for eating and socializing. ▌ Study in a quieter setting at school or at home. ▌ If some sound is needed, turn on a small fan to break the total silence.
Heather often studies in a student lounge area even though the fluorescent lighting bothers her to the point that her eyes do not focus well.	▌ Move to a room with windows so there is a combination of natural lighting and fluorescent lighting. ▌ At home, use a desk lamp and a ceiling light.
Marshall prefers studying at his kitchen table, but he realizes that he frequently leaves the table to get drinks or snacks. Work that would normally take an hour to finish at school is taking him much longer at home because of the frequent breaks.	▌ Modify the environment by removing all kitchen and food items from the table. ▌ Create a box of school supplies for the table to convert it into a work or study area. ▌ Sit facing away from the refrigerator. ▌ Resist the temptation to move from the table.

EXERCISE 5.1

My Ideal Study Area

PURPOSE: Your physical environment impacts your ability to use selective attention and to concentrate. To increase concentration, examine your physical space and modify it so it is more conducive to studying.

DIRECTIONS:

1. In the following chart (which continues on the next page), the items on the left are physical elements that can hinder or strengthen concentration. In the middle column, describe each physical element as it currently exists in your typical study area at home and at school.

2. In the right column, describe the changes you could make to your study area at home and your study area at school to create more ideal study areas.

Home	Current Study Area	Ideal Study Area
Noise		
Movement Nearby		

Home	Current Study Area	Ideal Study Area
Lighting		
Chair		
Work Surface		
Supplies		
School	**Current Study Area**	**Ideal Study Area**
Noise		
Movement Nearby		
Lighting		
Chair		
Work Surface		
Supplies		

CONCEPT CHECK 5.7

Which of the techniques do you predict will work effectively to deal with your internal and external distractors?

The **Say No Technique** involves resisting the urge to participate in an external or internal distraction.

The **No Need Technique** is the process of training yourself not to look up and not to break your concentration to attend to minor, familiar distractions.

The **Red Bow Technique** involves using a symbol to signal to others that you do not want to be interrupted or disturbed.

Internal and External Distractors

When you find yourself distracted and having trouble concentrating, the first step is to analyze the situation to determine the source of your distraction. Is it caused by an *internal distractor* or an *external distractor*? The second step is to select an appropriate technique to use to address the concentration problem. The following techniques are effective for dealing with distractors.

▌ The **Say No Technique** involves resisting the urge to participate in an external or internal distraction. When friends or family members ask you to drop your study schedule and participate in an activity with them, assertively just say *no*; suggest a different time to get together. You can also use the Say No Technique to tell yourself: no snack, no television now, no daydreaming, or no phone calls.

▌ The **No Need Technique** is the process of training yourself not to look up and not to break your concentration to attend to minor, familiar distractions. For example, if you study in the library, you know that occasionally someone will walk by, pull out a chair, or turn the pages of a book. You know the source of the distraction, so force yourself to keep your eyes and your attention on your own work. Tell yourself, "There is *no need* to look."

▌ The **Red Bow Technique** involves using a symbol, such as a red bow, to signal to others that you do not want to be interrupted or disturbed. On your door or in your study area, place a red bow or any other item or symbol to signal to others that you are studying and you want privacy. Ask them to respect your request for no interruptions unless an emergency occurs.

▮ The **Check Mark Technique** involves keeping a score card to record and reduce the number of distractions that you allow into your working memory. Each time you lose your concentration during a study block, make a check mark on a score card you keep on your desk. At the end of your study block, count the number of checks. Set a goal each time you study to reduce the number of check marks.

The **Check Mark Technique** involves keeping a score card to record and reduce the number of distractions that you allow into your working memory.

▮ The **Mental Storage Box Technique** involves placing any internal distractors into an imaginary box, putting a lid on the box, and shoving that box aside to be dealt with at a later time. Before you begin studying, identify any concerns, worries, or emotions that might interrupt your concentration. Place them inside your *mental storage box.* Tell yourself that you will deal with the contents of the box at a more appropriate time, and then do so.

The **Mental Storage Box Technique** involves placing any internal distractors into an imaginary box, putting a lid on the box, and shoving that box aside to be dealt with at a later time.

▮ The **Tunnel Vision Technique** involves picturing yourself in a tunnel and training your mind to stay centered and on course. In this one-way tunnel, if your mind wanders, steer it back into the center of the tunnel to avoid banging into the walls.

The **Tunnel Vision Technique** involves picturing yourself in a tunnel and training your mind to stay centered and on course.

▮ The **Emotional *E* Words Technique** involves refocusing your mind by using words that begin with *e* to create a positive attitude. Any time you find yourself dealing with negative emotions or attitudes toward a specific subject or an assignment, replace the negative energy by focusing your mind on positive energy words that begin with the letter *e*. For example, you might say *effortless, enthusiastic, excited, energetic, eager, effective, efficient, essential, excelling, excellent, expert, exhilarating,* or *educated.* In your mind, mentally rehearse with an image of yourself exhibiting these qualities. The result is an attitude adjustment that is more conducive to concentration and learning.

The **Emotional *E* Words Technique** involves refocusing your mind by using words that begin with *e* to create a positive attitude.

Each of the previous techniques for dealing with internal and external distractors are quick and easy to use. Familiarize yourself with each technique and practice using it several times so you can use it as needed to deal with a specific kind of distractor. These techniques will help you train your mind to stay focused and make better use of your working memory.

GROUP PROCESSING:
A COLLABORATIVE LEARNING ACTIVITY

Form groups of three or four students. Each group needs to have a chart to record information. Select one group member to be the group recorder. Complete the following directions.

1. Divide a large chart into two columns. In the left column, write as many different internal and external distractors that you might encounter when you study.

2. After you have listed the distractors, brainstorm techniques you can use to combat each distractor. List the techniques in the right column. Refer to the strategies listed in the Terms to Know on page 125 as well as the concentration strategies discussed in Chapter 2, pages 41 and 54, and Chapter 3, page 75.

3. Be prepared to share your list of distractors and techniques with the class.

CHECK POINT 5.1

ANSWERS APPEAR ON PAGE A4

True or False?

_____ 1. Using concentration strategies effectively increases working memory space for cognitive functions.

_____ 2. You can focus your mind more quickly on studying when you set learning goals, create a study ritual, and do a warm-up activity.

_____ 3. A person's physical environment has less of an impact on concentration than his or her emotional state of mind.

_____ 4. The take-charge, emotional *e* words, and the red bow techniques are designed to deal with external distractors.

Improve Your Grade
Online Practice 1:
Concentration

REFLECTIVE WRITING 5.1

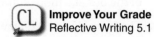

Improve Your Grade
Reflective Writing 5.1

On separate paper, in a journal, or online at this textbook's website, respond to the following questions:

1. *What* distractors do you encounter most frequently when you study? Be specific.

2. *When,* and *where* do you have the most problems concentrating when you study? What techniques can you learn to use more consistently to combat these problems?

MOTIVATION

2 ▶ *Define motivation and discuss factors that affect motivation and strategies to strengthen motivation.*

Motivation is the feeling, emotion, or desire that moves a person to take action.

Motivation is the feeling, emotion, or desire that moves a person to take action. Motivation is an internal process and an integral part of making changes, achieving goals, and pursuing personal growth. The following are important points about motivation:

▌ Motivation initiates action, contributes to changing behaviors, and determines the intensity and determination for achieving a goal.

▌ Motivation is the driving force that encourages people to "push on," to not give up, and to persevere.

▌ Once a person achieves a goal and experiences success, the accomplishment generates new motivation to tackle other challenges and create new goals.

▌ Motivation becomes the powerful, driving force behind the upward spiral of personal growth, confidence, and success.

The Incentive Theory of Motivation

The **Incentive Theory of Motivation** states that incentives and rewards are the driving forces behind people's choices and behaviors. People become motivated and activate specific behaviors in order to receive positive incentives and rewards. Children are good examples of incentive motivation: they behave in a specific way in order to receive a treat or receive your praise. Adults behave in the same way: they work hard to receive a paycheck (reward), or they study long hours to get into a pre-med program (reward). This theory also states that people refrain from specific behaviors that have negative consequences. For example, a student is motivated *not* to use a "cheat sheet" on a test because of potentially severe consequences. The following are important points about motivation based on incentives:

▌ Incentives become strong motivators only when the individual places a high value on the incentive and is willing to take action to obtain the reward.

▌ To work as motivators, the incentives and rewards must be obtainable. For example, most employees would not be highly motivated by an employer's offer of a week's paid vacation (incentive) if the goal set to receive the award is unrealistically high and most likely unobtainable.

▌ Two questions in a *goal organizer* (page 115) use the power of incentive motivation: *What benefits will you gain by achieving this goal?* This question focuses you on the incentives, the positive benefits and rewards, you will experience. If you value these rewards, you will strive harder to achieve them. *What consequences will you experience by not achieving this goal?* This question focuses on the negative consequences of not reaching your goal. If the negative consequences are detrimental to some aspect of your life, you will be motivated to take action to avoid the hardship or negative consequences.

Intrinsic and Extrinsic Motivation

Motivation is the driving force behind achieving goals. Two forms of motivation drive people to achieve their goals: intrinsic and extrinsic motivation. **Intrinsic motivation** is the driving force to take action that comes from within you. Intrinsic motivation is the most powerful and effective form of motivation because you "own" it, and you give it personal meaning, importance, and conviction. People with high intrapersonal intelligence use intrinsic motivation for personal development and self-understanding as well as a means for using their intuition and spirituality. The following are common sources of intrinsic motivation:

▌ Intrinsic motivation may stem from a desire to fulfill a basic need, such as food, shelter, or financial comfort.

▌ Intrinsic motivation may stem from an internal desire to engage in behaviors or actions that bring intrinsic rewards (feelings of pride, joy, increased self-esteem, or personal satisfaction).

▌ Intrinsic motivation may stem from a desire to affirm your self-image and prove to yourself that you are a person who does not shy away from goals, commitments, or hard work; you have the ability to achieve goals and excel beyond average levels of performance.

The second type of motivation is extrinsic motivation. **Extrinsic motivation** is the driving force to take action that comes from sources outside of yourself.

The **Incentive Theory of Motivation** states that incentives and rewards are the driving forces behind people's choices and behaviors.

CONCEPT CHECK 5.8

What examples can you give of children behaving in a positive way in order to receive a treat or a reward? What activities do you do in order to receive a reward?

Intrinsic motivation is the driving force to take action that comes from within you.

CONCEPT CHECK 5.9

Why is intrinsic motivation so powerful? What examples of intrinsic motivation can you give based on your personal experiences?

Extrinsic motivation is the driving force to take action that comes from sources outside of yourself.

CONCEPT CHECK 5.10

How does extrinsic motivation differ from intrinsic motivation? Which type of motivation do you tend to use more often? Give specific examples.

The motivator behind extrinsic motivation may stem from a desire to obtain an *extrinsic reward,* such as a prestigious award, a coveted prize, or monetary reward for work or performance. A desire to receive positive responses, praise, acceptance, or recognition from parents, family members, peers, co-workers, or a specific social group may be another type of extrinsic motivator. The following are important points about extrinsic motivation:

▮ Sometimes extrinsic motivation stems from expectations imposed on you by others. For example, you may be motivated to study hard and earn good grades because of academic or athletic scholarship requirements.

▮ Actions based solely on extrinsic motivation are often more difficult to achieve than actions based on intrinsic motivation. Having someone tell you that you *must* do something or you *must* behave in a certain way is a weak motivator and often ineffective.

▮ For extrinsic motivators to work, you must find a purpose or a value in complying with the external expectations. As you do so and as you gain momentum with your plan of action, extrinsic motivation converts to intrinsic motivation. Instead of working to please others, you are working to please yourself.

The Expectancy Theory of Motivation

CONCEPT CHECK 5.11

What example can you give that shows a low motivation due to your belief that you could not achieve the goal?

The **Expectancy Theory of Motivation** reflects a person's intensity or desire to achieve a goal and a belief in the likelihood of achieving that goal.

The **Expectancy Theory of Motivation** reflects a person's intensity or desire to achieve a goal and a belief in the likelihood of achieving that goal. When you believe you are worthy, capable, and sufficiently driven to take actions to achieve a goal, the likelihood of success increases. The excerpt in **Figure 5.4** explains the Expectancy Theory.

Self-Esteem and Motivation

Why are some people more motivated, more productive, and more successful than others? Part of the answer may be tied to their self-esteem. **Self-esteem** is the perception you have of yourself as a human being. Self-esteem includes your sense of personal pride and worthiness. The following are important points about self-esteem:

Self-esteem is the perception you have of yourself as a human being.

▮ Your self-esteem, your perception of yourself, is the result of your *perception* of past experiences, choices, behaviors, decisions, and consequences.

▮ Your self-esteem reflects past reactions of acceptance or rejection from family members, friends, teachers, or co-workers.

Individuals with high self-esteem tend to be highly motivated and experience a cycle of positive results. Their positive attitudes help them see mistakes or obstacles as opportunities to learn or to alter their approaches and strive to move forward with stronger conviction. They exhibit self-confident behaviors and feel in control of their lives. (See Exercise 11.3, page 321, for five common characteristics of people with high self-esteem.)

CONCEPT CHECK 5.12

How does the self-esteem cycle of a person with high self-esteem differ from the self-esteem cycle of a person with low self-esteem?

People with low self-esteem exhibit opposite characteristics: intrinsic motivation is lower; achievement of goals is less frequent and perceived as failure; obstacles are more difficult to overcome; and there is a higher feeling of lack of control for the events that occur in their lives. **Figure 5.5** shows the differences between the self-esteem cycles for people with low-self esteem and people with high self-esteem.

FIGURE 5.4

The Expectancy Theory of Motivation

Expectancy Theory, developed by Victor Vroom, is a very complex model of motivation based on a deceptively simple assumption. According to expectancy theory, motivation depends on how much we want something and on how likely we think we are to get it. Consider, for example, the case of three sales representatives who are candidates for promotion to one sales manager's job. Bill has had a very good sales year and always gets good performance evaluations. However, he isn't sure he wants the job because it involves a great deal of travel, long working hours, and much stress and pressure. Paul wants the job badly but doesn't think he has much

chance of getting it. He has had a terrible sales year and gets only mediocre performance evaluations from his present boss. Susan wants the job as much as Paul, and she thinks she has a pretty good shot at it. Her sales have improved significantly this past year, and her evaluations are the best in the company.

Expectancy theory would predict that Bill and Paul are not very motivated to seek the promotion. Bill doesn't really want it, and Paul doesn't think he has much of a chance of getting it. Susan, however, is very motivated to seek the promotion because she wants it *and* thinks she can get it.

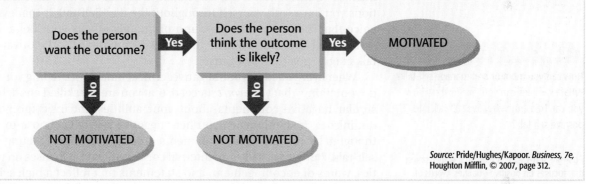

Source: Pride/Hughes/Kapoor. *Business, 7e,* Houghton Mifflin, © 2007, page 312.

FIGURE 5.5

Self-Esteem Cycles

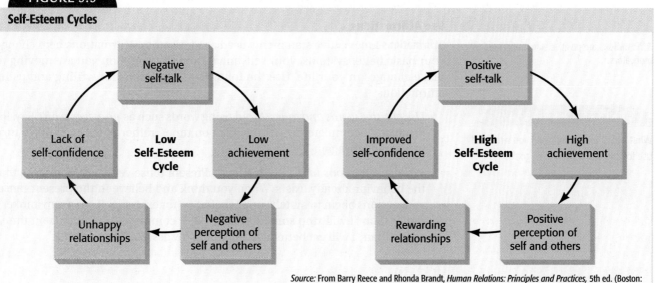

Source: From Barry Reece and Rhonda Brandt, *Human Relations: Principles and Practices,* 5th ed. (Boston: Houghton Mifflin Co., 2003), p. 71. Copyright © 2003. Reprinted by permission of Houghton Mifflin, Inc.

FIGURE 5.6

Strategies for Boosting Self-Esteem

▌ Let go of the past; focus on the present.
▌ Use positive self-talk.
▌ Use affirmations.
▌ Visualize success.
▌ Acknowledge yourself.

Since self-esteem is an integral part of motivation, exploring and implementing ways to boost self-esteem can increase motivation and lead to more positive outcomes. **Figure 5.6** shows five strategies for boosting self-esteem, changing your self-perception, and increasing your level of motivation.

Let Go of the Past; Focus on the Present

In many ways, we are the reflection of our past. Past experiences are strong influencing factors of who we are today, and understanding those influencing factors is important for self-understanding and growth. The expression, "Let it go," is often easier said than done, but it merits our attention. By choosing to use positive self-talk, affirmations, visualizations, and self-praise, you can shift your attention to the present and accentuate the positive elements that you are creating in your life at this very moment. Your positive attributes that you exhibit on an everyday basis can strengthen your positive self-perception that motivates and moves you forward.

Use Positive Self-Talk

Intrinsic motivation has a close relationship with *self-talk,* the internal conversations you have with yourself throughout the day. Self-talk is that ever-busy inner voice that monitors, critiques, and ultimately affects your behavior, choice of actions, self-esteem, as well as your level of confidence and motivation. Your self-talk may be positive or negative.

Whenever you hear your negative, critical inner voice telling you that you *can't* do something, that you *won't* succeed, that you are *not* skilled enough, or any other similar negative comments about your abilities, intrinsic motivation quickly diminishes. Instantly when you hear negative self-talk, choose to manage your thoughts by turning those statements around and counteracting with positive self-talk. **Positive self-talk** is an internal conversation that focuses on positive qualities, words of encouragement, and statements that reflect a high self-esteem and high self-efficacy. Statements such as "I am capable of doing this," "I have what it takes to succeed," and "I have the intelligence and skills to do well" turn *negative self-talk* into constructive, powerful, positive self-talk.

Use Affirmations

Affirmations are positive statements used as motivators. Affirmations help change your basic belief systems, your self-image, and the direction you are moving to make changes in your life. Use the following suggestions for writing and using affirmations:

▌ *Use positive words and tones.* Avoid using words such as *no, never, won't.* Say, for instance, "I complete my written work on time," rather than "I will never turn in a paper late again."

▌ *Write affirmations in the present tense.* Present tense verbs give the sense that the behavior already exists. When you think and believe in the present tense, your actions begin to match your beliefs. Say, for example, "I am a nonsmoker," rather than "I will stop smoking soon," or "I complete assignments on time," rather than "I will get better at completing my assignments on time."

CONCEPT CHECK 5.13

How can you monitor and manage self-talk? What examples can you give to show how you can transform negative self-talk into positive self-talk?

Positive self-talk is an internal conversation that focuses on positive qualities, words of encouragement, and statements that reflect a high self-esteem.

Affirmations are positive statements used as motivators.

CONCEPT CHECK 5.14

What *two* affirmations could you write and use to help you achieve two goals?

▌ *Write with certainty and conviction.* Avoid using words such as *want to, try,* or *hope to.* Say, for instance, "I exercise for thirty minutes every day," rather than "I want to exercise more each day," or "I manage my time well," rather than "I hope I can use my time-management schedule."

▌ *Keep the affirmation short and simple.* Brief, simple affirmations are easier to remember and repeat.

▌ *Repeat your affirmation frequently.* You can place your affirmation on cards around your house or inside your notebook. The more frequently you repeat your affirmation, the greater impact it has on your belief in the statements in the affirmation.

Visualize Success

Self-esteem, self-confidence, and intrinsic motivation are related to your personal belief systems about who you are and what you are capable of doing. In Chapter 3, you learned about the Memory Principle of Visualization and its powerful ability to imprint visual images in long-term memory. Visualizing yourself performing a task and achieving a specific goal imprints that image of yourself in your long-term memory. Use the following steps to imprint positive images of yourself into your memory:

CONCEPT CHECK 5.15

What Principles of Memory do you use when you visualize?

1. Close your eyes. Create a picture or an image of yourself, and "watch yourself" performing effectively in a specific situation. For example, you might see yourself working through the steps to perform a math equation, or studying in an ideal study area without encountering distractions, or standing comfortably and confidently in front of your class to give a speech.
2. In your visualization, "see" yourself receiving the rewards for your behavior or performance. *Feel* the sense of pride, accomplishment, or success.
3. Practice "rerunning" the visualization several times and recalling it from memory to use as a motivator.

Acknowledge Yourself

Your family members, friends, co-workers, and classmates may acknowledge and praise you for your efforts, your hard work, and your successes. Such positive feedback feels rewarding and helps build self-esteem and self-confidence.

However, you cannot expect nor rely on them to recognize or respond to all the positive accomplishments you experience on a daily basis. The person who can acknowledge and praise you on a regular basis is *you.* You are your best cheerleader, supporter, and motivator. Take time to recognize your accomplishments and your daily successes. Pat yourself on the back for each achievement, whether large or small. For example, when you successfully rework a math problem, revise and polish an essay, or learn to use a new software program to manipulate data, tell yourself, "Good job! You got that right!" Acknowledging yourself may seem trite, but words of self-praise reinforce positive actions and provide a steady stream of intrinsic motivation.

EXERCISE 5.2

Positive Self-Talk

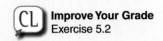 **Improve Your Grade**
Exercise 5.2

PURPOSE: Your self-talk affects your behaviors, beliefs, and performance. Increasing your awareness of and monitoring negative self-talk and converting it to positive self-talk bring positive results.

DIRECTIONS: For three days, pay attention to your inner voice and self-talk.

1. Record your negative self-talk. Next to the negative statements, convert them to positive statements.

2. Record any positive self-talk that you are aware of using. Your ultimate goal is to have more positive self-talk than negative self-talk occur throughout each day.

Self-Efficacy

Self-efficacy is the belief in your abilities to accomplish a specific task at a specific level of performance.

Self-efficacy is the belief in your abilities to accomplish a specific task at a specific level of performance. If your self-efficacy is high, you have a sense of self-confidence that you can take on a specific task and succeed at a desired level of performance. Your motivators initiate action and propel you to complete the task at a high level of performance even if it involves perseverance and overcoming challenges.

For example, Rachel, a drama student who has performed in the last three productions on campus, exhibited high self-efficacy when she auditioned for the leading role in a new performing arts production. Even though she had never had a leading role in a play, her past successes, experiences, and skill training formed her belief about her ability to take on a new challenge and deliver a stellar performance *in the field of drama.* After the audition, Rachel headed for the computer lab for the fourth time to tackle a computer lab assignment. She took a deep breath, shrugged her shoulders, and entered the room feeling as though she probably wouldn't get the application to run correctly once again. Rachel has a limited background working with computers, and she has had limited success with assignments in this course. Needless to say, her self-efficacy in the computer class is low.

Achievements, pleasant learning experiences, positive attitudes, and supportive environments cultivate high self-efficacy for specific tasks or types of activities. The following are important strategies for building self-efficacy:

> *Plan to succeed.* Create clear goals and plans of action as you approach new learning tasks. Use a goal organizer to increase your opportunity for success. One success leads to another. Obtaining success multiple times erases self-doubt and reinforces your belief in your ability to complete specific tasks on a high level of performance.

> *Use effective strategies.* Selecting effective strategies to complete a task results in positive attitudes and positive learning experiences. If one strategy is ineffective, modify your approach by selecting a different strategy to bring you the desired result. Choose to problem-solve rather than quit.

> *Use motivation to persevere.* Find meaningful motivators to keep your momentum to achieve your goals and build positive experiences.

CONCEPT CHECK 5.16

Can self-efficacy be high in one area and low in another? Why is this so?

CONCEPT CHECK 5.17

How does self-efficacy differ from self-confidence? What role does *interest* have in the development of self-efficacy?

True or False?

_____ 1. Extrinsic motivation based on physical or monetary awards tends to be the most powerful form of motivation.

_____ 2. Self-esteem and self-efficacy are based on other people's perceptions of you.

_____ 3. Self-esteem affects motivation, and motivation affects self-esteem.

_____ 4. As extrinsic motivators gain momentum, they often become intrinsic motivators.

_____ 5. Creating positive self-images and using positive words can alter your self-esteem.

 **Improve Your Grade**
Online Practice 2:
Motivation

STRESS MANAGEMENT

3 ▶ *Define stress and identify strategies and techniques for effective stress management.*

Stress is a reaction or response to events or situations that threaten or disrupt our normal patterns or routines. Stress is the wear and tear on our bodies due to physical, emotional, cognitive, and behavioral responses. The following are important points about stress:

Stress is a reaction or response to events or situations that threaten or disrupt our normal patterns or routines.

 Some stress is normal as we move through life making decisions and changing directions in our personal, work, and academic lives.

 In some situations, stress is beneficial. Stress can compel us to take action and to move in new directions. The increased adrenaline from stress can help us perform at higher levels.

 As stress increases, our ability to deal with and control the stress decreases.

 Early warning signs that stress is becoming more intense and moving into the danger level include headaches, backaches, insomnia, fatigue, anxiety attacks, mood swings, depression, forgetfulness, carelessness, and irritability.

 Excessive stress hinders performance and affects our cognitive abilities. Excessive stress affects working memory and long-term memory and reduces our ability to concentrate, solve problems, and make wise decisions.

 Excessive stress from unresolved issues has physical consequences: increased pulse rate, faster breathing, higher blood pressure, a weakening of the immune system, a decrease in the production of endorphins (a neurochemical that makes us feel happy), ulcers, heart attacks, strokes, and clinical depression.

 Learning to manage stress is a lifelong skill that affects the quality of life and longevity.

Stressors

How you *perceive* and *handle* external situations—rather than the situations themselves—is the cause of stress. People who handle stress best are those individuals who actively look for solutions and use techniques to alter their perception of

Stressors are situations or actions that cause stress.

CONCEPT CHECK 5.18

What stressors have you experienced recently? How did you react to these stressors?

external situations. **Stressors** are situations or actions that cause stress. When stressors enter into your life, often you can take some form of action to reduce or eliminate the stressors. For example, if an upcoming test is a stressor, you can create a plan of action and use specific techniques to take control of the situation. Other stressors, such as the terminal illness of a loved one, are out of your immediate control; the only control you have is how you handle your reaction to the stressor.

Stressors may be positive or negative. Divorce, personal injury, losing a job, or family problems are negative stressors. Events such as marriage or a vacation may be positive stressors. The number of stressors you face, both positive and negative, at one time affect your overall stress level. In 1967, Dr. Thomas H. Holmes and Dr. Richard H. Rahe developed a "stress test," the Social Readjustment Rating Scale (SRRS), to help individuals identify their stress levels. The stressors and the stress scores on SRRS remain applicable today. (See Exercise 5.3.)

EXERCISE 5.3

Stress Test

DIRECTIONS: Go to Exercise 5.3 in Appendix B, page A11, to complete the Social Readjustment Rating Scale. You will be asked to circle all the events (stressors) you have experienced in the last twelve months. Each event has a point value. After totaling all the point values for events, you will be able to find your stress level score.

Essential Strategies for Managing Stress

CONCEPT CHECK 5.19

In what ways can you use your interpersonal and intrapersonal intelligences to deal with stressors? Give specific examples.

In Chapter 1, you learned that interpersonal intelligence deals with your relationship with others and intrapersonal intelligence deals with your relationship with yourself. **Figure 5.7** shows seven Essential Strategies for Managing Stress. These strategies utilize your interpersonal and intrapersonal abilities.

Healthy Lifestyle

Your lifestyle and the choices you make in your daily and weekly habits and routines influence your level of stress and the way you respond to a variety of stressors. When you feel stress occurring in your life, and especially when you feel the stress is becoming excessive, take time to examine your habits, behaviors, and lifestyle choices. A basic look at your lifestyle patterns can begin by looking specifically at the areas of nutrition, exercise, and sleep since these three areas play important roles in reducing and coping with stress. **Figure 5.8** shows the lifestyle behaviors that affect the leading causes of death in the United States.

CONCEPT CHECK 5.20

What is the relationship between nutrition and stress? What foods are recommended for healthy nutrition?

Nutrition

Frequently people experiencing stress turn to fast foods and snacks that are high in sugar and fat. Foods high in sugar often produce an energy surge as they increase blood sugar in the body. However, the increased blood sugar quickly drops, thus

FIGURE 5.7

Essential Strategies for Managing Stress

▌ **Interact with others.** Many research studies show that social interaction can reduce stress, improve overall health and the immune system, stimulate cognitive processes, and stave off depression. Make time to spend with a close network of friends, create new friendships, or participate in student, church, or community activities.

▌ **Redirect your emotions.** Engaging in activities that create positive emotions reduces the intensity of your emotional reaction to stress and the tendency to dwell on negative situations. Redirect your emotions by spending time on a favorite hobby or activity; substitute negative emotions with positive ones.

▌ **Confide in others.** Get input and alternative perceptions of a stressful situation from others instead of hiding your feelings, which often compounds the stress and exaggerates the severity of the situation. Discussing your situation with others may thwart the tendency to make a mountain out of a molehill. If you cannot confide or share your feelings with friends, seek out an adviser or counselor on campus or in the community.

▌ **Take time to center yourself.** Engage in a mind-calming activity such as meditation, yoga, prayer, or biofeedback to center yourself and return to a state of calmness and serenity. Sitting in a sauna, soaking in a hot tub or warm bath, or sitting near a fountain of water can also be a mind-calming experience. Centering activities provide a way to block out and temporarily shield yourself from the rest of the world.

▌ **Keep a journal.** In a journal, describe your feelings or concerns privately and tap into some of your innermost thoughts in a nonthreatening way. Putting your emotions on paper often reduces the intensity of the emotions, disperses some of the negative energy, and helps you discover solutions or new directions to take with the situation.

▌ **Choose a healthy lifestyle** (nutrition, exercise, and sleep). See pages 140 and 142.

▌ **Practice relaxation techniques.** See pages 143 and 144.

FIGURE 5.8

Lifestyle Behaviors That Affect the Leading Causes of Death in the United States

This table shows five of the leading causes of death in the United States today, along with behavioral factors that contribute to their development

Cause of Death	Alcohol	Smoking	Diet	Exercise	Stress
Cancer	X	X	X		?
Heart disease	X	X	X	X	X
Stroke	X	X	X	?	?
Lung disease		X			
Accidents and injury	X	X			X

Source: Bernstein/Nash, *Essentials of Psychology,* © 2008, Houghton Mifflin, p. 391.

leaving the individual feeling less energetic than before eating the high-sugar foods or snacks. The following guidelines can help you make healthier lifestyle choices:

▌ Instead of eating foods loaded with sugar, choose foods that break sugars down more slowly and release energy over a more sustained period of time. Complex carbohydrates, such as those found in grains, cereals, rice, pasta, bread, and potatoes, protect blood levels from the roller coaster effect of highs and lows.

▌ Consume three to four helpings of fruits and vegetables each day. In addition to providing you with essential vitamins and minerals, these foods increase your brain's production of serotonin, a brain chemical that stabilizes mood swings and promotes a sense of happiness. Multivitamins can supplement your dietary needs for vitamins and minerals, but they are not a substitute for good eating.

▌ Limit your use of nicotine, caffeine, and alcohol; avoid non-prescription drugs. People often use more of these products when under stress, but they are not effective ways to cope with stress, and their health consequences may lead to more serious problems.

▌ Set aside fifteen to thirty minutes three times a day to sit down and enjoy a relaxing meal. Put work and other distractions aside so meals become a quiet time to enjoy and digest the food, or a time to socialize with others.

Exercise: Become More Active

Physical activity reduces the physiological effects of stress. Plan twenty to thirty minutes a minimum of three times a week to exercise (walk, run, swim, bike, lift weights, do aerobics, or play basketball, baseball, soccer, or golf). For more structure, sign up for a physical education course, a yoga class, an intramural sport, or a community exercise program or work out with a regularly televised exercise program. In addition to reducing your stress level and giving yourself a mental break from thinking about the stressor, the benefits of regular exercise are many:

▌ Exercise gets oxygen moving more smoothly to your brain; your concentration levels increase, and information enters and moves through your memory system more efficiently.

▌ Exercise improves your cardiovascular system, thus reducing your risk of more serious health conditions that may result from prolonged stress.

▌ Exercise strengthens your body, making it more resistant to the physical and emotional effects of stress. Your body becomes better equipped to handle stress when stress does occur.

Sleep

Strive to eliminate poor sleep patterns by establishing consistent sleep and waking times. Plan your time as best possible so you can get your sleep pattern on a regular schedule. Resetting your body's time clock requires training and often three or more weeks of scheduling consistency. Your goal is to create a pattern that gives you approximately eight hours of sound sleep, which results in your awaking each morning refreshed and ready to begin a new day. Recognizing the effects of stress on sleep patterns can alert you to the need to find strategies and help from others to deal more effectively with your stressors. The following are important points about sleep patterns during times of stress:

CONCEPT CHECK 5.21

What is the relationship between physical exercise and stress? What are the benefits of physical exercise?

CONCEPT CHECK 5.22

What is the relationship between hours of sleep and stress? How many hours of sleep do you get per night on a regular basis?

▌ Sleep patterns often become irregular and unpredictable. Lack of sufficient sleep becomes a stressor and makes it more difficult to manage other stressors that may also be occurring.

▌ Some individuals may experience *insomnia,* the inability to fall asleep; their hours of restful sleep are too few. If you experience insomnia, use the time to relax in a prone position; listen to soft music or spend the time visualizing or practicing relaxation techniques.

▌ Some individuals respond to stress by sleeping *too much*. Sleeping becomes an escape from the world. During their waking hours, the stressors may overwhelm them and render them nonproductive. They retreat again to sleep.

Relaxation Techniques

Relaxation techniques can help you reduce your stress levels and improve your emotional health. The goal behind relaxation techniques is to create a state of mind and body that perhaps can best be described as "Ahhhhhhh." In this state, the body is not tense and the mind is not wandering; you are open and ready to receive new information or expand on previously learned information. Relaxation techniques are effective in a wide variety of emotional situations: when you feel anxious, nervous, tense, stressed, apprehensive, hyperactive, restless, defeated, frustrated, or overwhelmed. The following are six relaxation techniques that are easy to learn and require only a few minutes of your time.

▌ The **perfect place technique** involves taking a mental vacation and visualizing a perfect, stress-free place to relax. To use this technique, close your eyes and breathe in slowly. Visualize a perfect place in the world where you feel relaxed, confident, safe, comfortable, and content. Continue breathing in and out slowly as you let the perfect place unfold in your imagination; add sounds, smells, sights, tastes, and tactile sensations to your perfect place. Make a mental picture of this perfect place. Through the power of association, you can recall the mental picture and the soothing sensations of this perfect place whenever you need to separate yourself in a healthy way from stress and stressful situations.

▌ The **soothing mask technique** involves using your imagination to create and pull a mask over your face to block out reactions to stress. Close your eyes and place your hands on the top of your head. Slowly move your hands down your forehead, down your face, and to your neck. As you do this, picture your hands gently pulling a *soothing mask* over your face. This mask removes other thoughts, worries, fears, or stresses from your mind. Keep your eyes closed for another minute. Feel the soothing mask resting on your face. Block out thoughts or feelings that are not related to your soothing mask. As you practice this technique, you will be able to do it without using your hands.

▌ The **relaxation blanket technique** involves visualizing yourself pulling a soft, warm blanket up to your neck to release tension. Sit comfortably in your chair. Close your eyes, and focus your attention on your feet. Imagine yourself pulling a soft, warm blanket up over your feet, up over your legs, lap, and chest until the blanket is snuggled around your shoulders and against your neck. Focus on the way your body feels warm and relaxed. Keep your eyes closed for another minute as you enjoy the warmth and comfort of the blanket.

CONCEPT CHECK 5.23

What effects can relaxation techniques have on the body and on the mind? Which relaxation techniques are most beneficial for you?

The **perfect place technique** involves taking a mental vacation and visualizing a perfect, stress-free place to relax.

The **soothing mask technique** involves using your imagination to create and pull a mask over your face to block out reactions to stress.

The **relaxation blanket technique** involves visualizing yourself pulling a soft, warm blanket up to your neck to release tension.

CONCEPT CHECK 5.24

Which techniques use visualization to create mental images?

The **breathing by threes technique** involves inhaling and exhaling slowly as a way to reduce stress.

▌ The **breathing by threes technique** involves inhaling and exhaling slowly as a way to reduce stress. You can do this technique with your eyes opened or closed. Inhale slowly through your nose as you count to three. Gently hold your breath as you again count to three. Exhale slowly through your nose as you count to three. Repeat this several times. You will feel your body begin to slow down and relax.

The **deep breathing technique** involves taking deep breaths and exhaling slowly as a way to reduce stress.

▌ The **deep breathing technique** involves taking deep breaths and exhaling slowly as a way to reduce stress. Take a deep breath to fill your lungs. You may think your lungs are full, but there is room for one more breath of air. Inhale once again. Now slowly exhale and feel your body relax. Repeat this deep breathing several times. If you feel lightheaded or dizzy after trying this exercise, you might want to select one of the other options.

The **deep muscle relaxation technique** involves tensing and releasing different groups of muscles as a way to reduce stress.

▌ The **deep muscle relaxation technique** involves tensing and releasing different groups of muscles as a way to reduce stress. Stress is often felt in one or more of these muscle groups: shoulders, arms, lower back, legs, chest, fingers, or face. Notice the amount of tension you feel in the various locations throughout your body. Then, make a clenched fist tight enough so that you can feel your fingers pulsating. Breathe several times and feel the tension in your fingers and your hands. Then breathe slowly and uncurl your fists until they are totally relaxed. Pay close attention to the different sensations as you go from tense to relaxed. Continue this with other muscle groups. Let the feelings of deep muscle relaxation and the feelings that the tension is washing away spread throughout your body.

CONCEPT CHECK 5.25

Which relaxation techniques emphasize breathing patterns? Which techniques do you prefer using?

EXERCISE 5.4

Textbook Case Studies

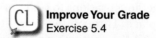 **Improve Your Grade**
Exercise 5.4

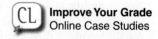 **Improve Your Grade**
Online Case Studies

DIRECTIONS:

1. Read each case study carefully. Respond to the question at the end of each case study by using *specific* strategies discussed in this chapter. Answer in complete sentences.

2. Write your response on paper or online at the Student Website, Exercise 5.4. You will be able to print your online response or e-mail it to your instructor.

CASE STUDY 1: Katlin feels that her life is spinning out of control. She is having problems at work and in one of her classes. She feels overwhelmed and stressed. She gets caught up in a lot of negative self-talk and irrational thinking, two characteristics that are not typical for her. She is not sure how these problems started, but they are affecting her sleep and her usu-

ally healthy eating patterns. She has been avoiding her closest friends; she does not want them to see her so stressed and "out of control." What can Katlin do to break this negative pattern and feel more in control of her life?

CASE STUDY 2: Debbie has disciplined herself to sit down to study during her scheduled study blocks. She sits in the living room at a large table that has her television, notebooks, supplies, and family pictures. Hours go by, and she has nothing to show for her time. She just cannot seem to get started. Her assignments seem long and tedious. She knows what needs to get done, but she cannot seem to motivate herself. She stares at her books and simply cannot focus her mind on studying. What strategies would you recommend Debbie use when she sits down to study?

Multiple Choice

_____ 1. Which statement is *not* true about stress?
   a. Stress results in physical, emotional, cognitive, and behavioral responses.
   b. With effective stress-management skills, a person can avoid experiencing stress.
   c. In some situations, stress can be beneficial.
   d. Stress is caused by the ways you perceive and handle stressors.

_____ 2. You can learn to handle stress by
   a. using your interpersonal and intrapersonal intelligences.
   b. shifting your focus from a negative stressor to a more positive activity.
   c. journaling your thoughts and learning from your insights.
   d. using all of the above.

_____ 3. You can learn to manage and reduce stress by
   a. examining and altering your eating, exercise, and sleep habits.
   b. telling everyone you know about your problems.
   c. getting an energy boost by eating foods with high sugar and fat content.
   d. using all of the above.

 Improve Your Grade
Online Practice 3:
Stress Management

PROCRASTINATION MANAGEMENT

4 *Define procrastination and identify strategies and techniques for effective procrastination management.*

Procrastination is a learned behavior that involves putting off or postponing something until a later time. Chronic procrastinators have ingrained certain behavioral and cognitive patterns into their way of "doing life." Quite consistently they choose low-priority tasks over high-priority tasks. Fortunately, because procrastination is a learned behavior, it can be "unlearned," reduced, or eliminated.

Do you know any procrastinators? You can often identify them by these characteristics:

▮ They accept and even boast about being procrastinators.

▮ They pride themselves on being able to do things quickly, at the last minute, and under pressure.

▮ They often wait for a "push," a threat of a specific consequence, a crisis, or some outside force to get the momentum to do what needs to be done.

▮ Their focus is on completing the task, and proving they can complete it in a short time frame, and not necessarily on the quality of the final product.

▮ They try to use their procrastination as a legitimate excuse for not performing on high levels or not completing projects.

Habitual or chronic procrastinators can create new behavioral and cognitive patterns that recognize the value of working first on high-priority tasks—even when they may not be as exciting or enjoyable as the low-priority tasks. Understanding when and why they procrastinate is the beginning step of the process of change.

CONCEPT CHECK 5.26

What false beliefs do some procrastinators have about their habit of procrastinating?

Procrastination is a learned behavior that involves putting off or postponing something until a later time.

Procrastinators put off or postpone tasks for a variety of reasons and tend to choose low-priority tasks over high-priority tasks. Often they rationalize or try to justify their behavior. When and why do you procrastinate?

CONCEPT CHECK 5.27

When do you tend to procrastinate? Give specific examples.

When You Procrastinate

Any time you find yourself avoiding a specific task or making statements such as "I'll do it when I am in the mood," "I have plenty of time to do it later," "I can let it slide a few more days," or "I will wait because I work better under pressure," recognize that you are procrastinating. Become aware of your procrastination patterns by answering the following questions.

1. *Are there specific kinds of tasks involved when you procrastinate?* For example, do you plan and follow through with studying for your computer class but procrastinate about studying for your writing or your math class? Do you complete specific household chores but procrastinate when faced with the laundry? Identify the specific kinds of tasks that you avoid most frequently; for those tasks, you will want to activate strategies to increase your momentum.

2. *Do you tend to procrastinate about beginning a specific task, or does procrastination appear during the middle of working on the task?* For example, do you struggle with setting time aside and sitting down to begin writing a paper? Do you make excuses for not beginning the paper? Or do you begin the paper but lose interest or motivation halfway through the process of writing it? Do you quit close to its completion? For example, do you put off typing the final version of the paper even though you have finished writing it? Understanding *when* in the process of a task you procrastinate can help you select strategies to complete tasks or goals more consistently.

3. *Do you start multiple tasks, jumping from one to another, and make less important tasks seem more important or urgent?* This behavior is a common sign of the onset of procrastination. Procrastinators can get so caught up in this whirlwind behavior that they do not realize all the busy work is a mask for avoiding specific tasks. When you find yourself scurrying around, sometimes aimlessly keeping busy, take time to identify the task you are avoiding.

Why You Procrastinate

CONCEPT CHECK 5.28

Why do you procrastinate? What reasons can you identify for putting off high-priority tasks and spending your time on low-priority tasks?

Reasons for procrastinating vary for different tasks, situations, and individuals. In some cases procrastinating will not have any serious consequences. For example, procrastinating about moving a stack of magazines to the garage or putting your compact disks back in their cases has no dire consequences. In other cases, procrastinating leads to increased stress and additional problems. Procrastinating about paying your bills, studying for a test, or filling your tires with air will have more serious consequences, some of which could alter your goals or course for the future.

CONCEPT CHECK 5.29

If a student procrastinates about working on a research problem, what might be the student's reason for procrastinating?

We have all procrastinated at one time or another. When you are aware of procrastinating, "dig deep" to uncover your reason for putting off something important that needs to be done. Do any of the following characters reveal one of your reasons for procrastinating?

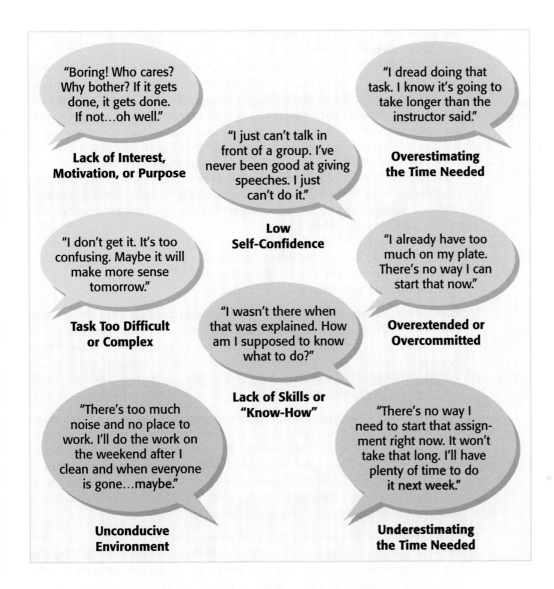

The following excerpt presents procrastination issues related to college students. In addition to the above eight reasons for procrastinating, this excerpt provides eight additional reasons why people procrastinate. Awareness of the various reasons will help you pinpoint the underlying reason for procrastinating, which can then lead to specific self-management strategies to address the issues and combat procrastination.

Procrastination and Its Causes

Author Maia Szalavitz in the following article, "Stand & Deliver" (*Psychology Today*, August 2003, pp. 50–54), provides information about procrastination and its causes.

Procrastination is not just an issue of time management or laziness. It's about feeling paralyzed and guilty as you channel surf, knowing you should be cracking the books or reconfiguring your investment strategy. Why the gap between incentive and action? Psychologists now believe it is a combination of anxiety and false beliefs about productivity.

Tim Pychyl, PhD, associate professor of psychology at Carleton University in Ottawa, Canada, tracked students with procrastination problems in the final week before a project was due. Students first reported anxiety and guilt because they had not started their projects. "They were telling themselves[,] 'I work better under pressure' or 'this isn't important,'" says Pychyl. But once they began to work, they reported more positive emotions; they no longer lamented wasted time, nor claimed that pressure helped . . . Psychologists have focused on procrastination among students because the problem is rampant in academic settings; some 70 percent of college students report problems with overdue papers and delayed studying, according to Joseph Ferrari, associate professor of psychology at Chicago's DePaul University.

Pychyl also found that procrastination is detrimental to physical health. College students who procrastinate have higher levels of drinking, smoking, insomnia, stomach problems, colds, and flu. So why can't people just buckle down and get the job done?

False Beliefs: Many procrastinators are convinced that they work better under pressure, or they'll feel better about tackling the work later. But, tomorrow never comes and last-minute work is often low quality. In spite of what they believe, "Procrastinators generally don't do well under pressure," says Ferrari. The idea that time pressure improves performance is perhaps the most common myth among procrastinators.

Fear of Failure: "The main reason people procrastinate is fear," says Neil Fiore, PhD, author of *The Now Habit*. Procrastinators fear they'll fall short because they don't have the requisite talent or skills. "They get overwhelmed and they're afraid they'll look stupid." According to Ferrari, "Procrastinators would rather be seen as lacking in effort than lacking in ability." If you flunk a calculus exam, better to loudly blame it on the half-hour study blitz than admit to yourself that you could have used a tutor the entire semester.

Perfectionism: Procrastinators tend to be perfectionists—and they're in overdrive because they're insecure. People who do their best because they want to win don't procrastinate; but those who feel they must be perfect to please others often put things off. These people fret that "No one will love me if everything I do isn't utter genius." Such perfectionism is at the heart of many an unfinished novel.

Self-Control: Impulsivity may seem diametrically opposed to procrastination, but both can be part of a larger problem: self-control. People who are impulsive may not be able to prioritize intentions, says Pychyl. So, while writing a term paper[,] you break for a snack and see a spill in the refrigerator, which leads to cleaning the entire kitchen.

Thrill-Seeking: Some procrastinators enjoy the adrenaline "rush." These people find perverse satisfaction when they finish their taxes minutes before midnight on April 15 and dash to the post office just before it closes.

Task-Related Anxieties: Procrastination can be associated with specific situations. "Humans avoid the difficult and boring," says Fiore. Even the least procrastination-prone individuals put off taxes and visits to the dentist.

Unclear Expectations: Ambiguous directions and vague priorities increase procrastination. The boss who asserts that everything is high priority and due yesterday is more likely to be kept waiting.

Depression: The blues can lead to or exacerbate procrastination—and vice versa. Several symptoms of depression feed procrastination. Because depressed people can't feel much pleasure, all options seem equally bleak, which makes getting started difficult and pointless.

From Maia Szolovitz, "Stand and Deliver," *Psychology Today,* Aug. 2003, pp. 50–54. Copyright © 2003, Sussex Publishers, Inc. Reprinted with permission.

EXERCISE 5.5

Procrastination Management Strategies

PURPOSE: By applying self-management skills and strategies, you can combat each of the sixteen common reasons for procrastinating.

DIRECTIONS: Work as a group, with a partner, or by yourself to complete the following directions.

1. On separate paper, create a chart such as the one shown below. Add sixteen rows on your chart.

2. In the first column, list the sixteen reasons people often procrastinate (pages 147–149).

3. In the second column, use your knowledge from previous chapters and personal experiences to list strategies a person could use to combat the reason for procrastination shown at the beginning of the row in column 1.

4. In the last column, list specific strategies from Chapter 5, page 150, for combating the reason for the procrastination.

Reason	General	Specific
Lack of interest, motivation, or purpose		

CONCEPT CHECK 5.30

What was the most recent task you procrastinated about doing? Why did you procrastinate? Which of the strategies in this chapter could you have used to stop your procrastination?

Essential Strategies to Combat Procrastination

Learning to reduce or eliminate procrastination can empower you, enhance your self-esteem, strengthen your self-discipline, and put you in greater control of your life. In addition to the time management, goal setting, motivation, and other self-management strategies that you have already learned, the following are ten additional strategies to combat procrastination.

▌ **Strategy 1:** *Use your intrapersonal intelligence.* Explore *when* and *why* you procrastinate about a specific task. Use those insights to identify appropriate strategies to deal directly with the underlying issues.

▌ **Strategy 2:** *Identify a purpose and meaning.* Avoid labeling a task as "meaningless, stupid, or boring" or expressing a negative attitude toward a task, as these attitudes and behaviors lower motivation and negatively impact your self-image. Find a purpose or a valid reason for the task. Use a goal organized; identify the benefits.

▌ **Strategy 3:** *Create an interest.* Engage a family member, a tutor, or a study group to work with you on the task. Seek alternative sources of information, such as a video, Internet searches, magazines, or books related to the topic. Once you become familiar with the topic, interest often increases.

▌ **Strategy 4:** *Take charge of the situation.* Gather up all the supplies or materials you need to get started. Select an appropriate work environment. *Take charge* and take responsibility of the situation.

▌ **Strategy 5:** *Prioritize and stick to the order.* When you feel overwhelmed or overextended, make a list of tasks that must be done. Use the ABC Method to prioritize them by their importance or prioritize them by completion date requirements. Tackle the high-priority tasks first. Schedule time on your weekly schedule to work on these tasks.

▌ **Strategy 6:** *Relax your personal standards.* If you tend to be a perfectionist, lower your unrealistically high standards or expectations. You can continue to produce quality without always having to "be the best." Avoid spending excessive time redoing parts of a task or the final outcome, such as a paper.

▌ **Strategy 7:** *Be flexible and willing to change.* Be willing to give up the attitude that "I have always done things this way." Be willing to try new strategies and to create new patterns of behaviors.

▌ **Strategy 8:** *Face your fear of failure.* Focus on your positive traits, your accomplishments, and the skills you have acquired. Use positive self-talk, affirmations, and emotional *e* words to negate self-doubts, self-criticism, and fear of failure. Build your self-confidence by mentally rehearsing the steps of the task several times before you begin.

▌ **Strategy 9:** *Visualize success.* Create a mental picture of yourself working through a task, feeling positive about your work, and completing the task on time.

▌ **Strategy 10:** *Make a contract with yourself.* Make a contract with yourself to stop using excuses for not getting things done. Begin by creating a plan of action (a goal). Push yourself to "just do it." End your contract with an incentive, such as an extrinsic reward.

REFLECTIVE WRITING 5.2

Improve Your Grade
Reflective Writing 5.2

On separate paper, in a journal, or online at this textbook's website, respond to the following questions:

1. Which strategies or techniques in Chapter 5 will you use to become a more effective self-manager? Be specific.

2. How will these strategies or techniques benefit you?

EXERCISE 5.6

Links

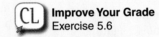
Improve Your Grade
Exercise 5.6

PURPOSE: The concept of self-management involves an integration of many different study skills and learning theories. Learning to use strategies from one category, such as motivation, can strengthen your self-management skills in other areas, such as goal setting, concentration, stress management, and procrastination management.

DIRECTIONS: Follow your instructor's directions for Exercise 5.6. You may be asked to work with a partner, in a group, or to respond in writing on separate paper or online at Exercise 5.6. Answer each of the following questions.

1. How does managing procrastination affect self-esteem?

2. How does a person's level of motivation affect concentration and stress?

3. How can stress management affect concentration, motivation, and procrastination?

4. How does a person's self-esteem cycle affect his or her self-talk and self-efficacy?

5. How do self-management skills affect the operations of working memory?

CHECK POINT 5.4

ANSWERS APPEAR ON PAGE A4

True or False?

_____ 1. Procrastination is a learned behavior that can be modified or eliminated.

_____ 2. Low self-efficacy can be one reason for procrastinating.

_____ 3. If a person starts a task and later procrastinates, he or she may fear failure or find the task to be too complex or difficult.

_____ 4. The most common myth among procrastinators is that they perform best under pressure.

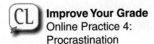
Improve Your Grade
Online Practice 4:
Procrastination

LEARNING OBJECTIVES REVIEW

1 *Define concentration and identify strategies to block out distractions and maintain a focused, disciplined mind.*

- Self-management is the ability to use strategies to deal constructively and effectively with variables that affect the quality of your personal life. Concentration is a self-management set of skills.

- Concentration is the ability to block out external and internal distractors in order to stay focused on one specific item or task. You can use specific strategies to increase your concentration when you study and free up your working memory for cognitive processes.

- An ideal study area involves careful attention to elements in your physical environment: noise, lighting, and workspace.

2 *Define motivation and discuss factors that affect motivation and strategies to strengthen motivation.*

- Motivation is the feeling, emotion, or desire that moves a person to take action.

- The Incentive Theory of Motivation states that incentives and rewards are the driving forces behind people's choices and behaviors. To be effective, the incentives must be valued and be realistically obtainable.

- Intrinsic and extrinsic motivation are driving forces behind achieving goals. In general, intrinsic motivation is more powerful than extrinsic motivation.

- The Expectancy Theory of Motivation reflects a person's intensity or desire to achieve a goal and a belief in the likelihood of achieving that goal.

- A person's self-esteem and self-efficacy are factors that affect motivation. You can use specific strategies to boost self-esteem and develop a stronger sense of self-efficacy.

3 *Define stress and identify strategies and techniques for effective stress management.*

- Stress is a reaction or a response to events or situations that threaten or disrupt our normal patterns or routines. Stress is normal and can be beneficial. Excessive stress has physical consequences and can hinder performance and cognitive functioning.

- Stressors, which can be positive or negative, are situations or actions that cause stress.

- You can learn to deal with stress more effectively by using a variety of stress-management techniques, choosing a healthy lifestyle (nutrition, exercise, and sleep), and using relaxation techniques.

4 *Define procrastination and identify strategies and techniques for effective procrastination management.*

- Procrastination is a learned behavior that involves putting off or postponing something until a later time. Identifying *when* and *why* you procrastinate is the beginning step to combating procrastination.

- Ten strategies can be used to overcome procrastination and take action to complete tasks.

CHAPTER 5 REVIEW QUESTIONS

ANSWERS APPEAR ON PAGE A4

Fill-in-the-Blanks

Write one word (key term) per blank to complete each sentence.

1. _____ distractors are disruptions caused by things in your physical environment.

2. The _____ _____ technique involves keeping score of the number of times you get distracted during a specific period of time.

3. The _____ Theory of Motivation states that people are motivated by the rewards that they can receive for their actions or performance.

4. _____ motivation is the most effective kind of motivation because you strive to accomplish something to please yourself.

5. Self-_____ is the belief in your ability to achieve a specific task at a specific level of performance.

6. A test, an argument, an illness, an engagement, or a promotion can all be considered _____ because they can be the source of stress.

7. The _____ _____ relaxation technique involves taking a mental vacation and visualizing a location that is peaceful, relaxing, and safe.

8. _____ may be caused by thrill-seeking, perfectionism, fear of failure, or false beliefs about working well under pressure.

Multiple Choice

____ 1. Concentration is
   a. the ability to block out distractions and focus on only one item or task.
   b. one of the Twelve Principles of Memory.
   c. a mental discipline that involves training your mind to maintain a focus.
   d. all of the above.

____ 2. Which techniques would work best for a student who wants to stop wasting the first half hour of a study block trying to "get started" on studying?
   a. Warm-up activities and using the take-charge technique
   b. Chunking technique and mental rehearsal
   c. Setting learning goals and creating a task schedule
   d. All of the above

____ 3. Procrastination
   a. may stem from lack of interest, fear of failure, or perfectionism.
   b. occurs when low-priority tasks take the place of high-priority tasks.
   c. is a learned behavior that can be altered by using effective strategies.
   d. involves all of the above.

____ 4. Which of the following strategies are *not* designed to convert a person's negative attitude to a positive attitude?
   a. Tunnel vision, intrinsic rewards, and deep breathing.
   b. Mental rehearsal and positive self-talk.
   c. Affirmations and emotional *e* words.
   d. Seeing success and strategies to increase self-esteem.

____ 5. Which of the following statements is *not* true about stress?
   a. Stress is normal and can help people move in new directions.
   b. Prolonged stress may affect physical, emotional, behavioral, and cognitive functions.
   c. Excessive stress requires prescription medications in order to avoid physical damage to the body.
   d. Excessive stress affects the functioning of working memory and long-term memory.

____ 6. Which of the following helps decrease or eliminate the habit of procrastination?
   a. Taking time to understand *when* and *why* procrastination occurs
   b. Using a weekly schedule, a task schedule, and goal organizers
   c. Creating a stronger interest in the task and finding a purpose for completing the task
   d. All of the above

Short-Answer Questions

On separate paper, answer the following questions. Use complete sentences and details and terminology from this chapter.

1. What are self-management skills? How do they affect your ability to perform well academically?

2. Discuss specific strategies you can use to improve your self-management skills in any one of the four sets of self-management skills presented in this chapter.

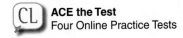 **ACE the Test**
Four Online Practice Tests

Developing Test-Taking Skills

LEARNING OBJECTIVES

1 *Identify and explain effective strategies for preparing for tests.*

2 *Identify and explain effective strategies for performing well on tests.*

3 *Identify and explain effective strategies for managing test anxiety.*

Chapter Outline

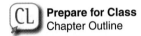

Prepare for Class
Chapter Outline

4 ▶ *Identify and explain ways to use mnemonics to prepare for tests.*

Tests in college are a standard method to assess your understanding of course material. In this chapter, you will learn effective strategies to prepare for tests, take tests, manage test anxiety, and use mnemonics to boost your memory. This chapter also includes inventories for you to use to assess the effectiveness of your study skills strategies and to examine indicators for test anxiety.

CHAPTER 6 PROFILE

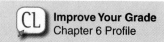

Improve Your Grade
Chapter 6 Profile

Developing Test-Taking Skills

ANSWER, **SCORE**, and **RECORD** your profile before you read this chapter. If you need to review the process, refer to the complete directions given in the profile for Chapter 1 on page 4.

ONLINE: You can complete the profile and get your score online at this textbook's website.

	YES	NO
1. I make a five-day study plan and summary notes before major tests.	_____	_____
2. I use the survival technique of cramming for most tests.	_____	_____
3. I use the Principles of Memory to prepare for tests.	_____	_____
4. On tests, I answer one question, or guess at an answer if necessary, and then move to the next question.	_____	_____
5. I use mental rehearsal, memory searches, and visualizations to try to remember information to answer test questions.	_____	_____
6. When I take tests, I tend to forget information that I studied, or I "go blank."	_____	_____
7. Difficulties I have on tests are usually due to factors that are beyond my control.	_____	_____
8. I am often nervous, feel sick, or have physical problems (headache, stomachache, clammy hands) right before a test or during a test.	_____	_____
9. I create some mnemonics for information that is difficult to remember.	_____	_____
10. I am confident in my test-taking skills and abilities.	_____	_____

QUESTIONS LINKED TO THE CHAPTER LEARNING OBJECTIVES:

Questions 1–3:	objective 1	Question 9:	objective 4
Questions 4, 5:	objective 2	Question 10:	all objectives
Questions 6–8:	objective 3		

TEST PREPARATION SKILLS

1 ▶ *Identify and explain effective strategies for preparing for tests.*

In college, tests are a way of assessing your understanding of information presented in your courses. Tests also indicate how well you have prepared, the effectiveness of your study methods, and your test-taking skills. Students who do not apply study skills on a regular basis often need to resort to *cramming*, which is an attempt to learn large amounts of information in a short period of time. Cramming is a survival technique that often backfires; frequently, students who cram become even more aware of how much *they do not know.* Feeling underprepared can create test anxiety and lead to poor test performance. By using the following strategies, you will learn how to enter testing situations with more confidence and preparedness, which will lead to better results and rewards for your work and effort.

Gathering Information About a Test

The more you can find out about an upcoming test, the better equipped you will be for preparing for and taking the test. Course materials, your instructor, and other students can provide you with valuable information. Use the following strategies to prepare for upcoming tests:

- *Course Materials:* First, review your course syllabus and class assignment sheets so you know specifically which chapters and topics will be included on the test. Gather together your notes and assignments for those chapters or topics as they tend to indicate the information that received attention in class.

- *Instructor:* Listen carefully to your instructor's description of the test and the topics or chapters that the test will cover. Sometimes your instructor will emphasize which materials you should review or need to know. If your instructor indicates the kinds of test questions that will appear on the test, jot these down as you may use different strategies for different kinds of tests.

- *Other Students:* Talk to other students who have already completed the course and tutors who are familiar with the course. Ask them for study suggestions and about the kinds of test questions to expect. Remember, however, that instructors do change test questions and formats, so do not feel overly confident about a test based on information you obtained from previous students or from tutors. If previous tests are available to examine, take the time to look at and practice with the tests.

Reviewing Your Study Tools and Materials

You have already learned a wealth of information and an array of strategies for learning, processing, and recalling information. The more strategies you use on a regular basis, the more prepared you will be for an upcoming test. To prepare for an upcoming test, begin by reviewing study tools that you have already created. If you have been using ongoing review, preparing for tests becomes a matter of "brushing up" or "refreshing" your memory. If you did not dedicate adequate time for ongoing review each week, you will need to dedicate more time to prepare for a test. **Figure 6.1** provides you with six Essential Strategies for Reviewing for Tests.

TERMS TO KNOW

summary notes   *p. 158*
five-day study plan   *p. 161*
four levels of response   *p. 165*
test anxiety   *p. 169*
locus of control   *p. 172*
systematic desensitization
  p. 172
acronym   *p. 175*
acrostic   *p. 176*
the Loci Method   *p. 178*

 Improve Your Grade
Online Flashcards
Glossary

CONCEPT CHECK 6.1

What kind of information should you gather about a test? Where can you find this information?

CONCEPT CHECK 6.2

What are the benefits of using ongoing review prior to the announcement of a test?

> ### FIGURE 6.1
>
> **Essential Strategies for Reviewing for Tests**
>
> ▌ **Review your lecture notes, textbook notes, and study tools that you have created.** Use Look-Away Techniques (reciting, visualizing, or writing from memory) to check your ability to recall information. If the feedback is positive, set those materials aside and move to other materials to review. If feedback is negative, reread the information and practice rehearsing it further.
>
> ▌ **Assess the effectiveness of your learning and review strategies.** Use the checklists in Exercise 6.1 and Exercise 6.3. Adjust your strategies if necessary.
>
> ▌ **Review associations, visualizations, and any mnemonics you previously created.**
>
> ▌ **For procedural knowledge, rework previous problems.** Rework problems from the textbook, from class lectures, and from your homework assignments. As you rework problems, talk to yourself to explain the steps and how to use the processes.
>
> ▌ **Review one final time the night before a test.** If you review before going to bed, and if you do not place any other kinds of stimuli such as television or a movie between your review time and sleep, your mind may continue thinking about and reviewing the information as you sleep.
>
> ▌ **Review an hour or so the day of the test.** This final review pulls information back into your working memory and puts you in a mindset for the subject matter.

Creating Summary Notes

Summary notes are specific notes that include information that you need to review further before the day of the test.

Summary notes are specific notes that include concepts, definitions, details, steps, or other information that you need to review further before the day of the test. Summary notes may also include notes that relate to specific information your instructor reminded you to study for the test. If you have used effective learning strategies and ongoing review, you already know and are able to recall many of the concepts and terms that a test will cover; these items do *not* need to appear on your summary notes. Summary notes are helpful to have before any test, but they are extremely valuable to have to prepare for midterm and final exams. **Figure 6.2** shows a variety of formats that are commonly used for summary notes. You will learn more about these formats in Chapters 10 and 11.

CONCEPT CHECK 6.3

What kind of information should you put in summary notes? How do they differ from your regular notes?

Predicting Test Questions

CONCEPT CHECK 6.4

Which types of test questions do you encounter most frequently?

Predicting test questions is an excellent method for preparing for tests and reducing test anxiety. Predicting test questions is even easier after you have taken one or two tests from a specific instructor and have a sense of the types of tests he or she uses. Understanding types of test questions is the first step. **Figure 6.3** shows test-question formats that are common in college courses.

FIGURE 6.2

Formats Commonly Used for Summary Notes

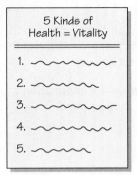

Lists/Categories of information to remember

Comparison charts to compare or contrast different subjects studied

Notes based on topics that include textbook and lecture information

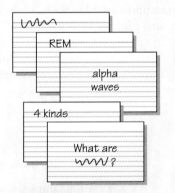

Flashcards of categories, terminology, and study questions

Chapter outlines made by using headings and subheadings

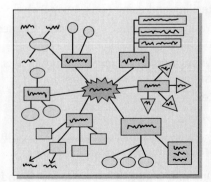

Visual mappings for individual chapters or topics that appear in several different chapters

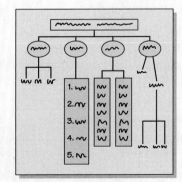

Large hierarchies made on poster paper to include several topics or chapters

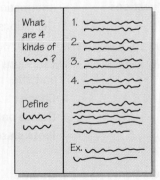

Cornell notes with study questions on the left for self-quizzing (see Chapter 9)

FIGURE 6.3

Test Question Formats

Kind of Question	Level of Difficulty	Includes	Requires
Recognition: Objective Questions	Easiest	True-False Multiple-Choice Matching	Read and recognize whether information is correct; apply a skill and then recognize the correct answer.
Recall Questions	More demanding	Fill-in-the-Blanks Listings Definitions Short Answers Problem Solving	Retrieve the information from your memory and then respond.
Essay Questions	Most difficult	Essays	Retrieve the information from memory, organize it, and use effective writing skills to respond.

Effective test preparation should include studying all the important material thoroughly so you are well prepared for any type of test question. However, many students prefer to modify their test-preparation strategies to reflect specific testing formats when the instructor announces the formats in advance. **Figure 6.4** provides you with a summary of the types of material you should focus on and practice strategies to use as you review for a specific type of test.

FIGURE 6.4

Predicting and Studying for Different Kinds of Tests

If You Predict . . .	Study This Kind of Information:	Practice May Include:
Objective Questions	▮ Definitions of key terms ▮ Categories or lists of information ▮ Details: names, dates, theories, rules, events	▮ Writing and later answering true-false, multiple-choice, and matching questions ▮ Working with a study partner to exchange practice questions
Recall Questions	▮ Information presented in lists ▮ Definitions of terminology ▮ Cornell recall columns (Chapter 9) ▮ Questions formulated before, during, and after reading ▮ Chapter summaries ▮ Details on visual notes (Chapter 11) ▮ Problem-solving examples	▮ Reciting and using Look-Away Techniques ▮ Writing summaries and answers to questions to practice expressing ideas ▮ Writing and answering fill-in-the-blanks, listings, and definitions questions ▮ Reworking math problems ▮ Writing the problem-solving steps ▮ Working with a study partner to exchange practice questions
Essay Questions	▮ Themes ▮ Relationships ▮ Major concepts	▮ Outlining chapters to see headings and relationships ▮ Reviewing notes for recurring themes ▮ Using strategies in Chapter 13

EXERCISE 6.1

Assessing Your Strategies Inventory

Go to Exercise 6.1, Appendix B, page A12, for the Assessing Your Strategies Inventory. Use this inventory based on the Twelve Principles of Memory to assess and then modify your study strategies. You can also use this inventory throughout the term to refine your approach to learning and reviewing course information.

Reviewing with Others

Review sessions are an effective way to receive immediate feedback about the topics you understand clearly and those that you need to review further. Review sessions also provide you the opportunity to verbalize, explain information in your own words, and answer practice test questions. *Study groups* are also an effective way to prepare for tests. If a study group does not exist, you can create one with members of your class. To be effective and time-efficient, a study group needs to have structure. As members of the group, you could agree to:

CONCEPT CHECK 6.5

What advantages have you experienced by attending review sessions and reviewing with a study group?

▌ Individually write practice test questions to present to the group

▌ Take turns leading a discussion for a specific topic that will be covered on the test

▌ Have each student summarize important information for specific chapters and provide group members with a set of summary notes for those chapters

▌ Bring study tools, such as flashcards, to use to quiz each other

Using a Five-Day Study Plan

A **five-day study plan** is a plan of action that helps you organize your materials and time to review for a major test, such as a midterm or a final exam. This plan promotes spaced practice and ongoing review; it reduces tendencies to procrastinate, cram, or have test anxiety. Use the following steps to create a five-day study plan.

A **five-day study plan** is a plan of action that helps you organize your materials and time to review for a major test, such as a midterm or a final exam.

Step 1: Be Specific and Realistic

Begin by making a list of all the topics and materials that you need to review for the upcoming test. Following is an example for a sociology course.

CONCEPT CHECK 6.6

How does a five-day study plan organize your materials and your time?

Topics/Materials to Review for Chapters 1–4:

Terminology	Lecture Notes	Textbook Notes
Study Guides	Chapter Reviews	Homework Assignments
Notes from Guest Speaker	Notes from Video	Two Short Discussion Papers

Step 2: Set Target Days and Times

Organize specific blocks of time on days 1, 2, 3, and 4 for review sessions. On day 5, dedicate all of your study time to reviewing your *summary notes*. Mark the study/review days and times on your calendar or your weekly schedule. Coordinate these times with other students if you are going to review with a study partner or study group.

Review Days and Times

Day 1	Day 2	Day 3	Day 4	Day 5
Monday Review:	Wednesday Review:	Friday Review:	Saturday Review:	Sunday Final Review:
8–9:00 AM	8–9:00 AM	8–9:00 AM	10:00 AM–12:00 PM	2–4:00 PM
3–4:00 PM	3–4:00 PM	3–4:00 PM	4–6:00 PM	7–9:00 PM

Step 3: Identify the Steps and a Plan of Action

Identify which chapters and which materials you will review on day 1, day 2, day 3, and finally on day 4. To avoid wasting review time, create a pattern or plan for reviewing each time you sit down. For example, your plan may be to use this sequence of review activities: read the study guide, review chapter summary, review terminology, review homework, review class handouts, review lecture notes, and review textbook notes. Throughout this review process, plan to make *summary notes for the information you feel you need to review further* on Day 5 and right before the test. Following is an example of a plan of action.

Example of a Plan of Action

Monday	Wednesday	Friday	Saturday	Sunday
8-9:00 AM	8-9:00 AM	8-9:00 AM	10-12:00 PM	2-4:00 PM
(Ch. 1) class study guide, homework Q, handouts	(Ch. 2) study guide, homework Q, video notes	(Ch. 3) class study guide, handouts, homework Q	(Ch. 4) study guide (no handouts), homework Q, 2 short papers	Review summary notes; self-quiz on Ch. 1 & 2
3-4:00 PM	3-4:00 PM	3-4:00 PM	4-6:00 PM	7-9:00 PM
(Ch. 1) lecture notes, textbook notes, Notes-Guest speaker	(Ch. 2) lecture notes, textbook notes	(Ch. 3) lecture notes, textbook notes	(Ch. 4) lecture notes, textbook notes	Review summary notes; self-quiz on Ch. 3 & 4

Step 4: Plan a Reward

At the end of each daily review time, use the intrinsic reward: the satisfaction that the studying is under control. Choose an intrinsic or an extrinsic reward for yourself *after* you complete your five-day study plan *and* after you complete the test.

For shorter tests, such as unit tests or tests for a module, you can use the same steps as those shown in the five-day study plan, but your plan will cover fewer days and less content. The important point is to identify what needs to be done and create a plan of action that organizes your time and your materials so you can review and prepare efficiently and thoroughly.

CONCEPT CHECK 6.7

What changes will you need to make to use the concept of a five-day study plan for tests other than major tests?

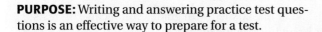

EXERCISE 6.2

Links

CL **Improve Your Grade**
Exercise 6.2

PURPOSE: Writing and answering practice test questions is an effective way to prepare for a test.

DIRECTIONS:

By yourself, with a partner, or in a small group, write one objective and one recall question for each of the following topics discussed in previous chapters. Your instructor may ask you to give your questions to your partner, to another group, or to the class to answer.

1. Linear and Global Learners
2. Multiple Intelligences
3. Feedback Model
4. Twelve Principles of Memory
5. Kinds of Time-Management Schedules
6. Scheduling Study Blocks
7. Motivation
8. Self-Management Skills

CHECK POINT 6.1

ANSWERS APPEAR ON PAGE A4

True or False?

_____ 1. Students who do not use ongoing review or a five-day study plan may need to resort to last minute cramming.

_____ 2. Participating in small study groups is always more effective and productive than using your time to review by yourself.

_____ 3. One effective strategy is to study thoroughly the day before a test and then enjoy a movie or

some type of recreational activity at night before you go to sleep.

_____ 4. The feedback you receive from Look-Away Techniques can help you determine what information to put into summary notes.

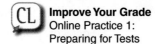

Improve Your Grade
Online Practice 1:
Preparing for Tests

EXERCISE 6.3

Academic Preparation Inventory

PURPOSE: Your grades on tests often reflect the effectiveness of your study and review strategies. Identifying your strengths and weaknesses before a test and after you receive test results provides you with an opportunity to identify which strategies work and which you need to modify or replace.

DIRECTIONS: Go to Exercise 6.3 in Appendix B, page A13, to complete the inventory.

Improve Your Grade
Reflective Writing 6.1

REFLECTIVE WRITING 6.1

On separate paper, in a journal, or online at this textbook's website, respond to the following questions:

1. For the majority of test-taking situations you encounter, do you enter the classroom feeling confident and well-prepared for the test? Explain your answer.

2. What specific test-preparation techniques do you use regularly because they have proven to be effective for you?

3. Overall, are you satisfied or dissatisfied with grades you receive on tests? Explain your answer by giving specific details.

TEST PERFORMANCE SKILLS

2 ► *Identify and explain effective strategies for performing well on tests.*

Feeling slightly nervous or apprehensive when you first enter the classroom or when the instructor distributes the test is a normal reaction to testing situations. Strive to use strategies to calm your nerves, establish a positive state of mind, and mentally prepare to do well on the test. The following are strategies to establish a positive mindset for tests:

▌ Arrive to class early. Rushing in at the last minute or arriving late adds stress and does not allow you time to mentally prepare.

▌ Use positive self-talk, a quick relaxation or visualization technique, or a concentration technique to focus your mind.

▌ Focus only on yourself; ignore other students and their nervous reactions to a test.

▌ If you have a few minutes before the test is distributed, mentally rehearse information from your summary notes. Or, if allowed, review your summary notes one final time.

▌ Listen carefully to the directions. Your instructor may announce corrections on the test, suggestions for completing the test, the amount of time available for the test, and other important directions.

Essential Test-Taking Strategies

In Chapters 12 and 13, you will learn specific strategies for taking objective tests, and for recall, math, and essay tests. After learning about general test-taking strategies in this chapter, you can familiarize yourself with the content in Chapters 12 and 13 by skimming through the chapters for a quick overview. You may "read ahead" in Chapters 12 and 13 at any time for test-taking strategies to use

CONCEPT CHECK 6.8

Why is the attitude you take with you into a testing situation important? What strategies can you use before a test to feel positive and confident?

CONCEPT CHECK 6.9

What strategies can you use within the first five minutes of receiving a test?

FIGURE 6.5

Essential Strategies for Taking Tests

▮ **As soon as you receive the test, jot down important information.** On the back of the test, in the margins of the test, or on separate "scratch paper," jot down formulas, mnemonics, lists, or facts that you may want to refer to quickly during the test.

▮ **Survey the test.** Glance through the test to become familiar with the types of questions on the test, the point value of different questions or sections on the test, and the overall length of the test. Be sure to check to see if questions appear on the backs of the test pages.

▮ **Budget your time.** Quickly estimate the amount of time you can spend on each section of the test. This is especially important if the test has short-answer or essay questions because they tend to take more time to write answers. If you wish, jot down estimated times to begin each section of the test.

▮ **Decide on a starting point.** Many students prefer to work through the pages of the test in the order in which the questions are presented, but you do not *have* to work in this order. You can begin with the part of the test that feels the most comfortable, has the highest point value, or with which you feel most confident.

▮ **Read all the directions carefully.** The number one cause of students making unnecessary errors on tests has to do with hastily reading directions and questions. Read directions slowly. Be sure you understand the directions before proceeding. To help yourself stay focused on the question, *circle key words* in the directions. Ask for clarification if the directions are not clear.

▮ **Use your test time wisely.** If you have time available after you have answered all the questions, check your answers. Do *not* change answers if you are panicking or feel time is running out. *Do* change answers if you can justify the change; perhaps other questions on the test gave you clues or helped you recall information that affects your original answer.

▮ **Do not leave answer spaces blank if you start to run out of time.** In most cases, you will automatically lose points if you leave an answer space blank. When you are running out of time, pick up your pace, read faster, spend less time pondering answers, and make a quick choice or use an educated guess for your answer if necessary. For essay questions, if you do not have time to write a complete answer, provide an outline or a list of points you would have developed further had you had sufficient time.

with specific kinds of test questions. The seven Essential Strategies for Taking Tests in **Figure 6.5** that you can use from the beginning to the end of a test-taking situation will apply to the information you will later learn in Chapters 12 and 13.

Four Levels of Response

To answer any type of test question involves conducting a memory search to locate and retrieve information from your long-term memory. Even objective test questions that offer you a choice of answers or require you to recognize whether a statement is true or false require memory searches.

Some students who have not yet learned effective test-taking strategies move through a test by reading a question, answering it with certainty or hesitancy, and then moving on to the next question. This approach works if students immediately know the correct answer for each question. When students are not able to answer all the questions immediately, using the four levels of response is a more effective approach to use. The **four levels of response** are stages students can use to answer test questions: *immediate, delayed, assisted,* and *educated guessing*. **Figure 6.6** describes the four levels of response to use to answer questions on tests.

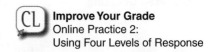

Improve Your Grade
Online Practice 2:
Using Four Levels of Response

CONCEPT CHECK 6.10

What four stages of answering questions do effective test-takers use?

The **four levels of response** are stages students can use to answer test questions: immediate, delayed, assisted, and educated guessing.

FIGURE 6.6

Four Levels of Response for Answering Questions

Levels of Response	Description
Immediate Response	▌ As soon as you read the question, you immediately know the answer. ▌ The question automatically triggers an association with information in your long-term memory. This is the payoff for effective studying. ▌ When there is no immediate response, move to the next level of response, delayed response.
Delayed Response	▌ When you cannot immediately respond, read the question a second time. ▌ Go into "retrieval mode." Try to stimulate an association or a retrieval cue. Think of things that you do know that are related to the question. Sometimes this activates chained associations and the correct answer "pops" into your working memory. ▌ Try *visualizing* the information as it appeared in your notes, in your study tools, in the textbook, or in the lecture, or try recalling your instructor's words or your own words when you recited the information. ▌ If no answer surfaces, *place a small check mark next to the question* and move to the next question. Plan to return to this question later. ▌ Move to the next level of response, assisted response.
Assisted Response	▌ After you have answered as many questions on the test as possible, return to the unanswered questions that are marked with a check mark. ▌ Reread the question to see if you can now answer it. Information from other questions may have trigged an association that helps you now answer the question. ▌ If you still cannot answer the question, search for clues in the test. Identify a key word in the question. Then, *skim through the test,* looking for other questions in the test that have that same key word. Reread those questions for clues that will help you find the answer you need. ▌ If none of these strategies result in an answer, move to the next level of response, educated guessing.
Educated Guessing	▌ Use educated guessing strategies only when all else fails. Educated guessing is a last-resort strategy that does not guarantee the correct answer. (See Chapters 12 and 13.) ▌ Educated guessing strategies are *never* more effective than answering a question using the other levels of response.

Computerized Tests

Computerized tests usually consist of multiple-choice questions. These tests may be written by the instructor, but more often they consist of a test bank generated by the textbook author or publisher. Some of the test banks randomly assign test questions of varying levels of difficulty; other test banks allow the instructor to tag the questions to be used on a test.

There are some advantages and disadvantages to taking computerized tests. One advantage is that you receive immediate feedback and a score for your test. When you answer correctly, the positive feedback increases your confidence level. Another advantage is that usually the time limits to complete a test are less rigid than when you take a test in class. Because you can control the pace for answering questions, you may feel less stress. One disadvantage is that any negative feedback that indicates an incorrect answer may cause stress and frustration. Also, most computerized tests do not allow you to go back to previous questions to change answers or use the test-taking strategy of assisted response. Finally, you usually do not get a printed copy of the test to review later when you study for your final exam.

If you have not already experienced computerized testing, chances are good that you will at some time during your college career. When you are faced with taking a test on a computer, gather as much information in advance about the computerized test-taking situation as possible. Ask questions such as the following:

CONCEPT CHECK 6.11

Do you prefer computerized tests over paper-pencil tests? Why or why not?

▌ Is there a tutorial or practice test? May I take the test more than once?

▌ Is there a time limit for completing the test?

▌ May I have blank scratch paper and pen to work out problems or to organize my thinking? Will I be able to preview all of the questions before I begin answering?

▌ Will I be able to get a printed version of the test to use for studying after the test is scored?

Allow yourself ample time to complete the test. For many students, taking computerized tests requires more time than taking tests in the classroom. Therefore, you will want to avoid going into the computer lab when you are rushed or pressed for time. Select a time of day when you feel mentally sharp and best able to concentrate. When you enter the lab, choose a computer that is not in the line of a steady flow of traffic so you will experience fewer distractions. **Figure 6.7** shows seven Essential Strategies for Taking Computerized Tests.

CONCEPT CHECK 6.12

If you have the option, when is the best time for you to go to a computer lab to take a computerized test?

Learning from Your Tests

Too often students receive their graded tests, look at the grade, and then stick the test into their notebooks. A more effective approach involves using the tests for valuable feedback and then analyzing the effectiveness of your learning strategies. (You can repeat Exercise 6.3 to analyze the strategies you used to prepare for a specific test.) With the information you learn from analyzing your test, create a plan of action to adjust your strategies and approaches to learning to bring even greater results on your next test.

FIGURE 6.7

Essential Strategies for Taking Computerized Tests

▌ **Understand the computer and the testing software commands.** Ask for help if you are unfamiliar with the computer or do not know how to log on. Read the directions carefully. Be sure that you understand how to enter answers and how to change or delete them. Find out if the software program allows you to return to previous questions.

▌ **Read and choose answers carefully.** Read the beginning of a multiple-choice question carefully, try to complete the question in your own words, and then examine the options given as possible answers.

▌ **Do not answer too quickly.** Once you have decided on your answer, reread the opening part of the question and complete it with *each* of the answer options. Select the answer that best completes the statement. You can often avoid careless mistakes by double-checking an answer before selecting it as the final answer.

▌ **If you receive feedback that you selected an incorrect answer, do *not* immediately move to the next question.** Reread the question and learn from your error because similar information may appear later

in the test in another form. This strategy keeps your mind focused on the material and reduces the tendency to move too hastily to the next question.

▌ **Pause and use a short relaxation technique if you find yourself tensing up, feeling discouraged, or getting irritated.** Working memory needs to remain free of mental clutter; stress or anxiety affect thinking processes. Breathing by threes, using positive self-talk, or stretching your arms, rolling your shoulders, or shaking out your hands can reduce stress.

▌ **Before you leave the test, jot down any questions that concerned or confused you.** Discuss these questions with your instructor. Make a brief list of topics you need to review or study further.

▌ **Discuss your computer test-taking skills with the lab assistant or your instructor.** After taking several tests, if you are uncomfortable with computerized tests, ask lab assistants and your instructor for additional test-taking strategies. Find out if other testing options are available. Talk with other students to learn their strategies.

Examine the Questions You Answered Correctly

Answer the following questions:

▌ What strategies did I use to learn this information?

▌ What was the original source of the information? Did I learn the information in class, through a homework assignment, from the textbook, or from a combination of sources?

▌ Was the information new to me or did I already know this information at the time it was presented?

Look for Patterns of Errors

CONCEPT CHECK 6.13

How can you use graded tests to improve your understanding and future performance on tests?

Repeat the process you used to examine the questions you correctly answered. For example, perhaps the information that you missed the most frequently appeared mainly in the textbook, or as information presented in class during lectures. This feedback makes you more aware of the need to focus greater attention on your textbook reading skills and strategies or on your notetaking skills for class lectures.

Correct Your Errors

You want to override or erase incorrect information and replace it with accurate information. Create and practice new associations so the next time you need to retrieve that information from your schemas, you will recall accurate information. Frequently during the course of a term, previously learned information appears again on future tests or as knowledge upon which new information is built.

CHECK POINT 6.2

ANSWERS APPEAR ON PAGE A4

True or False?

_____ 1. Students who use metacognition strive to use the results of their tests to analyze and modify their choice of learning strategies to use for that specific course.

_____ 2. Once you mark an answer, you should never go back and change that answer.

_____ 3. In the four levels of responding to a question, the third level of response involves searching for clues to the answer in other parts of the test.

_____ 4. When taking computerized tests, it is important to move through the test as quickly as possible to avoid forgetting information that appeared in earlier questions.

 Improve Your Grade
Online Practice 3:
Performing on Tests

TEST ANXIETY MANAGEMENT SKILLS

> **3** ▶ *Identify and explain effective strategies for managing test anxiety.*

In Chapter 5, you learned that *stress* is defined as your reaction or response to events or situations that threaten to disrupt your normal pattern or routine. With normal stress, a person is aware of the stress, aware of the source of the stress, and still able to control his or her reaction or responses. Stress specifically related to an upcoming test can be beneficial and motivate people to perform on higher levels; however, excessive stress that becomes test anxiety creates negative responses and consequences.

Anxiety occurs when the level of stress is excessive to the point that it hinders performance. Using stress-management techniques in Chapter 5 often can prevent stress from accelerating to the level of anxiety, but for individuals who do experience a bout with anxiety, knowing how to manage it can reduce its effects, duration, and intensity. When people experience a bout of anxiety, they no longer recognize the source of the excessive stress and have little or no control of the situation. They are reactionary rather than oriented to problem solving.

Test anxiety is a specific form of anxiety. **Test anxiety** is excessive stress that hinders a person's ability to perform well *before* or *during* a test. Test anxiety before and during a test can exhibit its presence in physical, emotional, cognitive, and behavioral forms. For example, a student might become ill, emotionally distraught, experience confused or disorganized thinking, or use avoidance strategies to procrastinate studying for a test. During a test, test anxiety affects cognitive processing and can immobilize thinking skills. A student may "go blank," make excessive careless mistakes, mark answers in the wrong place, or quit due to frustration. **Figure 6.8** shows common symptoms related to test anxiety.

Test anxiety is excessive stress that hinders a person's ability to perform well *before* or *during* a test.

CONCEPT CHECK 6.14

What symptoms might you exhibit if you experience test anxiety? If you have test anxiety, does it appear before or during a test?

FIGURE 6.8

Symptoms Related to Test Anxiety

Physical Symptoms of Anxiety	Rapid heartbeat Upset stomach, nausea Abnormal nervousness Tight muscles, tension	Blurred vision Increased blood pressure Shakiness	Headaches Clammy palms More than normal sweating
Emotional Symptoms of Anxiety	Fear, anger, frustration Irritable, short-tempered Fatigue	Feelings of hopelessness or lack of control of a situation	"Fight or flight" feelings Anxious, nervous, panicky Depression
Cognitive Symptoms of Anxiety	Mind filled with intrusive thoughts Poor concentration Inaccurate or limited recall Confusion, disorientation	Impulsive responses Negative self-talk Lack of clear thinking Misdirected attention "Going blank"	Fixating on one item too long Careless mistakes Overemphasis on negative thoughts
Behavioral Symptoms of Anxiety	Crying, sobbing Strained facial expressions	Slumped posture Procrastination	Shaky voice Aggressive behavior

Reviewing with other students and using available resources, such as online practice tests, can help you prepare for tests, strengthen your test-taking skills, and reduce or eliminate test anxiety. What other strategies can you use to control test anxiety and its effects on your performance?

CONCEPT CHECK 6.15

What creates test anxiety? How can statements students make about test anxiety indicate the source of their anxiety?

EXERCISE 6.4

Test Anxiety Inventory

PURPOSE: Some students may experience test anxiety, which impacts their test performance; other students may experience test-related stress that actually motivates them to perform well. This inventory provides you with information about test anxiety indicators you may experience.

DIRECTIONS: Go to Exercise 6.4 in Appendix B, page A14, to complete this inventory.

Sources of Test Anxiety

Test anxiety is a *learned behavior*. As such, it can be unlearned. If you experience test anxiety, begin by analyzing the source of your anxiety. In other words, what triggers your test anxiety? Sometimes listening to the kinds of comments you make about tests will help you identify the source of your test anxiety. *Underpreparedness, past experiences, fear of failure,* and *poor test-taking skills* are four common sources of test anxiety. **Figure 6.9** shows common student statements that relate to the four common sources of test anxiety.

FIGURE 6.9

Statements Relating to the Four Sources of Test Anxiety

Source	Common Student Statements
Under-preparedness	▌ I am nervous about this test because I did not have enough time to study or review. ▌ When I started reviewing, I realized how much I still needed to learn. ▌ Everyone else seems to know more than me. I should have studied more.
Past Experiences	▌ I never get decent grades on tests. ▌ I did not do well on the last test, so this probably will not be any different. ▌ Instructors write tricky tests that are not fair and do not let me show what I have learned.
Fear of Failure	▌ I am so worried that my grades will disappoint my parents. ▌ I am so concerned that my grades will affect my scholarship. ▌ My self-esteem gets deflated by my grades because I can never live up to my personal standards.
Poor Test-Taking Skills	▌ I have never been a good test-taker. ▌ I get nervous taking tests because I do not really know how to take tests or answer different kinds of questions. ▌ I make a lot of mistakes because I have problems understanding the directions or what kind of answers are expected. ▌ I could have done better if I had had more time to take the test.

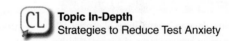

Topic In-Depth
Strategies to Reduce Test Anxiety

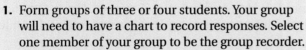

GROUP PROCESSING:
A COLLABORATIVE LEARNING ACTIVITY

1. Form groups of three or four students. Your group will need to have a chart to record responses. Select one member of your group to be the group recorder.
2. Create the following chart. In the "Strategies" column, brainstorm and list strategies students could

use to "unlearn" the behaviors and beliefs that cause test anxiety. Use your knowledge of strategies for Principles of Memory, self-management skills, as well as strategies from this chapter to recommend strategies to combat sources of test anxiety.

Source	Strategies
Under-preparedness	
Past Experiences	
Fear of Failure	
Poor Test-Taking Skills	

Strategies to Use *Before* a Test

In the Group Processing Activity, you and members of your group listed an array of strategies from previous chapters to deal with test anxiety. Following are a few such strategies that may have appeared on your lists.

CONCEPT CHECK 6.16

If your friend calls you a week before a midterm exam, and you sense that he or she is experiencing test anxiety, what strategies can you recommend to reduce or eliminate the test anxiety?

▌ Set learning goals.	▌ Make summary notes.
▌ Use ongoing review.	▌ Predict test questions.
▌ Recognize your strengths.	▌ Use effective study strategies.
▌ Use Look-Away Techniques.	▌ Use positive self-talk.
▌ Mentally rehearse.	▌ Recite and use feedback.
▌ Use schedules.	▌ Create plans of action.
▌ Use affirmations.	▌ Review with a partner.
▌ Improve motivation.	

Two new strategies, locus of control and systematic desensitization, also work effectively to help students with test anxiety reduce their excessive stress before a test.

Locus of Control

Locus of control is the degree to which a person feels power to control circumstances in his or her life.

Locus of control is the degree to which a person feels power to control circumstances in his or her life. Individuals with an *internal locus of control* feel that they have the power to control most situations or circumstances in their lives. They exhibit self-confidence and a high self-efficacy. When they do not do as well as expected, they accept responsibility for outcomes and use problem-solving techniques to create plans for improvement. Students with an internal locus of control experience test anxiety less frequently than students with an external locus of control.

CONCEPT CHECK 6.17

How does an internal locus of control differ from an external locus of control? Which locus of control is more empowering and beneficial?

Individuals with an *external locus of control* relinquish control and see other people or other situations as having the power and control over their circumstances. They blame others for their personal shortcomings instead of accepting personal responsibility. They tend to have low self-esteem, low confidence in their abilities, and high levels of frustration. Students with an external locus of control experience test anxiety more frequently and to greater degrees. To reduce test anxiety, the locus of control needs to shift from external to internal. **Figure 6.10** shows how attitudes and statements differ between people with an external and an internal locus of control.

Systematic Desensitization

Systematic desensitization is an anxiety-reducing strategy that involves a series of activities designed to reduce strong negative emotional reactions to an upcoming situation.

Systematic desensitization is an anxiety-reducing strategy that involves a series of activities designed to reduce strong negative emotional reactions to an upcoming situation. You can use this strategy before the day of a test by replacing your fear-based thoughts with positive thoughts that emphasize the successes you have already experienced. Systematic desensitization stops the fear from accelerating and getting blown out of proportion. You can use systematic desensitization in the following ways:

1. Make a list of specific situations or words that trigger your test anxiety. For example, "There will be a test next Monday" may trigger early test anxiety. After you have your list of *trigger situations or words*, visualize yourself reacting

FIGURE 6.10

Locus of Control

External Locus of Control	Internal Locus of Control
▮ I did not do well because my instructor does not like me.	▮ I need to adjust my attitude—quickly.
▮ This test is totally unfair.	▮ I take full responsibility; I was not prepared for this test.
▮ I could not study because of my children.	▮ I forgot to study the charts.
▮ All the questions were trick questions.	▮ I need to find more time to myself to study.
▮ I failed the test because it was poorly written.	▮ I am going to talk to the tutor about my test-taking strategies.
▮ My instructor did not even take the time to try to understand what I wrote.	▮ I am going to use more ongoing review every week.
▮ My instructor did not understand my situation.	▮ I am going to work to improve my writing skills.
▮ The textbook didn't explain this clearly.	▮ I can learn from this experience.

differently to those situations or words. See yourself responding in a more positive and constructive way. "Good. I have time to make a five-day plan, or I have stayed current with my work, so I can be ready for this test."

2. Predict and write practice test questions. Decide on an appropriate amount of time to answer the test questions. Create a test environment as close as possible to the real thing. If the classroom in which you will take a test is empty, be in that room when you take your practice test.

Strategies to Use *During* a Test

You can reduce or eliminate most test anxiety that occurs during a test by using the essential strategies for taking tests shown in Figure 6.5, page 165. The following strategies address specific symptoms that you might experience during a bout with anxiety during a test.

▮ *You go "blank" and are unable to recall the needed information.*

Strategies: 1. Use a quick relaxation technique to calm yourself down.
2. Use positive self-talk. Become your own cheerleader.
3. Reread the question in a whisper voice. Go into retrieval mode by conducting a new memory search. If necessary, place a check mark to return to the question later. Do not stay stuck on the question.

▮ *Your eyes start jumping from the printed line or skip over words when you read.*

Strategies: 1. Use your arm, a blank index card, or a blank piece of paper to block off the rest of the test. Restricting your vision to the question that you are contemplating helps your eyes stay focused on a line of information.
2. Use your pencil to point to each word as you read silently. Doing this keeps your eyes from skipping words or jumping to other lines of print.

CONCEPT CHECK 6.18

Have you ever had a fear escalate to the degree that the thing you feared became greatly over-exaggerated? What did you do to overcome your negative reaction?

CONCEPT CHECK 6.19

What may happen to your eyes, your concentration, and your cognitive skills when you are experiencing test anxiety? How can you combat these effects?

▌ *You notice yourself making excessive careless mistakes in selecting or marking the correct answer.*

Strategies:
1. Slow down the reading and answering process.
2. Activate your auditory channel by mouthing or quietly whispering the words as you read the directions, questions, and options for answers.
3. Highlight key words in the questions. Check to ensure that your answer relates to the key words.
4. Before moving to the next question, ask yourself: Does this answer make sense?

▌ *Your mind shifts away from the test and your concentration begins fading quickly.*

Strategies:
1. Become more active and interactive with the test. Circle direction words and highlight key words in directions and questions.
2. Use positive self-talk and force yourself to keep your eyes on the test. "I can do this. My eyes and my mind stay focused on the paper. I can figure this out."

By using the strategies in this chapter for preparing for and taking tests, you will see changes in your study habits and strategies and in your test results. These changes also affect your level of confidence, your self-esteem, your locus of control, and your ability to manage test anxiety.

CONCEPT CHECK 6.20

Which strategies for managing test anxiety do you think will work best for you? Why?

EXERCISE 6.5

Textbook Case Studies

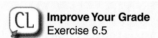 **Improve Your Grade**
Exercise 6.5

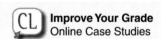 **Improve Your Grade**
Online Case Studies

DIRECTIONS:

1. Read each case study carefully. Respond to the question at the end of each case study by using *specific* strategies discussed in this chapter. Answer in complete sentences.

2. Write your responses on paper or online at the Student Website, Exercise 6.5. You will be able to print your online response or e-mail it to your instructor.

CASE STUDY 1: Adolpho has not been in school for fifteen years. He never learned how to study or take tests. He works hard, and he is able to respond in class and in study groups to questions that are related to the current assignment. However, when it is time to take tests that cover several chapters of information, he freezes and goes blank. What test-preparation and test-taking strategies would you recommend Adolpho start using?

CASE STUDY 2: Jenny does not study much for her communications class because she is taking the class for pass/no pass rather than a letter grade. As the end of the term approaches, she realizes that she may not have enough points to pass the class. She intends to deal with the situation the way she usually deals with tests—cramming in the day or two before the final exam. What test-preparation strategies would you suggest that Jenny use during the final two weeks of the term?

CHECK POINT 6.3

Multiple Choice

_____ 1. Which statement is *not* true about test anxiety?
   a. Students who have an internal locus of control frequently make excuses and see others as the source of their test anxiety.
   b. Students with test anxiety may exhibit physical, emotional, cognitive, or behavioral symptoms of excessive stress.
   c. Test anxiety is a learned behavior that may stem from under-preparedness, past experiences, fear of failure, or poor test-taking skills.
   d. Test anxiety is a learned behavior that can be controlled or eliminated.

_____ 2. When test anxiety occurs during a test,
   a. your eyes may jump around on the page.
   b. your mind may go blank or you may have confused thinking.
   c. you may find yourself making careless mistakes.
   d. you may experience all of the above.

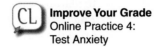

Improve Your Grade
Online Practice 4:
Test Anxiety

MNEMONICS

4 | *Identify and explain ways to use mnemonics to prepare for tests.*

Mnemonics are memory tools that serve as bridges to help you recall information from long-term memory. Mnemonics always involve creating some form of an association. You may want to use mnemonics, but sparingly, to create associations and retrieval cues for information that is otherwise difficult to recall. If you use mnemonics too extensively, they increase the amount of information you need to remember. If you do not memorize the mnemonic in its exact form, or if you do not practice translating the mnemonic back into its original meaning, it can hinder and confuse you rather than help you recall information accurately. In the Student Website, Topic In-Depth: Kinds of Mnemonics, you can learn how to use kinds of mnemonics that are not discussed in this section. In this section, the focus will be on creating acronyms, acrostics, word associations, picture associations, and the Loci Method for information that you want to remember and be able to retrieve from memory when you are taking tests.

CONCEPT CHECK 6.21

What mnemonics do you already use? Did you or someone else create the mnemonics you use?

Topic In-Depth
Kinds of Mnemonics

Acronyms

An **acronym** is a word or phrase made by using the first letter of key words in a list of items to remember. An acronym forms an association and works as a retrieval cue to recall the original items in the list. The mnemonic SAVE CRIB FOTO is an acronym for the Twelve Principles of Memory. A classic acronym is the word *HOMES* for the five Great Lakes in the northern United States: Huron, Ontario, Michigan, Erie, and Superior. For any acronym to work, you must practice translating the letters of the acronym back into the original words that the letters represent. For example, if you are asked to name the Great Lakes or name the Twelve Principles of Memory, giving the answer "HOMES" or "SAVE CRIB FOTO" would not suffice for an answer.

An **acronym** is a word or phrase made by using the first letter of key words in a list of items to remember.

Use the following steps to create an acronym:

1. *Write the list of items you need to remember.*
2. *Underline the **first letter** of each item in the list.* If an item in the list consists of more than one word, select only *one* key word to underline.
3. *Write the first letter of each key word on paper.*
4. *Unless the items in the list must be learned in the original order, rearrange the letters to form a word or a phrase.* If you do not have at least one vowel (*a, e, i, o, u,* and sometimes *y*), you will not be able to create an acronym that is a real word in English. A real word is easier to recall than a nonsense word, so strive to rearrange the letters to create a real word or phrase.
5. *Practice translating your acronym.* For your acronym to be useful to you, memorize the acronym, repeat it several times, and practice translating it back to the original words in the list of items.

Acrostics

If you are not able to create an acronym, you can always use the first letter of each key word to create an acrostic. An **acrostic** is a *sentence* made by using the first letter of key words in a list of items to remember. You can use the letters in their original order, or you can rearrange the letters to create the sentence. A classic example of an acrostic is the sentence *Please excuse my dear Aunt Sally.* The first letters of each word in this sentence represent the order of operations in math problems: parentheses, exponents, multiplication, division, addition, and subtraction. Note that you cannot add additional words to the sentence. Use acrostics sparingly as they tend to be more difficult to use effectively and result in one more piece of information you need to remember. As with acronyms, you must practice translating the acronym into the original words for items in your list.

EXERCISE 6.6

Creating Acronyms and Acrostics

PURPOSE: Acronyms are a common type of mnemonic used to remember items in a list. When you cannot create an acronym, you can create an acrostic.

DIRECTIONS: Create an acronym or an acrostic as indicated for the following items.

1. A pediatrician's advice for food a child should eat when he or she has a stomach flu: bananas, applesauce, toast, rice. (Letters to use: **b a t r**)
   Acronym: _____

2. Ten body systems in humans: skeletal, digestive, muscular, endocrine, circulatory, nervous, reproductive, urinary, respiratory, and integumentary. (Letters to use: **s d m e c n r u r i**)
   Acronym: _____

3. The seven coordinating conjunctions used to form compound sentences: for, and, nor, yet, but, so, or. (Letters to use: **f a n y b s o**)
   Acronym: _____

4. Vertical structures of the atmosphere, beginning with the closest to the Earth: troposphere, stratosphere, mesosphere, and thermosphere. (Letters to use: **t s m t**)
   Acrostic: _____
   _____

5. Skeletal (bone) structure of the arm: humerus, ulna, radius, carpals, phalanges. (Letters to use: **h u r c p**)
   Acrostic: _____
   _____

Word Associations

If you have strong language or musical skills, you can use those skills to create word associations that use *rhymes, jingles, short songs,* and *raps* that work as memory tools to recall information. The following examples of word associations demonstrate the use of linguistic and musical skills to create mnemonics:

▌ Use *i* before *e* except after *c* or when sounded like *a* as in *neighbor* and *weigh.*

▌ In fourteen hundred and ninety-two, Columbus sailed the ocean blue.

▌ Spring forward; fall back (daylight-saving time).

▌ Who invented dynamite? *Alfred Nobel had quite a fright when he discovered dynamite.*

▌ Which way should you turn to open a jar or tighten a bolt? *Righty tighty, lefty loosy.*

▌ What is the difference between *stalagmites* and *stalactites*? (Stalagmites are deposits of minerals that project upward from the floor of a cavern; stalactites project downward from the ceiling of a cavern.) You can use this jingle to differentiate between the two: *When the mites go up, the tights come down.*

▌ Use a familiar tune. Create lyrics with information you need to learn and sing them to a favorite tune or melody, such as "Happy Birthday" or "Rudolph the Red-Nosed Reindeer."

Picture Associations

To use picture associations effectively, you need to actively look for and think about ways to create simple associations that will be easy to remember and use to recall information. Actively search for a familiar object or picture to use in your association. Visualize the shape and colors of the objects. Sometimes picture associations are easier to remember if you exaggerate some part of an object by making it larger than its real size or if you turn them into whimsical cartoon figures. Add sounds and smells to the association when appropriate. **Figure 6.11** shows a picture association for Gardner's eight intelligences.

CONCEPT CHECK 6.24

What mnemonics do you know and use for common factual information? What mnemonics, if any, have you created this term for material you are studying?

CONCEPT CHECK 6.25

What picture associations have you created? Were they effective for recalling information? Why or why not?

FIGURE 6.11

Picture Association for the Eight Intelligences

▌ Linguistic
▌ Musical
▌ Logical-mathematical
▌ Spatial
▌ Bodily-kinesthetic
▌ Intrapersonal
▌ Interpersonal
▌ Naturalist

If you are adding letters to your picture, use large, bold capital letters. The following are suggestions for using picture associations to remember different kinds of information:

1. *To remember a person's name:* Associate the name with an object or another person you know with that name.
2. *To remember a definition:* Associate the meaning with an object that has a similar characteristic.
3. *To remember a specific number:* Find and visualize a number pattern within the number.
4. *To remember a cause-effect relationship:* Picture the items as an action movie.

The Loci Method

CONCEPT CHECK 6.26

Without looking on the website for examples, what picture associations can you create to remember these four kinds of information?

The **Loci Method** is a mnemonic technique that involves associating items or topics with specific rooms in a familiar building.

The **Loci Method** is a mnemonic technique that involves associating items or topics with specific rooms in a familiar building. *Loci* (pronounced lo-si), which means *locations,* dates back to the early times of Greek orators, who could deliver lengthy speeches without any written notes. Orators made mental notes by associating parts or topics of their speeches with familiar rooms or locations in a building. In their minds, as they walked through each room, they visualized items in the rooms that they associated with the topic to be discussed. With this technique they were able to deliver organized, fluent speeches to their audiences without using written notes. You can also use the Loci Method to memorize points you want to make in a speech, in an essay, or in a discussion. Use the following steps for the Loci Method:

1. *Make a list of the items you need to remember.*
2. *Draw a floor plan of a familiar location.*
3. *On paper or mentally attach pictures.* Attach a picture of the first item you need to remember inside the first location or room on your floor plan. You can exaggerate the size or shape of the picture or hang it in an unusual position to make it stand out in your memory.
4. *Continue attaching pictures.* Walk through the floor plan, attaching one item to each room.
5. *Practice visualizing.* Visually practice walking through all the rooms and reciting the important information associated with the items in the rooms.

CONCEPT CHECK 6.27

What Principles of Memory are activated when you use the Loci Method?

Assume that you are going to give a speech or write an essay for a history class about the end of the economic boom in the 1970s. You sketch the following map of the first floor of a building on your campus and you number specific locations that you will use in that sequential order. In this map, you show eight locations, but you may not need to use all eight locations for a specific set of information. Then you mentally attach a picture that represents the topic you would like to present in your speech or essay.

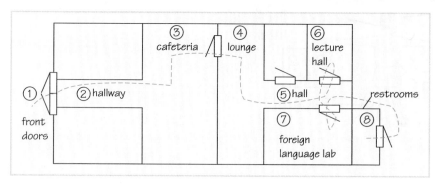

The bold faced items in the following list are the details you need to remember. After attaching one detail per location, memorize your map and the items placed in each location. Practice *visualizing* your map and *reciting* information associated to each location.

1. At the front door, picture a poster that says "**350 percent increase in oil prices**."
2. In the hallway, picture rows of oil barrels with large Xs on them for **Arab oil embargo**.
3. In the cafeteria, picture food prices: hamburgers $7.50, milk $3.00 for **high retail prices**.
4. In the lounge, picture posters on the walls of closed auto factories for **slump in auto industry**.
5. In the hall, picture people lined up for job interviews for **high unemployment**.

EXERCISE 6.7

Using the Loci Method

DIRECTIONS:

1. Identify a series of steps, a sequence of events, or a list of points that you want to include in a speech, an essay, or a discussion.

2. Draw a floor plan of a familiar building. Number the rooms to show the order that you will mentally walk. In each room, attach a picture that represents the item you need to remember.

3. Practice mentally walking through your building and reciting the information represented by the pictures in each room. Your instructor may ask you to recite your information in class.

CHECK POINT 6.4

ANSWERS APPEAR ON PAGE A4

True or False?

_____ 1. You will always be able to locate any information paired with a mnemonic and stored in long-term memory.

_____ 2. In acronyms, each letter at the beginning of each word in a sentence represents a specific item in a list of items you want to remember.

_____ 3. When you use mnemonics, you also use Memory Principles of Association, Visualization, Recitation, and Elaboration.

_____ 4. You can use mnemonics, such as picture or word associations, jingles, melodies, acronyms, or acrostics, as retrieval cues to help with later recall.

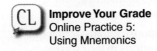 **Improve Your Grade**
Online Practice 5:
Using Mnemonics

REFLECTIVE WRITING 6.2

Improve Your Grade
Reflective Writing 6.2

On separate paper, in a journal, or online at this textbook's website, respond to the following questions.

1. Which specific skills in this chapter will help you the most in terms of preparing for tests, performing well on tests, and managing test anxiety? Discuss at least four skills and include specific strategies you intend to use.

2. How does your attitude toward taking tests affect your ability to perform well? How does your current attitude toward taking tests differ from your attitude at the beginning of the term? Explain with details.

LEARNING OBJECTIVES REVIEW

1 *Identify and explain effective strategies for preparing for tests.*

- Effective strategies to prepare for an upcoming test include: gathering information about a test, reviewing study tools, creating summary notes, predicting test questions, and reviewing with others.

- Three kinds of questions you will encounter on college tests include: recognition (objective) questions, recall questions, and essay questions.

- By using these steps in the five-day study plan, you can organize your materials and time to prepare effectively for a major test, such as a midterm or a final exam: (1) be specific and realistic; (2) set target days and times; (3) identify the steps and a plan of action; (4) plan a reward.

2 *Identify and explain effective strategies for performing well on tests.*

- To increase your performance on a test, you can use a variety of essential strategies to mentally prepare yourself, move through the test with confidence, and increase your test performance.

- By using the four levels of response for answering questions, you can respond to questions in four stages: immediate response, delayed response, assisted response, and educated guessing.

- Computerized tests differ from paper-pencil tests. Seven essential strategies provide you with ways to boost your computerized test performance.

- Tests not only provide you with a grade, but they also provide you with valuable feedback for assessing, modifying, or changing your learning strategies for even greater learning and performance on tests.

3 *Identify and explain effective strategies for managing test anxiety.*

- Test anxiety is excessive stress that affects performance. Symptoms of test anxiety may be physical, emotional, cognitive, or behavioral.

- Four common sources of test anxiety include: underpreparedness, past experiences, fear of failure, and poor test-taking skills.

- Test anxiety is a learned behavior that can be "unlearned" by using effective test anxiety management strategies before and during a test.

4 *Identify and explain ways to use mnemonics to prepare for tests.*

- Mnemonics are memory tools that serve as bridges to help you recall information from long-term memory.

- Five kinds of mnemonics can be used effectively for academic materials: acronyms, acrostics, word associations, picture associations, and the Loci Method.

- For any mnemonic to work effectively, you need to learn the mnemonic in its exact form and practice translating the mnemonic into the words or items it represents.

Multiple Choice

_____ 1. Effective use of mnemonics involves
  a. creating mnemonics only for information that is otherwise difficult to recall.
  b. creating acronyms and acrostics for every chapter in your textbook.
  c. limiting the use of mnemonics to information that appears in lists.
  d. all of the above.

_____ 2. Which of the following statements is *not* true about test-taking skills?
  a. Effective review strategies focus only on reviewing notes and homework assignments.
  b. Assessing the effectiveness of your study strategies before and after taking tests can provide you with valuable information.
  c. A final review before a test should occur as close to the test time as possible.
  d. You should avoid taking a computerized test when you are rushed for time.

_____ 3. A person with an external locus of control
  a. accepts responsibility for his or her situations and circumstances.
  b. shows a strong sense of self-confidence and control.
  c. blames others for his or her lack of success.
  d. reflects a strong intrapersonal intelligence.

_____ 4. Effective test-preparation skills
  a. reduce the necessity to cram for tests and use rote memory techniques.
  b. include time-management and goal-setting techniques.
  c. involve making summary notes and predicting, writing, and answering practice test questions.
  d. include all of the above.

_____ 5. In a five-day study plan, you
  a. begin by listing the topics and materials you need to review.
  b. use the same steps that you use to write effective goals.
  c. may set aside more than one study block for each day in the plan.
  d. do all of the above.

_____ 6. Which of the following statements is *not* true about test anxiety?
  a. A person's self-esteem and locus of control may contribute to test anxiety.
  b. Test anxiety can be productive and beneficial for many students.
  c. A person's lack of test preparation and test-taking skills may trigger test anxiety.
  d. Test anxiety is a learned behavior that can be altered, eliminated, or "unlearned."

_____ 7. Cramming
  a. is a survival technique used for under-preparedness.
  b. uses most of the Memory Principles.
  c. processes large amounts of information efficiently.
  d. is usually effective when used the day before a test.

_____ 8. Which of the following is *not* an effective test-preparation or a test-taking strategy?
  a. Leave some questions temporarily unanswered when taking a test.
  b. Read directions and questions carefully to avoid unnecessary mistakes.
  c. Use systematic desensitization activities to replace negative reactions with positive ones.
  d. Your original answer is usually the correct one, so avoid returning to questions to change the original answer.

Definitions

On separate paper, write a definition for the following terms. Each answer should include one or two sentences.

1. Internal locus of control
2. Acronym
3. Summary notes
4. Test anxiety

Short-Answer Questions

On separate paper, answer the following questions. Include details and chapter terminology in your answers.

1. Explain how associations are used in the first three levels of response for answering test questions.
2. Discuss four specific test-taking strategies that you can use to boost your test performance.
3. What are the advantages and disadvantages of using mnemonics such as acronyms and acrostics?

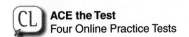
ACE the Test
Four Online Practice Tests

Online Resources

7 Strengthening Your Reading Skills

LEARNING OBJECTIVES

1 Explain how to use levels of reading, reading goals, and essential reading strategies when you read college textbooks.

2 Explain how to survey different kinds of reading materials and why surveying is important.

3 Explain how to identify and use paragraph elements (topics, main ideas, and key details) to strengthen reading skills.

Chapter Outline

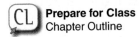

Prepare for Class
Chapter Outline

4 ▶ *Explain the importance of learning
definitions of terminology and
discuss strategies to use to identify
definitions in paragraphs.*

Strengthening your reading skills requires a variety of reading strategies, flexibility, and reading goals as you work with different kinds of textbooks and different levels of reading. Surveying before you conduct in-depth reading is a strategy that provides you with an overview and helps you establish schemas for new information. Working with paragraph elements, such as topics, main ideas, supporting details, definitions of terminology and meanings of unfamiliar words strengthens your reading skills and comprehension. Applying the skills in this chapter will increase your textbook reading performance and comprehension.

CHAPTER 7 PROFILE

Strengthening Reading Skills

CL **Improve Your Grade**
Chapter 7 Profile

ANSWER, **SCORE**, and **RECORD** your profile before you read this chapter. If you need to review the process, refer to the complete directions given in the profile for Chapter 1 on page 4.

ONLINE: You can complete the profile and get your score online at this textbook's website.

	YES	NO
1. Before I begin reading, I create a reading goal and a plan of action so I know what I intend to accomplish.		
2. I have one style of reading that I use with all reading materials.		
3. I do not waste time when I begin reading a new chapter; I start on the first page and read until I reach the end of the chapter.		
4. I skim through the chapter, read the chapter review questions, and read the summary before I start reading the chapter.		
5. I examine or preview the front and back sections of new textbooks before I begin using the textbook.		
6. When I read textbook chapters, I highlight or mark main ideas and important details in paragraphs.		
7. Finding a main idea or topic sentence in paragraphs is often confusing or difficult for me to do.		
8. I use different kinds of clues in sentences to help me identify the definitions of course-specific terminology or unfamiliar words.		
9. I create definition cards or vocabulary sheets that I can use to study and review course-specific terminology.		
10. I am confident in my ability to use reading and vocabulary strategies to strengthen my reading skills.		

QUESTIONS LINKED TO THE CHAPTER LEARNING OBJECTIVES:

Questions 1, 2: objective 1   Questions 8, 9: objective 4
Questions 3–5: objective 2   Question 10:   all objectives
Questions 6, 7: objective 3

THE READING PROCESS

1 *Explain how to use levels of reading, reading goals, and essential reading strategies when you read college textbooks.*

As a college student, you will spend thousands of hours reading thousands of textbook pages filled with information you will be required to learn. You cannot afford to spend your valuable time reading page after page in the *automatic pilot mode*, which is a state of mind in which you mechanically go through specific motions without registering information into your memory.

Reading is an active process of inputting information, encoding meaning, and creating associations that help you learn information from printed text. If you rush the process, do not take time to check your understanding, do not consciously make associations or pause to allow information to integrate or consolidate, you may find the need to reread the information several times before the information makes sense to you. Developing and strengthening your college-level reading skills will save you time and increase your academic performance.

 Improve Your Grade
Online Practice 1:
Levels of Reading

Levels of Reading

Making sense of what you read does not occur automatically. With some reading materials, you are able to read and quickly grasp the meaning of new information without much effort or struggle, yet with other reading materials, you need to work to understand, process, store, retrieve, and use the information. **Figure 7.1** shows four *different levels of reading*. **Levels of reading**—which include recreational, overview, thorough, and comparative—represent different reading skills and reading goals for different kinds of reading material. Using the correct level of reading for your college textbooks reflects your purpose and affects your ability to comprehend and use textbook information.

Overview Reading

Overview reading is the process of skimming or surveying reading materials without interruption in order to form a big picture or create a schema for the topic before engaging in thorough reading. Overview reading creates a mindset for more in-depth learning that will follow. You can use overview reading to:

▌ Survey a new textbook, chapter, or a test.

▌ Get a sense of the flavor of a short story, essay, play, or short excerpt by reading without stopping or pausing to analyze. This type of overview reading often stirs your imagination, creates an emotional experience to the words, immerses you in the material, and keeps the unity of the plot and the characters' actions moving steadily forward.

▌ Get a sense of the material in a difficult or complex section or chapter of a textbook without focusing on immediately understanding the details. Reading *slowly* all the way through can provide you with basic background information, lay a foundation for more thorough reading, and alert you to sections that seem confusing or complicated.

TERMS TO KNOW

levels of reading *p. 185*
overview reading *p. 185*
thorough reading *p. 186*
surveying *p. 190*
appendix *p. 191*
glossary *p. 191*
index *p. 191*
topic *p. 194*
main idea *p. 195*
topic sentence *p. 195*
supporting details *p. 197*
word clues *p. 201*
punctuation clues *p. 201*
word structure clues *p. 204*
context clues *p. 205*

 Improve Your Grade
Online Flashcards
Glossary

CONCEPT CHECK 7.1

Do you ever spend time reading a textbook only to discover you do not remember what you just read? Why do you think this happens?

Levels of reading—which include recreational, overview, thorough, and comparative—represent different reading skills and reading goals for different kinds of reading material.

CONCEPT CHECK 7.2

Is there a need for you to use all four levels of reading in your college courses? Why or why not?

Overview reading is the process of skimming or surveying reading materials without interruption in order to form a big picture or create a schema for the topic before engaging in thorough reading.

CONCEPT CHECK 7.3

When is overview reading appropriate for college textbooks? When is it not?

FIGURE 7.1

Levels of Reading

Levels of Reading	Description
Recreational Reading	▌ Use to read newspapers, magazines, short stories, poetry, or fiction. ▌ Read to be entertained, read for pleasure, or read to stay updated on current events.
Overview Reading	▌ Use for new material or difficult material. ▌ Survey or skim to create a *big picture* or framework before reading thoroughly. ▌ Read through difficult material uninterrupted and without stalling to become familiar with the topic before beginning thorough reading.
Thorough Reading	▌ Use for textbook or course-related materials. ▌ Use reading flexibility to adjust to levels of difficulty. ▌ Read slowly and systematically to allow your brain time to acquire and process new information and skills. ▌ Read to understand paragraph structures, organizational patterns, and to identify important information to record in notes. ▌ Use elaborative rehearsal strategies to practice new information.
Comparative Reading	▌ Use for two or more articles, excerpts, or books on the same subject. ▌ Compare or contrast, organize, and analyze for similarities and differences in points of view, rationale, implications, interpretations, models, or approaches.

Reading Flexibility for Thorough Reading

Thorough reading is the process of reading slowly and systematically in order to comprehend and process printed information. *Thorough reading* requires some flexibility on your part as you adjust to various levels of difficulty in both content and readability. Some textbooks are easy to read and understand; others require a considerable amount of attention and effort. In any given textbook, you may be able to read some sections more quickly, and then you need to slow down the reading process for more difficult sections.

> **Thorough reading** is the process of reading slowly and systematically in order to comprehend and process printed information.

Selecting an appropriate amount of material to read before pausing to think about or work with information further prevents overloading your working memory or going into *automatic pilot*, which results in little or no information registering in your memory. *Chunking* information into meaningful sized units requires reading flexibility. By using appropriate chunks of information, you give your working memory sufficient time to grasp, associate, and integrate information for understanding. The size of chunks of information will differ among students because of varying levels of reading and vocabulary skills, degrees of familiarity with subject and the specialized terminology, differences in background knowledge, and varying interest and motivational levels. **Figure 7.2** shows general reading flexibility guidelines to use for reading materials with different levels of difficulty or complexity.

CONCEPT CHECK 7.4

How does thorough reading differ from overview reading? Which of these two do you use more frequently?

FIGURE 7.2

Reading Flexibility Guidelines

Level of Difficulty	Kinds of Textbooks or Reading Materials	Reading Length
Easy	▌ Textbooks for career guidance, personal growth, developmental writing, personal health, literature, composition, or public speaking ▌ Fiction such as short stories, plays, or poetry	Stop at the end of each *page* to think about the information, create a visual image of the material, associate it with other information, formulate questions, or take notes.
Average	▌ Textbooks for history, sociology, economics, psychology, business, anthropology or political science ▌ Study guides or procedure manuals	Stop at the end of each *paragraph* to think about the information, create a visual image of the material, create associations, formulate questions, identify main ideas and important details, define terminology, or use some form of notetaking.
Difficult	▌ Textbooks for math, geology, computer science, chemistry, physics, anatomy and physiology, and other sciences ▌ Research journals, research studies, or professional articles	Stop at the end of each *sentence* or *group of sentences* to check your understanding, think about the information, create associations, formulate questions, define terminology, use some form of notetaking, or possibly work an example or practice the skill.

REFLECTIVE WRITING 7.1

 **Improve Your Grade**
Reflective Writing 7.1

On separate paper, in a journal, or online at this textbook's website, respond to the following questions.

1. What are your reading habits and interests? How often do you engage in recreational reading? What kinds of materials do you enjoy reading?

2. What type of reading is difficult or challenging for you? What specific difficulties do you encounter frequently?

Reading Goals and Plans of Action

Creating reading goals activates working memory. Your central executive responds to goal-oriented behavior and plans of action. Creating reading goals reflects your intention, your purpose, and your desired outcomes.

As you learn to work with a wide variety of textbooks, you will create numerous reading goals specific to the structure, subject matter, and level of complexity of each textbook. In Chapter 8, you will learn about strategies to strengthen comprehension as well as reading strategies to use in science, math, social science, and literature textbooks. **Figure 7.3** shows types of reading goals and plans of action that you can use to work with any of your textbooks.

CONCEPT CHECK 7.5

What specific reading goal do you have right now as you read this chapter? How does specifying a reading goal and a plan of action affect your reading performance?

FIGURE 7.3

Reading Goals and Plans of Action

▌ **Goal:** Become familiar with the textbook's organization and special features.
▌ **Plan of Action:** Survey the textbook at the beginning of the term.

▌ **Goal:** Get an overview of a chapter's structure, content, and length and create a "big picture" of the chapter.
▌ **Plan of Action:** Survey the chapter before reading thoroughly.

▌ **Goal:** Understand the main ideas and important details of each paragraph before continuing to read new paragraphs.
▌ **Plan of Action:** Underline or highlight main idea sentences and only key words in important details.

▌ **Goal:** Identify and understand terminology and definitions.
▌ **Plan of Action:** Use strategies to identify definitions; circle terms and underline key words in their definitions; create definition cards or vocabulary sheets.

▌ **Goal:** Identify and understand relationships, such as cause-effect, comparison-contrast, or chronological sequences.
▌ **Plan of Action:** Make notes in the margin or separate notes to show the relationships among key concepts or ideas; convert paragraphs into visual notes.

▌ **Goal:** Practice rehearsing and reviewing the important information in the chapter.
▌ **Plan of Action:** Create study tools to use in the rehearsal and review stages of learning.

Essential Reading Strategies

CONCEPT CHECK 7.6

Which Principles of Memory are used for the textbook reading strategies that appear in Figure 7.4?

Reading for understanding is a complex process that involves many cognitive functions. As you read a chunk of information, your working memory retrieves related information to help you understand new information. Working memory then integrates the new information with retrieved information and returns the unit of information back into long-term memory and the appropriate schemas. This interaction and exchange of information between the memory systems happens quickly and continually throughout the reading process. **Figure 7.4** shows nine Essential Strategies for Reading Textbooks. You can use these strategies to assist working memory with the process of reading.

FIGURE 7.4

Essential Strategies for Reading Textbooks

▌ **Begin with an attitude to learn.** Approaching a reading assignment with a positive, inquisitive, receptive attitude sends signals to working memory that this information is important.

▌ **Create reading goals for different reading stages and kinds of information.** Know your intention and what you want to accomplish before you begin any type of reading.

▌ **Be patient and do not rush the reading process.** Reading is an intake and an encoding process that requires time for your mind to mull over, absorb, process, and integrate the new information. Attempting to read quickly often results in rapid decay or fading of information without ever processing it.

▌ **Relate new information to existing schemas in your long-term memory.** Thinking about associations and linking different chunks of information lead to greater comprehension. Ask questions such as *What do I already know about this topic? How is it like and different from previous learning or what I have experienced? What are the important points and details?*

▌ **Recognize different levels of information as you read.** Strive to become an analytical reader who can recognize major themes, large concepts (schemas), main ideas, and important supporting details.

▌ **Learn terminology and definitions.** Understanding terminology lays the foundation for more complex learning and provides you with tools to communicate subject matter effectively to others.

▌ **Use spaced practice or spaced studying.** Spreading the reading process and activities over several different time periods actually cuts down total learning time. Avoid *marathon studying,* or in this case, *marathon reading,* which can overload your working memory.

▌ **Use elaborative rehearsal and active learning techniques as you read.** Actions that engage you in the reading and learning process help you maintain attention and concentration, encode information in new ways, and make stronger impressions of the information for memory.

▌ **Include some form of feedback as you study.** Use self-quizzing, reciting, and Look-Away Techniques to check the thoroughness and accuracy of your comprehension and memory.

CHECK POINT 7.1

ANSWERS APPEAR ON PAGE A4

Multiple Choice

_____ 1. Which of the following is *not* true about the reading process?
   a. Reading is a complex process of recalling and creating associations.
   b. You can use overview reading to survey or become familiar with new material before reading and studying the details more thoroughly.
   c. Chunking information into appropriate sizes of information that your working memory can process involves reading flexibility.
   d. One worthy reading goal involves knowing how to use skills so effectively that you can use your *automatic pilot* to read many of your college textbooks.

_____ 2. Effective textbook reading strategies include
   a. selecting meaningful and manageable sizes of information to process at one time.
   b. identifying a purpose and a process to use for reading a textbook.
   c. using spaced practice and including rehearsal techniques to reinforce concepts.
   d. all of the above.

 Improve Your Grade
Online Practice 2:
The Reading Process

SURVEYING READING MATERIALS

> **2** Explain how to survey different kinds of reading materials and why surveying is important.

Surveying is the process of previewing or skimming information to get an overview. As you learned in the section on overview reading, you can use surveying to get the "big picture" and set up schemas for all kinds of reading materials. You can also use surveying to preview tests. Surveying is an effective part of the reading process because surveying:

Surveying is the process of previewing or skimming information to get an overview.

- Enhances your motivation and your interest in the material
- Breaks inertia or the tendency to procrastinate about starting the reading process
- Boosts confidence in your ability to master new material
- Provides you with a general idea about the length and difficulty level of the material
- Helps you set realistic goals and manage your reading and studying time effectively

Surveying a Textbook

Surveying a new textbook before you begin reading specific chapters acquaints you with the book's philosophy, organization, and special features, and it provides you with suggestions for using the book more effectively. Surveying a textbook is a process that usually requires less than thirty minutes of your time at the beginning of the term. **Figure 7.5** shows the parts of a textbook to survey.

The Table of Contents

The **table of contents** provides you with an overview of the topics in the textbook, the organization of the topics (chronological or thematic), chapter headings and subheadings, page numbers, and other textbook features. Carefully examine the table of contents as it is the "roadmap" for the textbook. You can use the table of contents to quickly locate a chapter, view the major subheadings in the chapter, or check the length of chapters you are assigned to read.

The Introductory Materials

The **introductory materials** may include sections titled *Preface, Introduction, To the Teacher,* and *To the Student.* The **preface** (pronounced *prĕf' is,* not *prē face'*) or the *introduction* provides insight into the philosophy, objectives, and structure of the book, and may include background information about the author. While the sec-

---

CONCEPT CHECK 7.7

Even though surveying requires little of your time, how does it benefit you?

CONCEPT CHECK 7.8

Look at the first few pages of any textbook. What information appears on the title page and the copyright page?

CONCEPT CHECK 7.9

What are the front sections of a textbook that you should examine and read during the survey process?

CONCEPT CHECK 7.10

If students do not take time to read introductory information in their textbooks, what kind of valuable information will they miss?

Improve Your Grade
Online Practice 3:
Surveying a Textbook

FIGURE 7.5

Surveying a Textbook

1. **Front Matter:** title page, copyright page, table of contents, and introductory information

2. **Back Matter:** appendix, glossary, references/bibliography, and the index

tion titled *To the Teacher* may be interesting to read to see how the book is marketed to instructors, the section titled *To the Student* is of greater importance to you. Read the student-oriented introductory materials carefully for valuable suggestions, study strategies, and explanations of textbook features that will help you learn the textbook content and use the book effectively.

The Appendix

The **appendix** is the part in the back of a book that contains supplementary materials that were not included within the chapters. In a history textbook, for example, the Bill of Rights and the Constitution are important documents. However, due to their length, they may appear as supplementary materials in the appendix so as not to break the flow or disrupt the overall structure of the chapter. The appendix might also include answer keys; additional exercises; practice tests; supplementary readings; or important tables, graphs, charts, or maps. Textbooks with a wide variety of supplementary materials may have several appendixes.

The **appendix** is the part in the back of a book that contains supplementary materials that were not included in the chapters of the book.

CONCEPT CHECK 7.11

What kinds of materials appear in the appendixes of your various textbooks?

The Glossary

The **glossary** is a mini-dictionary in the back of a book that contains definitions of course-specific terminology. The glossary appears after the appendix. Definitions in a glossary are limited to the word meanings used in the textbook. (Use a standard college dictionary to locate multiple meanings of terminology.) Bold, italic, or colored print within textbook chapters often indicates words that appear in the glossary. If your textbook does not have a glossary, you can create your own glossary for each chapter. Use the following strategies with textbooks that have a glossary.

The **glossary** is a mini-dictionary in the back of a book that contains definitions of course-specific terminology.

CONCEPT CHECK 7.12

In addition to looking up definitions for terminology, what other ways can you make good use of a glossary?

▌ Each time you see words in special print in a chapter, review the glossary definitions. Sometimes the glossary definitions provide more details or more directly clarify the terminology.

▌ As you encounter terminology as you read your chapters, place a star next to or highlight those terms in the glossary. Use the glossary as a review tool to prepare for tests.

▌ Make separate definition cards or vocabulary sheets with the definitions of key terms to review to prepare for tests.

The Index

The **index** is an alphabetical listing of significant topics that appear in the book. The index is one of the most frequently used sections in the back of a textbook. You can use the index to quickly locate pages throughout the textbook that refer to a specific topic. In some textbooks you might find a *subject index*, an *author index*, or an *index of illustrations*. Frequently, topics are cross-referenced so they appear in more than one place in the index. The following strategies will help you use the index effectively:

The **index** is an alphabetical listing of significant topics that appear in the book.

CONCEPT CHECK 7.13

When might you need to refer to an index? How can it save you time?

▌ When you hear an unfamiliar term during a class discussion or lecture, write the word in your notes or in the margin of your textbook. After class, locate the term in the index of your book and read the pages indicated for explanations.

▌ When you are assigned a specific topic for a research paper, an essay, a writing assignment, a project, or a test, begin by locating the topic in the index. Then turn to the page numbers provided in the index and read or review the information.

EXERCISE 7.1

Surveying This Textbook

PURPOSE: Surveying a textbook takes fifteen to thirty minutes. The time spent surveying familiarizes you with the textbook structure and features and helps you use the textbook more effectively.

DIRECTIONS: Survey the front and the back section of this textbook. Then answer the following questions on separate paper.

1. Read the chapter titles in the Table of Contents. Which chapters contain the skills you feel you most need to learn or improve?

2. What did you learn from reading the introductory information? Had you previously read this infor-mation? If yes, how did it help familiarize you with this textbook? If not, how could this information have helped you use this textbook more effectively earlier?

3. What kind of information appears in the appendixes?

4. The glossary for this textbook is online. Have you used the online glossary and flashcards yet? What, if any, system or study tools have you started for working with terms and definitions?

5. How have you made use of the index so far this term?

Surveying a Chapter

Surveying a chapter before beginning the process of careful, thorough reading is a *warm-up* activity you can use at the beginning of a study block to help you focus your mind, create interest, and form a *big picture* of the chapter.

The benefits of surveying a chapter are numerous, yet doing so generally requires fewer than twenty minutes. For longer chapters, you can modify the pro-cess by surveying as many pages of the chapter as you think you can realistically cover in one or two study blocks; survey the remaining pages at the beginning of a future study block. **Figure 7.6** shows the parts of a chapter to include in surveying.

CONCEPT CHECK 7.14

What should you examine when you survey a chapter? How long should the process take you?

EXERCISE 7.2

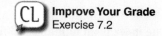

Surveying a Chapter

PURPOSE: Surveying activates working memory, eases you into a new chapter, creates a mindset for a new topic, and provides an overview of a chapter.

DIRECTIONS: Survey a chapter in this textbook that you have not yet read. Look at the chapter features that are shown in Figure 7.6. On separate paper, answer the following questions.

1. Which introductory features helped you begin to formulate a *big picture* of the chapter?

2. How long did it take you to survey the entire chap-ter? If you spent more than twenty minutes survey-ing the chapter, did you get sidetracked and begin some in-depth reading?

3. Which parts of the chapter provided you with the most information and helped you become most familiar with the content?

4. What do you find are the benefits of surveying a chapter before you begin thorough reading?

FIGURE 7.6

Surveying a Chapter

▌ **Introductory Materials:** Read the title of the chapter carefully; take a moment to think about the topic and relate the topic to information you already know. Read any lists, paragraphs, or visual materials that state the objectives for the chapter or introduce the chapter's content.

▌ **Headings and Subheadings:** Different print colors or fonts and different formats differentiate headings from subheadings. Move through the chapter by glancing over the headings and subheadings to see the "skeleton" structure of the chapter. Later, if you wish, you can use the headings and the subheadings to create a chapter outline.

▌ **Visual Materials:** Examine visual materials, such as charts, graphs, diagrams, pictures, and photographs. Read the information that appears with the visual materials.

▌ **Marginal Notes:** Marginal notes may be brief explanations, short definitions, lists of key points or objectives, or study questions that appear in the margins of the textbook pages. Marginal notes provide you with background details and emphasize important points to learn.

▌ **Terminology:** Skim over the terminology to get a general idea of terms you will need to learn. During surveying, do not spend time reading definitions for all the terminology.

▌ **End-of-the-Chapter Materials:** Read the chapter summary, list of key concepts, chapter review questions, or any other end-of-the-chapter materials. These materials highlight or summarize the important concepts and information you should learn in the chapter.

Surveying an Article or an Essay

Using surveying to preview an article, an excerpt, an essay, or any other short reading requires a minimal amount of time but can provide you with valuable information. Use the following steps to survey short readings:

1. *Think about the title.* Without reading the article or essay, what does the title mean to you? What do you predict that article will be about? What understanding or opinions do you already have about the subject?

2. *Identify the author.* If you are familiar with the author, think about the information you already know about the author. If there is a footnote or a byline about the author's affiliations with specific groups or organizations, additional publications, or other personal information, read it carefully and think of ways it might relate to the subject matter and the author's point of view.

3. *Read and think about any introductory material.* Introductory material for short articles often provides necessary background information about the topic and/or the author.

4. *Read the first paragraph carefully.* The thesis statement, the main point or purpose of the entire article, often appears in this paragraph.

5. *Skim through the rest of the article.* Read the headings, subheadings, and side notes.

6. *Read the concluding paragraph.* The concluding paragraph often restates the thesis statement and summarizes the main ideas in the article.

> **CONCEPT CHECK 7.15**
>
> Even though articles and essays are shorter, why is surveying still beneficial?

CHECK POINT 7.2

ANSWERS APPEAR ON PAGE A4

True or False?

_____ 1. Not taking the time to survey reading materials may reduce motivation, reduce your ability to relate information quickly to a schema, and increase procrastination.

_____ 2. Surveying is a process that is used only to become familiar with the front and back sections of a new textbook.

_____ 3. Since the table of contents of your textbook contains limited information of importance, you can skip surveying this section except for science textbooks.

_____ 4. Surveying a chapter involves reading headings, subheadings, visual materials, all the marginal notes, all the definitions, and all the review questions.

Improve Your Grade
Online Practice 4:
Surveying

GROUP PROCESSING:
A COLLABORATIVE LEARNING ACTIVITY

Form groups of three or four students. Then complete the following directions.

1. Individually, think of the last complete chapter that you read in any one of your textbooks. On separate paper, make a list of things you do when you read a chapter. Try to explain in chronological order how you go about completing a chapter.

2. Put all the lists together so that you and the members of your group can compare them. Do any of you use the same process? What do the lists have in common? Which approach seems most comprehensive? Be prepared to share your discussion with the rest of the class.

PARAGRAPH ELEMENTS

> 3 *Explain how to identify and use paragraph elements (topics, main ideas, and key details) to strengthen reading skills.*

For most textbooks, *thorough reading* involves reading one paragraph at a time; stopping to understand, analyze, and digest the important information in the paragraph; and then moving on to the next paragraph to repeat the process. You can understand the contents of a paragraph more easily when you can identify the following three paragraph elements and see their relationship to each other:

1. *The topic of the paragraph:* the subject
2. *The main idea of the paragraph:* the author's main point
3. *The important details of the paragraph:* details that support the main idea

The Topic of a Paragraph

The **topic** of a paragraph is a word or a phrase that states the subject of a paragraph. Every paragraph has a topic that tells what the author is writing about in a para-

CONCEPT CHECK 7.16

What specific kinds of information (elements) should you look for in a paragraph? How are they related to each other?

CONCEPT CHECK 7.17

Topics are short: one word or phrase. What is the topic of the paragraph below?

The **topic** of a paragraph is a word or a phrase that states the subject of a paragraph.

graph. By identifying the topic, you activate working memory and pull an appropriate schema into your conscious mind.

As you read a paragraph, begin looking for details that tell more about, explain, or give examples of the topic. These details cluster together to form meaning. You can use the following strategies to identify the topic sentence of a paragraph:

▮ Use overview reading to read the entire paragraph without stopping.

▮ Ask yourself: *In one word or one phrase, what is this paragraph about?*

▮ If you cannot state the topic, glance through the paragraph again and ask yourself: *Is one word repeated several times in the paragraph? Does that word work as the topic?*

The Main Idea

The **main idea** of a paragraph states the author's most important point about the topic of the paragraph. The **topic sentence**, also called the *main idea sentence*, is the sentence in a paragraph that includes the topic and states the author's main point or main idea for the paragraph. Sometimes after you read a paragraph, you can quickly identify the topic sentence; other times, you may need to reread the paragraph and actively search for the most important sentence that represents the main idea of the paragraph. The topic sentence is an essential key for understanding the information in a paragraph. Use the following tips to help you locate the topic sentence:

▮ **The topic sentence is like an umbrella.** It needs to be broad enough for all of the other sentences and supporting details in the paragraph to "fit under it." In a well-written paragraph, each sentence relates to or supports the topic sentence. Ask yourself the following questions to help you identify the topic sentence.

- What is the topic (subject) of this paragraph?
- Is there a "big picture" or "umbrella sentence" that contains this topic word?
- What is the main idea the author wants to make about the topic? Which sentence states the main idea?
- Which sentence is large enough to encompass the content of the paragraph?
- Do all the important details in the paragraph fit under this sentence?

▮ **Examine the first, the last, and then the sentences in the middle of the paragraph.**

- *First Sentence:* Topic sentences appear most frequently as the first sentence of paragraphs. This is particularly true in textbooks.
- *Last Sentence:* If the first sentence is not the "umbrella sentence," check the last sentence. Sometimes the last sentence summarizes the main points of the paragraph and thus states the main idea.
- *Other Sentences:* If the first and the last sentences do not state the main idea, carefully examine each sentence in the body of the paragraph.

Understanding, integrating, and processing textbook information are processes that you cannot rush. Strategies that focus on analyzing key elements in paragraphs help you unlock the meaning of printed passages. What strategies do you use to increase your reading comprehension and manage your textbook assignments?

The **main idea** of a paragraph states the author's most important point about the topic of a paragraph.

The **topic sentence**, also called the *main idea sentence*, is the sentence in a paragraph that includes the topic and the author's main point for the paragraph.

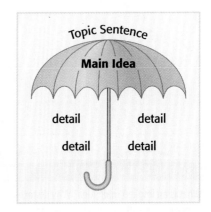

CONCEPT CHECK 7.18

How should you use highlighting to draw your attention to the topic sentence? How does this improve comprehension?

Highlight Topic Sentences

Highlighting or underlining the complete topic sentence in a paragraph is one way to make it stand out in your mind. Read the paragraph about knowledge workers (topic) in Example 1. Notice how highlighting the topic sentence creates a clearer impression of the topic and the author's most important point about the paragraph.

Example 1

Topic: Knowledge Workers

Knowledge workers, including, for example, computer scientists, engineers, and physical scientists, pose special challenges for managers. They tend to work in high-technology firms and are usually experts in some abstract knowledge base. They often like to work independently and tend to identify more strongly with their profession than with any organization—even to the extent of defining performance largely in terms recognized by other members of their profession.

From Ricky Griffin, *Principles of Management*, p. 213. © 2007, Houghton Mifflin.

In Example 2, the first sentence is an example of the biological approach that may be used by psychologists; however, the second sentence clearly states the main idea and is the sentence to highlight.

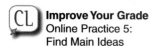

Improve Your Grade
Online Practice 5:
Find Main Ideas

Example 2

Topic: Biological Processes

Investigating the possibility that aggressive behavior or schizophrenia, for example, might be traceable to a hormonal imbalance or a brain disorder reflects the biological approach to psychology. As its name implies, the biological approach assumes that behavior and mental processes are largely shaped by biological processes. Psychologists who take this approach study the psychological effects of hormones, genes, and the activity of the nervous system, especially the brain. Thus, if they are studying memory, they might try to identify the changes taking place in the brain as information is stored there. Or if they are studying thinking, they might look for patterns of brain activity associated with, say, making quick decisions or reading a foreign language . . .

From Bernstein, *Psychology*, 5th ed., p. 3. © 2002, Houghton Mifflin.

Write Implied Main Ideas in the Margin

CONCEPT CHECK 7.19

What is an implied main idea? Why do textbooks infrequently use implied main ideas?

On occasion, you will encounter a paragraph that has *no stated main idea,* which means you will not find a topic sentence in the paragraph. This occurs when the main idea is *implied.* If you are not able to locate a topic sentence after carefully examining the first sentence, the last sentence, and the sentences in the remainder of the paragraph, look carefully at the details in the paragraph. Draw your own conclusion about the main idea. Write the main idea in the margin. Example 3 shows a paragraph with an *implied* main idea.

Example 3

Topic: Written Records

Some of the world's earliest civilizations have left written records that we cannot yet decipher and might never be able to read. These include India's Harappan civilization, which was centered in the Indus valley from before 2500 to some time after 1700 BCE; and the Minoan civilization of the Aegean island of Crete, which flourished from roughly 2500 to about 1400 BCE; and the African civilization of Kush, located directly south of Egypt, which reached its age of greatness after 800 BCE; but with much earlier origins as a state. For many other early civilizations and cultures we have as yet uncovered no written records. This is the case of mysterious peoples who, between approximately 6000 BCE and the first century CE, painted and carved thousands of pieces of art on the rocks of Tassili n'Ajjer in what is today the central Saharan Desert. It is also true of the Olmec civilization of Mexico, which appeared around 1200 BCE.

Supporting details

Formulated Main Idea:

We cannot use written records to learn about some early civilizations.

From Alfred J. Andrea and James Overfield, *The Human Record, 3rd ed.*, p. 34. Copyright © 1998 by Houghton Mifflin Company. Used with permission.

Important Details

Supporting details in a paragraph are facts, explanations, causes and effects, examples, and definitions that develop, support, or prove the main idea. In a well-developed paragraph, the details in each sentence must relate to the topic and the topic sentence, which states the main idea. Your goal as a reader is to use *Selectivity* to identify the important details that you need to learn and the details that provide understanding but are not essential to learn. Use the following tips to identify important supporting details:

Supporting details in a paragraph are facts, explanations, causes and effects, examples, and definitions that develop, support, or prove the main idea.

CONCEPT CHECK 7.20

What kinds of information in a paragraph can function as supporting details? What can you do to create a stronger impression of these details?

▮ Ask yourself: If I needed to explain the main idea to someone, what details would I want to include in my explanation? You can *highlight or underline the key words or phrases* in that paragraph that you would use in your explanation.

▮ Identify specific details that can serve as *retrieval cues* or associations to trigger recall of information later from your long-term memory. If the paragraph has multiple examples, select several, but not all, of the examples as memory cues.

▮ Be selective. Do not mark words such as *to, and, with, also,* and *in addition* because they are not key memory trigger words. Also, you do not need to mark a key word or the topic that appears multiple times.

▮ Carefully examine bulleted lists of information and notes that appear in the margins of your textbook. Key supporting details to learn often appear in these lists or notes.

The purpose of marking your textbooks, which includes highlighting or underlining, is to draw your attention to the most important information to study and to reduce the amount of information you need to review. Excessive marking defeats the purpose, so always be selective and limit the amount of highlighting or underlining you use in each paragraph. In Example 4, notice how a student highlighted the topic sentence completely and used Selectivity to identify and highlight only key words or phrases.

Example 4

Topic: Stalactites

Stalactites are stony travertine structures, resembling icicles, that hang from cave ceilings. They form as water, one drop at a time, enter the roof of a cave through a crack and deposits minute amounts of calcium carbonate. Initially, the center of each growing stalactite is a hollow tube, resembling a soda straw, through which the next drop enters the cave. Eventually precipitated travertine clogs the tube, causing the water to drip down the stalactite's outer surface, where it continues to deposit travertine and creates the irregular icicle shape of a typical stalactite.

From Chernicoff, Fox. *Essentials of Geology,* p. 203. © 2003, Houghton Mifflin.

EXERCISE 7.3

 **Improve Your Grade**
Exercise 7.3

Identifying Topic Sentences and Supporting Details

PURPOSE: Identifying the topic sentence of a paragraph provides a structure for identifying and understanding the important supporting details that you need to know.

DIRECTIONS: By yourself or with a partner, read each of the following paragraphs carefully. Highlight or underline the sentence that you think is the topic sentence for each paragraph. Then, selectively highlight or underline key supporting details.

1. In a family with two adults and children, for example, one of the adults may already have a job and the other may be choosing between working at home or working outside the home. This decision may be very sensitive to the wage and perhaps the cost of child care or consuming more prepared meals. In fact, the increased number of women working outside the home may be due to the increased opportunities and wages for women. The increase in the wage induces workers to work more in the labor market. Economists have observed a fairly strong wage effect on the amount women work.

From Taylor, *Economics,* pp. 327, 329. Copyright © 2004, Houghton Mifflin Co.

2. The human brain in late adulthood, however, is smaller and slower in its functioning than the brain in early adulthood. This reduction is thought to be caused by the death of neurons, which do not regenerate. Neurons die at an increasing rate after age 60. The proportion of neurons that die varies across different parts of the brain. In the visual area, the death rate is about 50 percent. In the motor areas, the death rate varies from 20 to 50 percent. In the memory and reasoning areas, the death rate is less than 20 percent. The production of certain neurotransmitters also declines with age.

From Payne and Wenger, *Cognitive Psychology,* p. 359. Copyright © 2004, Houghton Mifflin Co.

3. A solid has a definite shape and volume. In a *crystalline* solid, the molecules are arranged in a particular repeating pattern. This orderly arrangement of molecules is called a *lattice*. The molecules are bound to each other by electrical forces. Upon heating, the molecules gain kinetic energy and vibrate about their positions in the lattice. The more heat that is added, the stronger the vibrations become. When the melting point is reached, additional energy breaks apart the bonds that hold the molecules in place. As bonds break, holes are produced in the lattice, and nearby molecules can move toward the holes. As more and more holes are produced, the lattice becomes significantly distorted.

From Shipman et al., *An Introduction to Physical Science, 10th ed.,* p. 103. Copyright © 2003. Reprinted by permission of Houghton Mifflin Co.

CHECK POINT 7.3   ANSWERS APPEAR ON PAGE A4

True or False?

____ 1. A topic sentence is also known as a main idea sentence.

____ 2. In textbooks, the topic sentence appears most frequently as the last sentence in a paragraph.

____ 3. To identify a topic of a paragraph requires that you first identify the main idea.

____ 4. When highlighting or underlining supporting details in a paragraph, Selectivity is required to help you avoid over-marking.

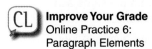

Improve Your Grade
Online Practice 6:
Paragraph Elements

EXERCISE 7.4

Textbook Case Studies

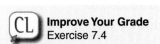

Improve Your Grade
Exercise 7.4

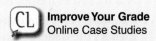

Improve Your Grade
Online Case Studies

DIRECTIONS:

1. Read each case study carefully. Respond to the question at the end of each case study by using *specific* strategies discussed in this chapter. Answer in complete sentences.

2. Write your responses on paper or online at the Student Website, Exercise 7.4. You will be able to print your online response or e-mail it to your instructor.

CASE STUDY 1: Justine reads all her textbooks the way that she reads paperback books. She begins at the beginning of the chapter and does not stop until she reaches the end of the chapter. She often finds that she needs to reread chapters two or three times before she can retain the information. What methods can Justine use to comprehend a textbook chapter better and spend less time rereading?

CASE STUDY 2: The instructor spent half the class time talking about a concept that was unfamiliar to Simon. Simon had not had a chance to read the last three chapters, so he thought perhaps the concept appeared in those chapters. When he sat down to work with a study partner, Simon started flipping through the chapters page by page and eventually located the section of information. What strategies would help Simon be a more efficient reader and student?

TERMINOLOGY AND VOCABULARY

 Explain the importance of learning definitions of terminology and discuss strategies to use to identify definitions in paragraphs.

Course-specific vocabulary and definitions are other details you will encounter in many college textbooks. Understanding course-specific terminology and definitions is one powerful way to strengthen your reading skills and lay a foundation for understanding the remainder of the paragraph. **Figure 7.7** summarizes five Essential Strategies for Working with Terminology.

As you read with an alert mind, you will notice many ways terminology and definitions appear in paragraphs. In Chapter 8, you will learn about different organizational patterns used in paragraphs; one such pattern is the definition pattern or definition paragraph. In a definition paragraph, the details throughout the paragraph define and explain one specific term. In other paragraphs, such as the paragraph in Example 5, you will find that more than one terminology word is defined. Example 5 shows how a student circled the terminology words and highlighted key words in the definitions.

CONCEPT CHECK 7.21

What strategies can you use to learn definitions for key terms?

FIGURE 7.7

Essential Strategies for Working with Terminology

▌ **Use bold or special print in textbooks to help identify terminology.** In most textbooks, the definition of the term is within the same sentence or in the following sentence.

▌ **Circle terminology words and highlight key words.** Circling the terminology words distinguishes them from other types of details in a paragraph, and selectively highlighting key words in the definition narrows your focus and reinforces the *paired associations.*

▌ **Use word clues and punctuation clues to identify the definitions.**

▌ **Use the textbook glossary to verify and learn more about the terminology words.**

▌ **Make definition cards or vocabulary sheets to recite, rehearse, and review definitions.**

Example 5

Topic: Changing Shape of the Earth's Continents

Have continents grown in more recent geologic time? Bordering North America on both the Atlantic and the Pacific coasts are rocks that are no more than 600 million years old. Recently gathered evidence indicates that many of these fault-bounded rock bodies, called ⟨**displaced terranes**,⟩ originated elsewhere but were transported by plate motion and attached, or *accreted*, to our continent by collisions. Some may have been island arcs that formed in an ocean basin and then were towed to a continental margin by subduction of the intervening ocean plate. Others are probably ⟨**microcontinents**,⟩ pieces of continental lithosphere broken from larger distant continents by rifting or transform faulting.

From Chernicoff, Fox. *Essentials of Geology*, p. 241. © 2003, Houghton Mifflin.

FIGURE 7.8

Common Word Clues in Definition Sentences

also	defined as	referred to as	known as	is/are called
is/are	to describe	mean/means	which is	or

Word Clues to Identify Definitions

A **word clue**, such as *defined as, is/are,* or *known as,* links the vocabulary word to its definition that appears in another part of the same sentence. In other words, a word clue links the two parts of a *paired association*. **Figure 7.8** shows word clues used frequently in sentences to define terminology.

When you search for the words in a sentence that define a word in bold or special print, *be selective*; do not automatically highlight all the surrounding words. Read and think carefully about which words are essential words for the definition. Remember, if the word is in special print and if your textbook has a glossary, the word will be defined clearly in the glossary. Refer to the glossary definition if you have difficulty separating the definition part of a sentence from other kinds of details.

In many textbooks, the terminology word appears first and is then followed by its definition. However, other sentence structures may be used. The definition may appear before the terminology word, or the terminology word may be inserted within parts of the definition. Reading and thinking carefully are essential for using information within a sentence to define a word. Following are two examples of using word clues to help locate definitions for terminology.

Word Clue: known as

For a time, researchers believed that anyone who displayed the pattern of aggressiveness, competitiveness, and nonstop work known as "Type A" behavior was at elevated risk for heart disease.

Word Clue: are called

Efforts to reduce, eliminate, or prevent behaviors that pose health risks and to encourage healthy behaviors are called health promotion.

From Bernstein, Nash. *Essentials of Psychology, 2nd ed.*, pp. 365 and 368. © 2002, Houghton Mifflin.

Punctuation Clues to Identify Definitions

Punctuation clues, such as commas, dashes, parentheses, and colons, signal the definitions of terminology within the sentence. The punctuation clues separate the definition from the other words in the sentence. Use the punctuation clues to help identify the words that are important parts of the definition and words that you should highlight for emphasis. Be aware, however, that each of these punctuation marks may serve other functions in sentences, so their appearance does not automatically mean they are functioning as definition clues. **Figure 7.9** shows the four kinds of punctuation clues with example sentences.

A **word clue**, such as *defined as, is/are,* or *known as,* links the vocabulary word to its definition that appears in another part of the same sentence.

CONCEPT CHECK 7.22

What are common word clues? How do word clues help you identify definitions?

Punctuation clues, such as commas, dashes, parentheses, and colons, signal the definitions of terminology within the sentence.

CONCEPT CHECK 7.23

What specific kinds of punctuation marks can help you locate definitions within a sentence? Do these punctuation marks *always* signal definitions? Explain.

FIGURE 7.9

Four Kinds of Punctuation Clues for Definitions

Punctuation Clue		Example Sentence with Example Highlighting
Commas	, ,	Stress may also intensify **functional fixedness**, the tendency to use objects for only one purpose.
Dashes	— —	**Chronic stressors**—stressors that continue over a long period of time—include such circumstances as living near a noisy airport, being unable to earn a decent living, residing in a high-crime neighborhood, being the victim of discrimination, and even enduring years of academic pressure.
Parentheses	( )	Stressors trigger a process that begins when the brain's hypothalamus activates a part of the autonomic nervous system, which stimulates the **medulla** (inner part) of the adrenal glands.
Colon	:	A related phenomenon is **catastrophizing**: dwelling on and overemphasizing the possible negative consequences of an event.

Source: Bernstein/Nash. *Essentials of Psychology, 2nd ed.,* pp. 351, 353, 355. © 2002, Houghton Mifflin.

EXERCISE 7.5

Using Punctuation and Word Clues

PURPOSE: Knowing how to use punctuation and word clues can help you identify the words in a sentence that define important terminology.

DIRECTIONS: Work with a partner to complete this exercise. In the following sentences, use punctuation and word clues to identify the definitions of the words in bold print. Underline or highlight the key words that define the terms. Be selective; include only words that are a part of the definition.

1. The unit of electric charge is called the **coulomb** (C), after Charles Coulomb (1736–1806), a French scientist who studied electrical effects. [p. 167]

2. Waves with relatively low frequencies, or long wavelengths, are known as **radio waves** and are produced primarily by causing electrons to **oscillate**, or vibrate, in an antenna. [p. 122]

3. The fourth and final factor in reaction rate is the possible presence of a **catalyst**, a substance that increases the rate of reaction but is not itself consumed in the reaction. [p. 326]

4. **Thermodynamics** means the dynamics of heat and deals with the production of heat, the flow of heat, and the conversion of heat to work. [p. 107]

5. The **neutron number** (N) is, of course, the number of neutrons in a nucleus. [p. 230]

6. The chemical reactivity of the elements depends on the order of the electrons in the energy levels in their atoms, which is called the **electron configuration**. [p. 272]

7. The outer shell of an atom is known as the **valence shell**, and the electrons in it are called the **valence electrons**. [p. 273]

From Shipman et al., *An Introduction to Physical Science, 10th ed.* Copyright © 2003. Reprinted by permission of Houghton Mifflin, Inc.

Definition Cards or Vocabulary Sheets

Because definitions of terminology from your textbook are so important, you can anticipate that knowing definitions will affect your performance on tests. More than 60 percent of most test questions are based directly on knowing and understanding the course terminology. To learn definitions and prepare for tests, preparing study tools to practice and review definitions is beneficial.

Create Definition Cards

One effective study tool involves using index cards to create a set of definition cards. On the front side of your index card, write the term. If you wish, include the chapter and the page number. On the back of your index card, write important information about the term. **Figure 7.10** shows an example of a definition card. To prepare for questions that evaluate your understanding of the terms, write three kinds of information on the backs of your cards:

- *The category to which the word belongs:* For example, write *A mnemonic*
- *The formal definition:* For example, write *A word or phrase made by using the first letter of key words in a list of items to remember.*
- *One or more additional details:* For example, write *Forms an association and works as a retrieval cue.*

Use your definition cards for self-quizzing and immediate feedback. Look at the front and then recite the information on the back. Turn the card over to check your accuracy. You can sort the cards into two piles: ones you know and ones you need to review further. If you anticipate fill-in-the-blank questions, reverse the order. Read the back and then *name and spell* the word on the front. Check your accuracy.

Create Vocabulary Sheets

Another way to study terminology and definitions is to create vocabulary sheets for each chapter. Vocabulary sheets are a form of *two-column notes.* In the left column, write the term. In the right column, write the three parts of a definition (the category, the definition, and one or more details). By creating vocabulary sheets, you create your own glossary of terms. **Figure 7.11** shows the beginning of a vocabulary sheet.

To study from a vocabulary sheet, cover up the right column with a piece of paper. Say the word and recite the definition. Remove the paper. Check your accuracy. Reverse the order. Cover the left column, read the right column, and then *say and spell* the term.

FIGURE 7.10

Example of a Definition Card

Front

Acronym

Back

— A Mnemonic

— A word or phrase made by using the first letter of key words in a list of items to remember

— Forms an association and works as a retrieval cue

FIGURE 7.11

Example of a Vocabulary Sheet

Terminology	Chapter 6
Acrostic	— A mnemonic — A word or phrase made by using the first letter of key words in a list of items to remember — Forms an association and works as a retrieval cue.
Acronym	

CONCEPT CHECK 7.24

How can you use definition cards to rehearse and review terminology and definitions?

CONCEPT CHECK 7.25

How does the information you write on vocabulary sheets differ from the information you write on definition note cards?

CONCEPT CHECK 7.26

What do you tend to do when you encounter an unfamiliar word when you read? Do you do something to figure out the meaning, or do you skip over the word?

Word structure clues involve using the meanings of prefixes, suffixes, base words, and roots in determine the general meaning of unfamiliar words.

EXERCISE 7.6

Definition Cards or Vocabulary Sheets

DIRECTIONS: Select any chapter in this textbook that you have already studied. Create a set of definition cards or vocabulary sheets for the terminology listed in the Terms to Know that appears in the front of the chapter. After creating your study tool, practice reciting the terminology and the definitions.

Meanings of Unfamiliar Words

Identifying and learning terminology and definitions definitely strengthen your reading skills and comprehension of paragraph-level information. However, paragraphs may contain other words, general words, that are unfamiliar to you. If you have limited understanding of a word in a paragraph, or if you just skip over an unfamiliar word, your understanding of the paragraph may be limited or inaccurate.

For example, do you know the meaning of the word *travertine*? If not, when you read the word in the previous Example 4 (page 198), did you skip over it, or did you use a dictionary to look up the meaning? Do you know the meaning of the words *accrete, subduction, lithosphere,* and *rifting* that were used in the previous Example 5 (page 200)? Any time you encounter unfamiliar words, recognize that understanding the meanings of those words can increase your understanding of the paragraph. **Figure 7.12** summarizes four Essential Strategies to Use with Unfamiliar Words. Use these strategies to increase your vocabulary and learn the meanings of unfamiliar words.

Use Word Structure Clues

Word structure clues involve using the meanings of prefixes, suffixes, base words, and roots to determine the general meaning of unfamiliar words. If using word structure clues results in a vague understanding of the word, refer to a dictionary

FIGURE 7.12

Essential Strategies to Use with Unfamiliar Words

▌ Use word clues and punctuation clues to identify definitions within the sentence.

▌ Use word structure clues to determine general meanings of words.

▌ Use context clues to determine general meanings of words.

▌ Use glossaries and dictionaries to look up meanings of unfamiliar words.

FIGURE 7.13

Word Structure Clues

WORD PARTS

prefixes	Units of meaning attached to the beginning of words
suffixes	Units of meaning attached to the end of words to indicate a specific part of speech (noun, verb, adjective, or adverb)
bases	English words that have meaning and can stand by themselves
roots	Units of meaning (often Greek or Latin) that do not form English words until other word parts are attached to them

prefix + Base Word or Root + suffix

re- + -ject + -ed

"back"   "throw"   past-tense verb ending

or glossary for a more complete definition. **Figure 7.13** shows the four word parts used in word structure clues plus a word structure model.

Using word structure clues to understand and recall terminology is an extremely valuable skill in science and health science courses, for much of the terminology used in those courses derives from Greek or Latin roots and word parts. Learning the meanings of structural word parts can save you time, increase your comprehension, and expand your vocabulary. For a list of prefixes, suffixes, and roots and their meanings, go to the Student Website, Topic In-Depth: Meaning of Word Parts.

CONCEPT CHECK 7.27

What courses have you taken in which knowing Greek or Latin roots or word parts helped you learn the vocabulary more readily? Give examples.

CL **Topic In-Depth**
Meaning of Word Parts

EXERCISE 7.7

Meanings of Roots

DIRECTIONS: Work with a partner or in a small group. Discuss the meaning of as many of the following word roots as possible:

anthro	derma	migra	phone	aqua	graph	ology
audio	helio	osteo	psych	biblio	hydro	ped
bio	macro	pathos	theo	cred	micro	phobia

Use Context Clues

Context clues are words in a sentence or in surrounding sentences that provide hints about the general meanings of unfamiliar words. By carefully reading the sentence with the unfamiliar word and then rereading the surrounding sentences, you can often pick up hints or context clues about the *general* meaning of the

Context clues are words in a sentence or in surrounding sentences that provide hints about the general meanings of unfamiliar words.

FIGURE 7.14

Kinds of Context Clues

Context Clue	Definition	Strategy	Example Sentence
Synonyms	words with exact or similar meanings	Try substituting a familiar word (a synonym) for the unfamiliar word.	***probity:*** The judge has a keen sense of recognizing a person's honesty and integrity. For that reason, the *probity* of the witness was not questioned.
Antonyms	words with opposite meanings	An unfamiliar word is understood because you understand its opposite.	***impenitent:*** Instead of showing shame, regret, or remorse, the con artist was *impenitent.*
Contrasts	words that show an opposite or a difference	Look for words such as *differ, different, unlike,* or *opposite of* to understand the differences.	***thallophyte:*** Because the fungi is a *thallophyte,* it differs from the other plants in the garden that have embedded roots and the rich foliage of shiny leaves and hardy stems.
Comparisons or Analogies	words or images that indicate a likeness or a similarity	Look for the commonality between two or more items.	***cajole:*** I sensed he was trying to *cajole* me. He reminded me of a salesman trying to sell me a bridge.
Examples	examples that show function, characteristics, or use of the term	Look for ways that the examples signal the meaning of the term.	***implosion:*** *Implosions* are not rare in Las Vegas. The most recent one collapsed an old, outdated casino to make room for a new megaresort. Dust and debris filled the air, but the nearby buildings suffered no damage.

CONCEPT CHECK 7.28

Why is it that sometimes when you encounter an unfamiliar word, you are able to get a sense of what the word means even though you cannot define it?

CONCEPT CHECK 7.29

Why does reading a paragraph with familiar words substituted for unfamiliar words improve comprehension? Describe times you have used this strategy.

word. Sometimes you simply get a "sense" of the meaning of a word by understanding the examples linked to it, relating it to personal experience, or drawing a logical conclusion. Other times, specific kinds of words signal the meaning of the unfamiliar. **Figure 7.14** shows five categories of words that often function as context clues to provide you with general meanings of unfamiliar words.

Once you have identified the meaning of an unfamiliar word, you can *substitute a familiar word for the unfamiliar word* to convert formal textbook language into a less formal, more personal conversational tone. Above each of the words in a paragraph that was unfamiliar to you, write a more common or familiar word. Reread the paragraph but substitute the common or familiar word for the unfamiliar word. The following example shows how this technique of substituting words adds clarity and improves comprehension of a difficult paragraph.

Few if any philosophies are as enigmatic [*puzzling*] as Daoism—the teachings of the Way (Dao). The opening lines of this school's greatest masterpiece, *The Classic of the Way and Virtue* [*morality*] (*Dao De Jing*), which is ascribed to [*associated with*] the legendary [*famous*] Laozi, immediately confront [*challenge*] the reader with Daoism's essential paradox [*contradiction*]: "The Way that can be trodden [*walked*] is not the enduring [*lasting*] and the unchanging Way. The name that can be named is not the enduring and unchanging name." Here is a philosophy that purports [*claims*] to teach the Way (of truth) but simultaneously [*at the same time*] claims that the True Way transcends [*exceeds*] human understanding. Encapsulated [*Contained*] within a little book of some five thousand words is a philosophy that defies [*resists*] definition, spurns [*rejects*] reason, and rejects words as inadequate.

From Alfred J. Andrea and James Overfield, *The Human Record, 3rd ed.*, p. 93. Copyright © 1998 by Houghton Mifflin Co. Used with permission.

REFLECTIVE WRITING 7.2

On separate paper, in a journal, or online at this textbook's website, respond to the following questions.

1. The reading process is complex and cannot be taught in one chapter of a textbook. However, by learning about and applying specific reading strategies, you can strengthen your reading skills. What strategies in this chapter will help you strengthen your reading skills?

2. On a scale of one to ten, with ten showing the most ability, how would you rate your ability to read and understand the textbooks you are currently using? What additional skills do you feel you need to acquire in order to rate yourself on an even higher level? Explain with details.

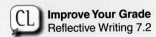
Improve Your Grade
Reflective Writing 7.2

EXERCISE 7.8

Links

PURPOSE: Effective study skills strategies support learning theories and understanding of how working memory processes information. Reminding yourself of *why* certain strategies are important provides you with a purpose for using the strategies.

DIRECTIONS: In a group of three or four students, discuss the following relationships:

1. The Principles of Memory—surveying materials
2. Adjusting reading rate—functions of working memory
3. Paired associations—terminology
4. Long-term memory schemas—paragraph elements

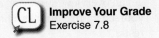
Improve Your Grade
Exercise 7.8

CHECK POINT 7.4

ANSWERS APPEAR ON PAGE A4

True or False?

_____ 1. Learning meanings of word parts can often help you learn terminology in health science and other science courses.

_____ 2. When you create study tools to rehearse and review terminology, they should show a category for the word, the definition, and at least one more detail that shows you understand the term.

_____ 3. You may be able to use word structure, punctuation, context, or word clues to determine the meaning of an unfamiliar word you encounter while reading.

_____ 4. Commas, quotation marks, semicolons, and dashes are the four common punctuation clues that help signal or identify definitions.

Improve Your Grade
Online Practice 7:
Terminology

LEARNING OBJECTIVES REVIEW

1 *Explain how to use levels of reading, reading goals, and essential reading strategies when you read college textbooks.*

- Reading is an active process of inputting information, encoding meaning, and creating associations—a process that cannot be rushed. By recognizing and using four levels of reading (recreational, overview, thorough, and comparative), you can adjust your reading goals and strategies to match the task.

- Reading flexibility guidelines suggest the length of material you should read before pausing to think about and work with the information.

- Reading goals activate working memory. Before starting a reading task, create a reading goal and a plan of action to make the best use of your time and achieve desired results.

- Nine essential reading strategies can help you strengthen your reading skills.

2 *Explain how to survey different kinds of reading materials and why surveying is important.*

- Surveying is the process of previewing or skimming to get an overview. Surveying can be used to familiarize yourself with textbooks, chapters, articles, essays, or tests.

- Surveying a textbook involves examining four parts in front and four parts in back of a textbook.

- Surveying a chapter involves examining six parts of the chapter before reading:
  - introductory materials
  - headings and subheadings
  - visual materials
  - marginal notes
  - terminology
  - end-of-chapter materials

- Surveying an article or an essay involves examining six parts of the printed materials.

3 *Explain how to identify and use paragraph elements (topics, main ideas, and key details) to strengthen reading skills.*

- Thorough reading for most textbooks involves reading one paragraph at a time and then pausing to analyze paragraph elements: topic, main ideas, and important details.

- The topic of a paragraph is the subject of the paragraph. The main idea states the author's most important point about the topic; it appears in the topic sentence. Strategies help you identify the topic and the topic sentence in a paragraph.

- Important supporting details in a paragraph include facts, explanations, causes and effects, examples, and definitions that develop, support, or prove the main idea.

4 ▸ *Explain the importance of learning definitions of terminology and discuss strategies to use to identify definitions in paragraphs.*

- Five essential strategies can help you work effectively with terminology:
  - Use bold or special print in textbooks to identify terminology.
  - Circle terminology words and highlight key words.
  - Use word clues and punctuation clues to identify the definitions.
  - Use the textbook glossary to verify and learn more about terminology words.
  - Make definition cards or vocabulary sheets to recite, rehearse, and review definitions.
- Use word structure and context clues to identify general meanings of unfamiliar words you encounter when you read.
- Substituting familiar words for unfamiliar words boosts your comprehension and recall ability.

CHAPTER 7 REVIEW QUESTIONS

ANSWERS APPEAR ON PAGE A4

True or False?

_____ 1. Learning the meanings of common prefixes, suffixes, and roots can sometimes help you unlock the general meanings of unfamiliar words you encounter in textbooks.

_____ 2. When you study from vocabulary sheets or definition cards, you are working with paired associations and using recitation and feedback.

_____ 3. Understanding the main idea of a paragraph helps you identify important details and understand the overall meaning of the paragraph.

_____ 4. One suggestion for saving time when you read is to skip over unfamiliar words as long as you understand the general meaning of the main idea of the paragraph.

_____ 5. When you use punctuation clues to define words, the definitions always appear between the two punctuation marks.

_____ 6. To read all college textbooks, you should first read through the entire chapter and then reread the chapter, stopping at the end of each page to take notes.

_____ 7. Marathon reading may overload your working memory and hinder your ability to process information effectively.

_____ 8. Overview reading involves identifying key ideas, determining the organization used in each paragraph, and analyzing the different parts of the overall topic.

Locating Definitions

In the following sentences, underline or highlight only the words in the sentence that define the term in bold print.

1. The advantage of the **binary system**, which uses only the digits 0 and 1, is that each position in a numeral contains only one of two values. (p. 134)
2. A **point** may be regarded as a location in space with no breadth, width, or length. (p. 253)
3. The property shared by these three numeration systems is that they are **additive**; that is, the values of the written symbols are added to obtain the number represented. (p. 118)
4. We have already studied **perimeter** (the length of the boundary of a polygon) and the area (the space enclosed by the polygon). (p. 395)
5. Primes that differ by 2 are called **twin primes**, and the smallest twin primes are 3 and 5. (p. 160)

From Bellow and Britton, *Topics in Contemporary Mathematics, 6th ed.* (Boston: Houghton Mifflin Co., 1997). Copyright © 1997. Reprinted by permission of Houghton Mifflin, Inc.

Short-Answer Questions

Write your answers on separate paper.

1. How does surveying assist working memory?
2. Why is it important to understand and be able to define course-specific terminology?

ACE the Test
Four Online Practice Tests

Online Resources

8 Learning from College Textbooks

LEARNING OBJECTIVES

1 Define active reading, and discuss active reading strategies and textbook reading systems to use with college textbooks.

2 Define and discuss the seven organizational patterns used to organize details in paragraphs.

3 Explain and use strategies to read and interpret six kinds of graphic materials.

Chapter Outline

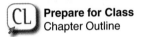 **Prepare for Class**
Chapter Outline

4 ▶ *Discuss strategies to use to read college textbooks for different disciplines and content areas.*

Many college students have reading habits and use techniques that they have established over many years of reading, yet those habits and techniques may be inadequate to handle the demands of college-level reading and comprehension. In this chapter, you will learn active reading strategies, which include selecting an effective reading system for your different textbooks, identifying and using different organizational patterns and graphic materials, and finally, using reading strategies specifically targeted for textbooks in different content areas. With the reading strategies in Chapter 7 and the strategies in this chapter, you can replace old reading habits and techniques with more effective ones designed to increase reading comprehension and performance.

CHAPTER 8 PROFILE

Learning from College Textbooks

ANSWER, **SCORE**, and **RECORD** your profile before you read this chapter. If you need to review the process, refer to the complete directions given in the profile for Chapter 1 on page 4.

ONLINE: You can complete the profile and get your score online at this textbook's website.

	YES	NO
1. I often go into "automatic pilot" when I read a textbook: I do not pay enough attention to the details and do not monitor my understanding.	_____	_____
2. The system I use to read textbooks includes surveying and some form of writing questions about the chapter content.	_____	_____
3. I use a variety of strategies when I read, and I adjust my strategies as needed to comprehend difficult-to-understand sections of information.	_____	_____
4. I use clue words and the order of details in paragraphs to identify the organizational pattern used by the authors.	_____	_____
5. I often have difficulty following the author's line of reasoning.	_____	_____
6. I know how to interpret information on pie charts, flow charts, tables, bar graphs, and line graphs.	_____	_____
7. I pose questions, compare data, and look for patterns and trends when I study visual materials.	_____	_____
8. I use the same reading strategies to read all of my textbooks.	_____	_____
9. I use different strategies to study factual information and procedural information.	_____	_____
10. I am confident in my ability to real all kinds of textbooks and select the most effective reading strategies for each textbook.	_____	_____

QUESTIONS LINKED TO THE CHAPTER LEARNING OBJECTIVES:

Questions 1–3: objective 1
Questions 4, 5: objective 2
Questions 6, 7: objective 3
Questions 8, 9: objective 4
Question 10:   all objectives

ACTIVE READING

 Define active reading, and discuss active reading strategies and textbook reading systems to use with college textbooks.

Comprehending what you read is a complex process that involves active learning and active reading. **Active reading** is the process of using effective strategies to engage working memory to achieve specific reading goals. Active reading places heavy demands on your working memory, demands your undivided attention, and cannot be done quickly or effortlessly. Your working memory requires time to:

▌ Attach meaning to printed words

▌ Associate chunks of new information with previously learned information

▌ Analyze information by identifying its individual parts, characteristics, patterns, and relationships

▌ Integrate information into existing schemas to form generalizations

▌ Evaluate the logic and accuracy of information

▌ Apply the information to new situations or to solve problems

Active Reading Strategies

Begin the process of becoming an active reader by committing yourself to the reading process. Create a mindset that reflects your intention to engage actively in the reading process to achieve your reading goals. **Figure 8.1** shows six Essential Strategies for Active Reading. You can use these strategies to improve your comprehension and your textbook reading performance.

REFLECTIVE WRITING 8.1

 Improve Your Grade
Reflective Writing 8.1

On separate paper, in a journal, or online at this textbook's website, respond to the following questions:

1. Which of your textbooks is the most challenging for you this term? Explain the kinds of challenges it presents and why the textbook is difficult for you to use effectively.

2. In a general sense, describe the current process you use to read textbook chapters.

Improve Your Grade
Online Flashcards
Glossary

Active reading is the process of using effective strategies to engage working memory to achieve specific reading goals.

CONCEPT CHECK 8.1

What kinds of demands does reading place on working memory and your central executive?

CONCEPT CHECK 8.2

Active reading strategies are not limited to those shown in Figure 8.1. What additional active reading strategies can you recommend?

FIGURE 8.1

Essential Strategies for Active Reading

▌ **Create a plan of action.** Instead of haphazardly tackling a textbook chapter or procrastinating about reading assignments, select an appropriate, systematic reading system to use to move you into the reading process and achieve your specific reading goals.

▌ **Read with a pencil in your hand.** Interact with printed materials by highlighting text, writing questions as you read, making notes in the textbook or on paper, creating pictures to show key concepts, or redrawing important visual materials.

▌ **Use knowledge of writing structures and organizational patterns.** Strive to "get into the writer's head" by identifying patterns used in paragraphs to organize details.

▌ **Distinguish between factual knowledge and procedural knowledge.** Select the best-suited strategies to learn, rehearse, and review the two kinds of information.

▌ **Learn how to read and interpret graphic materials.** Use the strategies in Figure 8.8, page 230.

▌ **Use all available resources.** Active readers are resourceful readers. They take advantage of: textbook resources, website enrichment materials, supplementary videos, computer lab software, lab manuals, study guides, tutors, or study groups.

Finding Meaning in Difficult Text

CONCEPT CHECK 8.3

How do you use metacognition when you encounter difficult text?

Using active reading involves developing an awareness of the strategies you use and monitoring your comprehension. As you read different types of material, become keenly aware of sections of material you understand and sections of material that puzzle you or are difficult to understand. Adjust your strategies to achieve greater comprehension. Use the following strategies when you encounter difficult-to-understand text:

▌ *Adjust your reading rate.* Slow down the intake process, which means slow down your reading rate. For difficult materials, you may need to read individual sentences or phrases slowly to allow your working memory time to make associations and attach meanings to words.

▌ *Use knowledge of writing structures.* A well-written paragraph has *unity* (all details relate to the main idea), *coherence* (ideas flow in a logical sequence), and *adequate development* (sufficient details to support the main idea). Likewise, paragraphs link together to develop a main point (the thesis, heading, or subheading in a chapter). Use this knowledge to identify levels of information and relationships among the concepts, main ideas, and details.

▌ *Be persistent.* Stay with a paragraph or section of material until you comprehend it. Reread the difficult section of material slowly at least one more time. Use strategies to analyze the paragraph, identify paragraph structure or patterns, and find relationships among the details and the main idea. Understanding later concepts may rely on understanding information in the difficult paragraph, so do not move on or skip the paragraph just because it is difficult.

CONCEPT CHECK 8.4

How can your speech patterns help you unlock the meaning of difficult paragraphs?

▌ *Verbalize by reading and talking out loud.* Reading out loud activates your auditory channel. Hearing yourself read can clarify information because the natural tendency, without any conscious effort, is to read in clusters or meaningful groups of words or phrases. When you talk or reason out loud, your own words may help you identify what you understand and which sections of information you do not clearly understand.

▌ *Ask questions to control your attention.* As you ask questions, your mind begins to search for answers. You might ask yourself: What don't I get here? How do these details fit together? What is the author trying to say here?

▌ *Visualize what you are reading.* Visualizing converts information from printed form (left brain) into pictures or visual images (right brain). Create strong visual impressions of the information or convert the information into a *movie in your mind.*

▌ *Chunk up or chunk down.* Consciously control the size of information you are trying to understand. When you *chunk up,* you look beyond the paragraph to determine how the paragraph fits into the bigger picture. Place the paragraph or section in context with the surrounding material. Reread the previous paragraphs and read ahead to the following paragraph or paragraphs to find the natural flow or progression of information. When you *chunk down,* you break the information into smaller units, perhaps as small as individual sentences, or phrases, to identify the meanings of details.

▌ *Use available graphic materials.* Examine any graphic materials associated with the difficult section of information. Shift back and forth between the printed text and the visual graphic until you can integrate the two forms used to explain a concept.

▌ *Convert information into pictures.* Draw pictures of the information presented in paragraphs. As you reread a paragraph, begin drawing a picture of the significant details. The process often forces you to find the relationships and the important details. **Figure 8.2** shows how converting a paragraph into a drawing clarifies printed information.

CONCEPT CHECK 8.5

What do you do to "chunk up"? How does it differ from "chunking down"?

FIGURE 8.2

Converting Paragraphs into Drawings

The Greenhouse Effect

A window pane transmits sunlight. It is nearly transparent, and much of the shortwave energy passes through. Only a little energy is absorbed to heat up the glass. However, the walls and furniture inside a room absorb a large part of the solar radiation coming through the window. The energy radiated from the furniture, unlike the original solar energy, is all long-wave radiation. Much of it is unable to pass out through the window pane. This is why the car seats get so hot on a hot, sunny day when all the windows are closed. Try putting a piece of glass in front of a hot object to see how the heat waves are cut off. A greenhouse traps energy in this way when the sun shines, and so does the atmosphere. From *Investigating the Earth,* American Geological Institute.

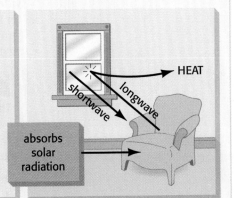

EXERCISE 8.1

Converting Words to Pictures

DIRECTIONS: Go to Exercise 8.1, Appendix C, page A26, to practice converting printed words into pictures for excerpts about environmental spheres, Celsius and Fahrenheit, and mass media.

CL **Improve Your Grade**
Online Practice 1:
SQ4R

CONCEPT CHECK 8.6

Can using a specific reading system reduce procrastination? Why or why not?

SQ4R is a six-step system for reading and comprehending textbook chapters: survey, question, read, record, recite, and review.

The SQ4R Reading System

Using a systematic approach for reading textbook chapters may take more time than you are used to spending for reading a chapter, but you will process and comprehend the information more thoroughly, eliminate the need to reread chapters multiple times in order to learn the content, and in the long run, save valuable study time.

One of the first textbook reading systems, SQ3R, was developed by Francis P. Robinson in 1941. The letters in the name of this system represent the five steps: survey, question, read, recite, and review. You may encounter other reading systems in your various textbooks, but when you analyze the steps in those systems, you will notice that many involve different labels for essentially the same steps because these steps are powerful processes that are proven to increase comprehension and enhance learning.

SQ4R is a six-step system for reading and comprehending textbook chapters: survey, question, read, record, recite, and review. SQ4R is based on SQ3R; a fourth "R" has been added to the system to remind students to take notes. As with any approach, skipping any one step weakens the system. To gain the most benefit from this system, use all six steps shown in **Figure 8.3** each time you use the SQ4R system.

Step One: Survey the Chapter

Surveying a chapter requires less than twenty minutes of your time. Surveying provides you with a preview of the chapter's contents, familiarizes you with the chapter features, and begins the process of activating or creating schemas upon which you can attach details. Refer to Figure 7.6, page 193, to review the process of surveying a chapter.

FIGURE 8.3

The Six Steps of SQ4R

1. **Survey** the chapter to get an overview.
2. Write **Questions** for each heading and subheading.
3. **Read** the information, one paragraph at a time.
4. Select a form of notetaking to **Record** information.
5. **Recite** the important information from the paragraph.
6. **Review** the information learned in the chapter.

Step Two: Write Questions

During the **question step**, turn the chapter title and each heading and subheading into a question. The ten or twenty minutes it takes to write questions is time well spent. You get one additional overview of the chapter, and you create a purpose for reading, focus your attention on upcoming information, and activate working memory. Use the following suggestions when you write your questions:

▌ *Strive to use a variety of questions.* Each question word elicits a different kind of response. For example, answers to:

> **what** questions name specific facts.
> **why** questions give reasons.
> **how** questions state steps or processes.
> **when** questions identify time periods.
> **which** questions identify specific items.
> **who** questions identify specific people.
> **where** questions identify specific locations.

▌ Modify or delete some words in headings and subheadings if necessary when you create questions. Write the questions directly in your textbook next to the title, headings, or subheadings, or write them on notebook paper or index cards, leaving space to write the answers later. Following are examples of questions for the beginning of this chapter. The italic print shows words added to the title, heading, and subheadings to create questions.

> **Title:** *What do I already know about* **Learning from College Textbooks***?*
> **Heading:** *What is* **Active Reading***?*
> **Subheading:** *What are* ~~Use~~ **Active Reading Strategies***?*

Step Three: Read Carefully

Some students feel that they should be able to "read fast" to get through chapters. Others read chapters—only to find at the end of the chapters that they do not remember much of what they had just read; consequently, they must reread at least one more time. The **read step** of SQ4R encourages you to read *carefully* and *thoroughly.* Use the following three suggestions for the *read step* of SQ4R:

▌ *Decide if overview reading would be beneficial.* Use *overview reading* when you want to get a "flavor" for the content, acquire some basic background information, or create a general schema for the information. Read without pausing to analyze information or take notes. Once completed, begin the essential thorough reading process.

▌ *Begin thorough reading.* For most textbooks, you should read *one paragraph at a time* and then stop to dissect, analyze, and comprehend the content of the paragraph. Identify the topic, main ideas, key details, and organizational patterns used in the paragraph.

▌ *Use strategies to unlock the meaning of difficult paragraphs.* Use the strategies on pages 214–215 to understand the information in difficult paragraphs.

Step Four: Record Information

After you read a paragraph or a section of information carefully, begin the **record step** by taking notes of the important information you will need to study, memorize,

CONCEPT CHECK 8.7

What are the benefits of converting headings and subheadings into questions? Have you ever used this technique?

CONCEPT CHECK 8.8

How does thorough reading in Step 3 differ from overview reading or recreational reading?

CONCEPT CHECK 8.9

What is the value of taking notes on textbook information? Do you usually take notes on textbook information? Why or why not?

learn, and use. Taking time to record information (take notes) benefits you in many ways. First, your notes become a *reduced or a condensed form* of the information you need to study and learn. Second, taking notes keeps you actively involved in the learning process and reduces the tendency for you to shift into *automatic pilot,* a state of mind where you mechanically read without processing information clearly. Third, taking notes holds information in working memory and provides more time for you to encode it for your long-term memory. Finally, creating a set of notes requires identification of key concepts and attention to key details and relationships among the details—processes that lead to improved comprehension.

With a repertoire of the following notetaking options that you will learn in Chapters 9 and 11, you can select a notetaking system that is appropriate for the type of textbook and content you are studying:

Annotation	Cornell Notes	Two- or Three-Column Notes
Outline Notes	Visual Mappings	Hierarchies
Comparison Charts		Index Card Notes

Step Five: Recite

Before you move on to the next paragraph, stop and use the **recite step**. Without looking at your notes or the textbook, recite the important points you read in the paragraph and recorded in your notes. Look back at the textbook or your notes to check your accuracy.

Continue to move through the chapter by using the Read-Record-Recite Cycle. The **Read-Record-Recite Cycle** is a thorough reading strategy that involves reading a section of information, taking notes, and explaining the information out loud before moving to new information. When you have completed this cycle for the entire chapter, move on to the final step of SQ4R.

The **Read-Record-Recite Cycle** is a thorough reading strategy that involves reading a section of information, taking notes, and explaining the information out loud before moving to new information.

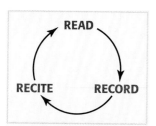

Step Six: Review

The **review step**, which includes both *immediate* and *ongoing review,* can be accomplished in a variety of ways:

▌ *Answer the chapter review questions* that appear at the end of the chapter.

▌ *Answer the questions you formulated during the* **question step**.

▌ *Study and recite from the notes that you took in the* **record step**.

▌ *Write a summary.* In paragraph form, summarize the important concepts and details.

▌ *Create additional study tools,* such as flashcards, outlines, study tapes, or visual notes.

▌ *Rework problems.* Rework problems from class or from your textbook. Compare the steps you used and your answers with those in the textbook. For language courses, copy sentences or grammatical exercises from the textbook. Rework the assignment, such as converting verb tenses, diagramming the sentences, or identifying parts of speech within sentences. Check your accuracy.

EXERCISE 8.2

Writing Questions in SQ4R

PURPOSE: Converting headings and subheadings into questions provides a purpose for reading and creates study questions to use to review chapter materials.

DIRECTIONS: Formulate questions for all headings and subheadings in this chapter. Use a variety of question words: *what, why, how, when, which, who,* and *where.* Write your questions in your textbook next to the headings and subheadings.

EXERCISE 8.3

Links

PURPOSE: Effective study skills strategies are powerful because they support learning theories and research. Understanding the reasons for using specific steps emphasizes the importance of using each step when you study.

DIRECTIONS: Work with a partner or in a small group. On separate paper, copy the SQ4R chart on the right. Label the six steps of SQ4R. Then, for each step of SQ4R, discuss which of the Twelve Principles of Memory (SAVE CRIB FOTO) are used in that step. Using any method you prefer, attach the appropriate Memory Principles to each section of the chart. Be prepared to share your results with the class.

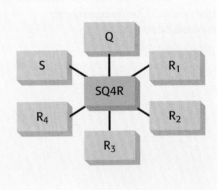

The Triple Q Reading System

The Triple Q System is an active reading system that focuses on formulating questions *before, during,* and *after* reading a chapter. After *surveying* the chapter, you can begin the process of formulating questions. **Figure 8.4** shows the three Q's in the Triple Q system.

Q₁ Write Questions Before You Read

Use the same suggestions for writing Q_1 questions as shown previously for the **question step** of SQ4R. Formulate a variety of questions for the title, headings, and subheadings by using the words *what, why, how, when, which, who,* and *where.*

The Triple Q System is an active reading system that focuses on formulating questions *before, during,* and *after* reading a chapter.

CONCEPT CHECK 8.13

Why do most reading systems begin with the process of surveying? What would be the consequences of skipping over the process of surveying before reading?

FIGURE 8.4

The Triple Q Reading System

Step	When to Use	What to Do
Q_1	Before reading	Write questions for the title, headings, and subheadings in a chapter.
Q_2	During the reading process	After reading a paragraph, write one or two study questions in the margin next to the paragraph. Highlight key words in the paragraph that answer each question.
Q_3	After reading a chapter	Write chapter questions to use to review the chapter and prepare for tests. Practice answering all your questions.

Q_2 Write Questions During the Reading Process

CONCEPT CHECK 8.14

How does the Q_2 step help you identify important details to study?

After you read and identify important concepts and details in a paragraph, think about the information and predict possible test questions that you might later encounter on the material. Then, do the following:

▍ In the margin, *write one or two study questions or test questions* that can be answered by the information in the paragraph. Use the *what, why, how, when, which, who,* and *where* question words as well as the following question words frequently used on tests:

List	Define	Describe	Identify	Discuss	Compare
Calculate	Show	Solve	Classify	Explain	Contrast

▍ Return to the paragraph. *Highlight key words* in the paragraph that provide details for answers to your questions. As shown in **Figure 8.5**, you can use different colors of highlighter pens to differentiate details if you wish.

Q_3 Write Questions After Reading a Chapter

Writing chapter questions after you finish reading a chapter while the information is fresh in your memory eliminates the need to spend time predicting and writing questions later when you prepare for tests. These questions also provide you with study tools to use to rehearse information, to self-quiz, and to use as a warm-up activity at the beginning of a study block.

CONCEPT CHECK 8.15

Give examples of higher level questions you can write in the Q_3 step.

In your textbooks and on your tests, you will encounter different types of questions. The Q_3 step provides you with a perfect opportunity to practice writing questions on different levels of difficulty. In 1956, a psychologist named Benjamin Bloom, along with several colleagues, developed *Bloom's Taxonomy*—a classification system for question types. **Figure 8.6** shows the six levels in Bloom's Taxonomy, beginning with the lowest level of questions (knowledge, also known as *recognition* or *recall*). When you write chapter questions, strive to include questions from the different levels of Bloom's Taxonomy chart. (Also see: Student Website, Topic In-Depth: Bloom's Taxonomy.)

Topic In-Depth
Bloom's Taxonomy

FIGURE 8.5

Using Q₁ and Q₂ Steps in an Excerpt

When *does* achievement motivation develop?	***Development of Achievement Motivation*** Achievement motivation develops in early childhood under the influence of both genetic and environmental factors. As described in the personality chapter, children inherit general behavioral tendencies, such as impulsiveness and emotionality, and these tendencies may support or undermine the development of achievement motivation. The motivation to achieve is also shaped by what children learn from watching and listening to others, especially their parents. Evidence for the influence of parental teachings about achievement comes from a study in which young boys were given a task so difficult that they were sure to fail. Fathers whose sons scored low on achievement motivation tests often became annoyed as they watched their boys work on the task, discouraged them from continuing, and interfered or even completed the task themselves (Rosen & D'Andrade, 1959). A much different response pattern emerged among parents of children who scored high on tests of achievement motivation. Those parents tended to (1) encourage the child to try difficult tasks, especially new ones; (2) give praise and other rewards for success; (3) encourage the child to find ways to succeed rather than merely complaining about failure; and (4) prompt the child to go on to the next, more difficult challenge (McClelland, 1985). Other research with adults shows that even the slightest cues that bring a parent to mind can boost some people's efforts to achieve a goal (Shah, 2003).
List factors that influence development of achievement motivation.	
How can parents support or undermine development of ach. motivation?	
Important point	

Source: Bernstein, Nash. *Essentials of Psychology* (Boston: Houghton Mifflin Co., 2008), page 317.

FIGURE 8.6

Levels of Questions in Bloom's Taxonomy

Level	Question Cues/Question Words
Knowledge	collect, define, describe, examine, identify, label, list, name, quote, show, tabulate, tell, what, when, where, who
Comprehension	associate, contrast, describe, differentiate, discuss, distinguish, estimate, extend, interpret, predict, summarize
Application	apply, calculate, change, classify, complete, demonstrate, discover, examine, experiment, illustrate, modify, relate, show, solve
Analysis	analyze, arrange, classify, compare, connect, divide, explain, infer, order, separate, select
Synthesis	combine, compose, create, design, formulate, generalize, invent, integrate, modify, plan, prepare, rearrange, rewrite, substitute, what if?
Evaluation	assess, compare, conclude, convince, decide, discriminate, explain, grade, judge, measure, rank, recommend, select, summarize, support, test

Adapted from Benjamin S. Bloom et al., *Taxonomy of Educational Objectives,* Fourth Edition. Copyright © 1984 by Pearson Education. Adapted by permission of the author and the publisher, Allyn & Bacon, Boston, MA.

CONCEPT CHECK 8.16

How can you get the most value from the three kinds of questions you write in the Triple Q System?

As you recall from Chapter 3, *elaborative rehearsal* is the process of thinking about, pondering, or working with and encoding information in new ways. The Triple Q Reading System elaborates on information through the use of questions. Questions by themselves are not sufficient for building memory. *Answering* the questions, reciting, and reviewing the answers are the processes that build memory.

Use the following three strategies for maximum benefits from your questions.

▌ *Recite answers.* Cover up the printed text. Recite by using your own words to answer the Q_1, Q_2, and Q_3 questions. Refer to your textbook to check the accuracy and completeness of the information you recited.

▌ *Create notes.* On separate paper or on index cards, copy the questions and provide the answers. These notes become valuable study tools to review and prepare for tests.

▌ *Review your questions and answers.* You can use your questions and answers as a warm-up activity at a beginning of a study block, for a quick review before a related lecture or discussion, as quizzing materials in a study group, or to prepare for an upcoming test.

A Customized Reading System

A **Customized Reading System** is a system you design for a specific textbook based on the author's suggestions and the chapter features.

SQ4R and Triple Q are effective textbook reading systems, but they are not the only systems available for you to use. A **Customized Reading System** is a system you design for a specific textbook based on the author's suggestions and the chapter features. Your goal with this system is to establish a consistent routine to use to study each chapter.

Step 1: Use the Author's Suggestions

Carefully read the To the Student or the Preface information in the front of the textbook. List the author's suggestions for reading and using the textbook.

CONCEPT CHECK 8.17

How could you use the chapter features for this textbook to customize a reading system?

Step 2: Use the Chapter Features

Examine the chapter features in the first few chapters. In some textbooks, such as composition and math textbooks, the chapter format and the chapter features "dictate" a reading process for you to use—work through each section and each feature in the order presented.

CONCEPT CHECK 8.18

What essential learning principles should you include in your customized system so it is effective?

Step 3: Create Your Customized System

Using the information learned by surveying, create a list of steps that you will use consistently and habitually to read and comprehend the information in each chapter. (See **Figure 8.7**.) To work successfully, your customized approach to reading the textbook should:

▌ Utilize effective study skills strategies that you are already know

▌ Include application of the Twelve Principles of Memory

▌ Incorporate at least one form of notetaking to organize and record information

▌ Include reworking problem sets or portions of homework assignments

▌ End with review activities

FIGURE 8.7

A Customized Reading System for a Math Textbook

Step 1: **Read the introduction, goals, and objectives.**

Step 2: **Read the definitions.** Create a vocabulary sheet or definition flashcards each time I encounter new terminology, formulas, equations, and symbols.

Step 3: **Study examples until I understand the problem type and steps involved.** Choose one example to memorize as a *prototype.* Create meaningful notes.

Step 4: **Practice new skills.** Rework the example problems. Check my accuracy.

Step 5: **Do new problem sets.** These usually mirror the problem types shown by the examples. Pay attention to underlying patterns. Apply the steps; check work.

Step 6: **Do mixed problem sets.** Look for underlying patterns. Match problem types to prototypes I have memorized. Apply the steps; check answers.

Step 7: **Do the real-world story problems.** Look for familiar underlying patterns. Apply RSTUV steps (page 246). Check work. Be sure to label units in the solution.

Step 8: **Review the chapter.** Read the chapter summary. Do review problems. Rework several examples and problems from the chapter. Recite and study the terminology, formulas, equations, and problem-solving steps.

CHECK POINT 8.1

ANSWERS APPEAR ON PAGE A5

True or False?

_____ 1. Surveying a chapter is a recommended reading strategy and is the first step in many reading systems.

_____ 2. You should use active reading strategies only for complex, difficult textbooks.

_____ 3. A student who uses metacognition adjusts strategies when initial strategies do not result in comprehending textbook information.

_____ 4. A Customized Reading System designed for one textbook can be used effectively for all other textbooks.

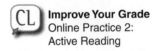 **Improve Your Grade**
Online Practice 2:
Active Reading

ORGANIZATIONAL PATTERNS

2 ▸ *Define and discuss the seven organizational patterns used to organize details in paragraphs.*

Organizational patterns are paragraph patterns that writers use to present details in a logical, meaningful order. Understanding organizational patterns helps you unlock the meaning of what you read, identify relationships among the details within a paragraph, and follow the internal logic and natural progression of information. Paragraphs may exhibit characteristics of more than one organizational pattern, but one dominant pattern reflects the purpose of the paragraph. In the following sections you will learn more about each pattern, its clue words, and diagram

Organizational patterns are paragraph patterns that writers use to present details in a logical, meaningful order.

CONCEPT CHECK 8.19

How can you differentiate one organizational pattern from another?

formats you can use to convert information into visual forms. A sample paragraph clarifies the key elements for each organizational pattern. You will encounter the following seven organizational patterns in your college textbooks:

▌ The *chronological pattern* presents details in a logical time sequence.

▌ The *process pattern* presents a specific procedure or order of steps to use to do, create, repair, or solve problems.

▌ The *comparison or contrast pattern* shows similarities and/or differences for two or more subjects.

▌ The *definition pattern* uses explanations, characteristics, examples, analogies, and negations to define a specific term.

▌ The *examples pattern* uses examples to expand a reader's understanding of a term, a concept, or a theory.

▌ The *cause/effect pattern* shows the relationship between two or more items by indicating which items or actions cause specific effects.

▌ The *whole-and-parts pattern* shows the individual parts, components, or entities that together create a whole object, concept, or theory.

The Chronological Pattern

Chronological Pattern	Clue Words	Diagram for This Pattern
▌ Details are presented in a logical time sequence: *chronological order.* ▌ Details happen in a specific, fixed order to reach a conclusion or an ending. ▌ This pattern is often used to tell a story (a narrative) or explain a sequence of events.	when then before next after first second finally	1. → 2. → 3. → 4. → Conclusion or Ending

CONCEPT CHECK 8.20

In what kinds of textbooks would you predict paragraphs with the chronological pattern will appear frequently?

Excerpt Demonstrating the Chronological Pattern:

While commercial farming was spreading, cattle ranching—one of the West's most romantic industries—was evolving. Early in the nineteenth century herds of cattle, introduced by the Spanish and expanded by Mexican ranchers, roamed southern Texas and bred with cattle brought by Anglo settlers. The resulting longhorn breed multiplied and became valuable by the 1860s, when population growth increased demand for beef and railroads facilitated the transportation of food. By 1870, drovers were herding thousands of Texas cattle northward by Kansas, Missouri, and Wyoming. On these long drives, mounted cowboys (as many as 25 percent of whom were African-American) supervised the herds, which fed on open grassland along the way. At the northern terminus—usually Abilene, Dodge City, or Cheyenne—the cattle were sold to northern ranches or loaded onto trains bound for Chicago and St. Louis for slaughter and distribution.

From Mary Beth Norton, David M. Katzman, Paul D. Escott, and Howard Chudacoff, *A People and a Nation, 5th ed.*, p. 496. Copyright © 1998 Houghton Mifflin Company. Used with permission.

The Process Pattern

Process Pattern	Clue Words	Diagram for This Pattern
▌ Details explain a procedure or how something works. ▌ Details may provide directions to complete a specific series of steps to do, create, repair, or solve something. ▌ Steps must be done in chronological order. ▌ Outcome is a finished product or a solution. ▌ Science, social science, and mathematics textbooks use this pattern frequently.	steps process procedure first second before after when as soon as next finally outcome result	1. → 2. → 3. → 4. → **End Product or Solution**

Excerpt Demonstrating the Process Pattern:

Frost Wedging   Water expands in volume by about 9% when it turns to ice. When water enters pores or cracks in a rock and the temperature subsequently falls below 0 degrees C (32 degrees F, the freezing point of water), the force of the expanding ice greatly exceeds that needed to fracture even solid granite. The cracks then become enlarged, often loosening or dislodging fragments of rock. This enlargement allows even more water to enter the crack, and the process is repeated. This frost wedging process is the fastest, most effective type of mechanical weathering. It is most active in environments where surface water is abundant and temperatures often fluctuate around the freezing point of water.

Source: Chernicoff/Fox, *Essentials of Geology,* p. 185. Houghton Mifflin, © 2003.

> **CONCEPT CHECK 8.21**
>
> Which of your textbooks frequently includes paragraphs with the process pattern?

The Comparison/Contrast Pattern

Comparison or Contrast Pattern	Clue Words	Diagram for This Pattern		
▌ Comparison shows likenesses and/or differences between two or more objects or events (the subjects). ▌ Contrast shows only differences between two or more objects or events. ▌ Several characteristics of "Subject A" and "Subject B" are compared or contrasted.	also similarly likewise but in contrast on the other hand however although while	**Characteristics**	**Subject A**	**Subject B**

CONCEPT CHECK 8.22

What are some clues you can use to identify paragraphs that use the comparison and contrast pattern?

Excerpt Demonstrating the Comparison/Contrast Pattern:

The Classical Period of music, art, and literature differed greatly from the subsequent Romantic Period. During the Classical Period, music, art, and literature, which were influenced by Greek and Latin traditions, emphasized formal rules, patterns, and structure. Complexity and heavy feeling or pressure cloaked all forms of art. Artists, musicians, and writers restrained emotions and suppressed or refrained from using creativity and originality. They honored and respected traditional standards. During the onset of the Romantic Period, however, musicians, artists, and writers sought to escape the formal, stiff, stifling rules of formality, set patterns, and inflexible structures. New forms of expression emphasized a light, joyful, and frivolous side of human nature. Society as a whole placed a high value on creativity, experimentation, and originality. Individuals received validation, and individual expression of emotions, passions, and the human soul became valued. Romantic art often depicted amoral love with an abundance of cupids and thinly clad nymphs. During this cultural revolution at the end of the eighteenth century, two opposing Periods with extremely different values collided.

Modifed from: Wong, *Paragraph Essentials*, p. 241. © 2002, Houghton Mifflin.

The Definition Pattern

Definition Pattern	Clue Words	Diagram for This Pattern
▍ Information throughout the paragraph defines a specific term. ▍ Explanations, characteristics, analogies, examples, and negations may be used to define a term. ▍ The term the paragraph defines often appears in bold print in the first sentence.	means is/are is defined as can be considered referred to as	WORD Key Points, Characteristics, Analogies, Examples

CONCEPT CHECK 8.23

In addition to the formal definition, what other details often appear in a paragraph with a definition pattern?

Excerpt Demonstrating the Definition Pattern:

Desertification is the invasion of desert conditions into formerly nondesert areas. Common symptoms of desertification include a significant lowering of the water table, a marked reduction in surface-water supply, increased salinity in natural waters and soils, progressive destruction of vegetation, and an accelerated rate of erosion. Desertification is an extremely clear example of how the interplay of the Earth's systems affects a region's human inhabitants.

Chernicoff/Fox, *Essentials of Geology, 3rd ed.* (Boston: Houghton Mifflin Co.), pp. 356–357. Copyright © 2003.

The Examples Pattern

Examples Pattern	Clue Words	Diagram for This Pattern
▮ An idea, term, or theory is expanded through the use of examples. ▮ One extended example may be used throughout the paragraph, or multiple examples may be used.	for example another example an illustration of this	

Excerpt Demonstrating the Examples Pattern:

History has shown that major innovations are as likely to come from small businesses (or individuals) as from big businesses. For example, small firms and individuals invented the personal computer and the stainless steel razor blade, the transistor radio and the photocopying machine, the jet engine and the self-developing photograph. They also gave us the helicopter and power steering, automatic transmissions and air conditioning, cellophane, and the 19-cent ballpoint pen. Today, says the SBA, small businesses supply 55 percent of all "innovations" introduced into the American marketplace.

Source: Griffin, *Principles of Management,* p. 114. Houghton Mifflin, © 2007.

CONCEPT CHECK 8.24

How does a paragraph with an examples pattern increase comprehension?

The Cause/Effect Pattern

Cause/Effect Pattern	Clue Words	Diagram for This Pattern
▮ Show the relationship between two items in which one item causes the other item to happen. ▮ One cause may have more than one effect or outcome. ▮ Several causes may produce one effect or outcome.	because since so therefore caused by result in	

Excerpt Demonstrating the Cause/Effect Pattern:

All humans respond bodily to stress, which is what enables us to mount a defense. Physiologically, the sympathetic nervous system is activated and more adrenaline is secreted, which increases the heart rate and heightens arousal. Then all at once the liver pours extra sugar into the bloodstream for energy, the pupils dilate to let in more light, breathing speeds up for more oxygen, perspiration increases to cool down the body, blood clots faster to heal wounds, saliva flow is inhibited, and digestion slows down to divert blood to the brain and the skeletal muscles. Faced with threat, the body readies for action.

From Brehm, Kassin, and Fein, *Social Psychology, 5th ed.* (Boston: Houghton Mifflin Co., 2002), p. 510. Copyright © 2002.

CONCEPT CHECK 8.25

What kinds of textbooks frequently use the cause/effect pattern in paragraphs? Explain your answer.

The Whole-and-Parts Pattern

Whole-and-Parts Pattern	Clue Words	Various Diagrams for This Pattern
▮ Focus is on the individual parts, components, or entities that together create the whole object, concept, or theory. ▮ The details identify, define, and explain each individual part of the whole item. ▮ Diagrams may include any *whole item* with its *parts* clearly identified and labeled. Science and social science textbooks use this pattern frequently.	parts X number of parts categories subsystems sections left right front back consists of is comprised of together make	

CONCEPT CHECK 8.26

Which Principle of Memory emphasizes the same relationships as emphasized by the whole-and-parts pattern?

Excerpt Demonstrating the Whole-and-Parts Pattern:

Creating a Marketing Mix

A business firm controls four important elements of marketing that it combines in a way that reaches the firm's target market. These are the *product* itself, the *price* of the product, the means chosen for its *distribution*, and the *promotion* of the product. When combined, these four elements form a marketing mix.

From Pride, Hughes, and Kapoor, *Business, 7th ed.*, p. 363. Copyright © 2002. Reprinted by permission of Houghton Mifflin, Inc.

EXERCISE 8.4

Creating Diagrams for Paragraphs

DIRECTIONS: Return to the paragraph examples on pages 224–228. Select any *two* paragraph examples to convert into diagrams. Use the diagram formats shown in the organizational chart for each type of organizational pattern. Be very selective; use only key words or phrases in your diagrams.

EXERCISE 8.5

Using the Triple Q System

DIRECTIONS: For each of the example paragraphs used on pages 224–228 to show the seven organizational paragraphs, practice using the Q_2 step to write questions in the margins. Highlight key words in the paragraphs that answer the questions.

CHECK POINT 8.2

ANSWERS APPEAR ON PAGE A5

True or False?

_____ 1. The comparison/contrast pattern, the cause/effect pattern, and the whole-and-parts pattern show relationships between two or more items.

_____ 2. All paragraphs exhibit characteristics of each of the organizational patterns, but only one pattern is dominant.

_____ 3. Writers use organizational patterns to show an internal logic for the order of details.

_____ 4. *When, before, steps, in contrast, means, for example, because,* and *subsystems* are clue words that help identify the kind of organizational pattern used in a paragraph.

Improve Your Grade
Online Practice 3:
Organizational Patterns

EXERCISE 8.6

Textbook Case Studies

 **Improve Your Grade**
Exercise 8.6

 **Improve Your Grade**
Online Case Studies

DIRECTIONS:

1. Read each case study carefully. Respond to the question at the end of each case study by using *specific* strategies discussed in this chapter. Answer in complete sentences.

2. Write your responses on paper or online at the Student Website, Exercise 8.6. You will be able to print your online response or e-mail it to your instructor.

CASE STUDY 1: Cecilia does not have problems reading the textbook words, but she often has problems following the author's line of thinking. She wants to learn new strategies that force her to think about relationships and see "the bigger picture." What strategies will help Cecilia tune in to the author's logical structures?

CASE STUDY 2: Several of Jeremy's "get-by" reading strategies that he acquired in high school are proving to be ineffective for his college textbooks. His current strategies involve looking through a chapter, reading the notes in the margins, examining graphs and charts, and reading the summary. He then reads only the sections of information that appear to have new or unfamiliar information. Jeremy visited the tutoring center to learn more effective strategies for his geology textbook. If you were the tutor Jeremy visited, what strategies would you recommend he begin using for his geology textbook?

GRAPHIC MATERIALS

3 ▶ *Explain and use strategies to read and interpret six kinds of graphic materials.*

Graphic materials are pictures, illustrations, diagrams, charts, tables, graphs, and other visual representations that convert verbal information into a mainly visual format. Many textbooks, especially science, social science, and mathematics textbooks, use graphic materials to convey important information about data, statistics, trends, and relationships. A picture is worth a thousand words, so learning how to read and interpret graphic materials is essential. To gain the greatest

Graphic materials are pictures, illustrations, diagrams, charts, tables, graphs, and other visual representations that convert verbal information into a mainly visual format.

Learning how to read and interpret graphic materials helps you understand data, identify relationships, and see trends. What kinds of graphic materials do you frequently encounter in your textbooks?

CONCEPT CHECK 8.27

In addition to adding visual appeal, what other purposes do graphic materials serve?

benefits from graphic materials, use the eight Essential Strategies for Working with Graphic Materials in **Figure 8.8**. You will encounter the following types of graphic materials in your college textbooks:

❚ *Photographs, illustrations,* and *diagrams,* which include cartoons, sketches, and drawings, provide background information and clarify concepts.

❚ *Pie charts* show and compare parts (sectors) to a whole.

FIGURE 8.8

Essential Strategies for Working with Graphic Materials

❚ **Carefully read the features in the graphic.** Read the titles, captions, legends, and labels that appear with graphic materials.

❚ **Examine the details carefully.** Look at sizes, colors, spatial positions, likenesses and differences, relationships, patterns, and trends.

❚ **Verbalize or "string ideas together."** Talk to yourself about the information. Use some of your own words to explain the information and the relationships you see.

❚ **Visualize the graphic.** Create a strong visual image or impression of the basic features of the graphic. Practice using this as a retrieval cue to recall and rehearse information.

❚ **Ask yourself questions about the content.** Create questions about specific parts of the graphic mate-

rials, questions that compare two or more items, and questions that focus on the cause-effect relationships, trends, and patterns.

❚ **Copy important graphic materials into your notes.** Unless the graphic materials are too complex, include them in your notes. Color-code the parts of the graphics and add labels and captions. For more complex graphics, list important points you learned from the graphic and list textbook page references for later review.

❚ **Expand the graphic materials in your notes.** Add your own reminders, details, or explanations to the graphics you copied into your notes.

❚ **Write a short summary under the graphics in your textbook or in your notes.**

▌ *Flow charts* show levels of organization or the directions in which information flows.

▌ *Tables* use columns and rows to organize information on various topics or to show data to use to solve problems.

▌ *Bar graphs* use vertical or horizontal bars to show frequency of occurrence of different subjects or data and to show trends.

▌ *Line graphs* plot information on a grid to form one continuous line to show trends and compare data.

Many graphic materials include captions and legends to help you interpret the information. A **caption** is a short explanation or description that accompanies a graphic. A **legend** defines or gives values for the symbols used in the graphic. Captions and legends provide you with essential information for understanding and interpreting the graphic materials, so read them carefully.

> A **caption** is a short explanation that accompanies a graphic.
>
> A **legend** defines or gives values for the symbols used in the graphic.

Photographs, Illustrations, and Diagrams

Survey any textbook and you will see an array of photographs, illustrations, and diagrams. To work with these graphic materials, use the Essential Strategies for Working with Graphic Materials in Figure 8.8.

> **CONCEPT CHECK 8.28**
>
> What is the purpose of photographs in textbooks? How do illustrations and diagrams help you understand printed text?

EXERCISE 8.7

Working with a Diagram

DIRECTIONS: Work with a partner. Refer to **Figure 8.9**, The Hydrologic Cycle, to answer the following questions.

1. What did you learn by reading the caption?
2. What are the important details in the diagram?
3. What does the diagram show? Verbalize or explain the flow of information in the diagram.
4. Visualize the basic structure of the graphic. After studying the diagram, use a Look-Away Technique. Practice using your visual memory to picture the diagram.
5. Create two questions about the details.
6. Write a short summary about the graphic.

FIGURE 8.9

The Hydrologic Cycle

All of the water that falls from the atmosphere onto the Earth's surface eventually enters the vast oceanic reservoir through one or more of the pathways of the cycle.

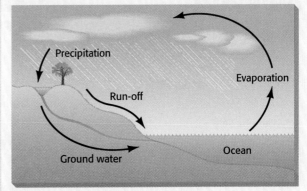

Figure 13.23 from Ebbing/Wentworth, *Introductory Chemistry*, p. 426. © 1998, Houghton Mifflin.

Pie Charts

Pie charts, also called circle graphs, show a whole unit (100 percent) divided into individually labelled parts or sectors.

Pie charts, also called circle graphs, show a whole unit (100 percent) divided into individually labelled parts or sectors. Pie charts are based on a whole-to-parts organizational pattern. **Figure 8.10** clearly shows the seven "selves" of a "whole person" as presented in a textbook for counselors; each sector of the pie is of equal proportion. If you were enrolled in the class using this textbook, after reading more detailed descriptions about each category of information, you could copy the chart into your notes and attach key words or phrases to each sector.

For some pie charts, you may need to estimate the percentage represented by each sector of the chart, or you may need to convert data into percentages. Frequently, however, pie charts provide exact percentages, making comparison of sectors easier and more accurate. (See **Figure 8.11**.) After examining the basic parts of a pie chart, compare and contrast sectors, make generalizations about the categories of information, and pose questions about the information.

CONCEPT CHECK 8.29

What questions could you pose to compare sectors in Figure 8.11? What generalizations could you make about the pie charts in Figures 8.10 and 8.11?

EXERCISE 8.8

Pie Charts

DIRECTIONS: Skim through any of your textbooks until you locate an example of a pie chart. Copy the chart on your own paper. Use the eight essential strategies (page 230) to understand and work with the pie chart. Be prepared to share your example of a pie chart in class.

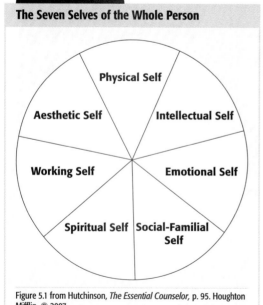

FIGURE 8.10

The Seven Selves of the Whole Person

Figure 5.1 from Hutchinson, *The Essential Counselor*, p. 95. Houghton Mifflin, © 2007.

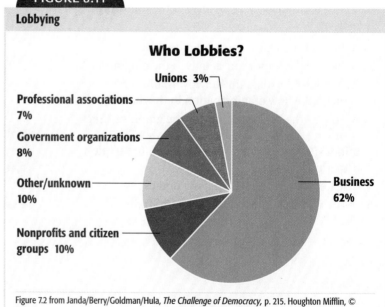

FIGURE 8.11

Lobbying

Figure 7.2 from Janda/Berry/Goldman/Hula, *The Challenge of Democracy*, p. 215. Houghton Mifflin, © 2008.

Flow Charts

Flow charts, also called organizational charts, show levels of organization or a directional flow of information from one level or topic to another. To remember information in flow charts, use the Essential Strategies in Figure 8.8, page 230: *Read*; *Examine*; *Verbalize/String Ideas Together*; *Visualize*; *Question*; *Copy*; *Expand*; and *Summarize*. In Chapter 5, you learned about the Expectancy Theory. **Figure 8.12** condenses one full textbook page of information about the Expectancy Theory into an easy-to-comprehend flow chart.

Flow charts, also called organizational charts, show levels of organization or a directional flow of information from one level or topic to another.

CONCEPT CHECK 8.30

How do flow charts differ from pie charts? What kinds of textbooks do you think frequently use flow charts?

EXERCISE 8.9

Learning from a Flow Chart

DIRECTIONS: Work with a partner. Refer to Figure 8.12 to complete the following directions.

1. Read the title, the caption, and examine the details in the chart.
2. Take turns verbalizing or stringing ideas together to explain the chart.
3. Create a visual impression of the chart. Look away and practice visualizing the chart.
4. Formulate two questions about the details in the chart.
5. Copy the chart on your own paper. Expand your chart in some way. (See Chapter 5, pages 134 and 135.)
6. Under your chart, write a short summary about the important information to remember.

FIGURE 8.12

The Expectancy Theory

Vroom's theory is based on the idea that motivation depends on how much people want something and on how likely they think they are to get it.

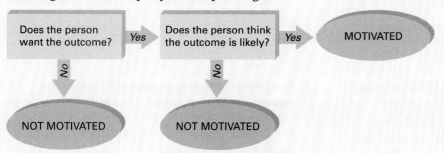

Figure 11.3 from Pride/Hughes/Kapoor, *Business, 7th ed.,* p. 312. Houghton Mifflin, © 2007.

Tables

Tables, also called comparison charts, grids, or matrixes, use columns and rows to organize information on various topics or to show data to use to solve problems.

Tables, also called comparison charts, grids, or matrixes, use columns and rows to organize information on various topics or to show data to use to solve problems. (See **Figure 8.13**.) Tables require careful reading as they often contain a considerable amount of data in the boxes or the *cells* of the chart.

FIGURE 8.13

Tables

Tables are used to compare:
1) one cell to another
2) one row to another
3) one column to another

	Column 1	Column 2	Column 3
Row 1	(cell)		
Row 2			
Row 3			
Row 4			

EXERCISE 8.10

Storing New Memories Table

DIRECTIONS: Work with a partner. Examine **Figure 8.14** and then follow the directions.

FIGURE 8.14

Storing New Memories Table

STORING NEW MEMORIES

Storage System	Function	Capacity	Duration
Sensory memory	Briefly holds representations of stimuli from each sense for further processing	Large: absorbs all sensory input from a particular stimulus	Less than 1 second
Short-term and working memory	Holds information in awareness and manipulates it to accomplish mental work	Five to nine distinct items or chunks of information	About 18 seconds
Long-term memory	Stores new information indefinitely	Unlimited	Unlimited

From Bernstein/Nash, *Essentials of Psychology*, p. 391. © 2008.

1. **Read the title and the caption.** Verbalize or string ideas together to explain the table.

2. **Visually memorize the skeleton of the chart.** The skeleton consists of the titles or labels for the columns and the rows. Look away and recite the skeleton.

3. **Read the information in each cell for the first column.** For example, read: *The function of sensory memory is . . . The function of STM and WM is . . . The function of LTM is . . .* Repeat the process by reading across the rows.

4. **Create questions based on the table.** Ask questions that compare the different cells, the different columns, and the different rows.

Bar Graphs

Bar graphs use vertical or horizontal bars to show frequency of occurrence for different subjects or data being graphed and to show trends. To read bar graphs, begin by reading the title and the caption. Then read the label that appears on the *horizontal line* called the *x axis* and on the *vertical* line, called the *y axis*. The axis that appears at the base of the bars identifies the data that is being graphed. The other axis shows the frequency of an occurrence or event, which may be shown in percentages, quantities, or a unit of measurement. Finally, use the height (or the length) of the bars to obtain information about each bar; compare the information. Exercises 8.11, 8.12, and 8.13 provide additional information about different kinds of bar graphs.

Bar graphs use vertical or horizontal bars to show frequency of occurrence for different subjects or data being graphed and to show trends.

CONCEPT CHECK 8.31

How does the format of bar graphs vary?

EXERCISE 8.11

A Histogram

DIRECTIONS: A *histogram* is a bar graph that shows a *range of values* at the base of the bars. Work with a partner. Examine **Figure 8.15** and answer the questions for the graph.

FIGURE 8.15

Stress Duration and Illness

Two hundred seventy-six volunteers were interviewed about recent life stress, then infected with a cold virus. As shown [below], the longer a stressor had lasted, in months, the more likely a person was to catch the cold. Over time, stress breaks down the body's immune system.

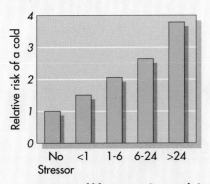

Figure 14.6 from Brehm/Kassin/Fein, *Social Psychology, 5th ed.,* p. 515. Houghton Mifflin, © 2002.

Questions:

1. How does the caption help you understand the bar graph?
2. Which axis shows the data being graphed? What do the number ranges represent?
3. Look at the vertical axis, the frequency data axis. What do the numbers represent?
4. What are *two* questions you could ask about this data?
5. What generalization could you make based on the data in the chart?

EXERCISE 8.12

Double Bar Graph

DIRECTIONS: *Double bar graphs* compare two kinds of data. A *legend* defines the colored bars. Work with a partner. After examining **Figure 8.16**, answer the questions about this bar graph.

FIGURE 8.16

Sources of Capital for Entrepreneurs

Small businesses get financing from various sources; the most important is personal savings.

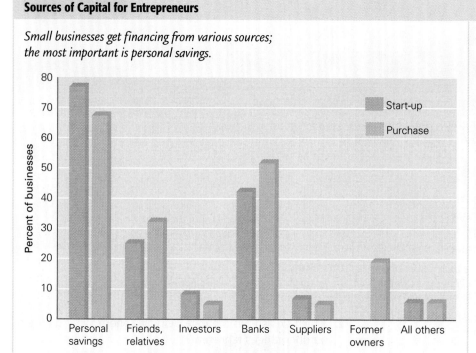

Questions:

1. What did you learn by reading the caption and the legend?

2. What information appears on the x axis? What appears on the y axis?

3. Estimate the percentages for each bar. Write the percentages on the top of the bars.

4. What *two comparison* questions could you pose for data in Figure 8.16?

Figure 6.2 from Pride/Hughes/Kapoor, *Business, 7th ed.,* p. 167. Houghton Mifflin, © 2002.

EXERCISE 8.13

Horizontal Bar Graphs

DIRECTIONS: Examine **Figure 8.17**. Notice that the topics being graphed appear on the *y axis*. The length of the bars shows the frequency rate. Because exact percentages or data appear at the end of the bars to avoid possible misinterpretations, the frequency axis is not labelled. Work with a partner. Answer the questions that appear next to the following bar graph.

FIGURE 8.17

Consumer Spending

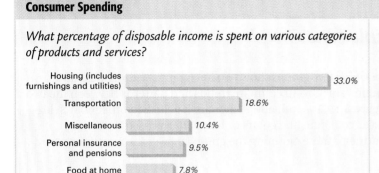

What percentage of disposable income is spent on various categories of products and services?

Category	Percentage
Housing (includes furnishings and utilities)	33.0%
Transportation	18.6%
Miscellaneous	10.4%
Personal insurance and pensions	9.5%
Food at home	7.8%
Food away from home	5.7%
Health care	5.4%
Entertainment	4.9%
Apparel and services	4.7%

Figure 13.5 from Pride/Hughes/Kapoor, *Business 7th ed.,* p. 375. Houghton Mifflin, © 2002.

Questions:

1. Does this graph reflect your disposable income expenditures?
2. Are the combined expenditures for "food away from home" and "entertainment" greater than or less than the "miscellaneous" expenditures?
3. What are two additional questions you can create to compare or contrast data?

Line Graphs

Line graphs, also called linear graphs, plot points on a coordinate grid or graph to form one continuous line to show trends and compare data. When you encounter line graphs, carefully read the *horizontal axis* and the *vertical axis* and then look for trends as well as increases, decreases, and changes in the occurrence of a particular action or event.

For example, in **Figure 8.18,** you can quickly notice a trend: a decline in the number of work force members belonging to unions. After identifying the trend, examine and compare the data for various years; look for patterns and ask yourself questions. Use the two coordinates to learn about any specific point on the graph. For example, in Figure 8.18, by drawing a vertical line from 1991 to the line in the graph, and then drawing a horizontal line from that point to the percentage axis, you learn that 16 percent of the work force belonged to a union in 1991. How does that percentage compare to the percentage in 2005? What are the percentage differences between 1985 and 1995? 1995 and 2005?

Line graphs, also called linear graphs, plot points on a coordinate grid or graph to form one continuous line to show trends and compare data.

CONCEPT CHECK 8.32

Which types of graphic materials are used to compare data? Which is best for identifying parts of a whole? Which are most effective for showing trends?

FIGURE 8.18

Unions

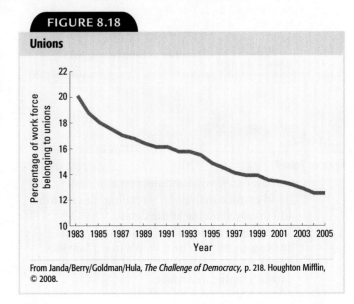

From Janda/Berry/Goldman/Hula, *The Challenge of Democracy,* p. 218. Houghton Mifflin, © 2008.

EXERCISE 8.14

Double Line Graph

DIRECTIONS: *Double line graphs* show two line graphs within one chart. Double line graphs are used to compare trends and patterns between the two subjects. In **Figure 8.19**, the individual lines are labelled; in other charts, legends may be used to define line colors or line patterns used in the chart. Work with a partner. After examining the graph, answer the questions about the graph.

FIGURE 8.19

Retrieval Failures and Forgetting

Tulving and Psotka (1971) found that people's ability to recall a list of items was strongly affected by the number of other lists they learned before being tested on the first one. When retrieval cues were provided on a second test, however, retroactive interference from the intervening lists almost disappeared.

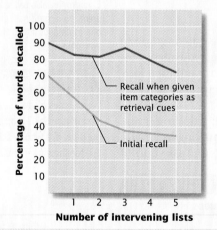

Figure 6.12 from Bernstein/Nash, *Essentials of Psychology*, p. 230. © 2008, Houghton Mifflin.

Questions:

1. How does the caption help you interpret the graph?

2. What happened when a person learned two additional lists and was tested on the first list without using any retrieval cues? What happened when retrieval cues were provided for a second test?

3. What is retroactive interference?

4. What can you conclude or summarize after studying this graph?

CHECK POINT 8.3

ANSWERS APPEAR ON PAGE A5

True or False?

_____ 1. In most cases, you can interpret and understand graphic materials by reading the caption and briefly glancing at the details.

_____ 2. "Stringing ideas together" is a strategy that involves using your own words to explain the information and the relationships between data in graphic materials.

_____ 3. Because graphic materials effectively condense printed information into visual forms, students should always copy the illustrations, graphs, or charts into their notes.

Improve Your Grade
Online Practice 4:
Graphic Materials

GROUP PROCESSING:
A COLLABORATIVE LEARNING ACTIVITY

Form groups of three or four students. Complete the following directions.

1. Each student needs to bring to the group at least one textbook used in another course. Take five minutes to skim through the various textbooks brought to the group.

2. Create the following chart. List the subjects of the textbooks that belong in each category of your chart. Be prepared to discuss your chart with the class.

Textbook Characteristics	Textbooks
Include photographs, illustrations, and diagrams:	
Include charts and graphs:	
Focus mainly on declarative (factual) knowledge:	
Focus mainly on procedural knowledge:	
Use factual (expository) writing styles:	
Use more figurative than expository writing styles:	
Present information in a narrative style:	
Present topics in a fixed, chronological sequence:	
Present topics based on specific themes:	

READING IN THE CONTENT AREAS

 Discuss strategies to use to read college textbooks for different disciplines and content areas.

Understanding the differences among textbooks from various content areas can help you select the most appropriate reading and study skills strategies to use for each textbook. Increasing your awareness of characteristics of different kinds of textbooks and the kinds of reading skills required for different content areas increases your understanding of the options you have for selecting appropriate strategies to use. **Figure 8.20** summarizes common reading skills and strategies for different content areas and kinds of textbooks.

Notice in Figure 8.20 that each of the content areas and subject matters involve working with declarative (factual) knowledge and procedural knowledge, two

CONCEPT CHECK 8.33

Based on your experiences with different courses and textbooks, do you agree with the information in Figure 8.20? Why or why not?

FIGURE 8.20

Common Reading Skills in Content Areas

Subjects	Declarative Knowledge	Procedural Knowledge	Organizational Patterns	Graphic Materials	Survey Chapter	Optional Overview Reading	SQ4R	Triple Q	Customized
Composition	X	X	X		X	X			X
Literature	X	X	X		X	X		X	X
Social Sciences	X	X	X	X	X	X	X	X	
Science	X	X	X	X	X	X	X	X	X
Mathematics	X	X	X	X	X	X			X

kinds of knowledge you first learned about in Chapter 3. The following are reminders about working with declarative knowledge:

▌ Use *elaborative rehearsal study strategies,* which involve working with information in new and creative ways, to learn factual information. These strategies may involve creating associations, mnemonics, visual mappings, and notes, as well as using processes that involve reciting and other Look-Away Techniques for feedback.

▌ Declarative knowledge includes learning definitions for terminology, symbols, and formulas; learning rules, patterns, and specific kinds of organizational structures; learning the parts of a whole and learning ways to analyze or interpret materials; and memorizing prototypes (models) that can be used to compare against other paragraphs or math problems.

The following are reminders about working with procedural knowledge:

▌ Procedural knowledge involves *learning to apply steps or processes* to achieve an outcome. In composition classes, you use procedural knowledge each time you generate ideas, gather and organize information, write drafts, edit, proofread, revise, analyze styles of writing, and critique work. In science and math classes, you use procedural knowledge each time you apply a series of steps to solve an equation or a problem.

▌ Strategies to learn procedural knowledge involve reworking and solving problems *multiple times*. Each time you rework familiar problems, the steps and processes become more internalized, more solidified in memory, and more routine.

▌ Learning procedural knowledge requires time. Trying to learn procedural knowledge quickly without using practice and repetition often leads to partial and inaccurate learning, "skill gaps" that cause problems later when you try to work with higher level skills, rote memory without understanding the how and why a process works, and a sense of confusion and frustration.

CONCEPT CHECK 8.34

Why are elaborative rehearsal strategies effective for factual knowledge but less effective for procedural knowledge?

▌ Repetition increases your problem-solving speed and accuracy; it helps you internalize the process so you can perform it automatically; and it helps you develop the ability to generalize the steps so you can apply them to new problems.

▌ Working problems multiple times provides you with feedback and the opportunity to correct any calculation or application errors.

EXERCISE 8.15

Textbook Reading Inventory

DIRECTIONS: Go to Appendix B, pages A15–A17, to complete the Textbook Reading Inventory.

Composition Textbooks

Composition courses encompass a wide range of writing skills—from grammar and sentence structure skills, to paragraph level skills, to essay skills involving writing for specific audiences, specific purposes, and within specific contexts. Becoming an accomplished writer involves acquiring:

▌ The foundation skills of grammar, punctuation, usage, and sentence structures

▌ A well-developed expressive vocabulary

▌ Broad background knowledge of many subjects

▌ Skills in organizing information and ideas effectively

▌ Analytical reading and critical thinking skills

▌ Effective research skills

Notice in Figure 8.20 that a *customized reading system* is effective for composition textbooks. Your instructors and authors of composition textbooks are aware of the difficulties and challenges many students experience with written expression. To address students' needs, composition textbooks include a variety of student-friendly features that you can use to work your way through a chapter: step-by-step explanations, clear examples, and ample exercises to practice skills.

Literature Textbooks

Most colleges offer a variety of literature courses with different purposes, content, and *genre* (categories of literature, such as poetry, drama/plays, and types of fiction). *Survey courses* involve the study of major writers and literary works from a specific period of time, nationality, or culture. Other literature courses may focus on specific genres, such as short stories, poetry, mythology, essays, or novels. For many courses, *Cliff Notes,* a special series of handbooks to help you interpret pieces of literature, are available study tools that you can use.

CONCEPT CHECK 8.35

How many college writing courses have you completed? Are the prerequisites required for writing courses necessary? Why or why not?

CONCEPT CHECK 8.36

How do literature courses differ from social science and science courses? Do you enjoy literature courses? Why or why not?

Literature textbooks use imagery and figurative language—such as symbolism, multiple meanings, and figures of speech—to convey images, evoke emotions, develop themes and characters, and engage readers in the action of the plots. Following are common figures of speech and terminology you will encounter and need to learn to interpret in literature textbooks:

▌ *Metaphors* compare one object to another *without using* the words *like* or *as*.

▌ *Similes* compare one object to another by *using* words such as *like* or *as*.

▌ *Personification* gives human qualities or capabilities to objects, ideas, or animals.

▌ *Alliteration* is the repetitive use of one letter sound at the beginning of a series of words.

▌ *Hyperbole* is the use of exaggeration to create a specific effect.

Read Two or More Times

CONCEPT CHECK 8.37

How do the reading goals for the first reading of a story differ from the reading goals for a second or third reading?

For the full emotional impact of the writing, read the selection at least two times. For the *first reading,* read through the complete selection, uninterrupted, to get an overview; do not stop to analyze or take notes. Let yourself get immersed in the content and the flow of the action. For novels, your overview reading may involve reading one chapter at a time. For the *second,* and possibly the *third reading,* read with the goal to use thorough reading strategies to analyze and interpret the key literary elements. Write comments next to important passages, take notes on paper, or create visual mappings or charts to show important details. With each reading you comprehend on a deeper level and create a stronger impression of the information.

Create Schemas

Studying literature involves creating schemas for different literary forms. These schemas identify specific sets of conventions or standards, characteristics, and literary terminology used to think about and analyze the structure, content, and purpose of different kinds of literature. As you study different literary forms, you can create visual mappings to show schemas with key elements to use in analyzing or discussing each of the various literary forms. To construct schemas, pay close attention to the standard features, frameworks, patterns, and aspects of literature emphasized by your instructor. **Figure 8.21** shows a visual mapping (schema) you could use to read and analyze short stories. After reading a story once to get an overview and an emotional response from the story, read to identify important details and attach those details to the visual mapping.

Social Science Textbooks

CONCEPT CHECK 8.38

What social science courses have you completed? How were the textbooks for those courses similar? How did they differ?

The term *social science* refers to a large category of academic disciplines that study societies and humanity from different perspectives. Many social science textbooks include topics that will be somewhat familiar to you because of your personal experiences. However, reading and studying social science textbooks involve moving beyond personal experiences and into an academic look at aspects of human relationships in and to society. Social scientists pose theories, create models, and examine trends based on research, scientific methods, and observational studies. Common fields of social science are listed on the next page.

FIGURE 8.21

Key Elements in a Short Story

Theme: The main point, the subject, the meaning, or the purpose

Setting: The location and the time of the story

Characters: The main character and the minor characters

■ **Physical characteristics:** age, gender, body type, facial features, race or ethnic group

■ **Social characteristics:** family, occupation, economic status, religion, political point of view, cultural background

■ **Psychological characteristics:** beliefs, motives, attitudes, personality, likes/dislikes, mental state of mind

■ **Moral characteristics:** values, conflicts, beliefs, ethics

Plot: Sequence of events from beginning to a turning point, and finally to a climax or conclusion

Point of View: Who tells the story, first, second, or third person

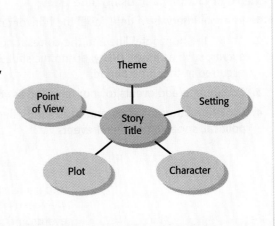

Common Fields of Social Science

Anthropology	Finance	Marketing
Archaeology	Foreign Policy	Philosophy
Business	Geography	Political Science
Counseling	History	Psychology
Criminal Justice	Information Science	Public Administration
Economics	International Relations	Sociology
Education	Law	Women's Studies
Ethnic Studies	Linguistics	

Use the Textbook Features

Each social science textbook has its own "style or personality." After working through one or two chapters in a specific social science textbook, you will become familiar with the format and standard features characteristic of your textbook. You will notice quickly that social science textbooks are rich with graphic materials designed to create interest and curiosity, explain concepts and theories, and condense statistics and data into visual forms that are easy to read and understand. As you work with social science textbooks, spend ample time reading and studying the graphic materials and relating them to the paragraphs that contain the more extensive details and explanations.

Create Time Lines for History Textbooks

History textbooks portray an event or series of events that occurred in the past. Unlike other social science textbooks, history textbooks use a narrative, story-telling approach to explain the unfolding of events influenced by specific individuals, groups, governments, and cultural factors, such as economics, religion, art,

CONCEPT CHECK 8.39

Why are time lines effective study tools to identify cause-effect relationships? What other kinds of textbooks might include data that you could present on time lines?

FIGURE 8.22

Creating a Time Line

Steps for Creating and Using Time Lines:

1. In equal intervals of time, label the horizontal line.
2. Above the horizontal line and the corresponding year, write the historical events, such as a war, treaty, economic shift, or political leadership that occurred in that time period.
3. Continue to add events to your time line as you work through the chapters.
4. Look for patterns, trends, and cause-and-effect relationships among the political, social, and cultural events.

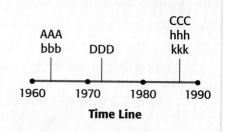

Time Line

and social structures. **Figure 8.22** shows the basic structure of a time line and the steps to use to create a time line that can increase your understanding of historical events and relationships.

Science Textbooks

CONCEPT CHECK 8.40

How do science textbooks differ from literature and social science textbooks?

The "hard sciences" or natural sciences include biology, chemistry, computer science, engineering, environmental science, geology, and physics. Science textbooks are densely written and filled with declarative knowledge and procedural knowledge. The study of the sciences also includes:

▌ Inductive arguments: observable experiments, evidence, or proof to arrive at a conclusion

▌ Hands-on, personal laboratory demonstrations, experiments, or observations

▌ Emphasis on understanding how parts relate to whole concepts or frameworks

▌ Conceptual understanding: understanding scientific concepts in order to solve problems in the appropriate context

▌ Problem-solving skills and analysis: knowing how to approach a problem, steps to solve a problem, and problem-analysis to explain the thinking processes used to reach a solution

▌ Applications: using concepts and problem-solving skills in everyday applications

▌ The scientific method: experimentation, hypotheses and theories, and laws

Acquire Background Knowledge

CONCEPT CHECK 8.41

What is the relationship between background knowledge and long-term memory schemas? How does background knowledge enhance comprehension?

When topics or concepts are new to you, you may lack background knowledge or experiences with the subject matter. Learning basic information about a subject creates a schema in memory upon which you can attach more in-depth or complex concepts and details. To lay a foundation for the new material, use the following suggestions:

▌ *Videos:* Check your science lab and library for available videos to view.

▌ *Internet:* Conduct Internet searches to locate and read articles about the subject.

❚ *Magazines:* Locate magazine articles related to the topic.

❚ *Surveying the chapter:* Survey the chapter before thorough reading and *before* the lecture on the topic.

❚ *Overview reading:* Conduct an uninterrupted overview reading of a chapter or a section of a chapter before thorough reading and *before* the lecture on the topic if possible.

Read Slowly and Thoroughly

Science textbooks are dense with complex scientific processes and reasoning, theories, predictions, explanations, evidence, patterns, numbers, symbols, formulas, graphic materials, and definitions. Because of the complexity of information in science textbooks and the critical thinking skills associated with the study of science, your reading goal for science textbooks is to read slowly, sometimes sentence by sentence, to comprehend, process, and integrate information. Another goal is to use your repertoire of reading and study strategies so you can adjust to the content and the textbook's level of difficulty.

Use a 3:1 Study Ratio for Some Science Classes

After surveying and possibly conducting an overview reading of a chapter, begin the process of thorough reading. For reading and studying science textbooks, you may need to use a 3:1 ratio in order to have ample time to read slowly and carefully, comprehend and integrate information, create notes or study tools, complete lab assignments, and finish textbook assignments.

Mathematics Textbooks

Studying mathematics is similar to studying a foreign language: it involves learning a language of symbols and formulas. Studying mathematics is also similar to studying fields of science: it involves learning and using formulas, equations, proofs, and problem-solving steps to reach solutions. The following points about studying math and using your math textbooks are important to remember:

❚ Studying mathematics involves learning a progression of concepts and skills, each building on previously learned information and setting a foundation for higher level skills. The process is ongoing, for there is always another higher level of mathematics to master.

❚ Working memory requires time to understand new abstract concepts, connect chunks of information, create associations, retrieve learned information, and perform a variety of functions to complete steps of a process.

❚ In learning math concepts, you often need to direct your mind to switch back and forth between new information and information stored in long-term memory. The process is complex and involves many cognitive processes, so strive to maintain undivided attention as you work with your math textbooks and notes.

❚ Provide ample time to process math skills. Study every day of the week; use a 3:1 study ratio; survey chapters or topics before lectures; schedule a study block shortly after class to begin working problem sets; and schedule time to work with a study partner or in a study group.

❚ Utilize all available resources: math lab videos, tutors, tutorials, or other supplemental materials.

CONCEPT CHECK 8.42

Is a 2:1 study ratio or a 3:1 study ratio more effective for your science courses? Explain why. For what other courses do you use a 3:1 study ratio?

CONCEPT CHECK 8.43

Are you currently using the recommended time-management principles for your math classes? Why or why not?

▌ Using a Customized Reading System is the often the most effective system to use for math textbooks. Use the three steps on page 222 to devise a step-by-step system to read and work with your math textbooks. See Figure 8.7, page 223, for an example of a Customized Reading System for a math textbook.

Study Examples and Memorize Prototypes

Study each example carefully, step by step, until you can follow the steps and understand the logic behind the process. Practice verbally explaining each step of the process to solve that type of problem; then express the same information using mathematical symbols and equations. Read the equation out loud.

Without referring to the text, rework the example problems and check your accuracy. Correct any mistakes immediately. Select one of the examples for each problem type to memorize and use as a *prototype* (model) that you can recall at later times as a reminder of the steps to use to solve that problem type. Problem sets that immediately follow new examples often mirror the example problems. Compare a new problem to the example problem to verify that both belong in the same category or type of problem. Then apply the problem-solving steps.

Use RSTUV to Read and Solve Problems

The **RSTUV Problem-Solving Method** is a five-step approach to solve math word problems. Each letter of RSTUV represents one step of this problem-solving approach.

▌ **READ** the problem, not once or twice, but until you understand it. Pay attention to key words or instructions such as *compute, draw, write, construct, make, show, identify, state, simplify, solve,* and *graph.*

▌ **SELECT** the unknown; that is, find out what the problem asks for. One good way to look for the unknown is to look for the question mark (?) and carefully read the material preceding it. Try to determine what information is given and what is missing.

▌ **THINK** of a plan to solve the problem. Problem solving requires many skills and strategies. Some of them are *look for a pattern; examine a related problem; make tables, pictures, and diagrams; write an equation; work backward;* and *make a guess.*

▌ **USE** the techniques you are studying to carry out the plan. Look for procedures that can be used to solve specific problems. Then carry out the plan. Check each step.

▌ **VERIFY** the answer. Look back and check the results of the original problem. Is the answer reasonable? Can you find it some other way?

From Bello and Britton, *Topics in Contemporary Mathematics, 6th ed.,* pp. 5–6. Copyright © 1997. Reprinted by permission of Houghton Mifflin, Inc.

CONCEPT CHECK 8.44

What is a *prototype,* and what is its use?

The **RSTUV Problem-Solving Method** is a five-step approach to solve math word problems.

CONCEPT CHECK 8.45

What are the benefits of using a system such as RSTUV to solve math equations and real-world story problems?

Check Point 8.4

True or False?

_____ 1. You can identify and use prototypes to recall steps of a process in composition, math, and science textbooks.

_____ 2. Factual knowledge is also called declarative knowledge; elaborative rehearsal strategies are recommended for learning factual knowledge.

_____ 3. Literature textbooks are the only type of textbook that uses figurative language.

_____ 4. You can strengthen your comprehension skills by acquiring background knowledge about an unfamiliar topic before you begin reading the textbook.

Improve Your Grade
Online Practice 5:
Different Textbooks

Reflective Writing 8.2

Improve Your Grade
Reflective Writing 8.2

On separate paper, in a journal, or online at this textbook's website, respond to the following questions:

1. Which skills in this chapter will benefit you the most in terms of improving your textbook reading and learning performance? Explain with specific details.

2. Discuss your results from the Textbook Reading Inventory (Exercise 8.15 on page 241). What did you learn about your current choice of strategies for different textbooks? What changes will you make in the way you read your textbooks?

LEARNING OBJECTIVES REVIEW

1 *Define active reading, and discuss active reading strategies and textbook reading systems to use with college textbooks.*

- Active reading is the process of using effective strategies to engage working memory to achieve specific reading goals. Six essential strategies can help students become more active readers.

- Nine additional strategies help students unlock the meaning and increase comprehension of difficult paragraphs. They include verbalizing, questioning, visualizing, chunking, and working with graphic materials.

- The SQ4R textbook reading system consists of six steps. After *surveying* and *questioning*, the next three steps use the read-record-recite cycle; the final step is *review*.

- The Triple Q system, which focuses on writing questions before, during, and after the reading process, begins after surveying a chapter. You can use question words from Bloom's Taxonomy to write questions on different levels of difficulty.

- The Customized Reading System is based on using the author's suggestions and the textbook features to devise a reading plan or system for a specific textbook.

2 *Define and discuss the seven organizational patterns used to organize details in paragraphs.*

- Seven organizational patterns are discussed:
    - The *chronological pattern* presents details in a logical time sequence.
    - The *process pattern* presents a specific procedure or order of steps to use to do, create, repair, or solve problems.
    - The *comparison or contrast pattern* shows similarities and/or differences for two or more subjects.
    - The *definition pattern* uses explanations, characteristics, examples, analogies, and negations to define a specific term.
    - The *examples pattern* uses examples to expand a reader's understanding of a term, a concept, or a theory.
    - The *cause/effect pattern* shows the relationship between two or more items by indicating which items or actions cause specific effects.
    - The *whole-and-parts pattern* shows the individual parts, components, or entities that together create a whole object, concept, or theory.

- Descriptions, clue words, diagrams, and an example paragraph appear for each pattern.

3 *Explain and use strategies to read and interpret six kinds of graphic materials.*

- Graphic materials convert verbal information into mainly visual formats. Photographs, illustrations and diagrams; pie charts; flow charts; tables; bar graphs; and line graphs are the six kinds of graphic materials you will encounter frequently in college textbooks.

- The following eight Essential Strategies for each type of graphic help you read, interpret, and effectively use the information presented in visual formats:
    - Read the title, captions, legends, and labels.
    - Examine the details carefully.
    - Verbalize or "string ideas together."
    - Visualize the graphic.
    - Ask yourself questions about the content.
    - Copy or refer to graphic materials in your notes.
    - Expand the graphic materials in your notes.
    - Write a short summary about the graphic material.

4 *Discuss strategies to use to read college textbooks for different disciplines and content areas.*

- Composition, literature, social science, science, and math textbooks each have unique characteristics. You can select the most appropriate reading systems and strategies for textbooks when you understanding the characteristics and skills commonly associated with specific fields of study.

- Eight essential strategies help you read, interpret, and effectively use the information presented in visual formats.

- A Textbook Reading Inventory is available to help you identify effective reading strategies that you are using and strategies that you can begin using to increase your reading performance.

True or False?

_____ 1. During active reading, new information and previously learned information appear together in working memory.

_____ 2. Formulating questions should only be done before you begin the reading process.

_____ 3. Surveying a chapter or doing overview reading before you begin the process of thorough reading helps create a mindset and schemas in memory for new information.

_____ 4. You can omit the fourth step of SQ4R without weakening this reading system.

_____ 5. The second step in SQ4R is the same as the first step in the Triple Q system.

_____ 6. Writing Q_2 questions in the Triple Q system also involves highlighting key words in the paragraph that answer the Q_2 questions.

_____ 7. A Customized Reading System allows students to create shortcuts to move through chapters quickly and focus only on the sections that are difficult for them.

_____ 8. The axes on bar and line graphs identify subjects being graphed and some type of frequency data.

Multiple Choice

_____ 1. Which of the following graphics are the least likely to show comparisons of data?
   a. Pie charts or circle graphs
   b. Photographs or illustrations
   c. Double bar graphs or double line graphs
   d. Tables

_____ 2. Which of the following organizational patterns frequently appear in science textbooks?
   a. Process pattern
   b. Definition pattern
   c. Cause-and-effect pattern
   d. All of the above

_____ 3. Which of the following are *not* common elements in literature textbooks?
   a. Graphic materials
   b. Figures of speech
   c. Chronological pattern
   d. Narrative language

_____ 4. Which of the following statements is *not* true or accurate?
   a. Pie charts are based on a parts-and-whole pattern for information.
   b. Tables condense large amounts of data into columns and rows.
   c. A histogram is a single bar graph that shows horizontal bars.
   d. Legends that accompany graphs define symbols, colors, or line patterns in the graphs.

Short-Answer Questions

Write your answers on separate paper.

1. Define the steps of SQ4R.
2. When is creating a Customized Reading System appropriate and effective?
3. What do active readers do to avoid slipping into *automatic pilot* when they read textbooks?

CL **ACE the Test**
Four Online Practice Tests

Online Resources

9 Developing Notetaking Skills

LEARNING OBJECTIVES

1 ▶ Discuss the rationale for taking notes and effective strategies to use with all notetaking systems.

2 ▶ Discuss and apply strategies for marking or annotating textbook passages.

3 ▶ Discuss and apply the five steps of the Cornell system for taking notes.

4 ▶ Discuss and apply effective strategies for creating two- and three-column notes.

Chapter Outline

CL **Prepare for Class**
Chapter Outline

5 ▶ *Discuss and apply effective strategies for taking informal outline notes.*

Effective notetaking is an essential skill for college students. In this chapter, you will learn about five powerful notetaking systems that lead to greater academic success: annotation, the five-step Cornell Notetaking System, two-column notes, three-column notes, and outlines. After learning to use all five notetaking systems, you will be equipped with the skills and ability to use the combinations of notetaking systems that are best matched to your individual textbooks and your preferences.

CHAPTER 9 PROFILE

Developing Notetaking Skills

ANSWER, **SCORE**, and **RECORD** your profile before you read this chapter. If you need to review the process, refer to the complete directions given in the profile for Chapter 1 on page 4.

ONLINE: You can complete the profile and get your score online at this textbook's website.

	YES	NO
1. I am selective when I take notes; I write down only the important ideas and details.		
2. I spend significantly more time rereading chapters than I spend studying from my notes.		
3. I highlight main ideas and only short phrases in my textbook to avoid highlighting too much.		
4. I write short notes or use abbreviations in the margins of my textbook.		
5. I copy as much word-for-word information as I can so my notes are accurate and detailed.		
6. I recite, reflect upon, and review my textbook notes.		
7. I use the same notetaking system for all of my textbooks.		
8. My notes summarize important charts, graphs, or pictures in the textbook.		
9. I avoid using an outline notetaking system because it is too confusing.		
10. I am confident about my ability to take effective notes and use a variety of notetaking systems for all my textbooks.		

QUESTIONS LINKED TO THE CHAPTER LEARNING OBJECTIVES:

Questions 1, 2:	objective 1	Questions 7, 8:	objective 4
Questions 3, 4:	objective 2	Question 9:	objective 5
Questions 5, 6:	objective 3	Question 10:	all objectives

TEXTBOOK NOTETAKING SKILLS

1 ▶ *Discuss the rationale for taking notes and effective strategies to use with all notetaking systems.*

Taking notes on textbook information moves you into an *active learning mode* that promotes thinking carefully about information and selecting what is important to learn and what is not. Taking textbook notes involves encoding information kinesthetically and visually, which together create stronger mental impressions of information. Notetaking also activates working memory and uses all Twelve Principles of Memory.

Textbooks are a focal point for learning and mastering course content. When you read a chapter in a textbook *before* the information is presented in class, you become familiar with the topics and the content of the chapter, and thus are better equipped to follow and understand class lectures, discussions, or activities. When you take notes *during* the reading process, you hold information longer in working memory, analyze information more carefully, and create notes you can use to rehearse and review. When you take notes *after* reading, they are often a different kind of notes that you use to reinforce learning. For example, perhaps initially you annotated your textbook; after reading, you decide to create outline notes to use for additional practice and review.

The Importance of Notetaking

Sometimes students are fooled by the fact that they seem to understand and temporarily remember what they read, so they feel there is no need to write down notes. However, information can fade over time or become confused with new information. Taking notes combats both memory fading and interference and backs up or reinforces memory. The following are additional important points about taking textbook notes:

▮ Research shows a high correlation between notetaking skills and test performance. The better students' notes are, the better are their grades.

▮ Your learning goal for taking textbook notes is to create a comprehensive set of notes that you can use to learn, rehearse, and review to help you master textbook information.

▮ Taking textbook notes involves condensing or reducing large amounts of information into more manageable units that are easier to study and review.

▮ Studying from well-developed notes is more time efficient than reading and rereading chapters of information. Effective textbook notes save you time in the long run.

▮ Learning to use specific notetaking systems is achieved more comfortably by first learning to use the systems to take textbook notes because you can control the pace, refer back to printed information, and learn the systems without the pressure of lecture situations.

 Improve Your Grade
Online Flashcards
Glossary

CONCEPT CHECK 9.1

How does taking notes affect your memory processes?

CONCEPT CHECK 9.2

When in the learning process should you take textbook notes?

CONCEPT CHECK 9.3

What benefits do you gain by taking notes?

Why do the essential strategies work for all notetaking systems? Which ones do you use consistently?

Essential Strategies for Textbook Notetaking

In the following sections, you will learn about five notetaking systems: annotation, Cornell notes, two-column notes, three-column notes, and outline notes. Each notetaking system differs in its structure, but all work effectively when you use the eight Essential Strategies for Textbook Notetaking as shown in **Figure 9.1**.

FIGURE 9.1

Essential Strategies for Textbook Notetaking

▌ **Understand what you read before taking notes.** Read a paragraph or chunk of information, pause, think about the information, be sure that you understand it, and then take notes.

▌ **Be selective.** Your notes should be a *condensed* version of the textbook, not a word-for-word copy of the textbook pages. Capture only the important concepts, main ideas, and supporting details in your notes.

▌ **Paraphrase or reword.** Shorten textbook explanations or information by using your own words to state main ideas and important details as long as your wording presents the information accurately.

▌ **Include textbook reminders in your notes.** Instead of copying large charts or lengthy sections of important text, write a reminder in your notes to see page XX in the textbook.

▌ **Label your notes.** As you progress through the term, you will have many pages of notes. To avoid confusion, include textbook chapter numbers and number each page of your notes.

▌ **Use spaced practice.** Make several contacts with your notes over different periods of time. You can use them as a warm-up activity to put you in the mindset of the subject the next time you sit down to study, or you can schedule time each week to review your notes for the week.

▌ **Use feedback strategies.** Use Look-Away Techniques, such as reciting or visualizing, to check the completeness and accuracy of your learning.

▌ **Review your notes.** Use immediate review to create a strong impression in memory. Use ongoing review to keep information active and accessible in working memory.

ANSWERS APPEAR ON PAGE A5

True or False?

___ 1. Taking textbook notes on textbooks that are easy to understand is not necessary.

___ 2. Students' test performance and grades are linked to the quality and use of their notes.

___ 3. Textbook notes should be condensed versions of textbook information.

___ 4. Notetaking encodes information in new ways and creates stronger memory impressions of material.

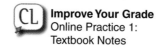

Improve Your Grade
Online Practice 1:
Textbook Notes

REFLECTIVE WRITING 9.1

Improve Your Grade
Reflective Writing 9.1

On separate paper, in a journal, or online at this textbook's website, respond to the following questions.

1. What kinds of notes do you currently take when you read your textbooks? Have your textbook notes proven to be effective? Why or why not?

2. What are the benefits you will gain by taking and studying from textbook notes?

ANNOTATION

2 ▶ *Discuss and apply strategies for marking or annotating textbook passages.*

Annotating is the process of highlighting, underlining, making marginal notes, or marking specific information in printed materials. By using this active learning process that involves interacting with printed text and holding information longer in your working memory, you reduce the risk of information fading or being displaced before you have time to process it.

> **Annotating** is the process of highlighting, underlining, marking marginal notes, or marking specific information in printed materials.

Annotating Important Information

Figure 9.2 shows five annotation strategies for marking or annotating your textbooks. Whenever you see the term *marking*, it includes *highlighting* or *underlining*, whichever is your preference. Highlighting (using different colors of highlighter pens) is preferred by most students because it tends to make information stand out more than underlining. However, you may substitute underlining for highlighting if you prefer.

In Chapter 7, you learned about highlighting the complete topic sentence, selectively highlighting key words or phrases that support the topic sentence, circling terminology, and highlighting key words in definitions. (See pages 196–198, 200.) Numbering steps or lists of information and making marginal notes complete the strategies for annotating textbooks.

> **CONCEPT CHECK 9.5**
>
> What should you highlight or mark? How can you avoid over-marking?

FIGURE 9.2

Annotation Strategies for Marking Textbooks

▌ Highlight the **complete topic sentence**, which states the main idea.

▌ Selectively highlight **key words or phrases** that support the topic sentence.

▌ **Circle terminology** and **highlight key words** in the definitions.

▌ **Enumerate steps** or lists of information.

▌ Make **marginal notes** to emphasize important ideas and integrate information.

FIGURE 9.3

Marking a Paragraph, Enumerating, and Making Marginal Notes

Earth System
1. atmosphere
2. hydrosphere
3. lithosphere
4. biosphere

The earth system contains a number of interconnected subsystems, often described as "environmental spheres." The four major subsystems are the ①(atmosphere) or the ocean of air that overlies the entire earth's surface; the ②(hydrosphere) or the water of the surface and near-surface regions of the earth; the ③(lithosphere) or the massive accumulation of rock and metal that forms the solid body of the planet itself; and the ④(biosphere) or the layer of living organisms of which we are a part. All four respond in various ways to the flow of energy and materials through the earth system.

From Holt Atkinson, *Reading Enhancement and Development,* 5e, pp. 218–219. © 1995 Houghton Mifflin Co.

Enumerate Steps or Lists of Information

Enumerating means "numbering." A paragraph with a topic sentence that uses words such as *kinds of, reasons, advantages, causes, effects, ways,* or *steps* often has a list of supporting details that are identified by ordinals. **Ordinals** are words that signal a numbered sequence of items. Ordinals, or "number words," such as *first, second,* or *third,* help you identify and focus your attention on the separate items. Enumerating serves as a memory device, for it is easier to remember a fixed quantity of items than it is an unknown quantity of items.

Use a pen to write the numerals (1, 2, 3) on top of the ordinals in a paragraph. Watch for words such as *next, another,* and *finally,* which are placeholder words used to replace ordinals. Read carefully and write a new numeral on these words as well. In **Figure 9.3**, notice how the topic sentence (the main idea sentence) is *completely highlighted,* key words of supporting details are highlighted, terminology is circled, and numbers create a list of items. Brief notes in the margin summarize the information.

A topic sentence that states there are "five reasons" for something, lets you know that you should find five details that give five reasons. If you do not find ordinals or placeholder words that mark each reason, search carefully to identify and mark the five reasons.

Write Marginal Notes

Marginal notes are brief notes written in the margins of textbook pages. Marginal notes give you a glimpse at the important points in a paragraph. To avoid cluttered or difficult-to-read marginal notes, be selective and brief. The following are kinds of information that work effectively as marginal notes:

numbered lists of key ideas	short definitions of terms
study questions	comments or reactions
diagrams or pictures	key words to define
definitions of unfamiliar terms	questions to ask in class
? for unclear information	

Ordinals are words that signal a numbered sequence of items.

CONCEPT CHECK 9.6

What is the value of enumerating items in your notes?

Marginal notes are brief notes written in the margins of textbook pages.

CONCEPT CHECK 9.7

If a textbook provides marginal notes, is there a need for you to make marginal notes? Why or why not?

Using brackets and abbreviations in the margins helps you avoid cluttered margins:

▌ *Use Brackets for Large Sections of Information:* Rather than over-mark or clutter the margins with too many details, draw a bracket next to large sections of information or entire paragraphs that are densely written. You can add a note or abbreviation next to the bracket.

▌ *Use Abbreviations to Call Attention to Specific Kinds of Information:* You can use abbreviations next to brackets to draw your attention to sections you want to return to for further studying. The following are abbreviations you may want to use.

EX.	= example or examples		**Q.**	= question
DIFF.	= differences		**CE.**	= cause-effect
SUM.	= summary		**RE.**	= reasons why . . . ?
F.	= important fact		**REL.**	= important relationship
IMP.	= important to reread		**FORM.**	= formula
DEF.	= lengthy definition		**H.**	= hypotheses

Figure 9.4 shows various forms of annotation, including the use of arrows to connect ideas, to emphasize main ideas, details, and terminology.

FIGURE 9.4

Feminism

Around 1910 some of those concerned with women's place in society began using a new term, *feminism* to refer to their ideas. Whereas members of the woman movement spoke generally of duty and moral purity, feminists—more explicitly conscious of their identity as women—emphasized rights and self-development. Feminism, however, contained an inherent contradiction. ① On the one hand feminists argued that all women should unite in the struggle for rights because of their shared disadvantages as women. ② On the other, they insisted that sex-typing—treating women differently than men—must end because it resulted in discrimination. Thus feminists advocated the contradictory position that women should unite as a gender group for the purpose of abolishing all gender-based distinctions.

DIFF.

IMP.

Norton, *A People and a Nation,* p. 616. Copyright © 1998 Houghton Mifflin Co. Used with permission.

EXERCISE 9.1

Practice Annotating Maslow's Hierarchy

PURPOSE: Annotating textbook passages identifies what information is important to learn. Studying from annotations requires less time than rereading and restudying textbook chapters.

DIRECTIONS:

1. Read the following excerpt one paragraph at a time. Use the strategies for annotating in Figure 9.2, page 255. Annotate the passage.
2. Go to Exercise 9.1 in Appendix B, page A18, for the Annotation Checklist. Check the appropriate answers to reflect the way you annotated the Maslow's Hierarchy excerpt.

Maslow's Hierarchy

Maslow (1970) suggested that human behavior is influenced by a hierarchy, or ranking, of five classes of needs or motives. He said that needs at the lowest level of the hierarchy must be at least partially satisfied before people can be motivated by ones at higher levels. From the bottom to the top of Maslow's hierarchy, these five motives are as follow:

1. *Physiological,* such as the need for food, water, oxygen, and sleep.
2. *Safety,* such as the need to be cared for as a child and to have a secure income as an adult.
3. *Belongingness and love,* such as the need to be part of groups and to participate in affectionate sexual and nonsexual relationships.
4. *Esteem,* such as the need to be respected as a useful, honorable individual.
5. *Self-actualization,* which means reaching one's full potential. People motivated by this need explore and enhance relationships with others; follow interests for intrinsic pleasure rather than for money, status, or esteem; and are concerned with issues affecting all people, not just themselves.

Maslow's Hierarchy of Motives

Abraham Maslow saw human motives as organized in a hierarchy in which motives at lower levels come before those at higher levels. According to this view, self-actualization is the essence of mental health; but Maslow recognized that only rare individuals, such as Mother Teresa or Martin Luther King, Jr., approach full self-actualization. Take a moment to consider which level of Maslow's hierarchy you are focused on at this point in your life. Which level do you ultimately hope to reach?

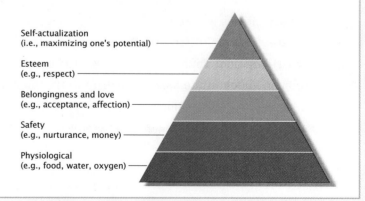

Self-actualization (i.e., maximizing one's potential)

Esteem (e.g., respect)

Belongingness and love (e.g., acceptance, affection)

Safety (e.g., nurturance, money)

Physiological (e.g., food, water, oxygen)

Maslow's hierarchy has been very influential over the years, partly because the needs associated with basic survival and security do generally take precedence over those related to self-enhancement of personal growth . . . But critics see the hierarchy as too simplistic. It doesn't predict or explain, for example, the motivation of people who starve themselves to draw attention to political or moral causes. Further, people may not have to satisfy one kind of need before addressing others; we can seek to satisfy several needs at once. Finally, the ordering of needs within the survival/security and enhancement/growth categories differs from culture to culture, suggesting that there may not be a single, universal hierarchy of needs.

To address some of the problems in Maslow's theory, Clayton Alderfer (1969) proposed *existence, relatedness, growth (ERG) theory*, which places human needs into just three categories: *existence needs* (such as for food and water), *relatedness needs* (e.g., for social interactions and attachments), and *growth needs* (such as for developing one's capabilities). Unlike Maslow, Alderfer doesn't assume that these needs must be satisfied in a particular order. Instead, he sees needs in each category as rising and falling from time to time and from situation to situation. When a need in one area is fulfilled, or even if it is frustrated, a person will be motivated to pursue some other needs. For example, if a breakup frustrates relatedness needs, a person might focus on existence or growth needs by eating more or volunteering to work late.

Source: Bernstein, Nash. *Essentials of Psychology*, Houghton Mifflin Co., 2008, pages 320–321.

Essential Strategies to Study from Annotations

To be truly effective, you need to practice using your annotations by personalizing, reciting, and working with the information in new ways. **Figure 9.5** shows five Essential Strategies for Studying from Annotations. Use these strategies to study your textbook annotations after you finish reading a paragraph, a group of paragraphs, or an end of a section in your textbook.

Reread Out Loud

When you reread only the marked information, it will sound broken or fragmented; however, you will hear yourself stating only main ideas and important supporting

CONCEPT CHECK 9.8

Why is rereading your highlighted and marked textbook not sufficient for boosting and challenging your memory? What steps should follow rereading your annotations?

FIGURE 9.5

Essential Strategies for Studying from Annotations

▌ Reread out loud only the marked annotations.

▌ Verbally string the ideas together by adding your own words.

▌ Recite without looking.

▌ Write summaries to reinforce the information.

▌ Use Figure 9.1 (page 254) strategies: spaced practice, immediate review, and ongoing review.

details. Read slowly so that your working memory has time to absorb the key points and to make associations.

Verbally String Ideas Together

Instead of reading fragmented annotated text, return to the text a second time to string ideas together more coherently. **Stringing ideas together** is the process of adding your own words to convert annotated text into full sentences and explanations. Verbalizing in this manner personalizes information as you state it in less formal language. Use transition words, such as *therefore, however,* or *also,* and ordinals, such as *first, second,* or *next* to list details or items. If you wish to create an auditory study tool, tape yourself stringing ideas together. Notice in the following example how textbook information from Figure 9.4 (page 257) is converted into a more conversational tone that is easier to remember.

> **Reading Annotations:** 1910 . . . feminism . . . woman movement . . . duty . . . moral purity . . . feminists . . . rights and self-development

> **Stringing Ideas Together:** In 1910, *the term* feminism *was introduced. Women who were a part of the* woman movement *emphasized* duty and moral purity. The feminists *in 1910, however,* emphasized *women's* rights and self-development.

Recite Without Looking

Take your eyes off the textbook and paraphrase; recite what you learned and explain the information using complete sentences. Glance down at the annotated information and marginal notes to check your accuracy. If you omitted important points or stated some information incorrectly, redo the reciting process and correct your errors.

Write Summaries

A summary gives you a written record of the information you stated out loud when you strung ideas together. Write a summary that includes the main ideas and the important details. Use your summary as a study tool to review for a test.

Stringing ideas together is the process of adding your own words to convert annotated text into full sentences and explanations.

CONCEPT CHECK 9.9

Explain how to "string ideas together" when you study from annotations.

EXERCISE 9.2

Stringing Ideas Together

Work with a partner. Complete the following directions.

1. Take turns using your annotations in Exercise 9.1 to "string ideas together" in coherent, complete sentences. Since stringing ideas together involves using your own words, your verbal presentation will differ from your partner's presentation.

2. Close your books. Recite the information you learned from Exercise 9.1. Ask your partner to check your accuracy and the completeness of your recited information.

CHECK POINT 9.2

Multiple Choice

_____ 1. Which of the following is *not* true about stringing ideas together from your annotated notes? Stringing ideas together
   a. should occur after you have created written summaries.
   b. involves connecting ideas by using transition words and informal language.
   c. involves activating the auditory channel by verbalizing and reciting information.
   d. may occur after each paragraph or after sections of information.

_____ 2. Annotating a textbook includes
   a. writing notes in the margins.
   b. highlighting topic sentences and key words.
   c. circling terminology and enumerating items in a list.
   d. all of the above.

Improve Your Grade
Online Practice 2:
Annotating

THE CORNELL NOTETAKING SYSTEM

3 ▶ *Discuss and apply the five steps of the Cornell system for taking notes.*

The **Cornell Notetaking System** is a five-step notetaking process used to take notes from textbooks or from lectures. This powerful notetaking system was designed by Dr. Walter Pauk at Cornell University more than forty-five years ago when he recognized students' need to learn how to take more effective notes. Many college and university instructors consider this the most effective notetaking system for college students.

The goal of the Cornell Notetaking System is to take notes that are so accurate and detailed that you *may not need to go back to the book to study*. The **Five *R*'s of Cornell** are record, reduce, recite, reflect, and review. To avoid weakening this powerful system, use all five *R*'s shown in **Figure 9.6** to record and study your notes.

To prepare your notebook paper for Cornell notes, draw a two-and-one-half-inch margin down the left side of your notebook paper. You do not need to draw a margin on the backs of your paper because you will be taking notes *only on the front side of your paper* and leaving the backs empty until the reflect step. (You may want to ask your campus bookstore if it carries Cornell or "law notebook" paper with the wider left margin.) At the top of the first page, write the course name, chapter number, and date. For all the following pages, just write the chapter number and the page number of your notes.

The **Cornell Notetaking System** is a five-step notetaking process to use to take notes from textbooks or from lectures.

The **Five *R*'s of Cornell** are record, reduce, recite, reflect, and review.

CONCEPT CHECK 9.10

What are the Five *R*'s of Cornell? Do these steps incorporate all Twelve Principles of Memory? Why or why not?

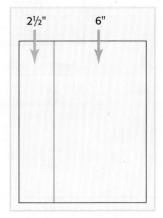

FIGURE 9.6

The Five *R*'s of Cornell

1. **Record** your notes in the right column.
2. **Reduce** your notes into the recall column on the left.
3. **Recite** out loud from the recall column.
4. **Reflect** on the information that you are studying.
5. **Review** your notes immediately and regularly.

Step One: Recording

The **record step** in the Cornell system involves taking notes in the right column.

The **record step** in the Cornell system involves taking notes in the right column. Read each paragraph carefully, decide what information is important, and then record that information on your paper. Your notes should be a *reduced version* of the textbook. Be selective. Carefully read the information in **Figure 9.7** to learn techniques for recording information in your notes.

CONCEPT CHECK 9.11

What strategies can you use to create organized notes with sufficient details?

Tips for Recording Notes

The headings (and subheadings) in the textbook are the *skeleton,* or outline, of the chapter. They serve as guides for identifying main categories of information. Details for your notes come from information under each heading. An effective notetaker organizes the details and gives them structure so they do not appear to be an endless stream of random details. Use the tips on the next page to organize your notes:

FIGURE 9.7

The Record Step of the Cornell System

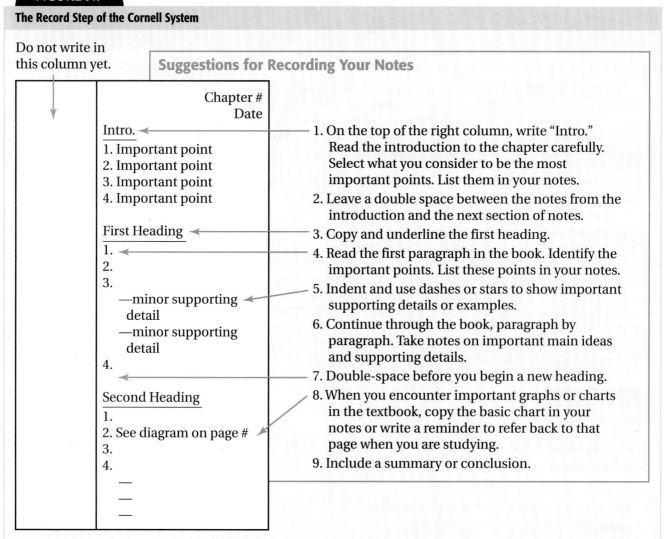

Do not write in this column yet.

Suggestions for Recording Your Notes

Chapter #
Date

Intro.
1. Important point
2. Important point
3. Important point
4. Important point

First Heading
1.
2.
3.
—minor supporting detail
—minor supporting detail
4.

Second Heading
1.
2. See diagram on page #
3.
4.
___
___
___

1. On the top of the right column, write "Intro." Read the introduction to the chapter carefully. Select what you consider to be the most important points. List them in your notes.
2. Leave a double space between the notes from the introduction and the next section of notes.
3. Copy and underline the first heading.
4. Read the first paragraph in the book. Identify the important points. List these points in your notes.
5. Indent and use dashes or stars to show important supporting details or examples.
6. Continue through the book, paragraph by paragraph. Take notes on important main ideas and supporting details.
7. Double-space before you begin a new heading.
8. When you encounter important graphs or charts in the textbook, copy the basic chart in your notes or write a reminder to refer back to that page when you are studying.
9. Include a summary or conclusion.

- *Introduction:* If the chapter has an introductory paragraph that lists key ideas presented in the chapter, create a heading that says <u>Introduction</u> and list the key ideas.

- *Headings and Subheadings:* Copy the textbook headings and the subheadings into your notes. Underline them so they stand out as main categories or topics. Do not number or letter the headings.

- *New Headings:* If you wish to regroup or reorganize information into headings or subheadings that are more helpful for understanding topics, you can create your own headings or subheadings in your notes.

- *Marginal Notes:* Carefully read marginal notes (or sidebars) that may appear in your textbooks. If this information does not appear within the regular text, include important points from the marginal notes in your notes.

- *Double Spacing:* To avoid crowded or cluttered notes that are difficult to study, leave a double space between each new heading or section of your notes. This visually groups or chunks the information into smaller units, which will help your memory.

- *Sufficient Information:* Your notes need to show the big picture and the small pictures (details), so be sure to record sufficient information to be meaningful later.

- *Meaningful Phrases or Short Sentences:* Shorten or paraphrase information. Avoid using only individual words or short phrases that may lose their meaning when you return to them later. If phrases by themselves are not meaningful units of thought, convert them into short sentences.

- *Annotations:* If you have already highlighted or annotated the information, move the same information into your notes.

- *Number Details:* Number the ideas as you include them in your notes. Numbering helps you create a stronger impression about the number of important points under each heading, and it breaks the information into smaller, more manageable units.

- *Minor Details:* You will frequently encounter minor details that belong under an idea that you already numbered. Indicate these details by *indenting* and then using *dashes* or *stars* before writing the details. Avoid more complicated formal outlining that mixes numbering and lettering.

- *Graphs and Charts:* You can *copy* smaller graphic materials into your notes or *summarize* the conclusions you make after studying the visual materials. For larger visual materials, simply include a reminder in your notes to go to a specific textbook page to review the materials.

Write a Summary or a Conclusion

Summaries or conclusions pull the main ideas together to help you see the big picture. If the book has a summary, include the summary as the last heading in your notes. If there is no summary, write your own summary for the chapter.

Step Two: Reducing

After you have finished taking notes for the chapter, you are ready to close the book and reduce your notes one step further. The **reduce step** in the Cornell system

The **reduce step** in the Cornell system involves condensing notes into the recall column on the left.

The **recall column** is the left column in the Cornell notes that shows headings, key words, and study questions.

CONCEPT CHECK 9.12

What are the *do's* and the *don't's* for creating the recall column?

The **recite step** in the Cornell system involves using information in the recall column to explain information out loud in your own words without referring to detailed notes.

CONCEPT CHECK 9.13

Why does reciting occur in so many learning strategies? How is it used in the Cornell system?

involves condensing notes into the recall column. The **recall column** is the left column in the Cornell notes that shows headings, key words, and study questions. See Figure 9.8 for an example of reduced notes in the recall column. Use the following tips to create an effective recall column that you can use during step three, reciting.

▌ *Copy Headings:* To structure and organize your recall column, copy the headings from the right column into the left column and underline them. The headings should appear directly across from the headings in your notes.

▌ *Reread Your Notes:* Reread a section of your notes to refresh your working memory. If your notes seem vague or incomplete, go back to the book, reread, and add more details to your notes.

▌ *Study Questions:* Under the headings in your recall column, write brief study questions about the information in the right column. Your study questions can be in an abbreviated form, such as *Why? Name the 6 . . . Related to* X *how?*

▌ *Key Words to Define:* In your recall column, across from your notes that define a key term, write *def.* and the *key word* to cue you later to recite the definition for the word.

▌ *Do Not Write Too Much:* Do not clutter the recall column with too much information. Do not write answers to your study questions or clues for definitions or lists of information; you want to challenge yourself in the next step to see if you can recall the information from memory.

Step Three: Reciting

The **recite step** in the Cornell system involves using information in the recall column to explain information out loud in your own words without referring to detailed notes. To avoid the tendency to look at your notes as you recite, use a blank piece of paper to cover your notes on the right side of your paper. **Figure 9.8** shows headings, study questions, and key words used to trigger reciting as well as suggestions for reciting.

Begin reciting by looking at and then telling about the information in the recall column. Use the following tips to recite from the recall column.

▌ *Explain in Complete Sentences:* Answer the questions, define terms, and tell what you remember about the key words. Talk out loud in complete, coherent sentences.

▌ *Use Feedback:* After reciting a section of information, pull down the paper that covered the right column. Check your accuracy and the completeness of your recited information. If you have difficulty reciting, or if you "go blank," pull down the paper, reread your notes, cover them, and try reciting again.

▌ *Adjust the Recall Column:* If the recall column did not have sufficient cues to direct your reciting or focus you on the important points, add more key words or study questions to the recall column. If you find that the recall column provided you with too much information that resulted in simply reading with little information left to recite from memory, cross out (or whiteout) some of the details before you recite again.

▌ *Track Your Progress:* If you wish, you can star items in the recall column that you recited with accurate details. You can check or place an arrow next to infor-

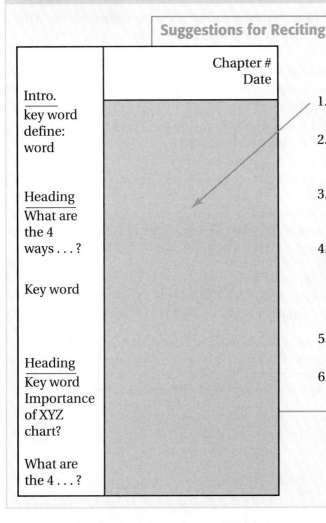

FIGURE 9.8

Reciting from the Recall Column

Suggestions for Reciting

Chapter #
Date

Intro.
key word
define:
word

Heading
What are
the 4
ways . . . ?

Key word

Heading
Key word
Importance
of XYZ
chart?

What are
the 4 . . . ?

1. Cover up the notes on the right.

2. Start at the top of the recall column. Read the heading and the first key word or question.

3. Explain the information. Talk out loud in complete sentences.

4. If you do not remember the information, uncover the right column. Reread the information. Cover it up and try reciting it again.

5. Move through your notes in this manner.

6. Adjust the recall column by adding new key words if needed.

mation that needs more practice and information that you need to recite more the next time you review.

Step Four: Reflecting

The **reflect step** in the Cornell system involves thinking seriously, comprehending, and using elaborative rehearsal strategies to work with information in new ways. The reflect step is a creative and highly individualized step, so no two students will create identical study tools or use the same rehearsal activities. This is the time for you to decide *what will work best for you.* Use the following tips for reflecting on your notes.

▌ *Think and Ponder:* Take time to think about the topic, relationships among details, and the importance of the information you are studying.

> The **reflect step** in the Cornell system involves thinking seriously, comprehending, and using elaborative rehearsal strategies to work with information in new ways.

CONCEPT CHECK 9.14

Why is the reflect step an individualized process? What might happen if you skip using this reflect step?

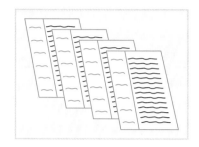

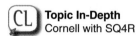
Topic In-Depth
Cornell with SQ4R

The **review step** in the Cornell system involves using immediate and ongoing review.

Immediate review is the process of rehearsing information before you end a learning task.

Ongoing review is the process of practicing information days and even weeks after the initial learning occurred.

CONCEPT CHECK 9.15

Should your review strategies differ for immediate and ongoing review? Why or why not?

■ *Line Up Your Recall Columns:* To see an informal outline and an overview of all the information in your set of notes, arrange the pages of your notes so you can see a lineup of all the recall columns.

■ *Write a Summary:* Look only at the information in the recall columns. Write a summary using full sentences and paragraphs to summarize the main ideas and important details.

■ *Write on the Back Side of Your Notes:* Use the back sides of your notes for reflect activities; make lists of information, write study questions, add diagrams or charts, or jot down questions you want to ask in class.

■ *Make Study Tools:* Reinforce your learning by creating study tools that you can use throughout the term: index card notes, visual mappings, charts, or mnemonics.

Step Five: Reviewing

The **review step** in the Cornell system involves using immediate and ongoing review. Use immediate review with your notes after you finish the reflect step. **Immediate review** is the process of rehearsing information before you end a learning task. This review helps create a stronger impression of the information before you set it aside and move on to something new.

Ongoing review is the process of practicing information days and even weeks after the initial learning occurred. Ongoing review is a Principle of Memory that keeps information active and accessible in your memory system. When you use ongoing review, use Look-Away Techniques to rehearse the information by visualizing or reciting the information in the recall columns of your notes. Ongoing review saves you time in the long run; when you prepare for tests or exams, you will not need to cram or spend excessive time "relearning" information.

EXERCISE 9.3

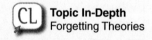
Topic In-Depth
Forgetting Theories

Taking Notes on Forgetting Theories

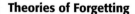

DIRECTIONS: Prepare your notepaper with the two columns for Cornell notes. In the right column of your notebook paper, take notes on the following information. Write and underline headings; number the important details. In the left column, create a recall column. To evaluate your notes, go to Appendix B, page A19, for the Cornell Notetaking Self-Assessment Checklist.

Theories of Forgetting

Five theories of forgetting offered by psychologists explain some of the reasons information may be forgotten or inaccessible in memory. The *Decay Theory* suggests that stimuli received by short-term memory (a part of working memory) may be too weak or unattended to, resulting in the stimuli simply decaying or fading away. Unattended or ignored stimuli decay from short-term memory within eighteen seconds, and thus are never processed or truly learned.

A second theory, the *Displacement Theory*, suggests another type of forgetting that also occurs in short-term memory. If too much information comes into short-term memory too rapidly, the short-term memory system in working memory becomes overloaded. Some of the stimuli already in short-term memory are shoved aside or displaced to make room for new stimuli. Displacement occurs because of short-term memory's limited capacity to hold, on the average, no more than seven chunks of information at one time. Once displaced, the stimuli drop out of the memory and processing centers.

The *Interference Theory* suggests two forms of forgetting that occur with learned information in long-term memory: retroactive and proactive interference. Interference can occur between items studied in the same session or between items studied many years apart. Both forms of forgetting are caused by interferences between old and new information during the imprinting or retrieval stages of learning. Forgetting due to interference often occurs when old and new information are similar in nature and characteristics of each are not highly differentiated.

Retroactive interference occurs when new information in working memory interferes with the retrieval process of old, previously learned information. The new information is fresher in working memory and overrides the ability to recall old information. For example, new information you are learning in a history class this term may hinder your ability to recall information you learned the previous term in a different history class.

Proactive interference occurs when old, previously learned information in long-term memory interferes with the ability to recall newly learned information, especially when the new information contradicts or does not integrate logically with previously learned information. For example, if you have spent several terms studying Spanish, this knowledge may make it difficult for you to switch to different language patterns to learn a language such as Japanese.

The *Incomplete Encoding Theory* suggests forgetting occurs due to incomplete encoding during the rehearsal process in working memory. If learning information is interrupted, information is only partially learned or understood. Strong enough impressions, retrieval cues, or associations are not created to recall information accurately. If some form of self-quizzing is not used, the learner may not be aware that information is not encoded clearly. When the stimuli are not imprinted clearly in long-term memory, recall produces partial or unusable information.

The *Retrieval Failure Theory* refers to the inability to conduct successful memory searches to locate information stored in long-term memory. Failure to retrieve information may be attributed to a weak organizational system for storing or filing the information, a lack of retrieval cues or associations, or it may be due to lack of use or practice pulling information back into working memory. Information that is not rehearsed or practiced still exists in memory, but it is not accessible. Anxiety, excessive stress, or emotionally disruptive thoughts may also hinder a person's ability to recall learned information.

Fortunately, a variety of study strategies that support the functions of working memory can be used to combat each of the five types of forgetting.

EXERCISE 9.4

Reciting from Your Recall Column

PURPOSE: Knowing how to use the recall column for reciting becomes easier with practice.

DIRECTIONS: Work with a partner. Take turns listening to each other recite and explain the information in the recall columns of your notes for Forgetting Theories, Exercise 9.3.

GROUP PROCESSING:
A COLLABORATIVE LEARNING ACTIVITY

Form groups of three students. Complete the following directions. Compile the responses on a large group chart.

1. Across the top of your chart, draw the five pictures shown below.

2. As a group, brainstorm and list all the important points you remember about each of the Five *R*'s of Cornell. Do not refer back to your textbook. You may be asked to share your chart with the class.

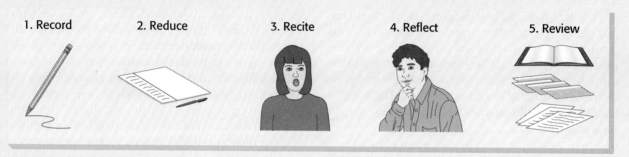

1. Record   2. Reduce   3. Recite   4. Reflect   5. Review

EXERCISE 9.5

Additional Cornell Notetaking Practice

DIRECTIONS: Practice taking Cornell notes by returning to Maslow's Hierarchy in Exercise 9.1 (page 258). Use your annotations in Exercise 9.1 to guide your choice of information to include in your Cornell notes for the same topic. Complete your notes by creating the recall column.

EXERCISE 9.6

Taking Cornell Notes from Textbooks

PURPOSE: Learning to use a new notetaking system effectively requires practice using the system for taking notes from a variety of textbooks. Your goal is to acquire the skills necessary to use the system comfortably and habitually.

DIRECTIONS: Follow your instructor's directions for *one* of the following notetaking assignments.

1. Take a complete set of notes, including a recall column, for specific pages in this textbook assigned by your instructor.

2. Take notes on any two pages of information from any textbook you are using this term. Your notes should begin with a textbook heading. Your instructor may ask to meet with you to compare your notes to the textbook pages or may ask you to include photocopies of the two textbook pages when you turn in your notes.

True or False?

_____ 1. The Five *R*'s of Cornell are *read, record, recite, reflect,* and *review.*

_____ 2. Headings are used to help organize information in both columns of Cornell notes.

_____ 3. An effective recall column includes questions without answers and terminology without the written definitions.

_____ 4. The Memory Principles of Selectivity, Elaboration, Recitation, Feedback, and Ongoing Review are used each time you create and study your Cornell notes.

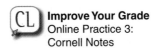

Improve Your Grade
Online Practice 3:
Cornell Notes

TWO- AND THREE-COLUMN NOTETAKING SYSTEMS

4 *Discuss and apply effective strategies for creating two- and three-column notes.*

Two-Column and Three-Column Notetaking Systems are alternatives to the Cornell Notetaking System. In each system, you begin your notes in the left column and then fill in the other one or two columns with details. As with all notetaking systems, to work effectively, you need to spend time rehearsing the information, using feedback systems, and incorporating immediate and ongoing review in your study blocks.

The Two-Column System

Two-column notes are a simplified version of Cornell notes. The **Two-Column Notetaking System** shows topics, vocabulary terms, and/or study questions in the left column and details or explanations in the right column. You can also include small diagrams or charts from the textbook in the left column followed by brief explanations in the right column. In this notetaking system, you can vary the width of each column to suit your needs and preferences. Creating two-column notes is a two-step process:

> **Step 1, Left Column:** Write a topic, vocabulary term, or a study question in the *left column.*
>
> **Step 2, Right Column:** Directly across from the item in the left column, write details or explanations. As with Cornell notes, be brief but not so brief that the information loses meaning over time. You can number details, use bullets for items in a list, or simply write the information in meaningful phrases or short sentences.

Two-column notes are easy to create and use when you take textbook or lecture notes. They are informal and reflect your preferences for the kinds of information you want to appear in each column. Following are three examples of two-column notes.

The **Two-Column Notetaking System** shows topics, vocabulary terms, or study questions in the left column and details or explanations in the right column.

CONCEPT CHECK 9.16

How is the Two-Column Notetaking System different from the Cornell system? In what ways are they similar?

Example 1: Forgetting Theories

Def.—Decay Theory	A forgetting theory that occurs in STM; stimuli too weak to process the information.
Forgetting Theories	1. Decay 2. Displacement 3. Interference 4. Incomplete Encoding 5. Retrieval Failure

Example 2: Multiplying Negative and Positive Numbers

When both numbers are positive	Answer is positive. Example: $4 \times 9 = 36$
When both numbers are negative	Answer is positive. Example: $-5 \times -4 = 20$
When one number is positive and the other is negative	Answer is negative. Example: $(-3) \times 4 = -12$

Example 3: Maslow's Hierarchy

What are the 5 classes of needs?	1. Physiological—ex. Food, water, oxygen, sleep 2. Safety—cared for (child); secure income (adult) 3. Belongingness and Love—part of groups & relationships 4. Esteem—respected as useful person 5. Self-Actualization—reaching full potential.
Critics of Maslow's Hierarchy	• Hierarchy too simplistic. Ex. Motivation to starve self for political statement doesn't follow the hierarchy. • People may not satisfy one need before working on others; seek to satisfy several needs at once. • Order of needs differs from culture to culture.
ERG Theory	(Students continue taking notes.)

Use the following tips to rehearse and review your two-column notes.

▌ *Cover the Right Column and Recite:* After you recite lists of information, definitions, or answer study questions, remove the paper to check the accuracy and completeness of your answer. Reread, cover the notes, and recite again if necessary.

▌ *Highlight Difficult Sections of Your Notes:* Use colored pens to highlight sections that you want to identify quickly for additional practice or review.

▌ *Use Immediate and Ongoing Review.*

EXERCISE 9.7

CL **Improve Your Grade**
Exercise 9.7

Two-Column Notes About the Forgetting Curve

PURPOSE: In order to select the best notetaking system for a specific notetaking situation, you need to know how to use each system comfortably. You may eventually have preferences, but in some situations, a notetaking system that is not necessarily preferred may be best suited for a specific textbook.

DIRECTIONS: Read the following excerpt one paragraph at a time, pause, and then create two-column notes. Use a combination of topics, key terms to define, and study questions in the left column.

How Do We Forget?

Hermann Ebbinghaus, a German psychologist, began the systematic study of memory and forgetting in the late 1800s, using only his own memory as his laboratory. He read aloud a list of nonsense syllables, such as POF, XEM, and QAL, at a constant pace, and then tried to recall the syllables.

Ebbinghaus devised the *method of savings* to measure how much he forgot over time. This method compares the number of repetitions (or trials) it takes to learn a list of items and the number of trials needed to relearn that same list later. Any difference in the number of learning trials presents the *savings* from one learning to the next. If it took Ebbinghaus ten trials to learn a list and ten more trials to relearn it, there would be no savings. Forgetting would have been complete. If it took him ten trials to learn the list and only five trials to relearn it, there would be a savings of 50 percent.

Ebbinghaus's research produced two lasting discoveries. One is the shape of the forgetting curve shown on the right. Even when psychologists have substituted words, sentences, and stories for nonsense syllables, the forgetting curve shows the same strong initial drop in memory, followed by a more moderate decrease over time . . . Of course, we remember sensible stories better than nonsense syllables, but the shape of the curve is the same no matter what

type of material is involved . . . Even the forgetting of events from daily life tends to follow Ebbinghaus's forgetting curve (Thomson, 1982).

Ebbinghaus also discovered just how long-lasting "savings" in long-term memory can be. Psychologists now know from the method of savings that information about everything from algebra to bike riding is often retained for decades . . . So, although you may forget something you have learned if you do not use the information, it is very easy to relearn the material if the need arises, indicating that the forgetting was not complete.

Source: Bernstein, Nash. *Essentials of Psychology,* Houghton Mifflin Co., 2008, pp. 227–228.

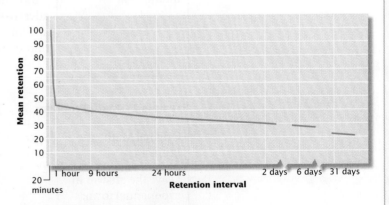

Ebbinghaus's Curve of Forgetting

Ebbinghaus found that most forgetting occurs during the first nine hours after learning, and especially during the first hour.

The Three-Column System

The Three-Column Notetaking System shows topics, vocabulary terms, or study questions in the left column followed by two categories of details in the remaining two columns.

The Three-Column Notetaking System shows topics, vocabulary terms, or study questions in the left column followed by two categories of details in the remaining two columns. Three-column notes work effectively for *comparative reading* to show information from two different sources for one specific topic. For example, if you are asked to read two separate articles about global warming, the global warming topics would appear in the left column. What each of the sources says about each topic would appear in the middle and the right columns.

Topic	Article 1	Article 2
Greenhouse Effect		
Climate Changes		
Burning Fossil Fuels		
Deforestation		

CONCEPT CHECK 9.17

Three-column notes are versatile because they can be used in many different ways. How can you use this notetaking system with your textbooks?

You can use three-column notes for additional notetaking situations. In the following Example 1, a topic or concept appears in the left column followed by a definition in the middle column and applications in the last column. In Example 2, a math problem appears in the left column followed by a blank middle column to be used later to rework the problem, and the original solution in the right column. In Example 3, math terms appear in the left column followed by examples in the middle column and explanations and rules in the right column.

Example 1   Definitions and Applications

Topic/Concept	Definition or Explanation	Applications—When, Where, How to Use
infomercial	A form of television advertisement that appears as a 15- to 30-minute program	Often used with exercise equipment and videos (ex. Tae-Bo), weight-loss programs, cosmetics, and "get rich quick" programs

Example 2   Math Problems

Fold this column back until you rework the problem.

Original Math Problem	Space to Rework the Problem	Original Solution from Textbook or Class
Leave the answer in exponential form: $4^5 \times 4^7$		$4^5 \times 4^7 = 4^{5+7} = 4^{12}$

Example 3   Math Terminology

Key Words	Examples	Explanations/Rules
$-n$	$-n$	Opposite of any number
	If $n = s$, Then $-n = -s$	
	$-(-10) = 10$ $-(-15)(-15) = -15$	Count the number of signs; even means $+$, odd means $-$
	Opposite of $-x$ is x	
Rational	Rational numbers are fractions (¼, ½, ¾)	A/B, $B/0$ is rational Division by 0 undefined
Numerator Denominator	numerator/denominator N/D	Numerator on top Denominator on bottom (D = Down)

Adapted from Nolting, *Math Study Skills Workbook*, pp. 50–51.

In Example 4, the topic appears in the left column followed by textbook notes on the topic in the middle column. *After* you take separate lecture notes, you can add class notes related to the topic to expand your three-column notes. In this example, the three-column notes serve as a study tool to pull together information from two sources: your textbook and the lecture. Because class lectures may present topics in an order different than your textbook notes, taking lecture notes directly in the right column is often not feasible.

Example 4   Combining Textbook and Lecture Notes

Topic/Concept	Textbook	Instructor/Lecture
Product life cycle	1. Introduction 2. Growth 3. Maturity 4. Decline	Class example: 3M (Post-it Notes) Sony digital cameras

To study from your three-column notes, use recitation. Cover the middle or the right-hand column, recite the information, and then check your accuracy. Continue to study from your three-column notes by covering the remaining columns, reciting, and then checking the accuracy of your explanations. For math notes that involve equations, rework the problems and then compare your results with the original problem and solution.

Check Point 9.4

Answers appear on page A5

True or False?

_____ 1. Three-column notes are always more difficult to create than two-column notes.

_____ 2. Unlike the Cornell system, you begin two-column notes by writing first in the left column.

_____ 3. The notetaker can use questions, terminology, diagrams, or key words for topics in the left column of two- or three-column notes.

_____ 4. You should always read the entire chapter before taking two-column notes.

Improve Your Grade
Online Practice 4:
2- and 3-Column Notes

Exercise 9.8

Textbook Case Studies

Improve Your Grade
Exercise 9.8

Improve Your Grade
Online Case Studies

DIRECTIONS:

1. Read each case study carefully. Respond to the question at the end of each case study by using *specific* strategies discussed in this chapter. Answer in complete sentences.

2. Write your responses on paper or online at the Student Website, Exercise 9.8. You will be able to print your online response or e-mail it to your instructor.

CASE STUDY 1: Labrishun learns by writing information and studying from handwritten information. After Labrishun had taken Cornell notes on two different chapters in her math textbook, she noticed that her notes were longer than the textbook chapters. She realized she had been copying everything from the textbook into her notes. What notetaking strategies or systems would you suggest Labrishun consider using?

CASE STUDY 2: With Cornell notes, Joey has learned to condense information effectively into the right column. In his recall column, Joey makes lists of important information, writes definitions for key terms, and writes study questions with their answers. He reads all the information out loud. What adjustments does Joey need to make in the way he uses his Cornell notes so he tests his memory more effectively?

The Outline Notetaking System

> 5 ▶ *Discuss and apply effective strategies for taking informal outline notes.*

You may already be familiar with formal outlines because many composition instructors require formal outlines with your essays or papers. Formal outlines are highly structured, logically organized, detailed notes that show levels of information and relationships among concepts and ideas. In formal outlines, you arrange the information in the order in which it is presented. By using Roman numerals, capital letters, Arabic numerals, lowercase letters, and numerals inside parentheses, you can show the relationship of the larger concepts to the smaller details. **Figure 9.9** shows the different levels of information in a formal outline.

FIGURE 9.9

Example of a Formal Outline

Title:

I. Main headings or topics use Roman numerals.

  A. Subtopics use capital letters.

  B. Subtopic

    1. Supporting details use Arabic numerals.

    2. Supporting detail

      a. Minor details use lowercase letters.

      b. Minor detail

        (1) Subideas of minor details use Arabic numerals inside parentheses.

        (2) Subideas of minor details

  C. Subtopic

Taking notes from textbooks and from lab projects provides you with a condensed version of the information to study and master. Which kind of notetaking system do you believe would be most effective for lab notes?

Formal outlines have standard requirements:

▎ *Alignment:* When you indent to show a subtopic of a larger category, place the new letter or the new number directly under the first letter of the first word that appears above in the larger category.

▎ *Two or More Subtopics:* Each level of the formal outline must have *at least two subtopics* under each category. If you do not have two items [A, B; 1, 2; a, b; or (1), (2)], try renaming the larger category so you do not end up with only one item under that category.

▎ *Roman Numerals:* Roman numerals are used for main topics. Roman numerals from one to fifteen are written as follows: I, II, III, IV, V, VI, VII, VIII, IX, X, XI, XII, XIII, XIV, and XV.

▎ *Arabic Numerals:* Arabic numerals (1, 2, 3, 4 . . .) are used for supporting details.

▎ *Wording:* Most outlines consist of key words and short phrases; full sentences are seldom used.

Informal Outlines

Outlines provide a *skeleton* or an overview of the basic structure of printed materials, or in this case, of a complete chapter. Some textbooks, including this textbook, provide chapter outlines in the chapter introductory materials; however, these chapter outlines may include only headings and subheadings and not include lower levels of information with specific details.

    The **Outline Notetaking System** involves using an informal outline structure for notes. When outlining a chapter, if you are not comfortable with the formal outline structure, you can modify the outlining "rules" for lower-level information.

CONCEPT CHECK 9.18

How can formal outlining be simplified so outline notes become easier to create?

The **Outline Notetaking System** involves using an informal outline structure for notes.

FIGURE 9.10

The Beginning of an Informal Outline

Chapter 9

I. Textbook Notetaking Skills

  A. Introduction

    1. Notetaking—active learning mode—think about what is imp.

    2. Involves encoding info kinesthetically & visually—stronger impression

    3. Activates working memory—Uses 12 Princ. of Memory

    4. Can use before, during, or after reading textbook

  B. The Importance of Notetaking

    1.

Instead, use Roman numerals (headings), capital letters (subheadings), and Arabic numbers (details), and then simply use dashes for minor details to avoid getting entangled or overly concerned about how to label lower levels of information: Should I use a "b" or should I use (1)? **Figure 9.10** shows the beginning of an informal outline for this chapter.

Outlining Before, During, or After Reading

You can use informal outlining for textbook notes *before, during,* or *after* reading a chapter. If your textbook does not provide a chapter outline, before reading, create a basic outline that shows only *headings* and *subheadings* to get an overview of the chapter and its main topics. Later you can use this basic outline for self-quizzing by reciting what you know about each heading and subheading and adding clue words. (See page 277.)

Some students prefer to use an informal outline to take textbook notes *during* the reading process. Using outlining during the reading process results in more comprehensive notes than outlines created before reading as an overview activity. Use the following tips to create outline notes as you read a chapter:

- *Headings and Subheadings:* Use the headings and the subheadings in your textbook as the skeleton for your outline. Use Roman numerals (I, II, III . . .) to label main headings. Use capital letters in the outline to label subheadings.

- *Details under Subheadings:* After labeling the subheading, read a paragraph under the subheading, pause, identify the important information, and then transfer that information into your notes. Number the individual items or details.

- *Minor Details:* Your informal outline is your personal set of notes, so use a clear, organized method for showing minor details. You may use lowercase letters or you may simply use dashes to indicate separate minor details.

Some students find value in creating informal outlines *after* they read the chapter. These outlines become study or review tools that follow some previously used form of notetaking, such as annotations, two-column notes, or Cornell notes.

CONCEPT CHECK 9.19

How do outline notes show different levels of information? How does understanding levels of information assist your memory?

Studying from Outline Notes

Outlines provide an excellent study tool to practice reciting and to give you immediate feedback about your level of understanding and recall of textbook information. Use the following tips to study from your outlines.

- *Read and explain line by line.* Begin with the first Roman numeral on your outline. Read the information on that line of the outline. Recite what you know about the topic. Speak in complete sentences. Move to the next line of information. Recite what you know; strive to integrate and link ideas together and explain relationships.

- *Check your accuracy and completeness of information.* As you recite, you will quickly become aware of your familiarity with the topic. Refer to your textbook to check your accuracy or to see what kinds of information you did not include in your reciting.

- *Add clue words to the right of the lines in your outline.* You can break away from the general structure of the outline at this point by jotting down key words or details that you did not initially include in your reciting. These clue words can guide you through the reciting process the next time you use your outline to review the contents of the chapter. Notice the clue words in the following example of an outline.

CONCEPT CHECK 9.20

How can you use each line in your outline notes to guide your reciting and trigger your memory?

B. Stress Responses
    1. Physical Stress Responses: The GAS *general adaptation syndrome* — alarm / resistance / exhaustion
    2. Emotional Stress Responses < fear, anger / diminish, persist, severe
    3. Cognitive Stress Responses — ruminative thinking; catastrophizing
    4. Behavioral Stress Responses

- *Use the outline to write a summary.* Many students learn and remember information more readily when they use their own words to explain and connect information in a logically sequenced manner and when they express themselves in writing. You can use the levels of information in your outline to organize and to write a summary. Include main ideas and briefly mention important supporting details.

EXERCISE 9.9

Creating Outline Notes

PURPOSE: Before you can know whether or not you like using a specific kind of notetaking system, you need to experience creating and studying from notes created with each system.

DIRECTIONS: Follow your instructor's directions for doing *one* of the following.

1. Use the Chapter 9 outline in the introduction of this chapter. With a partner, take turns reciting details for each part of the outline. Partners can check each other's accuracy and completeness of recited information.

2. Create a set of outline notes for this chapter. Include at least three levels of information: the heading, the subheading, and important supporting details. Compare your outline to the Chapter 9 expanded outline on the Student Website.

CHECK POINT 9.5

ANSWERS APPEAR ON PAGE A5

True or False?

_____ 1. You can use formal or informal outlining to take textbook notes.

_____ 2. Informal outline notes do not use Roman or Arabic numerals.

_____ 3. Reciting is one effective way to study from outlines.

_____ 4. Outline notes should always be created after you read the entire chapter.

 **Improve Your Grade**
Online Practice 5:
Outline Notes

REFLECTIVE WRITING 9.2

 **Improve Your Grade**
Reflective Writing 9.2

On separate paper, in a journal, or online at this textbook's website, respond to the following questions.

1. In what ways does taking textbook notes improve your performance in your classes?

2. Which notetaking system works best for each of your textbooks? Make a list of all the classes you are enrolled in this term. After carefully examining the textbooks for each class, state which notetaking system works best for each textbook and briefly explain why that system is the best choice to use.

EXERCISE 9.10

Links

DIRECTIONS: Work in a group or with a partner to complete the following chart. The top of the columns are labeled with the letters that represent the Twelve Principles of Memory. The rows show five notetaking options. After discussion, check the boxes to show which Principles of Memory are used in each of the notetaking systems. Use the space below the chart to create discussion notes. Be prepared to explain your answers.

	S	A	V	E	C	R	I	B	F	O	T	O
Annotation												
Cornell System												
Two-Column Notes												
Three-Column Notes												
Outlines												

DISCUSSION NOTES:

LEARNING OBJECTIVES REVIEW

1 *Discuss the rationale for taking notes and effective strategies to use with all notetaking systems.*

- Taking effective notes before, during, and after the reading process affects your ability to learn information, combats forgetting, and shows a high correlation to test performance.

- Eight essential notetaking strategies—including being selective, paraphrasing, and using spaced practice—work effectively for all notetaking systems.

2 *Discuss and apply strategies for marking or annotating textbook passages.*

- Annotating textbooks includes highlighting or underlining, marking, enumerating, and making marginal notes. Selectivity is essential when annotating.

- Marginal notes may include key terms, short questions, and abbreviations for kinds of information or sections of the text marked with a bracket.

- Studying from annotations involves rereading, stringing ideas together, reciting, and using additional activities to reinforce the learning.

3 *Discuss and apply the five steps of the Cornell system for taking notes.*

- The Cornell Notetaking System is a five-step process for taking comprehensive notes. The Five *R*'s of Cornell are *record, reduce, recite, reflect,* and *review.*

- The **record step** occurs in the right column. The **reduce** and the **recite steps** occur in the left column, the recall column.

- The **reflect step** involves activities that personalize and reinforce the information.

- The **review step** involves immediate and ongoing review.

4 *Discuss and apply effective strategies for creating two- and three-column notes.*

- Two-column notes show topics, vocabulary terms, or study questions in the left column and details or explanations in the right column. Rehearse and review by reciting columns.

- Three-column notes can be used for comparative reading, terminology with two additional categories of information, and math notes. Rehearse and review by reciting.

5 *Discuss and apply effective strategies for taking informal outline notes.*

- Formal outlines follow specific rules for ordering and labeling levels of information. You can use formal outlines for notes, or you can modify the lower levels of information to create informal outline notes.

- You can use textbook outlines or create outline notes before you read the textbook. You can also create more detailed outline notes during or after reading a chapter.

- Studying from outline notes involves reading each line of the outline, reciting information, and checking accuracy. Clue words may be added to assist with reciting.

CHAPTER 9 REVIEW QUESTIONS

True or False?

F   1. It is always best to read the whole chapter first and then go back to take notes.

T   2. All notetaking systems should result in a reduced version of textbook information.

F   3. If you are short on time, you will not weaken the system if you skip the fourth step of Cornell or skip rereading annotations and stringing ideas together.

F   4. It is not necessary to take notes on graphs, charts, or pictures because they are always easy to remember.

T   5. Annotating involves a variety of processes: marking main ideas, circling terminology, writing marginal notes, and possibly using abbreviations next to brackets.

T   6. Too much information in the Cornell recall column causes you to read and not do much reciting.

T   7. You can add more questions or key words to the Cornell recall column or outline notes if there are too few cues to help you recite.

T   8. The left column in two- and three-column notes usually shows terminology, study questions, or topics.

Application

Select *one* form of notetaking to take organized notes on the following excerpt.

Causes and Characteristics of Earthquakes

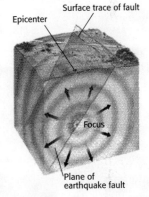

An **earthquake** is a trembling of the ground caused, most often, by the sudden release of energy in underground rocks. Most earthquakes occur where rocks are subjected to the stress associated with tectonic plate movement—that is, near plate boundaries. . . . The application of such stress may cause rocks to deform elastically and to accumulate *strain energy*, which builds until the rocks either shift suddenly along preexisting faults or rupture to create new faults. The result—earthquakes.

The precise subterranean spot at which rocks begin to rupture or shift marks the earthquake's **focus**. . . . Approximately 90% of all earthquakes have a relatively shallow focus, located less than 100 kilometers (60 miles) below the surface; indeed, the focus of virtually all catastrophic quakes lies within 60 kilometers (40 miles) of the surface. Large earthquakes seldom occur at greater depth because heat has softened rocks there and robbed them of some of their ability to store strain energy. A few earthquakes, however, have occurred at depths as great as 700 kilometers (435 miles). Deeper than this level, higher temperatures and pressures cause stressed rocks to deform plastically, rather than rupture or shift.

The point on the Earth's surface directly above any earthquake's focus is its **epicenter**. The greatest impact of a quake is generally felt at the epicenter, with the effect decreasing in proportion to the distance from the epicenter. After a major earthquake, the rocks in the vicinity of the quake's focus continue to reverberate as they adjust to their new positions, producing numerous, generally smaller earthquakes, or *aftershocks*. Aftershocks may continue for as long as one or two years after the main quake, shaking and further damaging already-weakened structures.

Source: Chernicoff; Fox. *Essentials of Geology,* Houghton Mifflin Co., 2003, pp. 198–199.

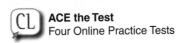
ACE the Test
Four Online Practice Tests

Online Resources

10 Listening and Taking Lecture Notes

LEARNING OBJECTIVES

2 *Discuss the notetaking options that are best suited for lecture, discussion, and math courses.*

1 *Discuss factors that influence the quality of listening; identify four kinds of listening you will encounter in school, work, and personal settings.*

Chapter Outline

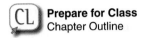 **Prepare for Class**
Chapter Outline

3 ▶ *Discuss and demonstrate use of effective notetaking strategies to capture main ideas and important supporting details in lecture notes.*

Understanding factors that affect your listening abilities and using effective listening strategies can help you improve your listening performance in all four kinds of listening: active, critical, empathic, and appreciative. Developing strong listening skills directly affects your ability to concentrate and take quality lecture notes. In this chapter, you will explore five types of lecture notetaking systems to use during lectures, discussions, and math courses. A variety of strategies will help you keep up with the speaker, identify important points for you notes, and organize your notes in meaningful ways. The result will be effective sets of notes that you can use to recite, rehearse, reflect, and review lecture information.

CHAPTER 10 PROFILE

Listening and Lecture Notes

ANSWER, **SCORE**, and **RECORD** your profile before you read this chapter. If you need to review the process, refer to the complete directions given in the profile for Chapter 1 on page 4.

ONLINE: You can complete the profile and get your score online at this textbook's website.

	YES	NO
1. I use different listening goals or purposes for different kinds of listening situations.	_____	_____
2. Internal and external distractors often interfere with my ability to concentrate during a lecture.	_____	_____
3. I often feel unprepared for class and unfamiliar with the lecture topic when I enter the classroom.	_____	_____
4. I know how to use several different kinds of notetaking systems, so I select the one that is best suited for each class, the instructor, and the content.	_____	_____
5. I avoid using outline notes—even when the instructor provides a basic outline before a lecture.	_____	_____
6. I stop taking notes when the speaker sidetracks from the topic.	_____	_____
7. I spend time going over my notes and filling in missing information as soon after the lecture as possible.	_____	_____
8. I have problems knowing what information to put into lecture notes.	_____	_____
9. I frequently paraphrase, abbreviate, and use shortened sentences in my lecture notes.	_____	_____
10. I am confident in my ability to use effective listening and lecture notetaking skills in my classes.	_____	_____

QUESTIONS LINKED TO THE CHAPTER LEARNING OBJECTIVES:

Questions 1–3: objective 1   Questions 7–9: objective 3
Questions 4–6: objective 2   Question 10:   all objectives

LISTENING SKILLS

> 1 *Discuss factors that influence the quality of listening; identify four kinds of listening you will encounter in school, work, and personal settings.*

Of the four verbal communication skills (listening, speaking, reading, and writing), listening skills are often the weakest. You may think that as long as you can hear, you are listening. However, hearing does not automatically assure that you are *listening*. Listening requires more than taking in sounds and being aware that words are being spoken.

Listening is a process that involves taking in auditory stimuli, holding the stimuli in working memory long enough to attach meaning to the words and interpret the speaker's message. Frequently, people incorrectly perceive *speaking* as an active process and *listening* as a passive process. The truth is that listening is an *active process* that engages the listener in a variety of mental processes.

Daly and Engleberg, in the textbook *Presentations in Everyday Life*, state that listening is what audiences are supposed to do when speakers talk. In fact, listening is our number-one communication activity. Although percentages vary from study to study, **Figure 10.1** shows how most of us divide up our daily communication time.

> One study of college students found that listening occupies more than half of their communicating time. In the corporate world, executives may devote more than 60 percent of their workday listening to others.
>
> Yet, despite all of the time we spend listening, most of us aren't very good at it. For example, immediately after listening to a short talk, most of us cannot accurately report 50 percent of what was said. Without training, we listen at only 25 percent efficiency. And of that 25 percent, most of what we remember is distorted or inaccurate.
>
> Source: Engleberg/Daly, *Presentations in Every Day Life, 2e,* Allyn and Bacon, © 2007, p. 29, 30.

As we all learn to increase our listening efficiency, the benefits will be apparent not only in the classroom, but also in our personal lives, our relationships, and our work environments. As indicated in **Figure 10.2**, developing effective listening skills is a topic of interest in more than college courses; businesses, organizations, and counseling settings all stress the importance of becoming an effective listener.

Listening is a process that involves taking in auditory stimuli, holding the stimuli in working memory long enough to attach meaning to the words and interpret the speaker's message.

CONCEPT CHECK 10.1

How does listening differ from hearing?

CONCEPT CHECK 10.2

Why is listening an active process?

FIGURE 10.1

Percentage of Time Used in Four Communication Activities

Communication Activity	Percentages
Listening	40–70
Speaking	20–35
Reading	10–20
Writing	5–15

FIGURE 10.2

More and Less Effective Listening Skills

Effective listening skills are a vital part of communication in organizations. There are several barriers that can contribute to poor listening skills by individuals in organizations. Fortunately, there are also several practices for improving listening skills.

From Griffin. *Principles of Management,* Houghton Mifflin, © 2007, p. 333.

More Effective Listening	Less Effective Listening
Stays active, focused	Is passive, laid back
Pays attention	Is easily distracted
Asks questions	Asks no questions
Keeps an open mind	Has preconceptions
Assimilates information	Disregards information

CONCEPT CHECK 10.3

Do you currently have more effective listener or ineffective listener characteristics? Explain.

CONCEPT CHECK 10.4

What role does your *central executive* play in the listening process?

So, why exactly is listening such a difficult process? The answer lies in understanding how our memory systems function. As you recall from Chapter 2, our sensory memory accepts input and within a matter of seconds, we need to identify information as important to avoid losing the stimuli completely. Once stimuli are in short-term memory, we need to attend to or concentrate on them to keep them active in working memory for further processing. To understand verbal messages, we need to continuously tap into long-term memory to associate the new information with information we already know or understand. The process is complicated and requires undivided attention, yet as indicated in Exercise 10.1, fluctuating attention is a natural process that occurs during listening. In addition, listening to speakers, taking in their visual materials, such as Power Point presentations, and in lecture situations, taking notes, result in divided attention—a true challenge for working memory. Effective listening requires rapid-fire shifting of attention to multiple stimuli and tasks.

EXERCISE 10.1

Role of Concentration in Listening

PURPOSE: Annotating skills improve through practice. The following excerpt provides you with meaningful information about the relationship between concentration and listening as well as provides you with the opportunity to practice your annotation skills. (See pages 255–257.)

DIRECTIONS: Read and annotate the following paragraphs. Include marginal notes.

Role of Concentration

Undoubtedly one of the most difficult tasks we have to perform as listeners is concentration. Motivation plays an important role in activating this skill. For example, if you really want to listen to a speaker, this desire will put you in a better frame of mind for concentrating than will anticipating that the speaker will be boring.

Two other factors that affect listening concentration are interest level and difficulty of the message. Some messages may be boring, but if you need to get the information, careful concentration is imperative. For example, you may not find the chemistry professor's ideas fascinating, but if you do not listen effectively, you probably will fail the next test. You also may find the information so difficult that you tune out. Again, if it is imperative for you to understand the ideas, then you have to force yourself to figure out what you do not understand and find a way of grasping the meaning.

We can think three to four times faster than the normal conversation rate of 125 to 150 words per minute. And because we can receive messages much more quickly than the other person can talk, we tend to tune in and tune out throughout a message. The mind can absorb only so much material. Indeed, the brain operates much like a computer: it turns off, recycles itself, and turns back on to avoid information overload. It is no wonder, then, that our attention fluctuates even when we are actively involved as listeners. Think back to any class you have attended. Do you recall a slight gap in your listening at times? This is a natural part of the listening process. When you tune out, the major danger is that you may daydream rather than quickly turn back to the message. But by taking notes or forcing yourself to paraphrase, you can avoid this difficulty.

Concentration also requires the listener to control for distractions. As a listener, you probably have a whole list of things that you have to attend to in addition to the speaker's message. Rather than attempting to dismiss them, control your concentration by mentally setting these other issues aside for the moment to give the speaker your full attention. It takes mental and physical energy to do this, but concentration is the key to successful listening.

Source: Berko, Wolvin, and Wolvin, *Communicating, 10e,* p. 89. Copyright © 2007 Allyn and Bacon.

Influencing Factors

CONCEPT CHECK 10.5

What factors influence your listening effectiveness?

Some poor listening habits are learned behaviors and often reflect our tendency to want to multitask as we listen. A person may begin listening to a speaker with the complete intention of "staying tuned in," listening attentively, following the ideas, and making every effort to understand the information, but then shifts suddenly to other thoughts, starts doodling, daydreaming, or making a grocery shopping or a to-do list. Poor listening habits may also be the result of the *lack* of training or instruction on how to be a good listener.

Good listening is similar to concentration: it is here one second and then it is gone. Good listening requires a conscious effort on your part to keep your mind focused on the speaker and his or her message. However, good listening involves more than good intentions. **Figure 10.3** shows five variables or factors that you need to monitor, control, and adjust to become an effective listener.

The way that you approach listening situations will be influenced not only by the five factors noted in Figure 10.3 but also by your own learning style preferences, which may influence your *listening style*. For example, linear learners often are also *linear listeners*. Linear listeners tend to listen for logical, sequential infor-

FIGURE 10.3

Factors That Influence Your Ability to Listen Effectively

Your Attitude *Positive attitude enhances listening ability; negative attitude hinders it.*	Your interest level in the topic Your attitude toward the subject Your attitude toward the speaker
The Topic *Familiarity enhances listening; lack of background hinders it.*	Your familiarity with the words, terminology, or topic Your personal background and cultural experiences Difficulty level of the course or presentation Quantity of information presented
The Speaker's Qualities *Positive speaker qualities enhance ability to listen; negative qualities hinder it.*	Speaker's tone of voice, rate of speech, speech patterns, and mannerisms Speaker's organization of the presentation Speaker's teaching/lecturing style, clarity in explaining information, and inclusion of sufficient examples and/ or providing evidence to support a point
External Distractors *Ability to block out distractors enhances listening; attending to distractors hinders it.*	Noise and movement in the listening environment Room temperature or lighting Interruptions or disruptions by others in the room
Personal Factors *Comfort, proximity to speaker, and positive physical and emotional state enhance listening; opposites of these factors hinder it.*	Length of time required to remain seated Sitting posture during the lecture Seating location in relation to the speaker Personal physical and emotional state at the time

mation; they focus on specific details that support a main point. Linear listeners need to use concerted effort to connect details to see the overall "big picture" when lectures or discussions are more global-thinking oriented. Global learners, on the other hand, often are also *global listeners.* Global listeners tend to focus on the overall picture supported by vivid examples, discussion, and group interaction. They need to use concerted effort to identify and remember specific details and sequential patterns when lectures are more linear-thinking oriented. When a speaker's speaking style does not match your listening style, without concerted effort, your concentration and effective listening skills tend to diminish and reduce your ability to capture the speaker's message.

CONCEPT CHECK 10.6

What is your listening style? In what kinds of situations are you an effective listener?

EXERCISE 10.2

Classroom Listening Factors Inventory

DIRECTIONS: Read each set of statements carefully. Check the statement that most reflects your behavior or attitude in a typical lecture class in which you are enrolled.

1. Interest Level:

___ A. I am not interested in the topic; in fact, it bores me.

___ B. I do not have a genuine interest in the topic, but I know it is important to learn.

___ C. I find ways to expand my interest in the topic, such as discussing it with others.

2. Seating Location:

___ A. I sit in the back of the classroom so I can see everything that goes on.

___ B. I sit in the middle of the classroom so I can see the screen or chalkboard clearly.

___ C. I sit in the front of the classroom so I have fewer distractions and a clearer view of visual materials.

3. Materials and Preparedness:

___ A. I often arrive to the classroom just as the lecture begins; I am seldom tardy.

___ B. I arrive with sufficient time to select a good seat and "settle in."

___ C. I arrive a few minutes early and prepared with sufficient paper, pens, my textbook, and class work.

4. Familiarity with the Topic:

___ A. I am curious at the beginning of each class about the topic for that day's lecture.

___ B. I use the course syllabus to identify the topic for the day's lecture; then I survey the corresponding pages in the textbook.

___ C. I read the textbook section or chapter for the lecture before class so I am familiar with the topic, definitions, and the kind of information I can find in the textbook.

5. Focused Attention:

___ A. I tend to "tune out" when the information is too technical or difficult to follow.

___ B. I am aware that my concentration fades in and fades out multiple times during the lecture; I refocus as quickly as possible.

___ C. I block out distractors so my concerted effort can be directed toward following the instructor's thinking and explanations.

6. Emotional Responses:

___ A. I immediately let an instructor know if I disagree with or dislike something he or she says during a lecture.

___ B. I am aware during a lecture of the times when I do not agree with the instructor's information or point of view.

___ C. I put my personal opinions aside so I can listen carefully to the information presented by an instructor before questioning or disagreeing with the information.

7. Asking Questions:

_____ A. I like to challenge the instructor by asking any questions as they pop into my mind.

_____ B. I jot down questions during a lecture and then ask them at an appropriate time.

_____ C. I ask open-ended clarifying questions to learn more about the topic; for example, I might ask: What are some ways this could be used? or Why is it important to . . . ?

8. Checking Understanding:

_____ A. I wait until after class to look at my notes to see what I understand.

_____ B. I ask questions or show my confusion at the point during a lecture when I do not understand what the instructor is presenting.

_____ C. At an appropriate time, I rephrase or paraphrase information that I do not understand clearly; for example, I might ask: Do you mean that . . . ? Is it correct then to say that . . . ?

9. Levels of Information:

_____ A. I know that everything the instructor presents is important to remember.

_____ B. I use verbal and nonverbal clues to identify the main points of a lecture.

_____ C. I use verbal, nonverbal, and visual clues, such as information the instructor writes on an overhead or presents on a slide, to identify important information.

SCORING YOUR INVENTORY:

How many responses did you have in each category? Write the number of responses:

A	B	C

Responses for A represent ineffective listening behaviors and attitudes.

Responses for B represent adequate listening behaviors and attitudes that you can further strengthen.

Responses for C indicate effective active learning behaviors and attitudes to use during lectures.

Kinds of Listening

Just as there is more than one way to read a book, write a paper, or speak to others, there is more than one way to listen. Different reading, writing, speaking, or listening activities involve different purposes or learning goals. For example, your purpose for:

▌ *reading* differs when you read a movie review, a magazine, a newspaper, a novel, a research report, and a textbook.

▌ *writing* may range from capturing feelings and memories in a diary, expressing yourself through poetry, communicating with a friend, writing a short story or an essay, summarizing an article, answering test questions, or preparing a report.

▌ *speaking* may be to gain someone's support, share personal experiences, vent emotions, teach or inform, clarify a situation, persuade, or promote.

▌ *listening* may be to understand new information, interpret and analyze a speaker's message, relate to another person's feelings, or enjoy and appreciate a message.

CONCEPT CHECK 10.7

What are different kinds of listening goals you might establish in your classes? Explain.

Understanding your listening goal each time you approach a listening situation can help you select appropriate strategies to strengthen your listening skills. **Figure 10.4** shows four kinds of listening and the listening goals for each.

FIGURE 10.4

Kinds of Listening and Listening Goals

Kinds of Listening	The Listening Goal Is to . . .
Active Listening	Understand and learn new information
Critical Listening	Understand, interpret, examine, and analyze a speaker's message
Empathic Listening	Understand and relate to another person's feelings and emotions
Appreciative Listening	Enjoy, appreciate, and acknowledge a speaker and his or her message

Active Listening

Active listening is the process of concentrating intently on a speaker's message with the goal of understanding the information as it is presented. Many of your college active listening experiences will occur in classroom settings: in lectures, in labs, in small groups, or in partner activities. **Figure 10.5** shows seven Essential Strategies to use in the classroom.

Active listening is the process of concentrating intently on a speaker's message with the goal of understanding the information as it is presented.

FIGURE 10.5

Essential Strategies for Active Listening

▌ **Create a clear listening goal.** Enter the classroom with an *intention* to listen to learn. Exhibit a positive attitude toward the subject, the speaker, and the experience. Strive to follow the speaker's chain of thoughts, sequence of details, relationships, examples, and logic.

▌ **Use concentration strategies.** Free up working memory space by eliminating as many external and internal distractors as possible, including disruptive thoughts. Make a concerted effort to maintain undivided attention.

▌ **Familiarize yourself with the topic *before* class.** Become familiar with the terminology, main concepts, and key details by previewing the chapter that will be discussed in class; read the chapter if time permits. Instead of hearing information for the first time, you will have already activated or started new schemas in your long-term memory for the information.

▌ **Keep an open mind.** Avoid prejudging information or the speaker. Set personal opinions aside so you can hear the speaker's message as it is presented.

▌ **Activate your visual skills.** Try to visualize information as it is presented. Turn on the "movie in your mind" to create a visual association with the verbal information.

▌ **Express an interest in the topic.** When appropriate, ask questions about points of interest or points that are confusing or unclear. Ask clarifying questions and paraphrase what you hear to check the accuracy of your understanding.

▌ **Participate in the learning process.** Be willing to respond to questions posed directly to you by the speaker. Volunteer to answer questions or to participate in verbal directions to do an activity or work a process.

CONCEPT CHECK 10.8

Which Principles of Memory do you use during active listening?

Critical Listening

Critical listening is the process of concentrating intently on a speaker's message with the goals of understanding, interpreting, analyzing, and critiquing the content of the message. Critical listening moves beyond active listening skills. It is a higher, more complex form of listening that involves critical thinking skills to examine, analyze, and critique the proof or evidence that is presented to support a specific point of view. Critical listening is difficult, if not impossible, to do without pre-existing background knowledge and familiarity with the topic. In addition to hearing the speaker's message without distorting it, critical listening requires separating your emotions and opinions from those of the speaker. Only after you hear the speaker's full message will you be able to analyze, evaluate, or critique the validity or logic of the information.

Critical listening challenges working memory due to the number of cognitive processes involved. For this reason, notetaking strategies for critical listening situations may differ from notetaking strategies used in active listening situations. To reduce the possibility of overloading working memory, focusing attention on the content of the message becomes more important than taking detailed notes. Notes taken during critical listening situations, such as with debates, may summarize important points in an argument with less recording of each step or detail in the presentation.

Empathic Listening

Empathic listening is the process of concentrating intently on a speaker's words with sincere intent to understand that person's feelings, emotions, and thoughts related to a specific topic or situation. Your listening goal is to *empathize* or relate to the other person. Empathic listeners pay attention to people's verbal and nonverbal clues in order to identify the emotion being exhibited (anger, frustration, disappointment, resentment, excitement, enthusiasm, self-pride, and so on) and relate to the speaker's situation, feelings, or point of view. In many empathic listening situations, the speaker wants someone to listen and understand; he or she does not necessarily want to be consoled or given advice.

Empathic listening skills are valuable in college courses that use group activities that encourage or require students to interact on more personal levels. An atypical or intense emotional response from another student during a group activity can be an indicator that you need to shift from active listening or critical listening to empathic listening. Listen to and observe what the person wants to communicate to you. Avoid being judgmental, criticizing, making negative comments, or telling the student that he or she is "wrong." Instead, use positive words or gestures to communicate that you *understand* the feeling or the situation—even if you do not agree with the other person.

Appreciative Listening

Appreciative listening is the process of listening to a speaker for the purpose of enjoying, appreciating, and acknowledging the speaker and the message in positive ways. Being drawn into a story by a captivating storyteller, laughing at an instructor's humorous anecdotes or examples in a lecture, marveling at the ease with which a student gives a class presentation, listening to an actor practice a scene from an upcoming play, or listening to someone describe a vacation to an exotic location are examples of appreciative listening.

Critical listening is the process of concentrating intently on a speaker's message with the goals of understanding, interpreting, analyzing, and critiquing the content of the message.

CONCEPT CHECK 10.9

How does critical listening differ from active listening? What was the last listening situation in which you used critical listening skills?

Empathic listening is the process of concentrating intently on a speaker's words with sincere intent to understand that person's feelings, emotions, and thoughts related to a specific topic or situation.

CONCEPT CHECK 10.10

Describe a situation in which you switched from one type of listening to empathic listening. How did your listening goal change?

Appreciative listening is the process of listening to a speaker for the purpose of enjoying, appreciating, and acknowledging the speaker and the message in positive ways.

Appreciative listening is not a passive, laid-back process. To feel the richness of words, to be moved emotionally by a message, or to experience overwhelming gratitude for a speaker and his or her message all require that you, the listener, take an active role by paying close attention to details, connecting with the speaker, and allowing emotional responses to occur. You can demonstrate your appreciation through nods of agreement, eye contact, facial expressions, compliments or expressions of gratitude, and, when appropriate, applause.

CONCEPT CHECK 10.11

Describe different situations in which you used appreciative listening.

EXERCISE 10.3

Using Four Kinds of Listening

PURPOSE: We engage in all four types of listening on a regular basis. By recognizing the type of listening involved in a situation, we can adjust our listening goals and strategies to the situation.

DIRECTIONS: Read the following descriptions of listening situations. Then write one of the following letters to indicate which kind of listening would be the most effective for each situation.

AC = Active   **C** = Critical
E = Empathic   **AP** = Appreciative

_____ 1. A debate about storing the nation's nuclear waste at Yucca Mountain in Nevada

_____ 2. A lecture that reviews a psychology textbook chapter

_____ 3. Four students' project that involves a ten-minute skit

_____ 4. A debate in a political science class between two guest speakers

_____ 5. An instructor's explanation of the steps to use to complete a lab project

_____ 6. A class discussion about the author's purpose and the thesis of a short story

_____ 7. A student expressing frustration about a disagreement with a tutor

_____ 8. An instructor reading three of his favorite poems written by American poets

_____ 9. A candidate for a county commissioner position giving a campaign speech

_____ 10. An instructor expressing his or her opinion about job reductions on campus

---

CHECK POINT 10.1

ANSWERS APPEAR ON PAGE A5

True or False?

_____ 1. Speaking is the most frequently used communication activity in college courses.

_____ 2. Listening is a challenging process partly due to the limited capacity and duration of working memory.

_____ 3. Your attitude, familiarity with the topic, internal and external distractors, and a speaker's qualities affect your ability to listen effectively.

_____ 4. Active listening is the only kind of listening that you will encounter in lectures.

 **Improve Your Grade**
Online Practice 1:
Listening Skills

Improve Your Grade
Reflective Writing 10.1

REFLECTIVE WRITING 10.1

On separate paper, in a journal, or online at this textbook's website, respond to the following questions:

1. During lectures, on a scale of one to ten with ten representing "highly effective," how do you rate your effectiveness as an active listener in lecture situations? Explain.

2. What are your greatest challenges in taking lecture notes? Do these difficulties occur in all lectures or just in lectures for specific classes? Be specific.

NOTETAKING SYSTEMS FOR LECTURES

2 *Discuss the notetaking options that are best suited for lecture, discussion, and math courses.*

Being familiar and comfortable with a variety of notetaking systems allows you to select the most appropriate and effective notetaking system to use for specific lecture styles and course content. **Figure 10.6** shows notetaking systems that are recommended for specific kinds of lectures; however, you can select from the other options if they seem better suited to your notetaking needs.

> **CONCEPT CHECK 10.12**
>
> Which notetaking options work best for each of your courses this term?

The Cornell Notetaking System

You can use the Five R's of the Cornell system for many of your lecture courses. (See Chapter 9, pages 261–266.) This system works most effectively when the instructor presents information in an organized, logical sequence. Any time you use the Cornell system for taking lecture notes, you can assess the quality of your notes by using the Cornell Notetaking Self-Assessment Checklist in Appendix B, page A19.

> **CONCEPT CHECK 10.13**
>
> How do Cornell notes for lectures differ from Cornell notes for textbooks?

During the course of a lecture, you may find that the instructor *sidetracks* by discussing information that does not seem to fit within the order or the outline of the topics. When you recognize that the instructor has sidetracked, continue to take notes on the *sidetracked information* as it may be important. Write sidetracked information on the *back side* of the previous page of notes, or include sidetracked information in your regular notes but place these notes inside a box to separate them from your regular notes. (See **Figure 10.7**.)

The Two-Column Notetaking System

The Two-Column Notetaking System is an effective notetaking option for lectures that move quickly from one topic to another, for math or science lectures, and for labs that focus mainly on problems, problem-solving solutions, or procedures and steps in a process. (See Chapter 9, pages 269–270.) You can also use two-column

FIGURE 10.6

Lecture Notetaking Options

	Cornell Notes	Two-Column Notes	Three-Column Notes	Outline Notes
Lectures *Mostly declarative knowledge: facts, definitions, examples, explanations*	✔ Write and underline headings and number details in the right column. Create the recall column after class.	✔ Write topics, terminology, and questions in the left column. Number details in the right column.		✔ Use I, II, III for topics. Use A, B, C for main ideas. Use 1, 2, 3 for details. Add a recall column if you wish.
Discussions		✔ Write questions or topics in the left column. Write comments and explanations in the right column.		
Math or Procedural Knowledge Content *Steps, processes, equations*		✔ Write the topic, process, or equation in the left column. Write the steps and the solution in the right column.	✔ Write the process or equation in the left column; write the steps in the middle column; write explanations in the right column. **OR** Leave the middle column empty for reworking the problem later. (See Figure 10.9.)	

FIGURE 10.7

Ways to Take Notes on Sidetracking

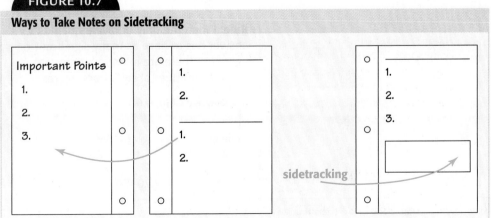

FIGURE 10.8

Two-Column Notes for Discussions

Topic or Question	Notes
Which of the major themes that we have discussed in class does this author use?	Short Story: 1. 2. 3.

CONCEPT CHECK 10.14

How can you use two-column notes for one or more of your classes?

CONCEPT CHECK 10.15

Can three-column notes be used effectively for straight lectures that focus on textbook concepts, terms, and explanations? Why or why not?

notes to capture main points made during discussions. As shown in **Figure 10.8**, write the discussion question in the left column; record students' responses and the instructor's comments in the right column.

The Three-Column Notetaking System

As discussed in Chapter 9, you can use the Three-Column Notetaking System for taking lecture notes in a math or a science class that involves using formulas or equations to solve problems. **Figure 10.9** shows terms and equations in the left

FIGURE 10.9

Three-Column Notes for Math Lectures

Problem—Directions	Rework the Problem	Solution—Rule
term: s.f.		s.f. = significant figure Method to express measured numbers properly; used in math. operations
6.8 cm/1.67 cm = ?	6.8 cm/1.67 cm = ?	6.8 cm/1.67 cm = 4.1 cm **Rule:** When multiply or divide quantities, answer has to have as many significant figures as there are in the quantity with the least number of significant figures. 6.8 cm/1.67 cm = 4.1 ↑ ↑ Limiting term 4.0718563 is rounded has 2 s.f. to 4.1 (2 s.f.)
9.7 m/4.4 m = ?	9.7 m/4.4 m = ?	9.7 m/4.4 m = 2.2045454 m = 2.2 m

Source: Modified from Shipman, Wilson, and Todd, *An Introduction to Physical Science, 10/e* (Boston: Houghton Mifflin Co., 2003), p. 15. Copyright © 2003. Reprinted by permission of Houghton Mifflin Co.

column and explanations and rules in the right column. The middle column is used after the lecture: fold the right column back or cover up the information so that it is not visible while you rework the problem. After reworking the problem, check the accuracy of your answer by comparing it with the information in the right column.

The Outline Notetaking System

The Outline Notetaking System works effectively for students who are familiar with and comfortable with outlining levels of information. Outline notes are also effective when the instructor provides you with an outline of the lecture at the beginning of the class. Using the outline as the skeleton of the main topics in the lecture, your goal then is to fill in the missing details. Under each heading, use numerals (1, 2, 3 . . .) for main points and lowercase letters (a, b, c . . .) for minor details under each numeral. **Figure 10.10** shows an example of an instructor's outline presented before the lecture begins. I-A shows the format to use for the details.

The Book Notes System

The Book Notes System is a form of notetaking that involves marking your textbook as the lecturer moves systematically through a chapter. Lecturing straight from the textbook is not very common, but does occur on occasion, such as in technical, reading, or composition courses. When an instructor moves systematically through the textbook chapter, discussing various headings, emphasizing certain details, demonstrating how to solve problems, or working textbook exercises with you in class, you can take notes directly in your textbook. Use the following strategies to take book notes:

❚ Use a specific colored marker to highlight the information the instructor discusses.

❚ Write notes in the margins to reflect any additional information or explanations.

❚ Use symbols, such as arrows or stars, to draw your attention to sections discussed.

❚ After class, use the textbook markings and marginal notes to develop a separate set of follow-up or summary notes on notebook paper if you wish.

Listening and taking lecture notes are two complex processes that require a repertoire of strategies for understanding, interpreting, organizing, and recording important information. What strategies do you use in lecture classes to capture important information for your notes?

FIGURE 10.10

Example of an Instructor's Lecture Outline

Outline for Feb. 5 Lecture

Health-Endangering Behaviors

I. Smoking
   A. Statistics/Studies
      1.
      2.
         a.
         b.
   B. Trends
   C. Treatments
II. Alcohol
   A. Statistics/Studies
   B. Health Consequences
   C. Treatments

CONCEPT CHECK 10.16

Do any of your instructors provide you with an outline at the beginning of a lecture class? If not, do you think they would welcome your suggestion? Why or why not?

The Book Notes System is a form of notetaking that involves marking your textbook as the lecturer moves systematically through a chapter.

CONCEPT CHECK 10.17

How do book notes differ from annotations made during the reading process?

CHECK POINT 10.2

True or False?

_____ 1. Effective notetakers use Cornell notes for lectures, outline notes for math courses, and two- and three-column notes only for notes made on textbook chapters.

_____ 2. The content of the lecture and the instructor's lecture style often determine which notetaking system would be the most effective to use.

_____ 3. Every student should master one specific notetaking system so he or she can use that system consistently for taking notes in every class that term.

_____ 4. Students should take some form of notes on information presented in lectures, discussions, labs, and problem-solving demonstrations.

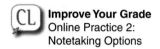

Improve Your Grade
Online Practice 2:
Notetaking Options

EFFECTIVE NOTETAKING STRATEGIES

3▸ *Discuss and demonstrate use of effective notetaking strategies to capture main ideas and important supporting details in lecture notes.*

The major difference between taking textbook notes and taking lecture notes is the rapidity with which you need to respond to stimuli, understand words and ideas, organize information in meaningful ways, and transfer it into notes—while at the same time taking in new information presented by the speaker. When taking lecture notes, keeping up with the speaker replaces the comfortable pace you use when taking textbook notes. Working memory is challenged.

Speaking, Thinking, and Writing Rates

Taking lecture notes requires you to adjust to your instructor's *rate of speech*. The **rate of speech** indicates an average number of words a speaker says per minute. In personal conversations, for example when you want to discuss serious issues or want to be sure the listener understands your points, you may speak slower than 100 words per minute. Other times in casual conversations, for example when you have exciting news to share, you may speak much faster than the normal rate of 125–150 words per minute for conversations. The average rate of speech during a lecture is 100–125 words per minute—a rate that provides a little more time to create basic understanding and to take notes.

You will likely encounter three general speaking rates instructors use during lectures: too slow, comfortable, or too fast. When an instructor speaks too slowly, you may have difficulty staying focused. Your *rate of thinking* far outpaces the instructor's rate of speech, so your mind tends to wander off the subject. The **rate of thinking** indicates an average number of words or small units of information a person thinks per minute. The average is 400 words per minute.

When an instructor speaks too fast, your *rate of writing* is too slow to capture the instructor's ideas on paper. The **rate of writing** indicates the average number of words a person writes per minute. An average rate of writing is thirty words per minute. When an instructor speaks at a comfortable pace, taking notes will still be demanding, but the discrepancies among speaking, writing, and thinking rates will not create as many notetaking difficulties. **Figure 10.11** summarizes average speaking, writing, and thinking rates.

CONCEPT CHECK 10.18

Why are lecture notes more difficult to create than textbook notes?

The **rate of speech** indicates an average number of words a speaker says per minute.

CONCEPT CHECK 10.19

What notetaking problems do you predict occur because of instructors' rates of speech?

The **rate of thinking** indicates an average number of words or small units of information a person thinks per minute (400 wpm).

The **rate of writing** indicates the average number of words a person writes per minute (30 wpm).

FIGURE 10.11

Speaking, Writing, and Thinking Rates	
Average Rates	**Words per Minute (wpm)**
Average Rate of Speech During Lectures	100–125 wpm
Average Rate of Writing	30 wpm
Average Rate of Thinking	400 wpm

Rate Discrepancies

Dealing with the discrepancies among the rate of speech in lectures, rate of writing, and rate of thinking requires flexibility and familiarity on your part with a variety of strategies you can use to adjust to specific lecture situations. **Figure 10.12** shows nine strategies to use to deal with discrepancies between rate of speech during lectures, rate of thinking, and rate of writing.

Maintain Undivided Attention

When your mind wanders, you start daydreaming, or you start doodling or tending to other tasks because of the large discrepancy between the speaker's slow rate of speech and your much faster rate of thinking, you may miss important information and find switching back into the listening mode more difficult to do. Your listening goal is to use strategies to keep your mind focused on the speaker and to maintain undivided attention, even though the presentation of information is not demanding. Use the following three strategies to deal with the discrepancy between a slow speech rate and a fast thinking rate:

■ **Strategy 1: Keep Writing**   Even if the details do not seem vital to your notes, write them down anyway. You can always cross out or eliminate them later. By continuing to write, you keep your working memory focused on the content of the lecture.

■ **Strategy 2: Mentally Summarize**   In your mind, run through the main ideas and the supporting details that have been discussed. Try to mentally summarize and list the details while you wait for new information to be introduced. You can also ask yourself basic questions, such as *Do I agree with this information? Is this the way it was presented in the textbook?*

■ **Strategy 3: Predict the Next Point or Answer to a Question**   With active listening, you can often "mentally tune in" to the speaker's outline or organizational plan for the lecture. Predict the next point that would naturally follow the sequential development of information, or mentally ask yourself a question that you think the next section of information will answer. Then listen carefully to determine if your prediction was correct or if your question was answered.

CONCEPT CHECK 10.20

What strategies can you use to minimize problems created by discrepancies between speaking and writing rates? Speaking and thinking rates?

FIGURE 10.12

Summary of Strategies for Dealing with Rate Discrepancies

■ Keep writing.
■ Mentally summarize.
■ Predict the next point or an answer to a question.
■ Paraphrase the speaker.
■ Use abbreviations and symbols.
■ Use modified printing.
■ Leave a gap and start writing again.
■ Shift to paragraph form.
■ Tape the lecture.

CONCEPT CHECK 10.21

Why does a speaker's slow rate of speech cause notetaking problems? What are possible solutions?

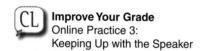

Improve Your Grade
Online Practice 3:
Keeping Up with the Speaker

CONCEPT CHECK 10.22

What is writing fluency? How does it affect the quality of your lecture notes?

Paraphrasing is the process of using your own words to rephrase or shorten a speaker's verbal information.

Increase Your Writing Rate

More often than not, notetaking problems occur because the rate of speech during a lecture is faster than your rate of writing. Your notetaking goal is *not* to write fast enough to write word for word; that is not feasible, practical, nor useful as notes should be *condensed* versions of information. Your goal is to develop a writing fluency or speed that is fast enough to write important information in your notes. Writing fluency is an essential notetaking skill; in fact, research studies show that writing fluency has the greatest impact on the quality of your notes. The following three time-saving strategies can improve your writing rate and fluency:

▌ **Strategy 4: Paraphrase**   **Paraphrasing** is the process of using your own words to rephrase or shorten a speaker's verbal information. Paraphrasing begins as a mental process that must be done quickly. As soon as you capture the speaker's words, interpret the information quickly, condense it using your own words, and write the shortened form. Your "sentences" do not need to be grammatically correct. You may omit words such as *the, an, and, there,* and *here* and other words that do not add to the overall meaning. Paraphrasing is perhaps one of the most difficult parts of notetaking, but with practice and familiarity with different instructors' lecture styles, your skills at paraphrasing will improve, and so will your writing fluency.

▌ **Strategy 5: Use Abbreviations and Symbols**   You can write faster by using abbreviations and symbols. When you find content-related words that you use frequently, create your own abbreviations for the terms or use common abbreviations, such as the following:

BC. for *because*	**PRES.** for *president*
EX. for *example*	**SOC.** for *social* or *sociology*
IMP. for *important*	**SOL.** for *solutions*
POL. for *politics*	**W/OUT** for *without*

Symbols are another form of abbreviations you can use to increase your writing speed. Symbols frequently appear in math notes, but can be used for other words as well. Following are common symbols you can use in your notes:

&	and	→	leads to; causes
@	at	<	less than
↓	decreases	>	more than; greater than
≠	doesn't equal	#	number
=	equals	+/−	positive/negative
↑	increases	∴	therefore
+	add; also	−	subtract
×	times	/	divide; per
( )	quantity	$p \wedge q$	conjunction *and*
~p	negation (not *p*)	$p \vee q$	disjunction *or*

▍**Strategy 6: Use Modified Printing** Modified printing is a style of handwriting that is functional and increases writing speed by using a mixture of cursive writing and printing. While taking notes, you can relax your handwriting standards and experiment with switching back and forth from printing and cursive writing to see if this increases your writing speed.

Do Not Stop When You Fall Behind

Most students at one time or another experience frustration from not being able to keep up with the speaker—even when using strategies to increase their writing speed. A normal tendency is to simply give up—stop taking notes and just listen. Sometimes that may not be a bad option, but later you may regret not having a written record of the information. Try using the following three strategies when you fall behind.

▍**Strategy 7: Leave a Gap and Start Writing Again** Instead of giving up, leave a gap in your notes and start taking notes again for as long as you can keep up with the instructor. After class, ask another student or the instructor to help fill in the gaps.

▍**Strategy 8: Shift to Paragraph Form** Sometimes becoming overly concerned with the notetaking format slows you down. If you find yourself spending too much time trying to decide how to number, label, or indent a detail, stop using your notetaking format and shift instead to writing paragraphs. Continue to paraphrase and use abbreviations or symbols in your paragraphs when possible. Later, when you have more time, you can reread the paragraph and organize it in a more meaningful way, such as making the recall column in Cornell notes or highlighting headings and numbering main ideas.

CONCEPT CHECK 10.23

How do you react to a notetaking situation in which you can no longer keep up with the instructor? What other ways can you deal with the situation?

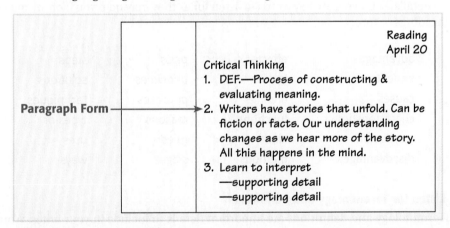

Paragraph Form ⟶

Reading
April 20

Critical Thinking
1. DEF.—Process of constructing & evaluating meaning.
2. Writers have stories that unfold. Can be fiction or facts. Our understanding changes as we hear more of the story. All this happens in the mind.
3. Learn to interpret
   —supporting detail
   —supporting detail

▍**Strategy 9: Tape the Lecture** If you consistently have difficulties keeping up with one instructor's style and rate of speech in lectures, ask your instructor for permission to tape the lectures. If permission is granted, sit near the front of the room. Start your tape recorder, and then begin taking notes on paper. If your tape recorder has a counter on it, when you run into notetaking problems or fall behind in your notes, jot down the counter number as it appears right then on your recorder. After class, return to specific sections of the tape so you can listen to the information one more time and add missing details in your notes. Your tape recorder should supplement, *not* replace, notetaking during the lecture.

Improve Your Grade
Online Practice 4:
Organizing Notes

CONCEPT CHECK 10.24

What are the characteristics of "quality notes?" Do you consider most or all of your notes to be quality notes? Why or why not?

Strategies to Organize Information

Quality notes show the structure, the levels of information, and sufficient details to support main ideas. If your notes are too brief and lack sufficient details, they will not be very helpful when you need to study the information or prepare for tests. By listening carefully for key words, you will be better equipped to identify main ideas and shifts made to supporting details.

Listen for Key Words Signaling Headings

The words in the following list often signal a new heading. When the words are repeated, they signal supporting details. For example, if the instructor says, "Let's look at the major <u>causes</u> of global warming," the word *causes* signals a new heading. As the lecture progresses, the instructor will use the word *causes* several more times to identify and explain each individual cause, which you can then number as details. Following are key words to listen for as they may help you identify major headings or topics.

advantages	effects	parts	steps
benefits	factors	principles	solutions
causes	findings	purposes	techniques
characteristics	functions	reasons	types of
conclusions	kinds of	rules	uses
disadvantages	methods	stages	ways

Listen for Terminology and Definitions

Terminology and definitions are important details to include in your notes. Word clues often signal definitions and help you identify key words to include in your notes. As previously discussed in Chapter 7, the following words signal definitions.

X means …	*X is defined as …*	*The definition of X is …*
X is also called …	*X, also referred to as …*	*X, also known as …*

When you hear these words, use the abbreviation *DEF* to signal that you are writing a definition. Or you may want to use the equal sign (=) symbol to connect a word to a definition. For example, you could write *paraphrasing* = *rephrasing or saying in your own words.*

Listen for Other Supporting Details

Dates, names, facts, statistics, and *examples* are additional kinds of supporting details that are important to include in your notes. These details develop, support, or "prove" the main idea and help you understand concepts more thoroughly.

Many instructors use *ordinals* (number words) to provide you with verbal clues for organizing the details in your notes. When you hear "first," make that point number 1 in your notes. Continue to use ordinals and *placeholder words* that *represent* a number: *first, second, next, also, in addition, another,* and *last* or *finally.*

Many instructors also include informative and interesting *examples* or *anecdotes* in their lectures. Why? Vivid examples serve as memory triggers or cues and create associations for a specific main idea or concept. For that reason, references to the example should be in your notes. Sometimes, however, the instructor may spend a considerable amount of time on an example, especially if it is an anecdote of a personal experience. Your notes only need to show the basic idea of the example; your notes do not need to "retell the whole story" with all its details.

Instructor Clues

As you become accustomed to your different instructors and their lecture styles, you will be able to use their verbal, visual, and nonverbal clues to help identify important information.

Listen for Verbal Clues

Key words such as *kinds of, steps, advantages of,* and so forth, are verbal clues that signal that the information is important. Other kinds of *verbal clues* may be even stronger signals of information that you should include in your notes. For example:

> "This is important. You need to know and understand this. This will be on the next test."
>
> "As I have already said ..." (ideas are repeated).
>
> "Be sure you copy this information (from the overhead or chalkboard)."
>
> "If you haven't already done so, be sure you read carefully the information on pages ..."
>
> "I can't emphasize enough the importance of ..."

A person's intonation (pitch of his or her voice), volume of voice, and rate of speech are also verbal clues. Listen to your instructor's patterns carefully. Does he or she speak louder, more enthusiastically, faster, slower, or at a different pitch when giving important information? Many speakers may not even be aware of the verbal patterns they use to emphasize important points, but skilled listeners can identify the patterns and use the information to help select the important ideas for their notes.

Watch for Visual Clues

Information that the instructor writes on the chalkboard or visual graphics that instructors display on a screen are visual clues that information is important. Include visual information as much as possible in your notes. If you recall seeing the same chart or visual information in your textbook, jot down a quick reminder to yourself to refer to the textbook chapter.

CONCEPT CHECK 10.25

What kinds of details are essential for quality notes? How can you quickly identify these details during a lecture?

CONCEPT CHECK 10.26

In what ways does your instructor provide you with clues to help you identify important information during a lecture?

CONCEPT CHECK 10.27

What specific nonverbal clues do each of your instructors use during a lectures? Do you think they are aware of their nonverbal patterns?

CONCEPT CHECK 10.28

How are math notes different from straight lecture or discussion notes? How are they similar?

Watch for Nonverbal Clues

Watch your instructor's *nonverbal clues* or patterns as well. Body stance, hand gestures, and facial expressions (forehead wrinkles, eyebrows rise) are nonverbal clues that communicate to observant listeners. If the instructor pauses to look at his or her notes or simply pauses to allow you time to write, the pauses are nonverbal clues. Writing information on the board, pointing to parts of it over and over, and circling words on the board are also nonverbal clues indicating that information is important.

Notetaking in Math Lectures

The majority of lecture time in math classes involves the discussion and explanation of solving math problems. Lectures include *declarative knowledge* (rules, definition, formulas, theorems, and problem solving steps) and *procedural knowledge* (application of steps to specific equations or word problems).

For the declarative knowledge, you can use any of the notetaking systems to capture this information. For the procedural knowledge, your notetaking goal is to copy the exact steps for solving a problem in your notes. In addition, you will want to include brief explanations or paraphrase the instructor's explanation of each step. If you miss some of the details, insert question marks; you can return to these question marks after the instructor completes the problem, or you can refer to your textbook to fill in the missing information. The following are four tips to increase your math notetaking skills.

▌ *Copy signs and symbols accurately.* Omitting a sign or symbol or copying it incorrectly will affect not only the quality of your notes but the accuracy of applying the steps to solve similar problems.

▌ *Listen and watch for patterns.* Problems solved in class consist of underlying patterns used to solve similar problems at a later time. Look for similarities in problem patterns.

▌ *Record explanations for steps.* Often the explanations remind you *when* to use a specific process and when *not* to use a specific process. They also tell you *why* a specific step is important.

▌ *Write reminders to see the textbook.* If you are already familiar with the chapter, some of the problems presented in class may also be explained in your textbook. If your instructor indicates the problem is from the textbook, use an abbreviation, such as TXBK next to the problem.

EXERCISE 10.4

Lecture Notetaking Checklist

DIRECTIONS: Select any set of lecture notes you have for any one of your courses. Go to Exercise 10.4 in Appendix B, page A21 to assess the quality of your lecture notes.

EXERCISE 10.5

Textbook Case Studies

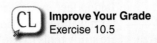
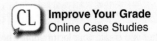
DIRECTIONS:

1. Read each case study carefully. Respond to the question at the end of each case study by using *specific* strategies discussed in this chapter. Answer in complete sentences.

2. Write your responses on paper or online at the Online Study Center, Exercise 10.5. You will be able to print your online response or e-mail it to your instructor.

CASE STUDY 1: Kimberly is very uncomfortable sitting in a classroom. She often feels like other students are watching her, so she sits in the back corner. She has a lot of problems taking notes. Her notes are too brief and ineffective for studying. She does not include information written on the board because she cannot see it clearly. At other times, she simply loses her concentration. When she does try taking notes, she cannot write fast enough to get all of the instructor's words on her paper. What would you recommend Kimberly do to improve her notetaking skills?

CASE STUDY 2: Alex has an outgoing, and sometimes overbearing, personality. He frequently annoys his classmates and instructors during lectures. He seems to verbalize every thought that enters his head. Thinking that he is participating in class, he often interrupts the instructor with irrelevant questions, or he asks the instructor to repeat information or to slow down so that he can write something down. He spends more time talking than listening and taking notes. What techniques does Alex need to learn in order to be a more effective listener and positive contributor to the class environment?

EXERCISE 10.6

Select a System and Take Lecture Notes

PURPOSE: Taking effective notes involves practicing effective notetaking skills in a variety of settings and with a variety of speakers.

DIRECTIONS:

1. Select any one of your classes you are enrolled in this term. Choose an appropriate notetaking system to use to take notes from one of the lectures in that class.

2. Your instructor may ask you to use the Instructor Questionnaire that is available for Exercise 10.6 in Appendix B, page A22.

3. On your own paper, identify the class, the topic, and the instructor's name. Then answer the following questions. Turn in your answers with a copy of your lecture notes.

   a. What problems did you have taking notes from this lecture?

   b. What are possible solutions for dealing with those problems? What strategies could you use to improve your notetaking skills for that course?

   c. How soon after the lecture did you study and review your notes? Were you able to understand your notes? Were they clear and did they have sufficient details? Explain.

4. If you would like to assess the quality of your notes, use the Exercise 10.4 checklist in Appendix B, page A21.

Working with Your Notes

CONCEPT CHECK 10.29

After you create your lecture notes, how can you use them effectively? Do your lecture notes replace or supplement your textbook notes? Explain.

Taking lecture notes helps you stay focused on the lecture and keeps your mind from wandering. The most significant purpose of taking notes, however, is to create study tools to use *after* the class has ended. As you learned in Chapter 4, scheduling a study block as soon after a lecture as possible gives you the opportunity to work with your notes while the information is still fresh in your mind. Use the following five strategies as soon after class as possible.

▌ *Complete Your Notes:* Add missing details, fill in gaps, and correct any misspelled key terms that appear in your notes. Confer with other students or your instructor, or refer to your textbook for missing information or correct spellings. If you chose to use the Cornell Notetaking System, complete the reduce step by creating the recall column.

▌ *Add More Structure to Your Notes:* If your notes lack a clear structure or appear disorganized, insert headings or number the individual details. Highlight specific concepts or key words or use a colored pen to circle terminology to create more structure for your notes.

▌ *Supplement Your Notes:* As you work with your notes, you may want to make lists of information, brief outlines of main ideas, or clarifying questions that you would like to ask in class. Each type of notetaking system recommends that you write only on the front side of your notebook paper. Use the back sides for adding supplementary notes or questions.

CONCEPT CHECK 10.30

Is rewriting your notes an effective use of your time? Why or why not?

▌ *Rewrite Your Notes When Justified:* Do not spend valuable time rewriting lecture (or textbook) notes simply for the sake of producing a neater set of notes. Students who are kinesthetic or highly visual learners may find value in rewriting or typing their notes on a computer. The physical process of rewriting boosts memory and encodes information in a form that is easier to recall. In such cases, rewriting notes, which may include reorganizing information, is a meaningful and effective use of time.

▌ *Recite, Reflect, and Review Your Notes:* The true value of your notes involves using them *after* the lecture. Spend time digesting the information, reciting the information, reworking problems, rehearsing, and reflecting. At the beginning of your next study block for the class, you can use your notes as a *warm-up activity*. Schedule time each week for *ongoing review*.

CHECK POINT 10.3

ANSWERS APPEAR ON PAGE A5

True or False?

_____ 1. The most common cause of notetaking problems is the discrepancy between thinking and writing rates.

_____ 2. If you think at 400 wpm and your instructor speaks at 80 wpm, you may need to use strategies, such as mentally summarizing, to stay attentive to the lecture.

_____ 3. Paraphrasing, using abbreviations, and modified printing are strategies to help you increase your writing fluency.

_____ 4. Quality notes show the skeleton of a lecture, plus clearly marked headings and sufficient supporting details, such as facts, definitions, examples, and explanations.

 Improve Your Grade
Online Practice 5:
Lecture Notes

REFLECTIVE WRITING 10.2

Improve Your Grade
Reflective Writing 10.2

On separate paper, in a journal, or online at this textbook's website, respond to the following questions.

1. Which strategies in this chapter were the most beneficial for helping you become a more effective listener? Be specific.

2. Which strategies in this chapter were the most beneficial for helping you take more effective lecture notes? Be specific.

EXERCISE 10.7

Improve Your Grade
Exercise 10.7

Links

PURPOSE: Many students have difficulty taking effective lecture notes. The problem often stems from the characteristics and functions of working memory.

DIRECTIONS: Work in groups of three or four students. Complete the following directions. Record your answers on a group chart that shows three columns.

1. Review working memory strategies in Chapter 2, pages 53–55.

2. Copy and complete the following chart. Begin by listing the ten strategies in Figure 2.5 for working memory (page 54). Then, write YES or NO in the middle column to indicate if the WM strategy is used actively during lecture notetaking activities; add brief explanations. Then, list strategies that you could use to minimize the problems with working memory during lecture notetaking.

Working Memory Strategies	Do Lecture Notes Use This Strategy?	Strategies to Overcome Problems:
Limit the number of items and the speed at which you take in stimuli.	NO. Many stimuli presented quickly.	
Create an interest/excitement.	(Continue with the chart.)	

LEARNING OBJECTIVES REVIEW

▶ *Discuss factors that influence the quality of listening; identify four kinds of listening you will encounter in school, work, and personal settings.*

- Listening skills are often the weakest of the four verbal communication skills. Listening is more than hearing; listening involves attaching meaning to a speaker's words.

- Factors, such as attitude, the topic, the speaker's qualities, external distractors, personal variables, and listening styles affect one's ability to listen effectively.

- Each of the following four kinds of listening involve different listening goals:
  - active listening
  - critical listening
  - empathic listening
  - appreciative listening

- Seven strategies promote active listening:
  - Create a clear listening goal.
  - Use concentration strategies.
  - Familiarize yourself with the topic *before* class.
  - Keep an open mind.
  - Activate your visual skills.
  - Express an interest in the topic.
  - Participate in the learning process.

▶ *Discuss the notetaking options that are best suited for lecture, discussion, and math courses.*

- Notetaking options for lectures classes that consist mainly of declarative knowledge include Cornell notes, two-column notes, and outline notes.

- The two-column notes are recommended for discussion classes; the two-column and three-column notes are recommended for math or science classes that involve more procedural knowledge.

- Outline notes work effectively when instructors provide students with lecture outlines.

- Book notes work effectively when instructors lecture directly from textbooks.

▶ *Discuss and demonstrate use of effective notetaking strategies to capture main ideas and important supporting details in lecture notes.*

- Some listening and notetaking difficulties occur due to discrepancies among rate of speech (100–125 wpm for average lectures), rate of thinking (400 wpm average), and rate of writing (30 wpm average).

- Nine strategies help students deal with rate discrepancies:
  - Keep writing.
  - Mentally summarize.
  - Predict the next point or an answer to a question.
  - Paraphrase the speaker.
  - Use abbreviations and symbols.
  - Use modified printing.
  - Leave a gap and start writing again.
  - Shift to paragraph form.
  - Tape the lecture.

- Quality notes show headings and include sufficient supporting details. By listening for key words, students can often identify main headings, terminology and definitions, and other supporting details, such as facts, names, dates, or examples.

- Instructors often provide verbal, visual, and nonverbal clues for identifying important information.

- For notes to be effective, students need to work with their notes by using reciting, rehearsing, reflecting, and reviewing activities.

Multiple Choice

_____ 1. Which of the following is the most frequently used form of communication?
   a. Writing
   b. Listening
   c. Reading
   d. Speaking

_____ 2. Your listening efficiency or ability may be influenced by
   a. your attitude toward the subject or the speaker and your interest in the topic.
   b. your emotional state, learning style preferences, and cultural background.
   c. the speaker's style of delivery, tone of voice, and rate of speech.
   d. all of the above.

_____ 3. Which of the following is _not_ true about writing fluency?
   a. Your writing fluency has minimal effect on the quality of your notes.
   b. Writing fluency refers to a person's rate of writing.
   c. A person with high writing fluency most likely knows how to paraphrase.
   d. A person with low writing fluency may fall behind taking notes during a lecture.

_____ 4. Listening goals
   a. vary for each of the four kinds of listening.
   b. involve understanding different kinds of information for different purposes.
   c. for critical listening involve higher-level thinking skills such as analysis.
   d. involve all of the above.

_____ 5. Which of the following is _not_ true?
   a. Linear listeners prefer a broad, open-ended discussion of a topic.
   b. Empathic listeners focus on a person's feelings without giving too much input.
   c. Global listeners prefer to get an overview followed by examples and discussion.
   d. Familiarizing yourself with the topic before class promotes active listening.

_____ 6. When taking lecture notes, strive to
   a. capture main ideas and important details.
   b. increase writing speed by using abbreviations and modified printing.
   c. listen for word clues that help you organize levels of information.
   d. do all of the above.

_____ 7. The best notetaking system to use in lecture classes is
   a. always the Cornell system.
   b. a notetaking system that works well with the lecturer's style and content.
   c. two-column notes with the topic or question on the right.
   d. a formal outline that shows specific levels of information.

_____ 8. Paraphrasing
   a. involves rephrasing and shortening a speaker's words.
   b. is an effective strategy to use to keep up with the speaker during notetaking.
   c. can be used to pose questions to the speaker.
   d. involves all of the above.

Short-Answer Questions

Write your answers on separate paper.

1. What strategies can you use to combat the effects of a discrepancy between the rate of speech and the rate of writing?
2. Explain how an instructor's lecture style and the content of the lecture affect your choice of notetaking systems to use during class.

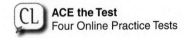 **ACE the Test**
Four Online Practice Tests

 **Online Resources**

11 Creating and Using Visual Notes and Study Tools

LEARNING OBJECTIVES

1 Describe strategies you use to tailor your approach to learning.

2 Explain and demonstrate how to create and use visual mappings.

3 Explain and demonstrate how to create and use hierarchies.

4 Explain and demonstrate how to create and use comparison charts.

310

Chapter Outline

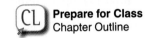

Prepare for Class
Chapter Outline

5 ▶ *Explain and demonstrate how to create and use index card notes.*

Tailoring your approach to learning involves becoming familiar with an array of strategies, learning to use the strategies, and then selecting those strategies that work most effectively for you and the content or course you are studying. Visual notetaking provides you with an avenue to use your visual skills and creativity to capture important information in the form of visual mappings, hierarchies, comparison charts, and index card notes. By learning to use all of these notetaking options, you will be better equipped to individualize the process of learning to achieve greater success.

CHAPTER 11 PROFILE

Creating Visual Notes and Study Tools

CL **Improve Your Grade**
Chapter 11 Profile

ANSWER, **SCORE**, and **RECORD** your profile before you read this chapter. If you need to review the process, refer to the complete directions given in the profile for Chapter 1 on page 4.

ONLINE: You can complete the profile and get your score online at this textbook's website.

	YES	NO
1. I use one specific notetaking system in all notetaking situations.		
2. I tailor my approach to learning by selecting different learning strategies and study tools to match the learning situation and materials.		
3. I draw various kinds of pictures to help me remember what I have read.		
4. I close my eyes or look up into the air to visualize or picture information.		
5. I recite information in diagrams and get immediate feedback on the accuracy and completeness of the information I recited.		
6. I try to visually memorize all the information in charts or diagrams.		
7. I know how to organize my notes into charts designed to compare and contrast information for different topics.		
8. I avoid making flashcards because they are too cumbersome to manage.		
9. I create index card notes that include definition cards, study question cards, and category cards with lists of information to memorize.		
10. I am confident in my ability to convert printed information into meaningful visual notes to study and learn new information.		

QUESTIONS LINKED TO THE CHAPTER LEARNING OBJECTIVES:

Questions 1, 2:   objective 1   Question 7:   objective 4
Questions 3, 4:   objective 2   Questions 8, 9:   objective 5
Questions 5, 6:   objective 3   Question 10:   all objectives

TAILORED APPROACH

▶ 1 *Describe strategies you use to tailor your approach to learning.*

Metacognition is the process of understanding *how* you learn, *what* you need to learn, and finally, *which* strategies or techniques would be the most effective or the best matched to the learning task and your learning process. In Chapter 1, you learned a variety of strategies for visual, auditory, and kinesthetic learners; in Chapters 2 and 3, you learned how your memory works and Memory Principles to use to enhance your memory systems; in Chapter 6, you were introduced to a variety of study tools for summary notes; in Chapter 7, you learned to create definition cards and vocabulary sheets; in Chapter 8, you learned strategies for learning from your textbooks, and in Chapters 9 and 10, you learned to use annotation, Cornell notes, two- and three-column notes, outline notes, and book notes for taking textbook or lecture notes.

Needless to say, using *all* of these study strategies for one chapter is not feasible. Instead, after experimenting with the various strategies, you should become increasingly more comfortable about *tailoring* or *personalizing* your approach to learning by selecting the combinations that work best for you in particular learning situations. After using a specific strategy to begin the learning process with new materials, you may at times choose to create additional notes or study tools to encode the information in new ways, elaborate or rehearse in greater depth to "cement" the information in memory, or to add more interest and creativity to the learning process. The following are possible combinations you may at times choose to use:

▌ Create Cornell notes, then create definition cards.

▌ Highlight and annotate, then create outline notes.

▌ Create two-column notes, then create a visual mapping or a hierarchy.

The combinations of notetaking systems and study tools is extensive; however, the choices are yours to make based on your preferences and effectiveness of various formats for specific information you are studying. In this chapter, you will learn additional strategies to add to your repertoire of strategy resources: visual mappings, hierarchies, comparison charts, and index card notes.

Creating Visual Notes

Visual notes are a form of notetaking that organizes information into diagrams that use colors, pictures, and shapes to help imprint information into visual memory. Visual notes, also called graphic organizers, include visual mappings, hierarchies, comparison charts, and index card notes. Many students prefer using visual notetaking systems to create reflect activities or study tools to review specific sections of information; however, some students become so proficient with visual notetaking that they can use it to take textbook and lecture notes. Visual notes are powerful and effective because they:

▌ Are based on Memory Principles that boost your ability to learn new information

▌ Incorporate the use of colors, pictures, symbols, and graphic formats that provide you with visual images and associations that work as memory retrieval cues

CONCEPT CHECK 11.1

In what ways do you use *metacognition* in your classes?

CONCEPT CHECK 11.2

How do you know which strategies work best in specific learning situations?

Visual notes are a form of notetaking that organizes information into diagrams that use colors, pictures, and shapes to help imprint information into visual memory.

CONCEPT CHECK 11.3

Why do you think visual notes are often considered right-brain notes and study tools? Why are they such powerful study tools?

▌ Provide structures to organize and rearrange information logically, they show relationships, and they identify different levels of information (topics, main ideas, supporting details)

▌ Utilize right-brain or global approaches to learning, with emphasis on creativity and visual memory skills

▌ Provide a way for you to personalize information in original, creative ways

▌ Promote effective recitation, lead to elaborative rehearsal, and increase concentration

▌ Involve multisensory approaches to learning

▌ Provide you with effective study tools to use for ongoing review

Identifying Information for Your Notes

CONCEPT CHECK 11.4

How can understanding paragraph elements help you create visual notes?

You cannot create effective visual notes if you do not understand the information you are reading. Visual notes are based on identifying the *topic* or subject, identifying the *main ideas* or headings, and identifying *important supporting details*. These are the paragraph element skills that you learned in Chapter 7, pages 194–198. Annotating printed materials before developing visual notes often helps you focus on the key elements to use in your visual notes; you can then use the highlighting as a guide for your notes. Use these suggestions for highlighting:

▌ Highlight, circle, place a box around, or write a large note in the margin showing the topic.

▌ Highlight headings and subheadings.

▌ Highlight the main idea or topic sentence in each paragraph.

▌ Highlight key words for important supporting details; circle terminology.

Studying Visual Notes

CONCEPT CHECK 11.5

What are the steps to use to study visual notes? What Principles of Memory do you use during each step?

As you strive to understand new information, analyze it, identify the different levels of information (topics, main ideas, supporting details), and then convert that information into meaningful visual forms, learning takes place. Each step of the process of creating visual notes helps you clarify and create a stronger impression of the information. However, to receive the most benefits from your visual notes, you need to spend time studying, visually memorizing, and reciting from your notes. **Figure 11.1** shows five Essential Strategies for Studying Visual Notes.

FIGURE 11.1

Essential Strategies for Studying Visual Notes

▌ **Imprint the basic structure (the skeleton) in your visual memory.** Look intently (stare) at the first two levels of information. Carve a mental image of the skeleton into your memory. Do *not* focus your attention on the lower-level details.

▌ **Visualize the skeleton of your notes.** Close your eyes, look away, or *look up and to the left* to recall the image. Practice visualizing or "seeing" the words, the shapes, and the colors in your visual notes. Look back at your notes to check your accuracy.

▌ **Recite the topic and the main headings.** Without looking at your visual notes, name the first two levels of information. Then begin reciting all that you remember about each heading. Explain in complete sentences. Look back at your visual notes to check the accuracy and completeness of the information you recited.

▌ **Use reflect activities for elaborative rehearsal.** Following are three suggestions.

1. Without referring to your notes, redraw the skeleton. Label each part.

2. Record yourself reciting information about each part of your visual notes.

3. Convert the information into a written summary, developing one paragraph for each heading and its details.

▌ **Use ongoing review.** Mentally rehearse and recite your visual notes frequently to keep the image sharp and the content fresh in your memory and readily accessible.

CHECK POINT 11.1

ANSWERS APPEAR ON PAGE A5

True or False?

_____ 1. Visual notes focus mainly on topics and main ideas or headings.

_____ 2. Reciting visual notes involves reciting main ideas as well as details.

_____ 3. Using metacognition involves picking and choosing the study strategies that work most effectively for you and that best match the materials you are studying.

_____ 4. Visual memory is the only type of memory used when you study visual notes.

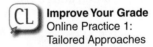
Improve Your Grade
Online Practice 1:
Tailored Approaches

REFLECTIVE WRITING 11.1

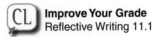
Improve Your Grade
Reflective Writing 11.1

On separate paper, in a journal, or online at this textbook's website, respond to the following questions:

1. What experiences have you already had with creating visual notes, such as visual mappings? Explain your reaction to this form of notetaking.

2. One aspect of metacognition is to select appropriate strategies for specific kinds of learning tasks or materials. In what ways do you currently tailor your approach to learning so it reflects your preferences or strengths? Give specific examples.

VISUAL MAPPINGS

2 ▷ *Explain and demonstrate how to create and use visual mappings.*

Visual mappings are diagrams that place the topic in the center of a diagram with main ideas branching off the center followed by details branching off the main ideas. Visual mappings are also called *cognitive maps, mind maps,* and *clusters.* You can use visual mappings to show:

- A chapter outline with its main headings and subheadings
- Levels of information in paragraphs that appear under one heading
- A topic or a subject presented in several chapters and lectures
- Lecture information
- Test review information in the form of summary notes
- Ideas brainstormed for a paper or a speech

> **Visual mappings** are diagrams that place the topic in the center of a diagram with main ideas branching off the center followed by details branching off the main ideas.

The Topic

The first step for creating a visual mapping is to identify the topic or the subject for your visual mapping. The topic may be the title of a chapter, the name of a lecture, or a specific subject. The topic is called *level-one information*; place it inside a geometric shape (circle, oval, triangle, or rectangle) or inside a picture shape. For example, if you are creating a visual mapping on the Brain Dominance Theory, you may want to use the picture in **Figure 11.2** as the center of your visual mapping.

Main Ideas or Headings

Level-two information consists of the main ideas associated with the topic. If you are creating a visual mapping for a textbook chapter, use the headings in the chapter for level-two information. Use the following guidelines for writing level-two information on your visual mapping:

- *Creating Your Own Headings:* In addition to the headings indicated in the printed materials, you can add headings, such as "Introduction" or "Summary." You can create a special heading to show a specific chart or diagram if it does not fit elsewhere on your visual mapping.

- *Spacing:* Visually appealing and uncluttered mappings are easier to visualize or memorize. Before you begin adding the level-two information, count the number of main ideas to decide how to space them evenly around the page. Place them relatively close to the topic so you will have room to add details later.

- *Organization:* The most common organization for this level-two information is clockwise, beginning at the eleven o'clock position. If there is a definite sequence to the information, such as steps that you must learn in order, you may add numbers to the lines that extend from the topic or add numbers inside the borders of level-two information.

FIGURE 11.2

The Topic for a Brain Dominance Theory Visual Mapping

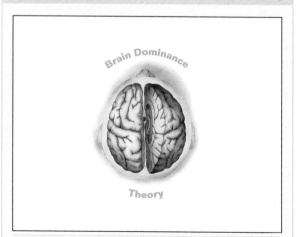

Source: Bernstein and Nash, *Essentials of Psychology,* 2nd ed. (Boston: Houghton Mifflin Co., 2002), p. 59. Copyright © by Houghton Mifflin Co. Used with permission.

❚ *Connectors:* Draw a line from the topic in the center to each main idea to connect the level-two subtopics to the main topic.

❚ *Borders, Shapes, or Pictures:* To make the main ideas or categories stand out, you can place a border or shape around each item on level two. You may use a different shape or a picture for each main idea if you wish. (See Exercise 3.5, page 87, for an example of adding pictures to level-two information on the Twelve Principles of Memory visual mapping.)

❚ *Colors:* Colors strengthen visual memory and create a stronger visual impression. Experiment with the use of colors: shade in the main ideas, use different colors for different levels of information, or add colors to pictures used as retrieval cues.

Keep in mind that visual mappings involve creativity, so a visual mapping that you create will be unique. Other students' visual mappings of the same topic will include similar information, but the visual presentations will vary. Students with artistic talent may create visual mappings that reflect those talents. Students with less artistic talent may use colors and shapes in interesting ways to create visually appealing mappings. **Figure 11.3** shows level-one and level-two information for a visual mapping for the SQ4R Reading System.

Supporting Details

Level-three information consists of major supporting details, the types of details that explain, support, or prove the main idea. Major supporting details are key words that work as retrieval cues to trigger recall of information. Later when you study your visual mapping and recite, you will convert these key words into full sentences to explain the information in greater detail. Use the following guidelines for adding level-three information to your visual mapping:

❚ *Key Words:* Use only key words on level three. Avoid using long phrases or full sentences as they will clutter your visual mapping.

❚ *Organization:* You can arrange the details in any order; they do not need to be organized in a clockwise direction.

❚ *Spacing:* Space them somewhat evenly around the main idea so each detail is clear and easy to read.

❚ *Quantity of Details:* Be selective. Include only as many major details as you need to help you remember key information about each main idea.

❚ *Horizontal Writing:* To make your mapping easy to read, keep all your writing horizontal. Avoid writing at a slant or sideways, or turning the paper as you write, resulting in words written upside down. Our visual memories are trained to recall writing that appears on horizontal lines.

CONCEPT CHECK 11.9

What are the benefits of using pictures and colors in visual mappings?

CONCEPT CHECK 11.10

Where is the starting position for the first heading on visual mappings? Is it important to always begin at that location? Why or why not?

CONCEPT CHECK 11.11

What is "level-three information" and how can you effectively include this information in your visual mappings?

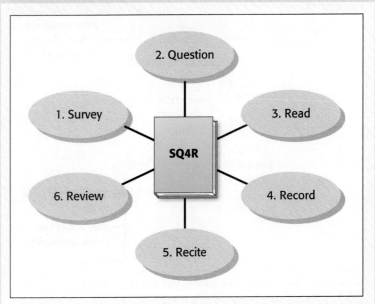

FIGURE 11.3

The SQ4R Reading System

▌ *Borders:* You do not need to add borders around level-three information if the details stand out clearly; however, including borders is an option.

▌ *Personalize with Pictures:* Pictures help imprint information in your visual memory and are often easier to recall than words, so include pictures when appropriate.

CONCEPT CHECK 11.12

Does a visual mapping provide an effective overview of a topic? Why or why not?

After reading a section about coping strategies in *Essentials of Psychology* by Bernstein and Nash (2nd edition, 2002, Houghton Mifflin Co.), a student chose to convert the information into a visual mapping. Carefully and selectively the student chose meaningful information for the visual mapping. Notice in **Figure 11.4** how much information you can learn about the topic of "Coping Strategies" even though you have not read this specific textbook information.

FIGURE 11.4

Visual Mapping for Coping Strategies

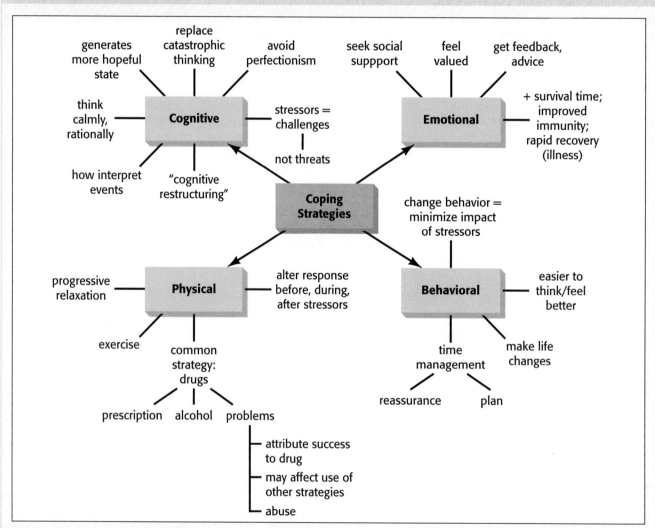

Source for information used in the visual mapping: Bernstein and Nash. *Essentials of Psychology,* 2nd ed. (Boston: Houghton Mifflin Co., 2002), pp. 370–371.

Minor Details

You will encounter situations in which you want to include *level-four information* on your visual mapping. *Level-four details* are minor details linked to an important supporting detail. Use the following guidelines for level-four information:

- *Be extremely selective:* Too many minor details will clutter your mapping and make it difficult to use as a study tool. Use only key words or short phrases, not full sentences.

- *Branch minor details off major details:* You can branch individual minor details off a major supporting detail as shown in Figure 11.4: "reassurance" and "plan" are minor details for "time management," one of the major details for Behavioral Coping Strategies.

- *Cluster minor details:* To avoid cluttering your visual mapping or branching information too widely across your paper, you can group or cluster minor details to save space. In Figure 11.4, notice how clustering is used under Physical Coping Strategies to show the *common strategy: drugs* and *three problems* associated with the drugs strategy.

- *Use larger paper:* When you plan to create more extensive visual mappings, work on unlined legal paper, drawing paper, or poster-sized paper. Crowded, cluttered visual mappings lose their purpose and their power if they are difficult to visualize.

- *Create separate visual mappings:* When you create a visual mapping for a chapter, you may find that you frequently need four or more levels of information to capture the important points. When this is the case, consider reorganizing the information into several different visual mappings; narrow the scope of each mapping by chunking the information into more meaningful units.

CONCEPT CHECK 11.13

What is "level-four information" and how can you include it in a visual mapping without cluttering up the diagram?

Studying from Visual Mappings

Studying from visual mappings strengthens your visual memory skills and provides you with visual images you can use to retrieve important information from memory. Use the Essential Strategies in Figure 11.1 on page 315.

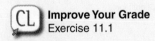

EXERCISE 11.1

A Visual Mapping for SQ4R

CL **Improve Your Grade**
Exercise 11.1

DIRECTIONS:

1. Review information about the SQ4R Reading System in Chapter 8, pages 216–218.

2. Expand Figure 11.3 by adding supporting major and minor details to the visual mapping.

3. Compare your visual mapping with the one that appears online for Exercise 11.1. Your visual mapping should contain similar material, but it should reflect your personalized design.

EXERCISE 11.2

Understanding Levels of Information

DIRECTIONS:

1. Work with a partner. Examine and discuss the visual mapping shown below.

2. Answer the following questions about the "Other Solar System Objects."

   a. What are the level-two headings for this visual mapping?

   b. Which parts of the mapping would you visually memorize as the skeleton?

   c. What details are provided for the heading "Background"?

   d. What level-three details are provided for asteroids?

   e. Where in the mapping do pictures help clarify information?

   f. Where are level-four details in this visual mapping?

   g. Which parts of the visual mapping should you not visually memorize, but you should refer to after you recite so you can check your accuracy?

3. You can read the excerpt used for this visual mapping by going to Exercise 11.2 in Appendix C, page A27.

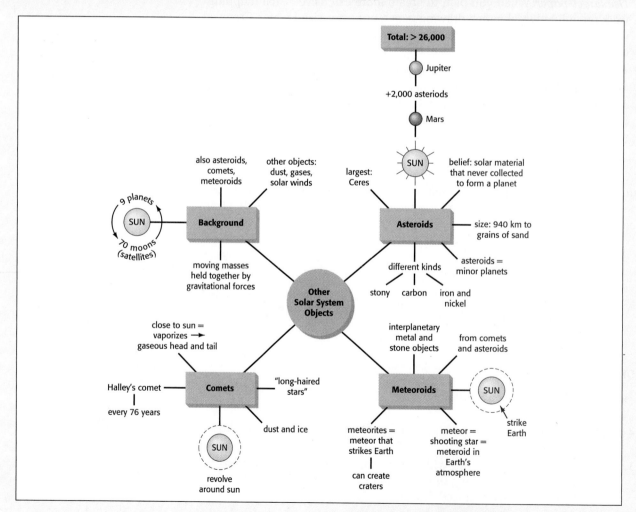

EXERCISE 11.3

Creating a Visual Mapping

PURPOSE: Converting printed information into visual mappings helps you identify levels of information and condense printed materials into visual forms that are easy to visually memorize.

DIRECTIONS: Read the following excerpt. Then create a visual mapping with at least three levels of information. Be selective with the details you include in your visual mapping. Use the tips in this chapter for creating and studying visual mappings.

Characteristics of People with High Self-Esteem

1. *People with high self-esteem are future oriented and not overly concerned with past mistakes or failures.* They learn from their errors but are not immobilized by them. They believe every experience has something to teach—if they are willing to learn. A mistake can show you what does not work, what not to do. One consultant, when asked whether he had obtained any results in trying to solve a difficult problem, replied, "Results? Why, I've had lots of results. I know a hundred things that won't work!" The same principle applies to your own progress. Falling down does not mean failure. Staying down does.

2. *People with high self-esteem are able to cope with life's problems and disappointments.* Successful people have come to realize that problems need not depress them or make them anxious. It is their attitude toward problems that makes all the difference. In his book, *They All Laughed: From Light-bulbs to Lasers,* Ira Flatow examines the lives of successful, innovative people who had to overcome major obstacles to achieve their goals. He discovered that the common thread among these creative people was their ability to overcome disappointing events and press on toward their goals.

3. *People with high self-esteem are able to feel all dimensions of emotion without letting those emotions affect their behavior in a negative way.* This characteristic is one of the major reasons people with high self-esteem are able to establish and maintain effective human relations with the people around them. They realize emotions cannot be handled either by repressing them or by giving them free rein. Although you may not be able to stop feeling the emotions of anger, envy, and jealousy, you can control your thoughts and actions when you are under the influence of these strong emotions. Say to yourself, "I may not be able to control the way I feel right now, but I can control the way I behave."

4. *People with high self-esteem are able to accept other people as unique, talented individuals.* They learn to accept others for who they are and what they can do. Our multicultural work force makes this attitude especially important. Individuals who cannot tolerate other people who are "different" may find themselves out of a job. People with high self-esteem build mutual trust based on each individual's uniqueness. These trusting relationships do not limit or confine either person because of group attributes such as skin color, religion, gender, lifestyle, or sexual orientation. Accepting others is a good indication that you accept yourself.

5. *People with high self-esteem exhibit a variety of self-confident behaviors.* They accept compliments or gifts by saying, "Thank you," without making self-critical excuses and without feeling obligated to return the favor. They can laugh at their situation without self-ridicule. They let others be right or wrong without attempting to correct or ridicule them. They feel free to express opinions even if they differ from those of their peers or parents. They are able to maintain an **internal locus of control**—that is, they make decisions for their own reasons based on their standards of what is right and wrong, and they are not likely to comply with the inappropriate demands of others. This internal control helps raise self-esteem every time it is applied.

Source: From Reece and Brandt, *Human Relations: Principles and Practices,* 5th ed. (Boston: Houghton Mifflin Co., 2003), pp. 63–64. Copyright © 2003. Reprinted by permission of Houghton Mifflin Company.

CHECK POINT 11.2

ANSWERS APPEAR ON PAGE A5

Multiple Choice

_____ 1. Which statement is *not* true about visual mappings?

    a. To avoid clutter, visual mappings should include only three levels of information.

    b. In a well-developed mapping, different levels of information are easy to identify.

    c. For consistency in "reading" a visual mapping, a standard format for ordering level-two information is recommended.

    d. Pictures, shapes, and colors strengthen visual memory and recall of information.

_____ 2. In visual mappings, level-one and level-two information

    a. should be visually memorized as the skeleton of the visual mapping.

    b. show the topic and its main headings.

    c. are the only levels of information that you should visually memorize.

    d. should do all of the above.

Improve Your Grade
Online Practice 2:
Visual Mappings

HIERARCHIES

> 3 ▶ *Explain and demonstrate how to create and use hierarchies.*

Hierarchies are diagrams that place the topic on the top line of a diagram with main ideas branching down from the topic followed by details branching down from the main ideas.

CONCEPT CHECK 11.14

How are hierarchies similar and how are they different from visual mappings? Which format is easier for you to use? Why?

CONCEPT CHECK 11.15

What kind of information do you include in a hierarchy skeleton? How do you use the skeleton when you study the material?

Hierarchies are diagrams that place the topic on the top line of a diagram with main ideas branching down from the topic followed by details branching down from the main ideas. Hierarchies arrange information in levels of size and importance from the top down. If visualizing mappings with lines extending in all directions is difficult for you, you may prefer the more organized structure of hierarchies. **Figure 11.5** shows two different ways to organize level-one and level-two information. SQ4R is the topic, so it appears on the top line. The six steps of SQ4R are the main ideas or headings, so they appear on the second level.

The Hierarchy Skeleton

You can use hierarchies to show the same kinds of information that you can show in visual mappings. The skeleton of a hierarchy, the parts of the hierarchy that you will visually memorize, are the topic and the level-two headings or main ideas. Begin by placing the topic or the subject on the top line. Then determine the number of main ideas to be placed under the topic. Branch *downward* to level two to write the main ideas. Use the guidelines listed on the next page for writing level-two information on your hierarchy.

FIGURE 11.5

Organizing Level-One and Level-Two Information

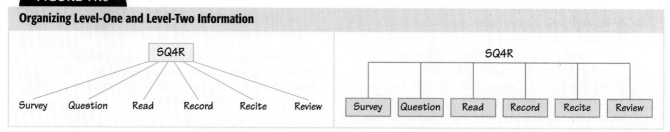

- *Use legal-size paper:* To have adequate room for the level-two and later the level-three information, consider using 8½" × 14" or legal size paper.

- *Space the main ideas evenly:* Spacing level-two information evenly helps avoid a cluttered or crowded look.

- *Use connectors:* Clearly connect levels of information by using lines.

- *Always write horizontally:* Your visual memory is not set up to visualize slanted writing, so imagine horizontal lines on your paper so you print on a horizontal plane.

- *Add colors, shapes, or pictures:* These visual features strengthen the visual image.

- *Add other level-two headings if necessary:* You can add headings, such as "Intro." for introductory information, or you may want a heading to show a specific graph or chart. For example, if you were to create a visual mapping for Maslow's Hierarchy, pages 258–259, you may want to add a heading to show the pyramid. If the printed material has a summary, you may want to add a final heading, "Summary."

Supporting Details

Be very selective. Use only key words or short phrases for level-three and level-four details. Because the lower levels on your hierarchy tend to have numerous supporting details, consider different ways to place the details on the paper. To avoid a cluttered or crowded look, you can stagger or arrange the details in a variety of layouts, as shown in **Figure 11.6**. As with visual mappings, do not attempt to visually memorize the supporting details. When you study your hierarchy, you will only glance down at the supporting details for feedback after you recite the information.

Studying from Hierarchies

Use the Essential Strategies in Figure 11.1 on page 315 to study your hierarchy. With frequent practice, you should be able to recall the skeleton with the first two levels of information in your hierarchy quickly and accurately. By reciting as you practice, you activate your auditory channel and strengthen your auditory memory and ability to recall the details.

CONCEPT CHECK 11.16

What strategies can you use to avoid a crowded or cluttered hierarchy when you add supporting details?

CONCEPT CHECK 11.17

How does studying hierarchies differ from studying visual mappings?

FIGURE 11.6

Arranging Details in Hierarchies

Equal-length lines—on the same plane

Unequal-length lines—staggered

Steps

One main line—spread-out lines

Chain

Half ladder

Full ladder

EXERCISE 11.4

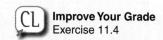

Improve Your Grade
Exercise 11.4

Converting a Visual Mapping to a Hierarchy

PURPOSE: Hierarchies are a "top down" visual representation of information. Hierarchies contain the same information that you would find in visual mappings.

DIRECTIONS:

1. A student made the mapping shown below during a lecture about vocabulary skills. The instructor began by identifying two kinds of vocabulary: expressive and receptive. The instructor then discussed six strategies for finding definitions for new vocabulary words.

2. On your own paper or on a large chart if you are working in a group, convert the visual mapping into a hierarchy. Show the three levels of information.

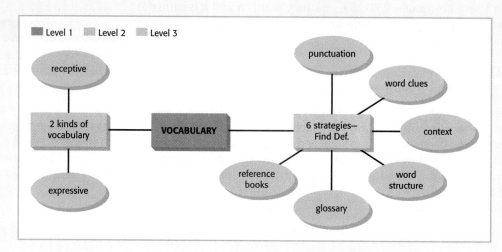

EXERCISE 11.5

Creating a Hierarchy

DIRECTIONS: Read the following excerpt on the topic "Communication Network." Highlight the topic, headings, and key words for details before you create your hierarchy. On separate paper, create a hierarchy to show three levels of information for this excerpt. Be selective.

Communication in Networks and Work Teams

Although communication among team members in an organization is clearly interpersonal in nature, substantial research also focuses specifically on how people in networks and work teams communicate with one another. A **communication network** is a pattern through which the members of a group or team communicate. Researchers studying group dynamics have discovered several typical networks in groups and teams consisting of three, four, or five members.

▪ *The wheel pattern.* All communication flows through one central person, who is probably the group's leader. The wheel is the most centralized network, because one person receives and disseminates all information.

▌ *The Y pattern.* This is slightly less centralized—two people are close to the center.

▌ *The chain pattern.* This offers a more even flow of information among members, although two people (the people at either end) interact only with one other person. This path is closed in the circle pattern.

▌ *The all-channel network.* This is the most decentralized, allowing a free flow of information among all group members. Everyone participates equally, and the group's leader, if there is one, is not likely to have excessive power.

Research conducted on networks suggests some interesting connections between the type of network and group performance:

▌ When the group's task is *relatively simple and routine,* centralized networks tend to perform with the greatest efficiency and accuracy. The dominant leader facilitates performance by coordinating the flow of information.

▌ When the task is *complex and nonroutine,* such as when making a major decision about organizational strategy, decentralized networks tend to be most effective because open channels of communication permit more interaction and a more efficient sharing of relevant information.

Managers should recognize the effects of communication networks on group and organization performance and should try to structure networks appropriately.

Source: Griffin. *Principles of Management,* Houghton Mifflin Co., © 2007, page 321.

EXERCISE 11.6

Creating Visual Notes for Your Textbook

DIRECTIONS:

1. Select a section from any one of your textbooks. On separate paper, convert information into a visual mapping *or* a hierarchy that has at least three levels of information. On the top of your visual notes, include the following information:

Name of the textbook: _____

Pages: _____

2. Go to Exercise 11.6 in Appendix B, page A23, to complete the Visual Notes Checklist. Include the checklist with your visual notes if you are asked to turn them in to your instructor.

CHECK POINT 11.3

ANSWERS APPEAR ON PAGE A5

True or False?

_____ 1. On hierarchies, larger concepts appear on the top levels and details appear on lower levels.

_____ 2. When you study hierarchies, you begin by visually memorizing the skeleton and then using the memorized skeleton to guide the reciting of details.

_____ 3. Unlike visual mappings, hierarchies usually do not include pictures or color.

_____ 4. Hierarchies tend to be more linear-learner oriented.

CL **Improve Your Grade**
Online Practice 3:
Hierarchies

EXERCISE 11.7

Textbook Case Studies

CL   **Improve Your Grade**
Exercise 11.7

CL   **Improve Your Grade**
Online Case Studies

DIRECTIONS:

1. Read each case study carefully. Respond to the questions at the end of each case study by using *specific* strategies discussed in this chapter. Answer in complete sentences.

2. Write your responses on paper or online at the Student Website, Exercise 11.7. You will be able to print your online response or e-mail it to your instructor.

CASE STUDY 1: Monica, a graphic arts student, feels that visual notetaking suits her learning style. The diagram below is her first attempt at creating a visual mapping for a section in her textbook about *Chronemics*. Monica was disappointed with the results. She found that her mapping was difficult to study from because it seemed "too busy" and "too disorganized." What techniques could Monica try that might result in a visual mapping that would be easier to use and study?

CASE STUDY 2: Mickey creates many visual mappings and hierarchies as a second form of notetaking after she has taken Cornell notes for a textbook or a lecture. She finds that the process of reorganizing and writing information in her own handwriting makes studying more interesting. However, she then sets them aside because she is not sure how to study from them. What strategies can Mickey use to study effectively from her visual notes?

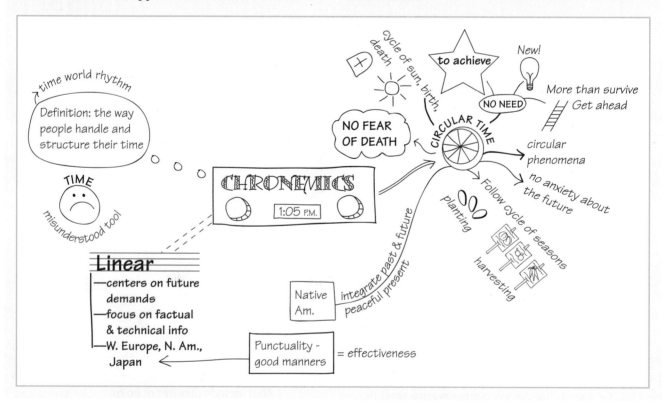

COMPARISON CHARTS

4 ▶ *Explain and demonstrate how to create and use comparison charts.*

Comparison charts are diagrams that organize information for two or more subjects into a chart or a grid with columns and rows. Comparison charts, also known as matrixes, grids, or tables, organize a large amount of information into a format that clearly compares and contrasts information for two or more subjects. You can easily create comparison charts on a computer by using the *tables* feature.

Comparison charts are diagrams that organize information for two or more subjects into a chart or a grid with columns and rows.

CONCEPT CHECK 11.18

What is the basic structure of a comparison chart? What kinds of information does it emphasize?

Labeling a Comparison Chart

The title of the comparison chart appears above the chart. **Figure 11.7** shows the categories or the characteristics that are being compared or contrasted placed at the top of each column. The subjects that are being compared or contrasted are placed at the beginning of each row.

In a comparison chart, *columns* run up and down, and *rows* run across the page. Important information about each subject is written inside boxes called *cells*. The number of columns and rows is determined by the information being covered.

Identify the Subjects

Begin by identifying the number of subjects discussed in the printed text information. If you have two subjects, your chart will have only two rows. Write the names of the subjects on the rows. Note, however, that you will find some variations of this format. Some tables or informational charts in textbooks place the subjects at the top of the columns instead of at the beginning of the rows, and they label the rows with the characteristics. You can also use this alternative format if it seems more effective for specific kinds of information.

Graphic programs on computers often facilitate the process of converting printed materials into visual graphics. In what ways do you use a computer to create study tools?

FIGURE 11.7

The Structure of a Comparison Chart

Title:

Subjects ↓ Categories →	Column 1 *Characteristics*	Column 2 *Uses*	Column 3 *Advantages*
Subject 1			
Subject 2			
Subject 3			

FIGURE 11.8

Other Solar System Objects

Objects	Location	Size	Origin	Kinds	Also Called	Other Characteristics
Asteroids						
Meteoroids						
Comets						

CONCEPT CHECK 11.19

The categories to use to label columns are not always immediately apparent in a textbook. What strategies can you use to identify meaningful categories for the columns?

Identify Categories

Identifying categories requires you to think carefully about and analyze the information you have read. What categories of information were discussed for all or most of the subjects? You can use the general category "Characteristics," but more specific categories are more useful. The number of categories you select determines the number of columns in your comparison chart. Once you have identified the categories, label the top of each column.

Figure 11.8 shows three rows for the subjects (*asteroids, meteoroids,* and *comets*) and six columns for the categories of information to be compared and contrasted. This comparison chart uses the visual mapping information that appeared in Exercise 11.2 on page 320. Notice how the comparison chart format draws greater attention to likeness and differences among the subjects.

Sometimes finding appropriate labels for the columns is difficult. Use the following process to help organize information and identify column headings:

▌ List each of the subjects across the top of a piece of paper.

▌ Under each subject, list important details associated with that subject.

▌ Look at your list of details. Can you group the details into larger categories?

▌ If you see a logical category of information under one subject, is that same kind of information also given for other subjects? If so, you have discovered an appropriate title for a category.

Figure 11.9 shows general categories that often appear in specific subject disciplines. You can use several of these categories if you are not able to identify more specific categories for your comparison chart.

FIGURE 11.9

Common Categories for Subject Disciplines

Literature	author tone theme setting main plot characters/traits actions
Sociology and Anthropology	culture location government religion beliefs education tribe family economy transportation foods tools imports/exports
History	events time period location leaders/rulers wars/conflicts influences
Psychology	kinds/types traits problems frequency duration symptoms causes methods functions uses studies
Science	terminology kinds/types causes effects relationships equations theorems problems solution applications

Completing a Comparison Chart

Once you have created the structure or the skeleton of the comparison chart, complete the chart by writing key details in the cells (the boxes). To avoid confusion, frustration, or errors with details, approach this task in an organized, systematic manner.

One Approach: Focus on one subject at a time. For example, in the comparison chart on *other solar system objects,* begin by identifying pertinent information about *asteroids.* Reread the textbook or source of your information; then, identify key words or short phrases that tell about the *location, size, origin, kinds, also called,* and *other characteristics.* Write these details in the cells. After you finish the cells for the first subject, move to the second subject (*meteoroids*) and continue the process until you have filled as many of the cells on the chart as possible.

Another Approach: Focusing on one *column* of information. For example, instead of focusing only on *asteroids,* you would focus your attention first on finding information about the *location* of asteroids, meteoroids, and comets; you would then move to information about the *size* of each of the subjects. The important point to remember is that your goal is to work in an organized, systematic manner to complete the cells in the comparison chart. Use the following guidelines for completing your comparison chart:

■ *Be selective:* Include only significant words or phrases. Avoid using full sentences.

■ *Use dashes or bullets* to separate two or more significant details in one cell.

■ *Leave cells blank if necessary:* Do not be concerned if information is not available to complete every cell; an occasional empty cell is acceptable. However, if information is not available for numerous cells under one category, the category is ineffective and needs to be renamed or eliminated.

Attaching Other Forms of Notes

On occasion, a printed section of material will contain important information that does not fit within the categories of your chart. When you encounter the following kinds of information, you may write a paragraph, create a list of the important points, or redraw the diagram outside of your comparison chart:

■ An introductory paragraph that "sets the scene" for the information

■ Definitions for terminology

■ Diagrams or charts with valuable information

■ A summary paragraph or conclusion

You can place these additional notes before or after the comparison chart, or if they are brief, between the title and the comparison chart. Remember, these are *your notes,* so you can modify or attach information in any way that is meaningful to you.

CONCEPT CHECK 11.20

Why is it important to select a systematic approach to use to complete each cell of a comparison chart?

GROUP PROCESSING:
A COLLABORATIVE LEARNING ACTIVITY

Form groups with three or four students. Then complete the following directions. Write your work on chart paper.

DIRECTIONS:

1. Copy the comparison chart Figure 11.8 "Other Solar System Objects" on chart paper, leaving ample space in the cells to add information.

2. Read the excerpt for Exercise 11.2 in Appendix C, page A27. Highlight key points if you wish before working on your comparison chart. As a group, discuss key words or phrases to place in each cell of your comparison chart.

3. Complete the chart. You may be asked to present your chart to the class.

Studying from Comparison Charts

CONCEPT CHECK 11.21

Why is studying from comparison charts more challenging to do than studying from other types of visual notes?

Use the *Essential Strategies for Studying Visual Notes* in Figure 11.1 on page 315. The skeleton that you need to imprint in your visual memory and visualize consists of the labels used for the columns and the rows. Do not focus your attention on visually memorizing the details within the cells.

Reciting from comparison charts is more demanding than for other types of visual notes. To facilitate the process, recite in a systematic way by using one of these approaches:

One Approach: Begin with the first subject in row 1. Recite what you remember about each category of information for that subject. Check your accuracy by looking at your chart. Continue in this manner for each of the subjects.

Another Approach: Begin with the first category of information in column 1. Recite the information you remember about the category for each of the subjects in your chart. Check your accuracy by looking at your chart. Continue in this manner for each of the columns.

EXERCISE 11.8

Diabetes Comparison Chart

DIRECTIONS: Read and highlight the following excerpt. Then convert the information into a comparison chart. You will need to identify categories to label the columns.

Type I and Type II Diabetes

Though both Type I diabetes and Type II diabetes are metabolic disorders that affect the way the body uses food, they are more dissimilar than similar. Type I diabetes, the insulin-dependent diabetes, affects 5% to 10% of the 16 million Americans who have diabetes. Type I diabetes surfaces during childhood or young adulthood; for that reason it is called *juvenile onset diabetes.* With Type I diabetes, the immune system attacks the pancreas and destroys its ability to make insulin. As a result, diabetics need to track the food they eat, their activity levels, and their blood sugar levels several times during the day. They must inject themselves with insulin to keep the body's sugar levels in balance.

Type II diabetes has different characteristics. Type II diabetes, the non-insulin-dependent diabetes, affects 90% to 95% of Americans who are diagnosed with diabetes. Type II diabetes usually surfaces after the age of forty. It is called *adult onset diabetes*. With this form of diabetes, the pancreas produces insulin, but the body and its tissues, especially its muscles, do not use the insulin effectively. Type II diabetes is linked to inactivity, weight gain, and obesity. Eighty

percent of the people with Type II diabetes are overweight. Type II diabetics can reduce or eliminate the health threats related to diabetes by lifestyle changes, more exercise, better nutritional habits, and possibly medication.

Even though Type I and Type II diabetes differ considerably in their time of onset, effects on the body, and forms of treatment, both are autoimmune disorders that must be diagnosed and treated in order to avoid serious, life-threatening health problems.

Source: Modified from Wong, *Paragraph Essentials*, Houghton Mifflin (2002), p. 259.

EXERCISE 11.9

Creating a Comparison Chart

DIRECTIONS: Go to Exercise 11.9 in Appendix C, page A28, to read, highlight, and create a comparison chart for "Industries That Attract Small Businesses."

CHECK POINT 11.4

ANSWERS APPEAR ON PAGE A5

True or False?

_____ 1. A standard format for comparison charts is to label the rows with the subjects, the columns with the topics or characteristics, and the cells with key words for details.

_____ 2. Comparison charts are limited to comparing or contrasting characteristics for one, two, or three subjects.

_____ 3. A completed comparison chart always has information in each cell of the chart.

_____ 4. A main difference between comparison charts and hierarchies or visual mappings is that likenesses and differences are more pronounced in comparison charts.

_____ 5. Study strategies for all forms of visual notes involve visually memorizing skeletons, reciting supporting details, and using feedback to check your learning accuracy.

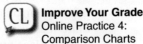

Improve Your Grade
Online Practice 4:
Comparison Charts

INDEX CARD NOTES

5 ▶ *Explain and demonstrate how to create and use index card notes.*

Index card notes involve creating three types of flashcards to use as study tools: definition cards, category cards, and question cards. Index card notes are effective study tools for learning definitions for terminology, lists of items under a specific category or steps in a process, or answers to questions you predict will appear in one form or another on an upcoming test. Index card notes work effectively to study both *declarative knowledge* (facts, dates, formulas, rules) and *procedural knowledge* (doing or applying steps to perform a process).

Index card notes involve creating three types of flashcards to use as study tools: definition cards, category cards, and question cards.

A Comprehensive Set of Index Card Notes

In Chapter 7, page 203, you learned that one way to study terminology is to create definition cards. In addition to definition cards, a comprehensive set of index card notes also includes *question cards* and *category cards*.

▌ *Question Cards:* Pose study questions for information that you are expected to learn. To prepare for a test, predict and write test questions on your index cards with the answers on the back. Question cards become excellent summary notes for test preparation.

▌ *Category Cards:* Write a category or topic on the front. On the back, list the items that belong to the category. To work effectively, do not clutter the back of the card with any additional details; you want to be able to visually memorize the list of items.

Figure 11.10 shows four examples of question, definition, and category index card notes.

To create stronger visual impressions of information on your index cards, use colors to write different kinds of information, and add pictures that you can use as retrieval cues. With practice, you can look up and to the left to picture the information on your cards.

Studying from Index Card Notes

Index card notes are portable and convenient to use. You can carry them in small plastic bags or hold them together with a rubber band and place them in the front of your binder. If you wish, you can also punch a hole in the top of the cards and attach them to a large metal ring. Use the following suggestions to study your index card notes:

▌ *Use the cards for self-quizzing.* Look at one side of the card and recite the information on the reverse side. Check the reverse sides of the cards for immediate feedback on the accuracy and completeness of the information you recited. Use your cards to self-quiz between classes, while waiting for transportation or for other events to occur, or any time when you have a few spare minutes.

▌ *Ask others to quiz you.* You can practice explaining information clearly by asking study partners, friends, or family members to use your cards to quiz you. Since all the information appears on the card, the person quizzing you does not necessarily need to know the information.

CONCEPT CHECK 11.22

Why is it important to include more than definition cards in your index card notes? What are the benefits of having all three kinds of cards?

CONCEPT CHECK 11.23

Why do you think many students believe index card notes are the most versatile notes to use to review for tests? Do you agree? Why or why not?

FIGURE 11.10

Kinds of Index Card Notes

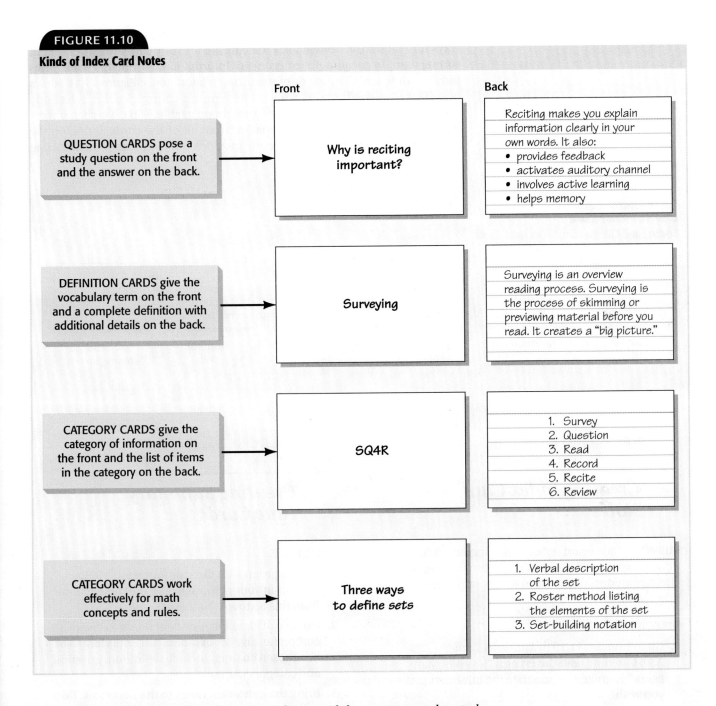

Front

Back

QUESTION CARDS pose a study question on the front and the answer on the back.

> Why is reciting important?

> Reciting makes you explain information clearly in your own words. It also:
> • provides feedback
> • activates auditory channel
> • involves active learning
> • helps memory

DEFINITION CARDS give the vocabulary term on the front and a complete definition with additional details on the back.

> Surveying

> Surveying is an overview reading process. Surveying is the process of skimming or previewing material before you read. It creates a "big picture."

CATEGORY CARDS give the category of information on the front and the list of items in the category on the back.

> SQ4R

> 1. Survey
> 2. Question
> 3. Read
> 4. Record
> 5. Recite
> 6. Review

CATEGORY CARDS work effectively for math concepts and rules.

> Three ways to define sets

> 1. Verbal description of the set
> 2. Roster method listing the elements of the set
> 3. Set-building notation

▌ *Sort the cards into two piles: the ones you know and the ones you need to study further.* Set aside the pile that contains the cards that you can explain accurately and with confidence. Focus your attention on the pile of cards that you need to study further. Continue rehearsing.

▌ *Use your cards as a warm-up activity at the beginning of a study block.* Working with your cards before you begin a new assignment puts you in the mindset for the subject, activates previously learned information, and promotes ongoing review.

▎ *Create reflect activities with your note cards.* You can use your cards in creative ways for elaborative rehearsal. First, shuffle all your cards together. Begin sorting them by meaningful *categories* of information. Sorting into categories provides practice grouping or reorganizing related items. **Figure 11.11** shows possible categories for note cards created for this course. Second, select one category of cards and spread those cards out on a table. Make a verbal or written summary that includes information from all of the cards. Stringing the ideas together logically and coherently provides you with practice associating related information.

FIGURE 11.11

Sorting and Categorizing Index Note Cards

What is another term for modality?	What is an internal distractor?	SAVE CRIB FOTO	sensory input	read— record— recite cycle	What is flex time?
Learning styles	Concentration	Memory Principles	Information Processing Model	Textbook skills	Time management

EXERCISE 11.10

Creating Index Card Notes

PURPOSE: Index card notes, which include definition, question, and category cards, provide you with effective study tools to use to review important information.

DIRECTIONS:

1. Go to Exercise 11.10 in Appendix C, pages A29–A30. Carefully read the excerpt "Kinds of Managers." Highlight or annotate the information if you wish.

2. Then create a *comprehensive* set of index card notes. Include *at least one question card, two category cards,* and as many *definition cards* as you think are important.

EXERCISE 11.11

Creating Summary Note Cards

DIRECTIONS:

1. Form a group with three or four students. Each student in your group selects a different chapter from this textbook for this exercise.

2. Outside of class, each student needs to create a comprehensive set of index card notes for his or her chosen chapter. Include definition, question, and category cards.

3. Bring the index card notes to the next class. Take turns using the sets of cards to quiz the other students in your group.

CHECK POINT 11.5

True or False?

_____ 1. You can use index card notes for elaborative rehearsal of definitions, lists, and study questions.

_____ 2. Index card notes are basically flashcards that include more than definitions for terminology.

_____ 3. When creating category cards, you should include brief details or definitions for each item that appears in the list of items.

_____ 4. Studying from index card notes involves recitation, feedback, and ongoing review.

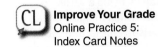
Improve Your Grade
Online Practice 5:
Index Card Notes

EXERCISE 11.12

Links

PURPOSE: You can use visual notes to show important information from a lecture, a section of a chapter, an entire textbook chapter, or information on one specific topic that appears in numerous sections of a textbook.

DIRECTIONS:

1. Work in a small group, with a partner, or on your own. Select *one* of the following topics that appears in multiple locations throughout this textbook: visualization, recitation, elaborative rehearsal, overview reading, or ongoing review.

2. Create a visual mapping, a hierarchy, a comparison chart, or index card notes to show multiple applications of your topic in study skills strategies and study tools. You may use the index in the back of this book as a starting point to locate information on your topic.

REFLECTIVE WRITING 11.2

Improve Your Grade
Reflective Writing 11.2

On separate paper, in a journal, or online at this textbook's website, respond to the following questions.

1. Which visual notetaking systems in this chapter appeal to you the most? Why?

2. Does creating visual notes and study tools affect your level of motivation and confidence for learning subject matter? Why or why not?

LEARNING OBJECTIVES REVIEW

1 ▶ *Describe strategies you use to tailor your approach to learning.*

- You are using metacognition when you personalize or tailor your approach to learning by using a variety of learning strategies. Visual notes, which include visual mappings, hierarchies, comparison charts, and index card notes, expand your repertoire of strategy resources for tailoring your approach to learning.

- To create effective visual notes, you need to understand and be able to identify different levels of information: topics, main ideas, and supporting details.

- Five essential strategies work effectively to study all forms of visual notes. Strategies involve imprinting, visualizing, reciting, reflecting, and using ongoing review.

2 ▶ *Explain and demonstrate how to create and use visual mappings.*

- Visual mappings show levels of information: level one shows the topic; level two shows the headings; and level three shows important supporting details.

- Using borders, shapes, pictures, and colors in visual mappings creates a stronger visual image to memorize.

- Studying from visual mappings involves using the five strategies used for all visual notes.

3 ▶ *Explain and demonstrate how to create and use hierarchies.*

- Hierarchies arrange levels of information from the top down. They also use borders, shapes, pictures, and colors to create strong visual images.

- A variety of strategies can be used to organize lower-level details to avoid cluttering the hierarchy and to facilitate the process of getting feedback after reciting.

- Studying from hierarchies involves using the five strategies used for all visual notes.

4 ▶ *Explain and demonstrate how to create and use comparison charts.*

- Comparison charts compare and contrast characteristics for two or more subjects. These charts consist of rows, columns, and cells.

- Creating comparison charts involves understanding printed information, analyzing it, and then identifying subjects and categories of information to compare or contrast.

- You can attach additional notes to your charts if important information does not fit within the categories you are using.

- Studying from comparison charts involves using a systematic approach to recite information that appears within the different cells of your chart.

5 ▶ *Explain and demonstrate how to create and use index card notes.*

- A comprehensive set of index card notes includes flashcards for definitions, categories and study questions. The key term, category, or question appears on the front; information or answers appear on the back.

- Index card notes are effective study tools to use for self-quizzing, elaborative rehearsal, warm-up activities, reflection activities, and ongoing review.

Multiple Choice

_____ 1. You can use visual mappings, hierarchies, and comparison charts to
   a. take lecture or textbook notes.
   b. create summary notes before a test.
   c. create study tools for elaborative rehearsal.
   d. do all of the above.

_____ 2. Visual notes involve which of the following Principles of Memory?
   a. Selectivity, Association, Visualization, Elaboration
   b. Concentration, Recitation, Intention, Big and Little Pictures
   c. Feedback, Organization, Time on Task, Ongoing Review
   d. All Twelve Principles of Memory

_____ 3. When you visualize your notes, you should
   a. first create a visual image of the skeleton.
   b. be creative and make changes each time you visualize.

   c. stare at the paper for at least fifteen minutes.
   d. keep your eyes focused on the notes when you recite.

_____ 4. Feedback
   a. is nonessential when you work with visual notetaking.
   b. lets you know how well you are learning.
   c. comes only in auditory form.
   d. requires that you work with a partner.

_____ 5. Which of the following is *not* a true statement about studying visual notes?
   a. You should begin by visually memorizing the skeleton of the notes.
   b. You can use them as study tools to rehearse and review information.
   c. You should recite details first, then main ideas, and then summarize the topic.
   d. You should recite the skeleton first and then details for each main idea.

Application of Visual Notetaking Skills

Read the following excerpt "Freedom." You may highlight or annotate it if you wish. Then select an appropriate form of visual notetaking to record the main ideas and the important details of this excerpt. Create your visual notes on separate paper.

Freedom

Freedom can be used in two major senses: freedom *of* and freedom *from*. Franklin Delano Roosevelt used the word in each sense in a speech he made shortly before the United States entered World War II. He described four freedoms: freedom *of* religion, freedom *of* speech, freedom *from* fear, and freedom *from* want. **Freedom of** is the absence of constraints on behavior. It is freedom to do something. In this sense, *freedom* is synonymous with *liberty*. **Freedom from** suggests immunity from something undesirable or negative, such as fear and want. In the modern political context, *freedom from* often connotes the fight against exploitation and oppression. The cry of the civil rights movement in the 1960s, "Freedom Now!" conveyed this meaning. If you recognize that *freedom* in the latter sense means immunity from discrimination, you can see that it comes close to the concept of equality. In this book, we avoid using *freedom* to mean "freedom from"; for this sense of the word, we simply use *equality*. When we use *freedom,* we mean "freedom of."

Source: Janda/Berry/Goldman/Hula. *The Challenge of Democracy,* Houghton Mifflin Co., © 2008, page 11.

ACE the Test
Four Online Practice Tests

Online Resources

12 Developing Skills for Objective Tests

LEARNING OBJECTIVES

1 ▶ Explain how to use essential strategies for answering true-false questions.

2 ▶ Explain how to use essential strategies for answering multiple-choice questions.

3 ▶ Explain how to use essential strategies for answering matching questions.

Chapter Outline

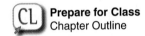

Prepare for Class
Chapter Outline

4 ▶ *Discuss the advantages and disadvantages of using educated guessing, and describe ways to use educated-guessing strategies.*

In addition to the valuable test-taking skills you learned in Chapter 6, you can increase your performance on tests by learning to use specific strategies for answering three kinds of objective questions: *true-false, multiple-choice,* and *matching.* In this chapter, you will learn ten educated-guessing strategies that can help you analyze questions more effectively and increase your odds for selecting the correct answer after you have tried all other methods for answering the questions. The strategies in this chapter will help you comprehend and respond to objective questions with more confidence and accuracy.

Chapter 12 Profile

Developing Skills for Objective Tests

ANSWER, **SCORE**, and **RECORD** your profile before you read this chapter. If you need to review the process, refer to the complete directions given in the profile for Chapter 1 on page 4.

ONLINE: You can complete the profile and get your score online at this textbook's website.

	YES	NO
1. True-false questions confuse me because I do not understand what they are asking.		
2. I understand the importance of modifiers such as *no, never, some, few, always,* and *often* and know how they can affect the meanings of questions.		
3. I recognize when a multiple-choice question is testing a definition or a cause/effect relationship.		
4. I turn each part of a multiple-choice question into a true-false question before I select a final answer.		
5. I have a system for answering matching questions so that I do not use an answer twice.		
6. I know how to look for paired associations in matching tests.		
7. I know how to use educated-guessing strategies, but I only use them as a last resort to answer questions.		
8. The first time I work through a test, I leave blank the answers that I do not know and then return to them when I have time.		
9. I make too many careless mistakes on objective tests.		
10. I am confident in my ability to answer objective test questions without making many mistakes.		

QUESTIONS LINKED TO THE CHAPTER LEARNING OBJECTIVES:

Questions 1, 2:   objective 1   Question 7:   objective 4
Questions 3, 4:   objective 2   Questions 8–10: all objectives
Questions 5, 6:   objective 3

TRUE-FALSE QUESTIONS

1 ▶ *Explain how to use essential strategies for answering true-false questions.*

True-false questions are one of the most basic forms of objective questions, for they take less time to read and can easily be scored by hand, by scoring machines, or by computers. Students sometimes feel that some true-false questions are "trick questions" because they do not know how to read and interpret the questions correctly. In this section, you will learn the "tricks" for understanding and answering true-false questions.

Essential Strategies for True-False Questions

In Chapter 6, you learned many valuable test-taking skills: how to study, review, and prepare for tests; how to use essential strategies for taking tests (Figure 6.5, page 165); and how to conduct memory searches to locate information. As you acquire additional strategies specifically tailored to objective tests, continue to use the test-taking strategies you learned in Chapter 6.

Using the Four Levels of Response is one strategy you are encouraged to use for all forms of objective tests. The following is a summary of the Four Levels of Response:

▌ *Immediate Response:* After you carefully read the question, if you immediately know the answer, write the answer with confidence.

▌ *Delayed Response:* If you do not immediately know the answer, reread the question carefully and then conduct a memory search. Recall what you do know about the topic; strive to trigger an association that will link you to the answer. *If you cannot answer with certainty, leave the answer space empty. Place a check mark next to the question and return to it after you have answered as many questions as possible on the remainder of the test.*

▌ *Assisted Response:* Return to the unanswered questions, the ones with the check mark reminder next to them. Use other parts and other information in the test for clues or associations that can help trigger recall and help you select an answer.

▌ *Educated Guessing:* Use an educated-guessing strategy if all else fails.

Because true-false questions usually consist of one sentence, some students have the tendency to read and respond to the questions quickly; they believe that true-false questions are "easy." However, if that were the case, students would seldom make mistakes on the true-false sections on tests. **Figure 12.1** shows seven Essential Strategies for True-False Tests.

Items in a Series

As indicated in Figure 12.1, a statement is true only when the entire statement is true. One common way for instructors to write false statements is to place one item that does not belong in a series of items. That one item turns the statement into a false statement. Items in a series are separated by commas, so use the

CONCEPT CHECK 12.1

What are the four levels of response? How do you apply the first three levels when you answer objective questions?

CONCEPT CHECK 12.2

Which of the strategies in Figure 12.1 will help you the most with true-false tests?

FIGURE 12.1

Essential Strategies for True-False Tests

❚ **Read the statement carefully.** Pay attention to *every* word in the statement. If you tend to misread questions, *point to each word* as you read and *circle the key words.*

❚ **Be sure you completely understand the statement.** Read it a second time if necessary. For clarity, translate difficult words into your own words. Create a visual picture of the information.

❚ **Be objective when you answer.** Do not personalize the question by interpreting it according to what you do or how you feel. Instead, answer according to the information presented by the textbook author or your instructor in class.

❚ **Mark a statement as *True* only when the statement is completely true.** If any one part of the statement is inaccurate or false, you must mark the entire statement *False.*

❚ **Do not add your reasoning or argument to the side of the question.** Frequently, the only information that the instructor will look at is the *T* or *F* answer, so other notes, comments, or clarifications will be ignored during grading.

❚ **If you are taking a true-false test using paper and pencil, make a strong distinction between the way you write a *T* and an *F.*** Trying to camouflage your answer so it can be interpreted as a *T* or an *F* will backfire. Unclear letters are usually marked as incorrect.

❚ **Pay close attention to key elements: items in a series, modifiers, definition and relationship clues, and negatives.** One single word can affect the meaning and the accuracy of a statement.

CONCEPT CHECK 12.3

How can you quickly identify items in a series of items? Why is it important to pay attention to items in a series?

comma as a signal to check each item carefully. The words in bold print in the following examples turn the statements into false statements.

    _F_ 1. Effective lecture notes show ***details of all examples***, *main ideas, important details,* and *sketches of visual materials* used by the instructor.

    _F_ 2. *Active listening, critical listening,* ***informal listening***, and *appreciative listening* are the four kinds of listening, each with different purposes.

Modifiers

Modifiers are words that tell to what degree or frequency something occurs.

Modifiers are words that tell to what degree or frequency something occurs. There is a huge difference between saying that something *always* happens and saying that something *sometimes, often,* or *seldom* happens. Pay close attention to modifiers, for a single modifier alters the meaning of the statement.

Identify 100 Percent Modifiers

100 percent modifiers, also called **absolute modifiers**, are words that indicate absolutes, which means there is a total degree without any exceptions.

Modifiers can be shown on a scale. The 100 percent modifiers are on the extreme ends of the scale. **100 percent modifiers**, also called **absolute modifiers**, are words that indicate absolutes, which means there is a total degree without any exceptions. Words such as *best* or *worst* show the extremes and indicate that there is *nothing* that is better or worse; they are absolutes. In **Figure 12.2**, the 100 percent modifiers appear in the first and the third columns. In the following examples, the 100 percent modifiers appear in boldface print.

____F____ 1. Sentences with absolute modifiers are **always** false.

____F____ 2. Sentences with absolute modifiers are **never** false.

____T____ 3. Well-written true-false statements have **only** one correct answer.

Identify In-Between Modifiers

In-between modifiers are words that indicate something occurs in varying degrees or frequency. The in-between modifiers appear in the middle column of Figure 12.2. In-between modifiers allow for more flexibility, variance, or exceptions because they indicate that a middle ground exists where situations or conditions do not occur as absolutes (100 percent of the time). In the following examples, the in-between modifiers appear in boldface print.

____T____ 1. Spaced practice is **usually more** effective than massed practice for studying textbook information.

____T____ 2. **Sometimes** students can reduce stress by changing their sleep or their eating habits.

____F____ 3. Look-Away Techniques **seldom** provide students with effective feedback.

In-between modifiers are words that indicate something occurs in varying degrees or frequency.

CONCEPT CHECK 12.4

How do modifiers affect the meaning of sentences? How do 100 percent modifiers differ from in-between modifiers?

FIGURE 12.2

Kinds of Modifiers

100 Percent	In-Between	100 Percent
all, every, only	some, most, a few	none
always, absolutely	sometimes, often, usually, may, seldom, frequently	never
everyone	some, few, most	no one
everybody		nobody
best	average, better	worst
any adjective that ends in *est,* which means "the most," such as largest, smallest . . .	any adjective that ends in *er,* which means "more," such as larger, smaller . . .	least, fewest
Absolute Phrases: is/are definitely with certainty beyond a doubt without exceptions	Other Words: perhaps possibly maybe tend to	

How can you use modifiers to help you choose a true or false answer?

Improve Your Test-Taking Skills

Understanding how to use modifiers can improve your performance on objective tests. Use the following tips to improve your test-taking skills:

1. Actively look for and circle 100 percent and in-between modifiers in statements.
2. For 100 percent modifiers, ask yourself: *Is this accurate? Does this happen or occur all the time without any exceptions?* If you answer "yes," then the statement is true. If you answer "no," then the statement is false.
3. For in-between modifiers, ask yourself: *Is this accurate? Does this happen or occur this frequently or to this degree?* If you answer "yes," the statement is true. If you answer "no" the statement is false.

EXERCISE 12.1

Items in a Series and Modifiers in Questions

ANSWERS APPEAR ON PAGE A5

PURPOSE: Carefully check each statement for the accuracy of each item in a series. Check whether or not the modifiers accurately represent the frequency or degree that something occurs in the statement.

DIRECTIONS: Write *T* for true statements and *F* for false statements.

_____ 1. Diagrams can be created to show these organizational patterns in paragraphs: process, definition, examples, and cause/effect.

_____ 2. The steps in the SQ4R reading system are survey, quiz, read, record, recite, and review.

_____ 3. Declarative knowledge involves working with factual details while procedural knowledge works with applying steps, procedures, and formulas.

_____ 4. Vowels, prefixes, suffixes, and roots are the four parts of a word to examine when you use word structure clues.

_____ 5. You can create associations by using visualizations, acronyms, acrostics, and the Loci Method.

_____ 6. Students with strong study skills always use the 2:1 ratio for studying.

_____ 7. Some form of assessment is used in all college-level, graded courses.

_____ 8. Students with a high self-efficacy are often self-motivated and goal-oriented.

_____ 9. Students who procrastinate and who experience test anxiety never perform well on tests.

_____ 10. Fear of failure is definitely the most common reason students experience test anxiety.

Definition Clues

Definition clues are words that signal that the question is evaluating your understanding of the meaning or the definition of terminology.

Definition clues are words that signal that the question is evaluating your understanding of the meaning or the definition of terminology. **Figure 12.3** shows common definition clues and the sentence pattern that often is used in statements that test your understanding of definitions.

In the following examples, the definition clue appears in boldface print. Notice that the definition clue appears between the terminology word and the definition.

_T_ 1. Annotating **is** the active learning process of marking textbooks to show main ideas and supporting details.

_F_ 2. Marathon studying **is also known as** distributed practice.

_T_ 3. A traditional IQ test **measures** intellectual abilities in the areas of verbal, visual-spatial, and logical mathematics.

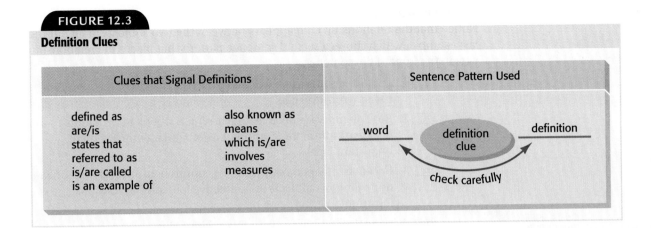

FIGURE 12.3

Definition Clues

Clues that Signal Definitions		Sentence Pattern Used
defined as	also known as	
are/is	means	word → definition clue → definition
states that	which is/are	check carefully
referred to as	involves	
is/are called	measures	
is an example of		

Use the following tips to improve your test-taking skills:

1. Actively look for and circle definition clues. Underline the terminology word.
2. Ask yourself: *What is the definition I learned for this word?* Compare your definition to the definition that is given.
3. If your definition matches the test question definition, answer *true.* If there is a discrepancy, analyze the test question definition carefully because it may be saying the same thing but simply using different words. If the definitions are not the same, answer *false.*

Relationship Clues

Relationship clues are words that signal the question is evaluating your understanding of the relationship between two subjects. Relationships often show cause/ effect—one item causes another item to occur. Relationships may also show other organizational patterns: chronological, process, comparison/contrast, and whole/ parts. (Refer to Chapter 8, pages 223–228, for additional clue words used in organizational patterns.) **Figure 12.4** shows common relationship clue words and a sentence pattern that often is used in statements that show relationships.

CONCEPT CHECK 12.6

What are examples of definition clues? What sentence pattern is often used for definition test questions?

Relationship clues are words that signal the question is evaluating your understanding of the relationship between two subjects.

CONCEPT CHECK 12.7

What are examples of relationship clues? How does a common sentence pattern for relationship questions differ from the pattern used for definition questions?

FIGURE 12.4

Relationship Clues

Clues that Signal Relationships		Sentence Pattern Used
increases	result	
produces	since	
reason	so, so that	Subject A → relationship clue → Subject B
affects	creates	check carefully
because	decreases	
causes	effects	
before/after	differs	
consists of	leads to	

In the following examples, the relationship clue appears in boldface print. Notice that the relationship clue appears between the two subjects in all but the last example, which shows a second sentence pattern that places the relationship clue in the front of the sentence.

____T____ 1. Linking a picture to a word **creates** an association that you can use as a retrieval cue.

____F____ 2. Rote memory is effective for learning textbook information **because** it promotes comprehension and memorization of important facts.

____F____ 3. **Because** rote memory promotes comprehension and memorization of important facts, it is effective for learning textbook information.

CONCEPT CHECK 12.8

What strategies can you use to analyze a relationship that appears in a true-false question?

Use the following tips to improve your test-taking skills:

1. Actively look for and circle relationship clues. Underline the key words for the two subjects involved in the relationship.
2. Ask yourself: *What do I know about how these two subjects are related to each other?* Once you have a relationship idea in mind, compare your idea with the one presented in the question.
3. If your idea matches the relationship in the question, and if the relationship is logical, answer *true*. If your idea does not match the relationship in the question, analyze the statement more carefully. Question the accuracy and the logic of the relationship as it is stated in the question. If the relationship is not accurate or logical, answer *false*.

EXERCISE 12.2

Definition and Relationship Clues

ANSWERS APPEAR ON PAGE A5

PURPOSE: Carefully check each statement for definition and relationship clues. Use the sentence pattern to identify the terminology word and its definition or the two subjects in a relationship.

DIRECTIONS: Write *T* for true statements and *F* for false statements.

_____ 1. The Loci Method refers to a type of mnemonic that uses a familiar location as the setting for creating picture associations.

_____ 2. Intrusive thoughts, stress, and use of selective attention cause working memory to overload and work less efficiently.

_____ 3. The central executive is the part of working memory that holds stimuli for less than two seconds.

_____ 4. The Principle of Elaboration involves working with information in new ways.

_____ 5. Performing well on tests is often the result of creating strong retrieval cues, using ongoing review, and using effective test-taking strategies.

Negatives

Negatives are words or prefixes in words that carry the meaning of "no" or "not."

Negatives are words or prefixes in words that carry the meaning of "no" or "not." Negatives affect the meaning of the sentence; if you ignore or miss them, the meaning of the sentence is the opposite of the correct meaning. For example: *The ABC Method is **not** a goal-setting technique* becomes *The ABC Method is a goal-setting technique.* **Figure 12.5** shows common negatives.

In the following examples, the negatives appear in boldface print. You may notice that sometimes questions with one or more negatives can be confusing and can leave you wondering what the question really means. The tips below the examples provide you with helpful strategies.

   _F_ 1. A **dis**organized desk is **not** an external distractor.

   _F_ 2. The Principle of Selectivity is **not** used during the fourth step of SQ4R.

   _T_ 3. Using chained associations is **not im**practical during a test when you need to conduct a memory search to find an answer to a question.

Use the following tips to improve your test-taking skills:

1. If a question with a negative word or prefix confuses you, *cover up the negative.* If the sentence has two negatives, cover up *only one* negative.
2. Now read the sentence with one negative covered up or ignored. Decide if that statement is true or false.
3. If the statement with the negative covered up makes a *true* statement, the answer to the original question will be the opposite: *false.* If the statement with the negative covered up is a false statement, the answer to the original question will be the opposite: *true.* Try using this technique on the previous example questions.

FIGURE 12.5

Common Negatives

Negative Words	Negative Prefixes	
no	dis	(disorganized)
not	im	(imbalanced)
but	non	(nonproductive)
except	il	(illogical)
	in	(incomplete)
	ir	(irresponsible)
	un	(unimportant)

CONCEPT CHECK 12.9

What are examples of *words* that work as negatives? How can you understand what a questions means if the negatives confuse you?

EXERCISE 12.3

Answering True-False Questions

ANSWERS APPEAR ON PAGE A5

PURPOSE: Performing well on true-false tests involves first *knowing* the information, and second, knowing how to understand and answer the questions.

DIRECTIONS: Read the following true-false questions. Pay close attention to items in a series, modifiers, definition and relationship clues, and negatives. Write *T* for true and *F* for false.

_____ 1. When you create a goal organizer, you identify benefits you will gain, obstacles you may encounter, and resources you could use.

_____ 2. The recall column in the Cornell system should have headings, key words, study questions, and answers to the questions.

_____ 3. Concentration is defined as the ability to focus on two or more things at one time without being distracted.

_____ 4. Ongoing review is essential in the Cornell system but is optional in the SQ4R system.

_____ 5. In a formal outline, Roman numerals are never used to label supporting details under a subheading.

_____ 6. Reciting is important because it utilizes the auditory channel and creates associations.

_____ 7. You should always begin by studying your favorite subject first so that you can get motivated.

_____ 8. The central executive in the Information Processing Model is not a part of long-term memory.

_____ 9. The right hemisphere of the brain coordinates movement on the right side of the body and processes mental activities that involve creativity and generalized thinking.

_____ 10. Because test anxiety is a learned behavior, it cannot be unlearned.

CHECK POINT 12.1

True or False?

_____ 1. In true-false questions, it is important to read every word because a single word can change the meaning of the statement.

_____ 2. Some true-false statements may have more than one answer depending on your personal experiences.

_____ 3. *Always, best, larger, never,* and *none* are 100 percent or absolute modifiers.

_____ 4. In-between modifiers indicate that something occurs in varying degrees of frequency.

_____ 5. One effective strategy for true-false questions involves circling clue words for definition, relationship, and false statements.

Improve Your Grade
Online Practice 1:
True-False Questions

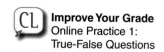

REFLECTIVE WRITING 12.1

Improve Your Grade
Reflective Writing 12.1

1. Some students prefer taking tests that involve objective questions, such as true-false or multiple-choice. Others prefer short-answer tests or essay tests. What are your preferred types of test questions? Why do you prefer those types?

2. Which of the strategies and tips discussed so far in this chapter for answering true-false questions are most helpful for you? Be specific and explain your answer.

MULTIPLE-CHOICE QUESTIONS

2 ▸ *Explain how to use essential strategies for answering multiple-choice questions.*

Careful reading is also essential for answering multiple-choice questions correctly. For most multiple-choice questions, there are two parts to the question: the stem and the options. The **stem** is the beginning of a multiple-choice question before the options for answers appear. The **options** are the choices of answers to use to complete a multiple-choice statement. Usually there are four options, but some tests use three options and others use five or six options. Unless the directions say otherwise, there will be only one correct answer.

> The **stem** is the beginning of a multiple-choice question before the options for answers appear.
>
> The **options** are the choices of answers to use to complete a multiple-choice statement.

Essential Strategies for Multiple-Choice Questions

Your goal when you are taking multiple-choice tests is to read stems and their options carefully and then select the option that best completes the statement. During this process, you want to identify and eliminate the distractors. **Distractors** in multiple-choice questions are the incorrect answers or options. Knowing with certainty that an option is a distractor reduces the number of options you need to consider carefully as possible correct answers. **Figure 12.6** shows six Essential Strategies for Multiple-Choice Tests.

> **Distractors** in multiple-choice questions are the incorrect answers or options.

FIGURE 12.6

Essential Strategies for Multiple-Choice Tests

▮ **Read the directions carefully.** Even though most multiple-choice tests direct you to choose *one answer,* do not automatically assume that is the case. Some directions state that *more than one answer may be correct,* or *mark all the correct answers.* If no mention is made about the number of answers to choose, always select only one.

▮ **Read all of the options before you select your answer.** Do not stop as soon as you find an acceptable answer; a later option may be a more comprehensive or a better answer.

▮ **Choose the *best* answer.** One or more of the answers may be correct, but the answer that is the most inclusive (includes the most or the broadest information) is the *best* answer.

▮ **Select "All of the above" only when every option is correct.** If all the options are the same level of information (one is not a larger category under which the other items belong), and all options contain accurate information, only then should you select "All of the above."

▮ **Avoid careless mistakes.** To avoid writing the wrong letter on the line, *circle* the letter of the *best* answer and then write the letter on the line. You may not need to use this strategy all the time, but it is effective when you get nervous, work too quickly, or your eyes skip around as during a bout with test anxiety.

▮ **Use the two-step approach for answering multiple-choice questions.**

The Two-Step Approach for Multiple-Choice Questions

The following two-step approach for answering multiple-choice questions increases your accuracy rate and your test-taking performance. Use it often so you become familiar with the process and it becomes habitual.

Step One: Finish the Stem in Your Mind

Read the stem carefully and, without looking at the options, quickly finish the stem in your mind. This step puts you in retrieval mode and into a schema related to the statement. Then glance down to see if any of the options are similar to what you had in mind. For practice, how would you complete each of the following stems in your mind?

_____ 1. A mnemonic is _____

_____ 2. When you trade time on your weekly schedule, you _____

_____ 3. Howard Gardner's eighth intelligence _____

Step Two: Create True-False Statements

Read the stem of a multiple-choice question with just one of the options; the result is a one-sentence statement that you can treat as a true-false statement. Continue by creating true-false statements by combining each option with the stem. Use the strategies that you have already learned for answering true-false questions.

CONCEPT CHECK 12.10

If you quickly see the correct answer, should you immediately write the answer on the line? Why or why not?

CONCEPT CHECK 12.11

As soon as you read the stem of a multiple-choice question, what should you do next?

> CONCEPT CHECK 12.12
>
> In what ways are multiple-choice questions similar to true-false questions?

If the statement is *false*, it is a distractor—an incorrect answer. *Cross off that option.* If the statement is true, *it may be the correct answer.* You won't know for sure until you have read all the options with the stem. After using this process for each option, focus on the options that you did not cross off. Select the *best* answer from those options.

The following example demonstrates the use of this strategy:

> _b__ 1. Maslow's Hierarchy of Needs suggests that
>   a. physiological needs have the greatest influence on human behavior. (F)
>   b. human behavior is influenced by a hierarchy of five different levels of needs. (T)
>   c. safety and esteem needs must be satisfied before a person can work on the other four levels of needs. (F)
>   d. human behavior is influenced by needs. (T)

Both b and d are true statements. Answer b is more comprehensive and inclusive. Answer b includes the information stated in option d. Answer b is the *best* option.

"Not" Questions

> CONCEPT CHECK 12.13
>
> What is a "not" question? What strategies can you use to answer "not" questions?

The majority of multiple-choice questions begin with a stem that is completed with one of the four options. However, you will encounter another type of multiple-choice question: a "*not*" question. A "*not*" question asks you which of the options is *not true* or does *not belong* in the same category as the other options. Following is an example of a "not" question.

> _c__ 1. Which of the following statements is <u>not</u> true about systematic desensitization?
>   a. It is a strategy to use to decrease test anxiety. (T)
>   b. It replaces negative emotional responses with positive ones. (T)
>   c. It involves a four-step process or system to use during a test to reduce stress. (F)
>   d. It may involve visualizing a different response to words that trigger anxiety. (T)

To answer this type of objective question, read each option carefully. All the options that are *true* statements are distractors. The option that is *false* is the correct answer.

GROUP PROCESSING:
A COLLABORATIVE LEARNING ACTIVITY

Form a group of three or four students. Complete the following directions on a large chart:

1. Brainstorm all the kinds of problems you have experienced taking paper-pencil or computerized objective tests. List all these problems on your chart.

2. Have students take turns selecting a problem on the chart, suggesting strategies to eliminate the problem, and then leading a group discussion about the problem. Continue until solutions for all of the problems have been discussed.

EXERCISE 12.4

Answering Multiple-Choice Questions

ANSWERS APPEAR ON PAGE A5

DIRECTIONS: Use the two-step approach for answering multiple-choice questions. Write the letter for the *best* answer on the line.

_____ 1. The central executive in your memory system
   a. coordinates most brain activities and cognitive functions.
   b. manages the flow of information into and out of long-term memory.
   c. initiates goal-directed behavior.
   d. integrates sensory information.

_____ 2. Which of the following statements is *not* true about visualization?
   a. You can use it to visualize the skeleton of a visual mapping or hierarchy.
   b. It never involves staring at an object as a way to make a visual impression.
   c. You can use visualization as a Look-Away Technique, or to reduce stress, and to increase comprehension when you read.
   d. It involves picturing information in your head without looking at the physical form.

_____ 3. Look-Away Techniques
   a. always involve reciting.
   b. are used mainly when you read.
   c. help you ignore unimportant information.
   d. provide feedback.

_____ 4. The five steps in the Feedback Model are
   a. action, goal, feedback, comparison, yes.
   b. goal, action, feedback, comparison, results.
   c. feedback, action, comparison, yes, no.
   d. goal, feedback, comparison, action, results.

_____ 5. The principle of Big Picture–Little Pictures
   a. encourages you to identify individual facts and details.
   b. is based completely on rote memory.
   c. recommends that you process information only in clusters.
   d. recommends that you try to "see the trees" *and* "see the forest" when you study.

CHECK POINT 12.2

ANSWERS APPEAR ON PAGE A5

Multiple Choice

_____ 1. Options in a multiple-choice question may
   a. contain definition or relationship clues.
   b. form true statements.
   c. include items in a series separated by commas.
   d. involve all of the above.

CL **Improve Your Grade**
Online Practice 2:
Multiple-Choice Questions

_____ 2. Which of the following is *not* a recommended strategy for multiple-choice tests?
   a. Circle correct answers instead of writing them on the line.
   b. Turn the question into a series of four true-false statements.
   c. Finish the stem in your mind before looking at the options.
   d. Cross off and eliminate distractors and then focus on the remaining options.

MATCHING QUESTIONS

3 ▸ *Explain how to use essential strategies for answering matching questions.*

Matching questions consist of two columns of information. The left column often consists of key words or terminology. The right column contains definitions, descriptions, events, examples, or other factual information that matches with the items in the left column. Matching questions are created through the use of *paired associations*. The following are examples of paired associations you may encounter on matching tests:

- Words and their definitions
- Dates and events
- Problems and their solutions
- People and what they did
- Terms and their function or purpose
- Causes and effects

Essential Strategies for Matching Questions

When you are faced with matching questions on tests, you will reduce careless errors and increase your test performance by answering the matching questions in a systematic way. **Figure 12.7** shows five Essential Strategies for Matching Tests.

CONCEPT CHECK 12.14

What are examples of paired associations that may appear in matching tests?

CONCEPT CHECK 12.15

Do you tend to get confused on matching tests or make frequent errors? What systematic approach can you use to increase your performance?

FIGURE 12.7

Essential Strategies for Matching Tests

- **Read the directions carefully.** Usually each item on the right can be used only once; if an item can be used more than once, the directions should say so.

- **Count the items in each column.** If the lists contain an equal number of items, each item will be used once. If the list on the right contains more items than the list on the left, some items on the right will be extra and will not be used.

- **Read the list with the shorter entries.** Usually the column on the left will have the shorter entries. Reading through the items in the column familiarizes you with the topics and the kinds of paired associations you may be working with: people, events, dates, or vocabulary terms. If items are about equal length, read the left column.

- **Start with "a," the first item at the top of the right column.** Scan the items in the left column to find a match. Once you see a definite match, write the letter on the line and *cross off the letter you used so you do not reuse it.* Do not write an answer unless you are certain that it is correct.

- **Use the four levels of response to work your way through the matching test.**

The Four Levels of Response for Matching Questions

The four levels of response help you move through the test in a systematic way. Unlike true-false and multiple-choice questions, if you *incorrectly* match an item on the right with an item on the left, the result will be two incorrect answers rather than one. Remember, you can write one answer on each space next to the left column, so placing an incorrect answer on a line forces the answer that should have been placed there to be placed elsewhere (the second incorrect answer). Using a step-by-step, systematic approach increases your test performance.

CONCEPT CHECK 12.16

Why does one mistake on a matching test result in at least one additional mistake?

Immediate Response

If you can find the match for an item, and you know with certainty that it is a correct match, write the letter of that item next to its match in the left column. *Cross off the letter* of the answer you used so you do not try to reuse it, which will cause confusion and frustration.

Delayed Response

Look for *word clues* and *grammar clues* that can help you find the item on the left that goes with the item on the right. For example, if you are working with a lettered item from the right column, and you see *system, technique,* or *rule,* narrow your focus by looking for choices in the left column that deal specifically with some type of system, a technique, or a rule.

When you read and connect the item on the left with the item on the right, a meaningful "thought unit" or sentence should emerge. To find this meaningful connection, *mentally chatter your way* to the answer. For example, based on the example in Figure 12.8, a conversation with yourself might go like this: *Which one of these has to do with belief in one's abilities? Not that one—beliefs don't have anything to do with chunking. Not that one. Oh, this might be it. Yes, self-efficacy is the belief in one's own abilities.*

If you are not able to identify the correct answer after trying one or more of the previously mentioned techniques, *leave the answer space blank*; do not guess. Use a check mark in the left margin as a reminder that you need to return to this question later. Move on to the next item. Always work your way from the top down to the bottom of the list.

Assisted Response

Scan through other sections of the test to look for any of the key words used on either side of your matching list. Other parts of the test may have information that helps you recall associations or jogs your memory about the information in the matching questions. If you cannot find any clues in other parts of the test, move on to educated guessing.

CONCEPT CHECK 12.17

How can assisted response help you answer objective questions? Do you ever use assisted response?

Educated Guessing

If none of the previous techniques helped you find matches for specific items, use educated guessing. If you put nothing on the line, it will be wrong; you might as well take the remaining items that you could not match and fill in any empty lines with any of those remaining letters.

Figure 12.8 shows the steps you can use to answer matching test questions. Review these steps by reading through the circled items one through seven.

FIGURE 12.8

Steps for Answering Matching Questions

1. Directions say to use each answer once.

2. Two answers are extra and won't be used.

5. Use delayed response. Use helper words to try to connect the items that you do not know well.

6. Use assisted response. Use the rest of the test for assistance in finding more answers.

7. Use educated guessing. Fill in any remaining blanks with letters you did not already use.

Matching

Match the items on the left to the items on the right. Write the letter of each answer on the line. Each item on the right may be used only one time.

3. Read the shorter list.

4. Start with "a." Do only the ones you know.

_h_	1. working memory	a. permanent storage center
____	2. motivation	b. associating items together
_a_	3. long-term memory	c. short-term memory and feedback loop
_j_	4. affirmations	d. feeling, emotion, or desire that elicits an action
_f_	5. chunking	e. feedback
____	6. sensory stimuli	f. group into bigger units or break into smaller units
_b_	7. linking	g. procedural memory
_i_	8. central executive	h. conscious mind
____	9. self-efficacy	i. manager/organizer of WM
____	10. result of self-quizzing	j. positive statements written in present tense
		k. belief in one's own abilities
		l. words, sounds, pictures

Improve Your Grade
Reflective Writing 12.2

REFLECTIVE WRITING 12.2

On separate paper, in a journal, or online at this textbook's website, respond to the following questions.

1. Examine two or more objective tests you have taken in any of your classes. Analyze any questions you answered incorrectly. Look for the use of *items in a series, modifiers, negatives, definition* and *relationship clues* in the questions. What did you discover by examining your previous tests?

2. How would the objective test-taking strategies in this chapter have helped you perform better on those tests? What do you notice now about those tests and the questions that you were not aware of at the time you took the tests? Be specific in your answers.

EXERCISE 12.5

Matching Problems and Solutions

ANSWERS APPEAR ON PAGE A5

DIRECTIONS: Read each problem on the left. Then find the solution on the right. Write the letter of the solution on the line. You may use each answer only once.

_____ 1. I highlight too much.

_____ 2. I don't know how to study from underlining.

_____ 3. When I read, I need to find a way to make important terminology stand out more clearly.

_____ 4. I have trouble finding the topic sentence.

_____ 5. I have problems finding definitions for key words in the book.

_____ 6. I don't feel like I really understand how to use the textbook features very well.

_____ 7. I need a fast way to look up page numbers to find information in my book.

_____ 8. The instructor said to check our work with the answer keys in the book, but I can't find any answer keys in my chapters.

_____ 9. I have trouble getting started when I have a reading assignment. I'm just not motivated to "dig right in" and do the serious reading.

_____ 10. I go into automatic pilot every time I try to read pages in my textbook.

_____ 11. I can't write fast enough to write down everything the instructor says in a lecture.

_____ 12. When the instructor talks too slowly, my mind wanders to other things.

_____ 13. My notes are a jumbled mess. The information all runs together.

a. Circle the words that you need to be able to define.

b. Survey the book at the beginning of the term.

c. Use punctuation clues, word clues, word structure clues, and context clues.

d. Try to organize with headings and numbered details. Leave spaces between headings.

e. Only mark the main idea and the key words for details.

f. Read one paragraph at a time. Stop. Take time to comprehend what you read.

g. Use your own words to string together the ideas you marked.

h. Use the index.

i. Survey the chapter first as a warm-up activity.

j. Paraphrase with shortened sentences. Abbreviate. Use symbols.

k. Check the first and the last sentences to see if one has the main idea that controls the paragraph.

l. Keep writing, anticipate new points, question ideas, or mentally summarize.

m. Check the appendix of the book.

CHECK POINT 12.3

ANSWERS APPEAR ON PAGE A5

True or False?

_____ 1. Reading the column with the shorter entries gives you an overview of the topics and gets you started on matching the items more quickly.

_____ 2. As soon as you see a match that could be correct, you should write the letter on the line and continue looking for paired associations.

_____ 3. One way to check your accuracy is to talk to yourself about the way two items match or belong together.

CL **Improve Your Grade**
Online Practice 3:
Matching Questions

EXERCISE 12.6

Textbook Case Studies

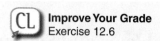 **Improve Your Grade**
Exercise 12.6

 **Improve Your Grade**
Online Case Studies

DIRECTIONS:

1. Read each case study carefully. Respond to the question at the end of each case study by using *specific* strategies discussed in this chapter. Answer in complete sentences.

2. Write your responses on paper or online at the Student Website, Exercise 12.6. You will be able to print your online response or e-mail it to your instructor.

CASE STUDY 1: Sarah has the ability to organize and express ideas well on essay tests. However, she struggles with objective tests. She often feels that she does not understand what true-false questions mean, and she gets very confused and frustrated trying to select the correct answer on multiple-choice questions. What strategies can you recommend to help Sarah improve her performance on objective tests?

CASE STUDY 2: Tim rolls his eyes and groans any time he sees a matching test. He tends to mismatch too many items, which then leaves him with items that cannot be matched at all. He moves through the right and the left columns in random order as he tries to find things that "belong together." He starts erasing and changing his answers and ends up duplicating answers and writing answers on the wrong lines. What suggestions would you give Tim that would help him approach matching tests in a more organized, systematic way?

EDUCATED GUESSING

 4 *Discuss the advantages and disadvantages of using educated guessing, and describe ways to use educated-guessing strategies.*

Educated guessing is the fourth level of response for answering objective test questions. Educated guessing involves using specific strategies to improve your odds for supplying the correct answers on objective test questions.

Understanding educated-guessing strategies often improves critical reading skills, for you learn to notice the significance of individual words and details in questions. Even though educated-guessing strategies may help you gain a few additional points on a test, the strategies do not always result in correct answers. The following are important points to know about educated guessing:

▌ The phrase *educated guessing* is used instead of simply *guessing* because you do use some background information, logic, and common sense to approach questions that you cannot answer through immediate, delayed, or assisted response. Educated guessing truly does involve more thinking skills than randomly selecting an answer or guessing without thinking.

▌ Educated guessing is not foolproof or guaranteed to produce the correct answer. These strategies only increase the odds that you will reach the final answer. Because they do not always work, do not become overly confident about taking tests simply because you know how to use educated guessing.

▌ Limit the use of educated-guessing strategies to situations in which nothing else has produced an answer. Educated guessing is a last resort! It never replaces studying and knowing the answers.

CONCEPT CHECK 12.18

What are the benefits of using educated guessing?

Figure 12.9 summarizes ten educated-guessing strategies that apply to true-false and multiple-choice questions. Remember that multiple-choice questions may be seen as a series of true-false questions, so the same strategies used for true-false questions will apply to multiple-choice questions. Each strategy is explained with greater details in the sections that follow.

Guessing TRUE

For true-false questions and for multiple-choice questions in which you use the stem with each option to form a true-false statement, guess TRUE for statements that have in-between modifiers or when you need to make a "wild-shot guess."

Guess True: In-Between Modifiers

The *in-between modifiers* make room for exceptions or for the statement to sometimes apply and sometimes not apply. If you are using educated guessing, and you see an in-between modifier in a question or an option, guess *true*. Notice how the in-between modifiers work in true-false and multiple-choice questions.

___T___ 1. Reviewing notes from a previous paragraph can **sometimes** be used to help understand a difficult paragraph.

___T___ 2. People **often** use empathic listening to try to understand another person's feelings.

_____ 3. Intrapersonal intelligence is an intelligence that
   a. **always** shows leadership and group charisma.   (F)
   b. **often** involves a special interest in personal growth and insights.   (T?)
   c. **seldom** is combined with linguistic or interpersonal intelligence.   (T?)
   d. is **never** taught in schools.   (F)

Options *a* and *d* have 100 percent modifiers. If guessing strategies are used, these would be marked *false*. Both option *b* and option *c* have in-between modifiers, so by using guessing strategies, they would be marked *true*. Therefore, guess one of these two options. However, before you purely guess, think it through more carefully. Option *c* is not accurate information; option *b* makes sense and is the correct answer. If you didn't know this, by reducing the choices to two options, you have a fifty-fifty chance of guessing correctly.

Guess True: The "Wild-Shot Guess"

For true-false questions, if there are no modifiers to use, and there is no relationship shown, you will need to take a "wild-shot guess." If you run out of time on a test and simply must guess, *guess true*. There is a logical reason for this. When instructors write tests, they usually prefer to leave the correct, accurate information in your mind. They know that you are likely to remember what you read. Therefore, they tend to write more true statements than false statements.

FIGURE 12.9

Summary of Ten Educated-Guessing Strategies

1. Guess *true* if there is an in-between modifier.
2. Guess *true*, the "wild-shot guess," if there are no other clues in a true-false statement.
3. Guess *false* if there is a 100 percent modifier.
4. Guess *false* if there is a relationship clue.
5. Guess *false* if the statement is obviously incorrect.
6. Guess one of the **middle numbers** when numbers are the options.
7. Guess one of the **"look-alikes"** when two options are almost identical.
8. Guess the **longest** or **"most inclusive"** option.
9. Guess *c*, the "wild-shot guess," if there are no other clues.
10. Guess **"All of the above"** in specific situations.

CONCEPT CHECK 12.19

Can you use some of the educated-guessing strategies for true-false questions with multiple-choice questions as well? Why or why not?

CONCEPT CHECK 12.20

Why do in-between modifiers appear in more *true* statements than do 100 percent modifiers?

CONCEPT CHECK 12.21

Why is the "wild-shot guess" for true-false questions the answer *true*? Do you agree with the reasoning? Why or why not?

Guessing FALSE

For true-false questions and for multiple-choice questions in which you use the stem with each option to form a true-false statement, guess FALSE for statements that have 100 percent modifiers, relationship clues, or options that obviously are incorrect answers.

Guess False: 100 Percent Modifiers

The *100 percent modifiers* are the *absolutes,* meaning that they are the extremes; no exceptions are allowed. Few things happen or exist without exceptions, so the odds are in your favor that questions or options with 100 percent modifiers will be false. Guess *false.* Notice how the 100 percent modifiers work in true-false and multiple-choice questions.

> **CONCEPT CHECK 12.22**
>
> What educated-guessing strategies can you use when you find a modifier in a true-false or a multiple-choice question?

___F___ 1. Attendance in college is required in **every** class.

___F___ 2. **Always** begin by studying your favorite subject first.

_____ 1. The prefix *intra-*
  a. is never used in English words.
  b. always means "between."
  c. means "within" or "inside of."
  d. None of the above

___F___ a. The prefix *intra-* is (never) used in English words.
___F___ b. The prefix *intra-* (always) means "between."
Correct Answer ⟶ ___T___ c. The prefix *intra-* means "within" or "inside of."

Guess False: Relationship Clues

Cause/effect and explanation through reason are two common kinds of relationships questioned on tests. If you cannot figure out the answer about a relationship, guess *false.* Why? Relationship questions often involve higher-level thinking skills, and test writers can easily write questions to show false relationships. Notice how the true-false and multiple-choice questions do not show a true or accurate relationship.

> **CONCEPT CHECK 12.23**
>
> Why does the educated-guessing strategy for sentences with relationship clues suggest using the *false* answer? What true-false question can you write that uses a relationship clue and has *true* for an answer?

___F___ 1. Lack of motivation is the **reason** unsuccessful students avoid using time management.

___F___ 2. Cramming is not recommended **because** it uses only eight of the Twelve Principles of Memory.

_____ 1. Systematic desensitization
  a. <u>causes</u> a person to react more mildly to criticism. (F)
  b. works <u>because</u> the immune system is strengthened. (F)
  c. should <u>never</u> be used to avoid undesirable situations. (F)
  d. helps a person change his or her negative reaction to specific events. (T)

Guess False: Obviously Incorrect Answers

If you read statements that are ridiculous, foolish, insulting, or use unfamiliar terms, mark them *false* in true-false questions and mark them as distractors in multiple-choice questions. If you have attended class regularly and have done all the reading assignments, and you encounter unfamiliar terms on a test, odds are in your favor that the statement is false, or it is a distractor in a multiple-choice question. Notice how this works in the following examples.

___F___ 1. Howard Gardner's multiple intelligences theory applies only to people with IQs over 175.   (*ridiculous*)

___F___ 2. Howard Gardner's Theory of Multiple Intelligences added an eighth intelligence called psychic/intuitive.   (*unfamiliar terms*)

___d___ 3. When you don't know the answer to a test question, you should
    a. try using the rest of the test to trigger your memory.   (T)
    b̶. try looking at another student's answers.   (*ridiculous*)   (F)
    c̶. cry.   (*ridiculous*)   (F)
    d. use delayed or assisted response before guessing.   (T)

___a___ 4. Interpersonal intelligence is
    a. seen in people with social and leadership skills.   (T)
    b̶. associated with immaturity.   (*ridiculous*)   (F)
    c̶. not a useful quality in school beyond the first grade.   (*silly*)   (F)
    d̶. a form of type B behavior.   (*unfamiliar term*)   (F)

Educated Guessing for Multiple-Choice Questions

Five educated-guessing strategies apply specifically to multiple-choice questions. These strategies help you use educated guessing when options are numerals/numbers, have "look-alike" answers, or vary in length and content. They also include a "wild-shot guess" and discussion about the option that says "All of the above."

Guess a Middle Number

When the options in a multiple-choice questions are numbers, chances are better that the correct answer is one of the numbers in the middle range. Therefore, treat the highest and the lowest numbers as distractors; eliminate them. That leaves you with two options. Try to reason through to make the better choice of the remaining two options. If any one of the other guessing strategies applies (such as choose *c*), incorporate that strategy as well to choose your answer.

CONCEPT CHECK 12.24

In the following options for answers, which would you eliminate and which would you consider as a final answer: 38, 14, 46, 21?

    1. An average rate of thinking speed is
    a̶. 800 words per minute.   (Eliminate the highest.)
    b. 600 words per minute.   ⎧Choose between
    c. 400 words per minute.   ⎩these two options.
    d̶. 200 words per minute.   (Eliminate the lowest.)

Guess One of the "Look-Alikes"

Some questions have two options that look almost the same except for one or two words. Chances are good that the correct answer is one of these two options. Eliminate the other options and focus on these two "look-alikes." Carefully think through and associate the information with what you have learned. If you can't decide, choose either one.

CONCEPT CHECK 12.25

What is a "look-alike" answer? Is it a distractor or a possible answer?

_____ 1. Compared to the left hemisphere of the brain, the right hemisphere of the brain
　　a. understands spoken language better.
　　b. has better logical abilities.
　　c. perceives words better.
　　d. perceives emotions better.

Focus on *c* and *d* because they are "look-alikes." Now try to reason your way through this. You have already eliminated *a*, which deals with language. Because *c* also relates to language, it, too, must be incorrect. This leaves you with *d* as the correct answer, which it is. (Notice in this case how the guessing strategy to use *c* does not work—there are no guarantees!)

Guess the Longest or Most Inclusive

This guessing strategy is based on two premises. First, sometimes more words are needed to give complete information to make a correct answer. Second, an answer that covers a wider range of possibilities is more likely to be correct.

Look at the *length* of the options. If one option is much longer than the others, choose it. Also look at the *content* of the answers. Sometimes two or three answers may be correct to some degree, but one answer contains more information or a broader idea. This answer is the most inclusive. Notice how the *most inclusive answer* in the following example is the best answer.

_____ 1. Test anxiety can be reduced by focusing on
　　a. yourself and ignoring others.
　　b. outward thoughts and actions.
　　c. your strengths and accomplishments.
　　d. the four strategies to reduce test anxiety.

All of the answers are correct to some degree. However, *d* is the longest and includes a wider range of information. The answers *a*, *b*, and *c* fit under the information given in *d*.

Guess C: The "Wild-Shot Guess"

For multiple-choice questions, many instructors favor the *c* answer for the correct answer. If you try writing some of your own multiple-choice questions, you may find that you, too, tend to put more correct answers in the *c* position than in any other position. The position of *c* seems to hide the answer best and force the reader to read through more of the options.

Guess "All of the Above"

If you know for certain that two options are correct, but you are not sure about the third option, and the fourth option is "All of the above," choose "All of the above." This is a safe guess since you know that two options are correct. If you do not know for certain that two are correct, and you have found no other clues to help you, you can choose "All of the above." However, be aware that this strategy is not very reliable, especially if "All of the above" is used throughout the test.

CONCEPT CHECK 12.26

What does the "most inclusive option" mean? How is it used as an educated-guessing strategy?

CONCEPT CHECK 12.27

If two different educated-guessing strategies conflict with each other, how will you decide which answer to use?

CONCEPT CHECK 12.28

When is guessing the option "All of the above" a fairly reliable guess to make? When is this option less reliable?

Performing well on tests involves learning effective strategies for taking tests. How you read questions, contemplate answers, and select the answers requires careful attention to details. What test-taking skills have you learned recently that increase your scores on tests?

Educated-Guessing Strategies

This entire textbook emphasizes strategies to boost your memory and strengthen your learning strategies, so at first glance teaching how to make educated guesses may seem contradictory to the philosophy of this textbook. However, you may be required at some time to take a standardized test that tests you on information that you possibly have not yet learned in your courses or through other experiences. In such situations, educated guessing can help you improve your performance.

If you would like to practice these skills further, go to the Student Website, Topic In-Depth: Educated-Guessing Worksheets for true-false and multiple-choice questions that come from sources other than this textbook. You can also practice by trying to answer questions in textbooks for courses that you are not enrolled in or subjects that are somewhat unfamiliar to you. Remember, time spent practicing educated guessing *could* be time spent studying to learn and imprint information into your own memory system!

 **Topic In-Depth**
Educated-Guessing Worksheets

CHECK POINT 12.4   ANSWERS APPEAR ON PAGE A5

True or False?

_____ 1. Educated guessing used correctly involves more than randomly selecting an answer.

_____ 2. Students who know all the educated-guessing strategies are able to guess more than 90 percent of the answers correctly.

_____ 3. The "wild-shot guess" for multiple-choice questions is *c*; the "wild-shot guess" for true-false questions is *f*.

_____ 4. In-between modifiers appear more frequently in false statements.

_____ 5. In multiple-choice questions, statements with middle numbers, relationship clues, or definition clues tend to be distractors, not the correct answers.

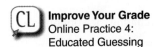 **Improve Your Grade**
Online Practice 4:
Educated Guessing

EXERCISE 12.7

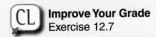 **Improve Your Grade**
Exercise 12.7

Links

PURPOSE: Study skills throughout this textbook are integrated. Each supports research based on learning theories and functions of working memory, and each works effectively because of other underlying strategies and Principles of Memory. This exercise provides you with an opportunity to express your understanding of these links.

DIRECTIONS: Work in a small group or with a partner to discuss the relationships between the following pairs of items.

1. Retrieval cues and levels of response for answering questions

2. Recognition level tasks and long-term memory

3. Test anxiety and objective test-taking skills

4. Self-management skills and test-taking skills

LEARNING OBJECTIVES REVIEW

1 ▶ *Explain how to use essential strategies for answering true-false questions.*

- The Four Levels of Response work effectively for all objective questions.
- Seven essential strategies can improve your performance on true-false questions.
- When answering true-false questions, check items in a series, identify 100 percent/absolute modifiers and in-between modifiers, definition and relationship clues, and negatives.

2 ▶ *Explain how to use essential strategies for answering multiple-choice questions.*

- Multiple-choice questions consist of stems, options, and options that are distractors.
- Six essential strategies can improve your performance on multiple-choice questions.
- When answering multiple-choice questions, use a two-step approach: finish the stem in your mind, and then turn the stem plus the options into four true-false statements.
- Answer "not" questions by evaluating each option as a true-false statement.

3 ▶ *Explain how to use essential strategies for answering matching questions.*

- Matching questions use paired associations.
- Five essential strategies can improve your test performance on matching questions.
- Use the Four Levels of Response to answer matching test questions.

4 ▶ *Discuss the advantages and disadvantages of using educated guessing, and describe ways to use educated-guessing strategies.*

- Educated-guessing strategies can help you read questions more carefully and increase your performance on objective tests. However, avoid over-relying on educated guessing.
- Ten guessing strategies can help you improve your test performance on true-false and multiple-choice questions.

CHAPTER 12 REVIEW QUESTIONS

ANSWERS APPEAR ON PAGE A5

True or False?

___F___ 1. If you cannot give an immediate response on an objective test question, you should use educated guessing and move quickly to the next question.

___T___ 2. The words *reason, because,* and *since* are often relationship clues.

___F___ 3. All items listed in a series must be false before you can use a false answer.

___F___ 4. True-false statements that use negatives are always false.

___T___ 5. The "most inclusive option" in a multiple-choice question may be the best answer.

___F___ 6. A multiple-choice "not" question has a negative in each option.

___T___ 7. If a multiple-choice question has four options, the question should be read as four true-false statements.

___T___ 8. Using word clues and grammar clues may help you match paired items during the delayed-response step of answering questions on a matching test.

Multiple Choice

_____ 1. Objective test questions
a. require students to pay careful attention to all the words in the question.
b. involve recognition level tasks.
c. are often best answered after comparing the information in the question to information in one's memory.
d. involve all of the above.

_____ 2. Which of the following parts of a multiple-choice question should you use with each option to form a true-false statement?
a. distractors
b. directions
c. stem
d. modifiers

_____ 3. Educated guessing should be used after
a. the recall step of response.
b. the immediate-response step.
c. all other options have been tried.
d. the delayed-response step.

_____ 4. When you first read the stem of a multiple-choice question, you should
a. decide you really do not like the question.
b. turn it into a true-false question.
c. finish the stem with your own words and then see whether an option matches your words.
d. identify the distractors immediately by using educated-guessing strategies.

_____ 5. Which of the following is _not_ true about modifiers?
a. 100 percent modifiers are also called absolute modifiers.
b. The words _always, everyone, never,_ and _every_ are not absolute modifiers.
c. The words _maybe, sometimes, most,_ and _seldom_ are not absolute modifiers.
d. Modifiers indicate the degree or the frequency that something occurs.

Matching

Match the items on the left to the items on the right, writing the letter answer on the line. You may use each answer only once.

_____ 1. Paired associations
_____ 2. 100 percent modifiers
_____ 3. In-between modifiers
_____ 4. Relationship clues
_____ 5. Prefixes with negative meanings
_____ 6. Recognition questions
_____ 7. Delayed response
_____ 8. Assisted response
_____ 9. Stem
_____ 10. Distractors

a. words such as _sometimes, often, some, perhaps_
b. units of meaning at the beginning of words that mean "no" or "not"
c. guessing _true_ or the letter _c_
d. the linking of two ideas together
e. the beginning part of a multiple-choice question
f. answers that you immediately know
g. options that are incorrect answers
h. involves rereading, looking for clues, and doing memory searches
i. words that are absolutes
j. objective questions
k. a response you give after you skim the test for clues
l. words that often show cause/effect

CL **ACE the Test**
Four Online Practice Tests

Online Resources

LEARNING OBJECTIVES

1 ▶ *Explain how to use essential strategies for answering recall questions, which include fill-in-the-blank, listing, definition, and short-answer questions.*

2 ▶ *Explain how to use essential strategies for answering math test questions.*

Chapter Outline

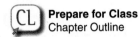 **Prepare for Class**
Chapter Outline

3 ▶ *Explain how to use essential strategies for answering essay test questions.*

In this chapter you will learn effective strategies for answering recall questions (fill-in-the blanks, listing, definition, and short-answer questions) and increasing your performance on math tests. Finally, strategies for essay tests—the most challenging type of test for many students—will guide you step-by-step through the process of developing an effective essay answer. You can use many of the exercises in this chapter to review content that you have studied throughout the term in previous chapters.

Chapter 13 Profile

Recall, Math, and Essay Tests

ANSWER, **SCORE**, and **RECORD** your profile before you read this chapter. If you need to review the process, refer to the complete directions given in the profile for Chapter 1 on page 4.

ONLINE: You can complete the profile and get your score online at this textbook's website.

	YES	NO
1. My answers on questions that require lists of information or short answers are often incomplete or inaccurate.	_____	_____
2. I often have difficulty recalling a specific word to complete a fill-in-the-blank question.	_____	_____
3. Open-ended questions that have many possible answers are difficult for me to answer.	_____	_____
4. I use the formal textbook definition to write a one-sentence answer for most questions that ask me to define a term.	_____	_____
5. I often make careless mistakes on math tests or do not show all of the steps I use to solve problems.	_____	_____
6. I know how to analyze my answers on math tests so I can identify my pattern of errors.	_____	_____
7. I understand the different answers required for questions that use the direction words *define, explain, compare, summarize,* or *evaluate.*	_____	_____
8. I use my course syllabus, the table of contents of my textbook, and my class notes to predict themes or topics that might appear in essay questions.	_____	_____
9. Organizing my ideas and providing sufficient details in paragraphs are problems that I have when I answer essay questions.	_____	_____
10. I am confident in my ability to adequately prepare for and perform well on recall, math, and essay tests.	_____	_____

QUESTIONS LINKED TO THE CHAPTER LEARNING OBJECTIVES:

Questions 1–4:	objective 1	Questions 7–9: objective 3
Questions 5, 6:	objective 2	Question 10: all objectives

REFLECTIVE WRITING 13.1

Improve Your Grade
Reflective Writing 13.1

On separate paper, in a journal, or online at this textbook's website, respond to the following questions:

1. What are your greatest concerns about taking tests that are not objective tests? Why do you have these concerns?

2. How do you rate your overall performance and grades on recall and essay tests? What areas do you consider your weakest areas for these kinds of tests?

 Improve Your Grade
Online Flashcards
Glossary

RECALL TEST QUESTIONS

1 *Explain how to use essential strategies for answering recall questions, which include fill-in-the-blank, listing, definition, and short-answer questions.*

Recall questions are test questions that require you to retrieve (recall) information from long-term memory: fill-in-the-blank, listing, definition, and short-answer questions. Unlike objective questions that involve *recognition tasks*, recall questions involve *recall tasks*, which require you to conduct memory searches, locate, and retrieve pertinent information from memory without any direct clues or information to recognize as accurate or not.

Recall questions are test questions that require you to retrieve (recall) information from long-term memory: fill-in-the-blank, listing, definition, and short-answer questions.

Fill-in-the-Blank Questions

Fill-in-the-blank questions are recall questions in the form of sentences that have one or more missing words. You can predict that the majority of answers for fill-in-the-blank questions will relate to terminology. To prepare for these tests, spend ample time reading definitions from your flashcards, vocabulary sheets, or notes, and then *recalling from memory* and *writing* the words for those definitions as those are often the words used to complete fill-in-the-blank statements.

To answer fill-in-the-blank questions, begin by carefully reading the sentence and noting what type of word is needed; often the word needed is a noun naming an object, concept, step, process, or person. Then decide what key words will complete the sentence correctly. Following are examples of fill-in-the-blank questions.

1. A _____ learner is a "right-brain dominant person" who tends to be intuitive, creative, and visual.
2. _____, _____, _____ on _____, and Ongoing _____ are the last four Principles of Memory represented by the mnemonic "FOTO."
3. _____ _____ is also known as your conscious mind.

In question 1, the answer is a single word: *global*. In question 2, the answer is four individual items in a series, indicated by the commas: *Feedback, Organization, Time on Task*, and *Review*. In question 3, the answer is a two-word answer: *Working memory*. See **Figure 13.1** for five Essential Strategies for Fill-in-the-Blank Tests.

CONCEPT CHECK 13.1

How do objective questions and recall questions differ?

Fill-in-the-blank questions are recall questions in the form of sentences that have one or more missing words.

CONCEPT CHECK 13.2

What visual clues in a question can help you figure out what kind of answer is necessary?

CONCEPT CHECK 13.3

Can you use educated guessing for this kind of recall question? Why or why not?

FIGURE 13.1

Essential Strategies for Fill-in-the-Blank Tests

▌ **Write only *one* word on each blank line.** When you read the full sentence, it must make sense and be grammatically correct. If it is not, search for a different word for the blank.

▌ **Understand the kinds of answers for more than one blank.** Use comma clues to recognize series of items. When you see two or more blank lines, a comma between the blanks indicates a series of items. If no commas separate the blanks, the answer is a two-word answer.

▌ **Conduct a memory search for the answer.** Use key words in the statement to trigger associations. For example, ask: *What do we call . . . Where did I learn about . . . Who . . . What other things do I know related to this?*

▌ **Use assisted response.** If you cannot come up with a word to complete the sentence, place a *check mark* next to the question and move on. After you have answered the remaining questions on the test, skim through the test looking for clues or for a word to complete the question.

▌ **Write a *substitute word,* a *synonym,* or even a *phrase* to complete the sentence.** A synonym is a word with a similar meaning. Even though the substitute word, synonym, or phrase may not be the *exact* word required to complete the sentence, you may receive partial points for your answer.

A **synonym** is a word with a similar meaning.

EXERCISE 13.1

Answering Fill-in-the-Blank Questions

 Improve Your Grade
Online Practice 1: Fill-in-the-Blanks
Online Practice 2: Fill-in-the-Blanks

DIRECTIONS: Work with a partner or by yourself. Complete each statement by writing one word on each blank line.

1. The _____ _____ technique is a concentration technique for letting other people know that you do not want to be disturbed.

2. The beginning part of a multiple-choice question is called the _____.

3. _____ time consists of a few hours each week added to your time-management schedule to allow for any extra study time beyond your regular study blocks.

4. The _____ Method helps you prioritize goals according to their degree of importance.

5. When you use the second step of the Cornell system, you use selectivity to decide what information to place in the left column, which is called the _____ column, of your notes.

6. Each time you link together two items in memory, you create an _____ that then works as a retrieval _____ to retrieve information at a later time.

7. An _____ is a "memory trick" or a memory tool that you can create by taking the first letters of each of the key words in a list to create a mnemonic sentence.

8. _____ memory, _____ memory (which includes short-term memory and the central executive), and long-_____ memory are the three main memory centers in the Information Processing Model.

Listing Questions

Listing questions are recall questions that ask for a specific list of ideas, items, or steps that belong together in a specific category. Listing questions often begin with the direction word *list, name,* or *what are.* Unless the directions say otherwise, answers on listing questions are words or phrases, not complete sentences. You can predict listing questions as you read and take notes. Any time you see a list of items or steps in a process, create a study tool—such as an index card or a mnemonic—for those lists. Chapter objectives and chapter summaries are other sources for lists of information to learn.

Closed and Open-Ended Questions

Two kinds of questions may be used for listing questions: closed questions and open-ended questions. **Closed questions** are questions that require specific answers. Some closed questions, such as questions about the steps used in a specific procedure, require that you list the items in their original order. The following are examples of *closed* listing questions:

1. What are the Four Levels of Response to use for answering objective questions? (*Specific order required: Immediate, Delayed, Assisted, Educated Guessing*)

2. List the four most common ways to encode information to process into memory. (*Nonspecific order:* linguistic, visual, motor, semantic)

Open-ended questions are questions that have many possible answers. To answer open-ended questions, you can list a variety of answers as long as the items in your answers relate to or belong in the category of the question. Some students find open-ended questions easier to answer because they can take information from different chapters and parts of the course to answer the question. Other students, however, find open-ended questions more difficult because the questions do not refer to a specific list of ideas or information previously studied *as a list.* The following are examples of open-ended questions that have many possible correct answers.

1. List four subintelligences of Gardner's musical intelligence.

2. List five *reflect activities* a student could use during the fourth step of the Cornell notetaking system.

Essential Strategies for Listing Questions

In addition to predicting listing test questions and creating study tools that show lists to learn, you can increase your performance on listing tests by using the five Essential Strategies for Listing Tests in **Figure 13.2**.

Listing questions are recall questions that ask for a specific list of ideas, items, or steps that belong together in a specific category.

CONCEPT CHECK 13.4

What three listing questions can you create for information you learned in this textbook?

Closed questions are questions that require specific answers.

CONCEPT CHECK 13.5

How do open-ended and closed questions differ? Do you have a preference for either type of question? Why or why not?

Open-ended questions are questions that have many possible answers.

CONCEPT CHECK 13.6

What strategy can you use if you cannot recall all the items necessary to answer a listing question?

FIGURE 13.2

Essential Strategies for Listing Tests

▌ **Underline the key words in the question.** This helps you focus on what kind of information you need to include in your answer.

▌ **Identify the question as a closed or an open-ended question.**

▌ **Conduct memory searches for answers.** Use the key words you underlined in the question to trigger associations and answers. Ask yourself questions: *What else belongs here? What other things are related to the answers I already listed?*

▌ **Place a check next to the list if you were not able to complete it.** After you have answered the questions on the remainder of the test, use assisted response by using other parts of the test to locate items to complete your list.

▌ **Write a substitute word, synonym, or phrase to complete the list.** An empty space brings only one result: no points for your answer—so attempt to complete the list.

EXERCISE 13.2

Answering Listing Questions

CL **Improve Your Grade**
Online Practice 3: Listing Questions

DIRECTIONS: Work with a partner or by yourself. Underline the key words in each question. On the line, write *O* for open-ended question and *C* for closed question. On separate paper, list answers for each question without referring to other pages in your textbook or your notes.

_____ 1. What are the steps, in order, for the Feedback Model?

_____ 2. List five strategies to reduce or eliminate procrastination.

_____ 3. List five traits or characteristics of linear learners.

_____ 4. What are the eight intelligences in Howard Gardner's Theory of Multiple Intelligences?

_____ 5. Name the four most common sources of test anxiety.

Definition Questions

Definition questions are recall questions that ask you to define and expand upon a word or terminology.

Definition questions are recall questions that ask you to define and expand upon a word or terminology. For definition questions, a one-sentence answer that simply provides a formal definition of a term often is insufficient and does not earn you the maximum points for the question. For more comprehensive answers for definition questions, include three levels of information:

CONCEPT CHECK 13.7

What are the three parts of a well-developed answer for a definition question?

1. *Name the category associated with the term.* To identify the category, ask yourself: In what group or category of information does this belong? In what chapter (topic) did this appear? What is the "big picture" word or schema for this word?
2. *Give the formal definition.* Give the course-specific definition you learned from your textbook or from class lectures.
3. *Expand the definition with one more detail.* **Figure 13.3** shows seven methods and examples for expanding an answer on a definition question.

FIGURE 13.3

Methods to Expand a Definition Answer

Method	Example
Add one more fact.	Distributed practice often occurs when the 2:1 ratio is used.
Give a synonym.	Distributed practice is the same as spaced practice.
Give an antonym, a contrast, or a negation.	Distributed practice is the opposite of marathon studying or massed practice.
Give a comparison or an analogy.	Distributed practice is like working on a goal a little every day instead of trying to complete all the steps in one block of time.
Define the structure of the word.	The root of *neuron* is *neuro,* which means nervous system.
Give the etymology.	The term *locus* comes from the Latin *loci,* which means *place,* so locus of control refers to a place where there is the control.
Give an application.	Surveying can be used to become familiar with a new textbook, chapter, article, or test.

Study Examples of Weak and Strong Answers

Notice in the following example the difference between a weak answer and a strong answer for a definition question about *distributed practice*.

Question:	**Define the term *distributed practice.***
Weak Answer:	It means you practice at different times.
Strong Answer:	Distributed practice is a time-management strategy that is also related to the Memory Principle of Time on Task. It means that study blocks are spread or distributed throughout the week. Distributed practice, also known as spaced practice, is the opposite of marathon studying.

Category ——————→ (Strong Answer, lines 1–2)
Definition ——————→ (lines 3–4)
One more detail ——————→ (lines 5–6)

CONCEPT CHECK 13.8

Explain why part of a definition answer is objective and part is more personalized or subjective.

CONCEPT CHECK 13.9

How are associations used to answer definition questions?

Essential Strategies for Definition Questions

Course-specific terminology lays the foundation for understanding ideas, concepts, and relationships, so throughout this textbook, learning terminology has been emphasized. When you study for any test, predicting definition questions is relatively easy and is facilitated by textbook features, such as key words in boldface print or lists of important terms in each chapter. Test-preparation strategies should always include self-quizzing activities that include reciting or writing definitions. **Figure 13.4** shows four additional Essential Strategies for Definition Tests.

FIGURE 13.4

Essential Strategies for Definition Tests

▌ **Read the question carefully; underline the word you need to define.**

▌ **Use paired associations and chained associations.** Use paired associations to recall the definition linked to the word you need to define. Use chained associations to retrieve additional information related to the topic to use to expand the definition.

▌ **Include three or more sentences in your answer.** Include the category of the word, a formal definition, and one additional detail.

▌ **Use assisted response.** If you are not able to define the word after conducting a memory search, place a check mark next to the question, and move to another question. Later, use other parts of the test for clues you can use to complete your answer.

EXERCISE 13.3

Improve Your Grade
Online Practice 4: Definition Questions

Answering Definition Questions

DIRECTIONS: On your own paper, define each of the following terms. Use the three-part format for your answers: category, definition, and expansion with one more detail.

1. Define the term *reciting*.
2. You have learned many study strategies in this course. These strategies have one common characteristic: they all emphasize elaborative rehearsal. Define *elaborative rehearsal*.
3. Learning involves intellectual and emotional growth. Self-talk has the power to enhance the learning process, but it can also hinder the learning process. In this course, the focus has been on the power of positive self-talk. Define *positive self-talk*.

> ### FIGURE 13.5
>
> **Essential Strategies for Short-Answer Tests**
>
> ▌ Circle the direction word and underline the key words.
>
> ▌ Determine if the question is closed or open-ended.
>
> ▌ Make a mental plan or short list of key ideas to use in your answer.
>
> ▌ Write a strong, focused opening sentence.
>
> ▌ Expand your answer by adding additional sentences with specific details.
>
> ▌ If necessary, use other parts of the test to locate additional details to expand your answer.
>
> ▌ Proofread and correct any spelling or grammatical errors.

Short-Answer Questions

Short-answer questions are recall questions
that require a short paragraph for an answer.

Short-answer questions are recall questions that require a short paragraph for an answer. Three to seven sentences usually suffice. Sometimes answers for these recall questions look like "mini-essays," and at other times they look like expanded "listing questions" that use sentences to explain the items in a listing. With short answers, both the content of your answer and your writing skills are important. Some instructors will grade higher when you use correct grammar, punctuation, and spelling. **Figure 13.5** summarizes seven Essential Strategies for Short-Answer Tests. Details for these strategies follow.

CONCEPT CHECK 13.10

How are short-answer and listing questions similar? How are they different?

Pay Attention to Direction Words and Key Words

Direction words are words in test questions
that signal a specific kind of answer that is
required.

Direction words are words in test questions that signal a specific kind of answer that is required. To get full points for your answer, your response must reflect the expectation associated with the question word. **Figure 13.6** shows common direction words used for short-answer questions.

FIGURE 13.6

Direction Words for Short-Answer Questions

Direction Word	What Is Required
Discuss/Tell	Tell about a particular topic.
Identify/What are?	Identify specific points. (This is similar to a listing except that you are required to answer in full sentences.)
Describe	Give more specific details or descriptions than are required by "discuss."
Explain/Why?	Give reasons. Answer the question "Why?"
Explain how/How?	Describe a process or a set of steps. Give the steps in chronological (time sequence) order.
When?	Describe a time or a specific condition needed for something to happen, occur, or be used.

As soon as you identify a direction word in a question, *circle it*. Review in your mind what is required by this direction word. Because you want to respond quickly, become very familiar with the direction words and the type of answer each requires. Then, underline key words in the question; you will want to include these key words in your response. Each of the following test questions has the same subject: *visual mappings*. However, answers will vary slightly because of the different direction words used.

> (Why) is recitation important to use while studying a visual mapping?
>
> (Explain how) to create a visual mapping.
>
> (How) should you study from a visual mapping?
>
> (When) should you use visual mappings?

CONCEPT CHECK 13.11

Do you know the meanings of all the direction words? To find out, cover the right column in Figure 13.6. Read the direction words in the left column and define them.

Make a Mental Plan or a Short List of Key Ideas

Look at the key words underlined in the question as you will want to use these key words in your answer. Determine if the question is a *closed question* with specific answers or an *open-ended question* with many possible answers. Conduct a *memory search* for appropriate details for your answer. Then, either make a mental plan or jot down a short list of points that you will want to present in sentence form. Do only what is expected; do not pad the answer with unrelated information or attempt to write an essay.

Write a Strong, Focused Opening Sentence

You will not have space to write a long answer, so begin your answer with a sentence that is direct and to the point. Do not beat around the bush or save your best information for last. The first sentence, when well written, lets your instructor know right away that you are familiar with the subject and your answer is "on target." The first sentence of your answer:

CONCEPT CHECK 13.12

Why is the first sentence of your short-question answer so important?

▌ Should clearly state the main idea of your answer

▌ Should include the key words from the question

▌ Should show that you are responding appropriately to the direction word

▌ May possibly indicate the number of items that you will discuss

▌ May possibly list a series of items you will discuss

Figure 13.7 shows differences in quality in three opening sentences. The first one does not get to the point. The second and third examples are direct, focused, and show confidence.

FIGURE 13.7

Examples of Opening Sentences

Question:	(Why) is recitation important in the learning process?
Weak:	Recitation is important because it helps a person learn better.
Strong:	Recitation, one of the Twelve Principles of Memory, is important in the learning process for three reasons.
Strong:	Recitation is important in the learning process because it involves the auditory channel, feedback, and practice expressing ideas.

CONCEPT CHECK 13.13

Describe characteristics of a well-developed answer for a short-answer question.

Expand Your Answer with Details

Expand your answer with appropriate details to support your opening sentence and show that you understand the question. Use course-related terminology in your answers. Notice the difference between the weak answer and the strong answer in **Figure 13.8**.

FIGURE 13.8

Weak and Strong Answers

Weak: Recitation is important because it helps a person learn. Everyone wants to do the very best possible, and recitation helps make that happen. When you recite, you talk out loud. You practice information out loud before a test.

Strong: Recitation is important in the learning process because it involves the auditory channel, gives feedback, and provides practice expressing ideas. When a person states information out loud and in complete sentences, he/she encodes information linguistically and keeps information active in working memory. Reciting also gives feedback so that a person knows immediately whether or not the information is understood accurately and on the level that can be explained to someone else. Taking time to recite also provides the opportunity to practice organizing and expressing ideas clearly.

EXERCISE 13.4

Answering Short-Answer Questions

DIRECTIONS: Select *two* questions from the following list. Write your answers on separate paper. You may be asked to read your answers to other students or to the class.

1. Explain why *rote memory* is not a reliable method for studying most college materials.
2. Explain how *locus of control* affects a person's response to his or her grade on a test.
3. Discuss important functions of the central executive in working memory.
4. What are the four different kinds of listening?
5. Describe situations when marathon studying can be effective.

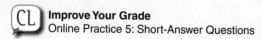
Improve Your Grade
Online Practice 5: Short-Answer Questions

EXERCISE 13.5

Links

PURPOSE: Predicting, writing, and answering practice test questions are excellent ways to prepare for a final exam. This Links exercise provides you with the opportunity to create review tools for your final exam.

DIRECTIONS:

1. Write five of each of the four kinds of recall questions: fill-in-the-blanks, listing, definition, and short-answer. Use information from any of the chapters in this textbook for your questions.
2. Make four copies of your questions. Meet with four other students. Use the review questions from all members of the group to practice answering the questions.

CHECK POINT 13.1

True or False?

_____ 1. When you do not know the exact answer, you may be able to earn partial points in fill-in-the-blank and listing questions by giving synonyms or phrases to complete your answer.

_____ 2. Open-ended questions require a specific answer with items in the answer presented in their original order.

_____ 3. For most definition questions, writing the formal textbook definition with accuracy is an appropriate and sufficient answer.

_____ 4. Each of the following direction words requires a different kind of response: *how, discuss, tell, when,* and *explain how.*

Improve Your Grade
Online Practice 6:
Recall Questions

EXERCISE 13.6

Textbook Case Studies

DIRECTIONS:

1. Read each case study carefully. Respond to the question at the end of each case study by using *specific* strategies discussed in this chapter. Answer in complete sentences.

2. Write your responses on paper or online at the Student Website, Exercise 13.6. You will be able to print your online response or e-mail it to your instructor.

CASE STUDY 1: Jake takes effective notes in his science class. He does well on multiple-choice tests but frequently has difficulty with listing and short-answer questions. He often finds it difficult to complete lists

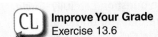

Improve Your Grade
Exercise 13.6

Improve Your Grade
Online Case Studies

or provide depth in his response to short-answer questions. What test-taking strategies do you recommend for Jake?

CASE STUDY 2: In Heather's medical terminology class, many of her tests include definition questions that ask students to explain specific terminology. She writes, verbatim, the definition stated in the textbook. However, she seldom receives full points for her answer. She does not understand what else is required since her answer defines the word with accuracy. What test-taking skills could you explain to Heather to help her increase her test performance?

MATH TEST QUESTIONS

> 2 ▶ *Explain how to use essential strategies for answering math test questions.*

Performing well on math tests requires an alert mind ready to manage a variety of thinking processes and tasks that result in an exact correct answer. Unlike tests for many other subjects that assess your understanding and ability to recall specific *declarative knowledge,* math tests assess your ability to apply *procedural knowledge* you have learned to *new* problems. Math tests emphasize using *skills* that you acquired through practice and repetition, skills that you cannot memorize or master the night before a test. The skills needed to perform well on tests are learned through homework assignments and practice sets that involve working multiple problems and applying problem-solving steps repetitively to the point that you can use the steps to solve new problems that are of the same type with accuracy and speed in a timed setting.

CONCEPT CHECK 13.14

How do math tests differ from other kinds of tests?

FIGURE 13.9

Essential Strategies for Math Tests

▌ **Survey the test and create a plan for budgeting your time.** Skim through the test to familiarize yourself with the types of questions, different test question point values, and the length of the test. Create a quick plan for budgeting your time for each section.

▌ **Begin with familiar problems.** You do *not* need to work problems in the order they appear in the test. By starting with familiar problems, you create the mindset for the math test and build confidence.

▌ **Circle direction words and underline key words.** Read the directions and the question carefully. Circle the direction words; be sure that you understand them. Underline key words in the questions to help you maintain a focus on what is essential.

▌ **Identify and think about the pattern of the problem.** Identify the type of problem involved, recall a prototype, and use the steps for that type of pattern. Ask yourself: *What problems did I study that are similar? What is the pattern? How did I solve problems with this pattern? What prototype did I memorize?*

▌ **See the problem clearly.** Examine the available information. Identify what information is needed, what information is missing, and what information is irrelevant to solving the problem. Try listing the known facts, drawing a simple picture of the problem, or expressing the problem in an algebraic formula.

▌ **Devise a strategy and solve the problem.** Mentally talk or explain to yourself the steps you will use to solve this problem; then apply the steps. Show your work for each problem-solving step.

▌ **Use the RSTUV Problem-Solving Method.** See Chapter 8, page 246.

▌ **Check your work one final time.** If time permits, checking your results can help you eliminate common errors such as omitting labels on story problem answers, using the incorrect mathematical sign of operation, or calculating incorrectly.

Essential Strategies for Math Tests

CONCEPT CHECK 13.15

What are the first things you should do after you read a new math problem to solve?

The essential strategies in Chapter 6 to use during a test apply to math tests as well (page 165). However, the following sections address additional strategies for working specifically with math tests. **Figure 13.9** shows eight Essential Strategies for Math Tests.

Working Memory During Tests

Your working memory needs to perform a variety of cognitive functions as you work through the various steps to solve problems on math tests. Sometimes you and your working memory need a boost to get back on track and working efficiently. Use the strategies in the following sections when you get "stuck" on specific problems.

Go into Retrieval Mode

CONCEPT CHECK 13.16

Explain how to "go into retrieval mode" to solve problems.

Do some type of movement, such as shaking your head, breathing in and out a few times, or using a quick relaxation technique. This activates new activity in working memory to get your mind "unstuck." Look away from the problem and turn your thoughts inward. Ask yourself what you already know about this kind of problem. Try recalling the prototype (model) problem you memorized for this pattern and the steps or formula you used to solve that problem. Use other associations to trigger recall of the related information.

Shift Your Mind

Let your mind shift back and forth between the problem and your memory. Processing math and solving math problems involves a variety of mental activities. Read the problem, shift your eyes off the problem for a few seconds, and start a new memory search for possible things to do to solve the problem. Look back at the problem. This shift between problem and memory searches may occur several times before the necessary information is located in long-term memory and pulled back into working memory for use.

CONCEPT CHECK 13.17

When should you intentionally shift your focus away from a problem?

Mentally Visualize or Reconstruct Information

If you are working on an application problem or a word/story problem, picture the known information and the information you need to find to solve the problem. As you read the following example, try visualizing the story. Then use your skills to answer the questions. As you solve the two questions, be aware of or "watch" your thinking processes and the many functions of working memory.

> **Question:** After playing tennis for 2 h, Ruben ate a banana split containing 650 calories and a fudge brownie containing 250 calories. Playing tennis uses 720 calories per hour. (Visualize this story scene.)
>
> a. Without doing the calculations, did the banana split and the fudge brownie contain more or fewer calories than Ruben burned off playing tennis?
>
> b. Find the number of calories Ruben gained or lost from these two activities.

Give Working Memory a New Problem

If you have tried a variety of strategies to solve a problem, or if you have spent too much time on one individual problem, place a check mark next to the question and move on to another problem. Complete as many problems on the remainder of the test as possible. Do not read or respond hastily. Your working memory needs time to shift from one concept and process to new thinking and problem-solving steps for another problem. If time permits, return to the problem with the incomplete solution. You may be able to see the problem differently and find the solution.

Ten Common Test-Taking Errors

When you receive your graded tests, do an error analysis on the test. Look at the kinds of errors you made and correct the errors so you replace the incorrect thinking about the problem or the process with the correct information. The following are ten common test-taking errors students discover during error analyses.

CONCEPT CHECK 13.18

Which of the ten test-taking errors do you commit the most frequently?

1. *Missing more questions in the first third or the last third of a test:* Errors in the first third of a test (the easiest problems) can be due to carelessness. Errors in the last part of the test can be due to the fact that the last problems are more difficult or due to increasing your test speed to finish the test.
2. *Not completing a problem to its last step:* Take time to review the last step to be sure you show all your work right up to the end of the problem.
3. *Changing test answers from correct to incorrect:* Changing answers without a logical reason for doing so is a sign of panic or test anxiety. Keep your original answer unless you locate an error in your work when you review your work a final time.

4. *Getting stuck on one problem and spending too much time on it:* Set a time limit for each problem. Working too long on a problem without success will increase your test anxiety and waste valuable time that could be better used solving other problems or reviewing your test.

5. *Rushing through the easiest part of the test and making careless errors:* Work more slowly and carefully. Review the easiest problems first if you have time to go back over your work during the allotted test time.

6. *Miscopying an answer from your scratch work to the test:* Systematically compare your last problem step on scratch paper with the answer written on the test. Always hand in your scratch work with your test.

7. *Leaving answers blank:* If you cannot figure out how to solve a problem, rewrite the problem and try to do at least the first step.

8. *Solving only the first step of a two-step problem:* Write *two* in the margin of the test when you first read the problem. This reminds you that you need to show two steps or two answers to the problem.

9. *Not understanding all the functions of your calculator:* To avoid major testing problems, take time to learn all the functions of your calculator *before* the test.

10. *Leaving the test early without checking your answers:* Use the entire allotted test time. Remain in the room and use the time to check each problem.

[Adapted from Paul Nolting, *Math Study Skills Workbook,* pp. 92–95. Copyright © 2000. Reprinted with permission of Houghton Mifflin, Inc.]

EXERCISE 13.7

Error Analysis

DIRECTIONS: Refer to any previous math test (or a science test with equations) that has been graded. Analyze which of the ten kinds of errors you made on the test and list them on separate paper. Create a plan of action to adjust your study, review, or test-taking strategies to reduce or eliminate these kinds of errors on future tests.

CHECK POINT 13.2

ANSWERS APPEAR ON PAGE A5

True or False?

_____ 1. While solving a math problem, working memory must stay focused on only one process until the solution is completed.

_____ 2. On a math test, it is best to begin with the most difficult questions so you do not run out of time to solve them.

_____ 3. Answering math problems often involves identifying patterns, recalling the steps to use for each pattern, and using this information to devise a strategy.

_____ 4. The RSTUV Problem-Solving Method includes these steps: *read, survey, think, use,* and *visualize.*

_____ 5. You can "go into retrieval mode" to recall a formula, a pattern, steps, or get "unstuck" in your thinking.

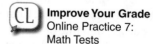 **Improve Your Grade**
Online Practice 7:
Math Tests

> ## GROUP PROCESSING:
> ### A COLLABORATIVE LEARNING ACTIVITY
>
> **PURPOSE:** Form groups of three or four students. Your group will need to have a chart to record information. You may be asked to share your chart with the class.
>
> **DIRECTIONS:**
>
> 1. Brainstorm ways members in your group prepare for essay tests. On your chart, list all the study strategies or systems that members of your group use.
>
> 2. List all the kinds of problems that you encounter when taking essay tests. Include weaknesses you have noticed in your answers and graded tests.

ESSAY TEST QUESTIONS

3 *Explain how to use essential strategies for answering essay test questions.*

Essay questions require an organized composition that develops several main ideas that are related to one thesis sentence. The thesis sentence directly states the main point of your entire essay. The following are important points about answering essay questions:

- Answering essay questions is demanding and requires that you know the information thoroughly, be able to pull the information from your memory, and write about relationships rather than individual facts.

- The way you express the information and the relationships needs to follow a logical line of thinking.

- Essays also require a sound grasp of writing skills (grammar, syntax, and spelling) and a well-developed, expressive vocabulary.

- To prepare for essay tests, include elaborative rehearsal activities that involve categorizing main ideas under concepts and themes; looking for relationships and patterns; and working with information in new ways.

If essay writing is intimidating to you, be assured that with practice you can strengthen your essay-writing skills. Begin by using the three Essential Strategies for Preparing for Essay Tests in **Figure 13.10**.

Essay Test Formats

The most difficult essay tests are those in which your instructor does not announce the topics or the questions in advance, tests in which you cannot use your book or other materials while writing essay answers, and tests with time limitations. Regardless of the essay test format, spend ample time using the Essential Strategies for Preparing for Essay Tests in Figure 13.10.

Essay questions require an organized composition that develops several main ideas that are related to one thesis sentence.

CONCEPT CHECK 13.19

Do the skills in Figure 6.1 (page 158) and Figure 6.5 (page 165) in Chapter 6 apply to essay tests? Why or why not?

CONCEPT CHECK 13.20

What different kinds of essay test formats have you encountered in your classes? Which are easier for you and which are difficult?

FIGURE 13.10

Essential Strategies for Preparing for Essay Tests

▍ **Identify ways subjects are organized.** Use course objectives, your course syllabus, course outlines, the textbook table of contents, and chapter outlines to identify a subject's organization: themes, theories, models, or sequential skill development.

▍ **Create summary notes that include textbook, lecture, and homework information.** Essay questions often require you to compare, contrast, summarize, explain, discuss, or apply information about major themes, theories or models. Create summary notes to group related information that you could use in predicted essay questions.

▍ **Predict, write, and answer practice test questions.** Work with a partner or in a study group to create essay questions and answers. Set a realistic time limit to compose your answers. If you practice expressing your ideas on paper *before the test,* dealing with essay questions on the test is much less stressful and intimidating.

Developing effective test-taking skills involves practice, effort, time, and metacognitive strategies to adjust and improve your performance on tests. What "old" test-taking habits have you replaced with new, more effective strategies?

Topics Are Announced in Advance

When the *topics* for the essay questions are announced in advance, generate detailed notes on the topics. Gather pertinent information; use the index of your textbook to locate information on the topic; reread the pages indicated in the index; and prepare a set of summary notes. Predict possible questions, organize your information, and practice writing answers to the questions you predicted.

Questions Are Announced in Advance

When the *questions* are announced in advance, gather and organize pertinent information; practice writing essay answers. If you are given a list of essay questions from which the actual test questions will be selected, use the index in your textbook, gather pertinent information, and then create and memorize an outline or organizational plan for your answers. Practice writing answers for each question. Work with a study partner or in a study group; compare responses.

Open-Book Essay Tests

Begin by organizing materials for an open-book essay test. Become familiar with the index of your book so you can look up topics quickly. Use a special highlighter to mark important facts (dates, names, events, statistics, and terminology) and quotations you may wish to use in your answer. Use tabs to mark significant pages such as those with important summary charts, tables, lists, steps, or visual materials.

Take-Home Essay Tests

For take-home essay tests, plan your time well. A major problem some students face with take-home essay tests is not allowing sufficient time to develop polished essay answers. Create a plan of action, similar to a five-day study plan, to organize your materials and efficient use of your time. Set your completed essay aside for a day; then, reread it; proofread for spelling, grammar, and mechanics; revise if you see ways to strengthen it; and type the final version. Instructors tend to expect higher quality essay answers on take-home tests than on classroom essays, so do not wait to write your answer the night before it is due.

Essential Strategies for Writing Essay Answers

By planning sufficient time to organize and prepare for an essay test, you will be better prepared to enter an essay test-taking situation with confidence and a feeling of preparedness. On some essay tests, you will be given one essay question to answer. On other tests, you may be required to answer two or more essay questions. Use the following tips when you are required to answer more than one essay question:

- *Examine the essay questions carefully.* If you are given choices of questions to answer, do not automatically choose the questions that look the shortest or the easiest. They are usually more general and more difficult to answer than longer questions that tend to be more specific.

- *Begin with the question that is most familiar.* Starting with a question that you can answer with confidence boosts your confidence level and puts you in the "essay mode."

- *Budget your time carefully.* Allow sufficient time to answer all questions or to at least write some information for each question. If you run short on time, turn in your outline or organizational plan to show the main points you intended to discuss.

Figure 13.11 provides you with six additional Essential Strategies for Essay Tests. The sections following the chart provide additional details.

FIGURE 13.11

Essential Strategies for Essay Tests

- **Read the question carefully and identify the question as closed or open-ended.**

- **Circle the direction word and underline key words in the question.** Quickly review in your mind the kind of answer that will be required for this direction word. Plan to use the key words in your introductory paragraph as well as throughout parts of your essay.

- **Write a strong *thesis sentence.*** A thesis sentence, usually the first sentence of your essay on a test, directly states the main point you want to make in the entire essay.

- **Plan the main points of your essay before you begin writing.** Taking time to develop an organizational plan speeds up the writing process in the long run and keeps you focused on answering the essay question without getting sidetracked.

- **Use a five-paragraph format.** This format uses an introductory paragraph, three paragraphs in the body of the essay, and a concluding paragraph.

- **Proofread and revise if time allows.**

CONCEPT CHECK 13.21

Why are time-management skills essential for preparing for essay tests?

CONCEPT CHECK 13.22

Do these strategies address all of the essay-taking problems you listed in your Group Processing activity on page 379?

Direction Words

CONCEPT CHECK 13.23

What might be the results if you ignore the direction word or do not understand it?

Some of the direction words used in short-answer questions also appear in essay questions. Understanding the direction words is essential for your essay to address the question as it is posed. **Figure 13.12** shows direction words for essay questions and the type of responses expected in your answer. Spend time learning these direction words and their meanings.

FIGURE 13.12

Direction Words for Essay Questions

Direction Word	What Is Required
Compare	Show the similarities and differences between two or more items.
Contrast	Present only the differences between two or more items.
Define	Give the definition and expand it with more examples and greater details.
Trace/Outline	Discuss the sequence of events in chronological order.
Summarize	Identify and discuss the main points or the highlights of a subject. Omit in-depth details.
Evaluate/Critique	Offer your opinion or judgment and then back it up with specific facts, details, or reasons.
Analyze	Identify the different parts of something. Discuss each part individually.
Describe	Give a detailed description of different aspects, qualities, characteristics, parts, or points of view.
Discuss/Tell	Tell about the parts or the main points. Expand with specific details.
Explain/Explain why	Give reasons. Tell why. Show logical relationships or cause/effect.
Explain how	Give the process, steps, stages, or procedures involved. Explain each.
Illustrate	Give examples. Explain each example with details.
Identify/What are	Identify specific points. Discuss each point individually. Include sufficient details.
When	Describe a time or a specific condition needed for something to happen, occur, or be used. Provide details and any relevant background information.

EXERCISE 13.8

Understanding Essay Questions

PURPOSE: Reading and understanding the kind of answer that is expected for essay test questions is an important starting point for performing well on essay tests. Use the strategies in this exercise each time you encounter an essay test question.

DIRECTIONS: Work with a partner or in a small group. Read each question carefully. On the line, write *C* if the question is a closed question and *O* if the question is an open-ended question. Then circle the direction word and underline key words that you would use in your answers.

_____ 1. Contrast the opinions and sentiments expressed by the people of Panama and the American people in 1977 in regard to the ownership and rights to the Panama Canal.

_____ 2. Explain why gross national product is or is not a reliable indicator of a nation's standard of living.

_____ 3. Why should business take on the task of training the hard-core unemployed?

_____ 4. What are the major differences between the economic model of social responsibility and the socioeconomic model?

_____ 5. Define the goal of affirmative-action programs and tell how the goal is achieved.

_____ 6. Explain the differences between general partners and limited partners.

_____ 7. In the late 1990s, environmental issues remained high on the international list of global problems. Attention to environmental issues in the form of global warming is again in the forefront. Summarize the global environmental issues that may have the greatest impact on the welfare of the world's population.

_____ 8. Discuss the changes made in Washington in the post-Watergate years to place greater restrictions on the executive power of the president of the United States.

Thesis Sentence

A **thesis sentence** is a strong, focused sentence that states the main point of an entire essay. The thesis sentence for an essay test should be the first sentence on your paper. The thesis sentence should clearly state the topic of the essay, include key words that are a part of the question, and show that you understand the direction word. A thesis statement may also indicate the number of points you plan to discuss.

The thesis statement is important to you and to your instructor. For you, it serves as a guide for developing the rest of your essay. It suggests the basic outline of main ideas to develop with important supporting details. For the instructor, it serves as an immediate indicator that you understand the question and know the answer. Because of the significance of the thesis statement, take time to create a strong, direct, confident opening sentence. **Figure 13.13** shows examples of two essay test questions, the meaning of the directions words, and examples of strong thesis statements.

A **thesis sentence** is a strong, focused sentence that states the main point of an entire essay.

CONCEPT CHECK 13.24

How does a well-developed thesis statement help you plan your essay?

FIGURE 13.13

Thesis Sentences

Question	Direction	Possible Thesis Statement
(Discuss) the characteristics of each of Howard Gardner's multiple intelligences.	Discuss = tell about What are the eight intelligences?	Each of Howard Gardner's eight intelligences has clearly recognizable characteristics.
(Explain why) elaborative rehearsal is more effective for college learning than rote memory strategies.	Explain why = give reasons What are the reasons? How many reasons?	Elaborative rehearsal is more effective than rote memory because more Memory Principles are used and information in memory is in a more usable form.

An Organizational Plan

Organizational plans for an essay provide an overview of the main ideas you plan to include in your essay.

For many students, organizing information is the most difficult part of writing essays. Many students wander off course or lack a clear vision of the main ideas they want to include in their essays. After writing or drafting a thesis statement, make an organizational plan before you begin writing. **Organizational plans** provide an overview of the main ideas you plan to include in your essay. Outlines, visual mappings, hierarchies, and basic lists are four common organizational **plans you** can quickly develop for your essay answer.

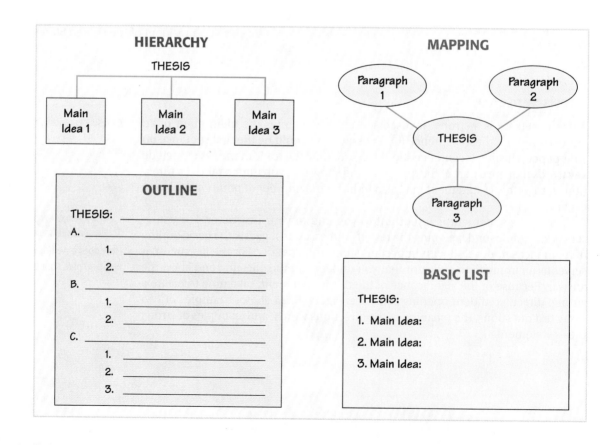

FIGURE 13.14

Key Elements in a Five-Paragraph Essay

Paragraph	Details
Introductory Paragraph (one paragraph)	▍ Includes the thesis statement ▍ Indicates that you understand the direction word ▍ Repeats key words from the essay test question
Body of the Essay (three paragraphs with three different main ideas)	▍ Expands *each category or section* of information in your organization plan into separate *paragraphs* ▍ States a main idea in each paragraph and develops the main idea with details, such as facts, examples, reasons, or definitions ▍ Limits one main idea per paragraph
Concluding Paragraph (one paragraph)	▍ Briefly summarizes your essay or draws a conclusion ▍ Leaves a clear picture in your reader's mind of the main points ▍ Repeats key words from the essay test question

The Five-Paragraph Format

A strong thesis statement and an organization plan that shows the information you want to include in your essay lead naturally to the next step, the actual writing of your essay that clearly explains your thoughts and demonstrates your understanding of the topic. For many students, the *five-paragraph essay* is a format that works well for most essay test questions. The **five-paragraph essay format** consists of an introductory paragraph, three paragraphs in the body of the essay to develop three separate main ideas, and a concluding paragraph. (Note, however, that you can expand this format to a six- or a seven-paragraph essay if you have more than three main ideas to develop in the body of the essay.) **Figure 13.14** shows you key elements of each part of the five-paragraph essay.

Examine the example of an open-ended essay test question shown at the right. Notice how the student identified the direction word and key words, created a thesis statement (not shown), and developed an organizational plan, including details for each main idea. This plan provides the student with a step-by-step outline that can guide the writing process.

The **five-paragraph essay format** consists of an introductory paragraph, three paragraphs in the body of the essay to develop three separate main ideas, and a concluding paragraph.

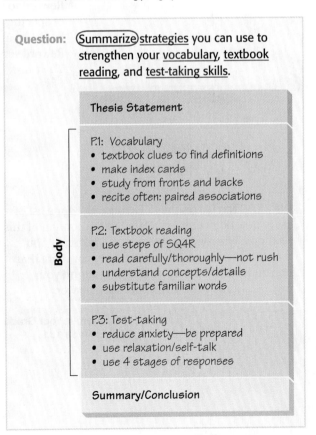

Question: Summarize strategies you can use to strengthen your vocabulary, textbook reading, and test-taking skills.

Thesis Statement

Body

P.1: Vocabulary
- textbook clues to find definitions
- make index cards
- study from fronts and backs
- recite often: paired associations

P.2: Textbook reading
- use steps of SQ4R
- read carefully/thoroughly—not rush
- understand concepts/details
- substitute familiar words

P.3: Test-taking
- reduce anxiety—be prepared
- use relaxation/self-talk
- use 4 stages of responses

Summary/Conclusion

CONCEPT CHECK 13.25

What is the purpose of each paragraph in the five-paragraph essay format?

CONCEPT CHECK 13.26

What do you need to do to avoid an under-developed essay answer?

Performing Well on Essay Tests

In addition to the essential strategies presented in Figure 13.10, the following tips can help you improve your performance on essay tests.

▍ *Weigh the value of different questions.* If one question is worth more points, take more time to develop that answer or to return to that answer later and add more information to strengthen your answer.

▍ *Use complete sentences to express your ideas.* Short phrases, charts, or lists of information are not appropriate for an essay.

▍ *Use supporting details so your essay will not be underdeveloped.* Include facts such as names, dates, events, and statistics; include definitions, examples, or appropriate applications of the information you are presenting. Do not make the mistake of assuming that information is obvious or that your instructor knows what you are thinking or clearly sees the connection. Write as if your reader is *not knowledgeable* about the subject.

▍ *Use course-specific terminology in your answers as much as possible.*

▍ *Strive to write as neatly as possible.* Illegible handwriting will hurt your grade. If you need to delete some of the information, delete it by crossing it out with one neat line or by using correction fluid.

▍ *Strengthen your essay by making the following revisions:*
 - Replace slang or informal language with formal language or course terminology.
 - Reword to avoid using the word *you.* Replace the word *you* with the word *I* or specific nouns, such as *students.*
 - Replace vague pronouns such as *it* with the name of the specific item.
 - Reword sentences to avoid weak "sentence starters" such as *There is . . . There are . . . Here is . . .* or *Here are.*

▍ *Consider writing on every other line.* This gives you space to revise or add information if time permits before the test time ends.

▍ *Consider using a laptop to write essay answers.* If your keyboarding skills are good and you have a laptop computer, ask if you can write your essay on the computer and turn in the disk. Work tends to appear neater and easier to read and is less likely to include spelling errors.

▍ *Learn from your tests.* Writing strong essay answers becomes easier with practice. When you get your essay tests back, read the comments and suggestions. Analyze your essays and ask yourself questions: *Did I predict this question? Did I answer questions directly and in an organized way? Did I include sufficient details?* Adjust your studying and test-taking skills as needed to perform even better on the next essay test.

CONCEPT CHECK 13.27

What kinds of words or expressions should you avoid using in a formal essay?

EXERCISE 13.9

Practice Writing Essay Answers

DIRECTIONS: Go online to Exercise 13.9 for a list of essay questions that are related to the content of this textbook. Follow your instructor's directions. You may be asked to answer one question or more than one question. You may be asked to submit your organizational plan with your essay answer.

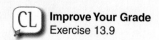

Improve Your Grade
Exercise 13.9

CHECK POINT 13.3

ANSWERS APPEAR ON PAGE A5

True or False?

_____ 1. The first paragraph of an essay should begin with a thesis statement followed by one or more sentences that use key words from the question.

_____ 2. The direction words *contrast, discuss,* and *summarize* are similar in meaning.

_____ 3. In the five-paragraph essay, you can use as many main ideas as needed to express your view of the topic.

_____ 4. An organizational plan shows the main ideas but not necessarily all the details for your essay.

CL **Improve Your Grade**
Online Practice 8:
Essay Questions

REFLECTIVE WRITING 13.2

CL **Improve Your Grade**
Reflective Writing 13.2

On separate paper, in a journal, or online at this textbook's website, respond to the following questions.

1. What does *metacognition* mean to you?

2. In what specific ways have you learned to use *metacognition* this term?

LEARNING OBJECTIVES REVIEW

1 *Explain how to use essential strategies for answering recall questions, which include fill-in-the-blank, listing, definition, and short-answer questions.*

- Recall questions include fill-in-the-blanks, listing, definition, and short-answer questions. Because all recall questions require you to pull information from your memory, memory searches and associations are used frequently to identify appropriate answers.

- Immediate, delayed, and assisted response can be used for recall questions. Even though educated guessing does not work for these questions, you can often use a substitute word, a synonym, or even a phrase in an attempt to earn partial points for some answers.

- Listing and short-answer questions may be closed or open-ended questions.

- Well-developed answers for definition questions include identifying a category for the word, writing a formal definition, and adding one more detail to expand the definition.

- Short-answer questions involve writing a paragraph with a strong opening sentence that clearly states the main idea and indicates that you understand the direction word.

2 *Explain how to use essential strategies for answering math test questions.*

- Math tests involve using procedural knowledge and skills to solve new math problems. Seven essential strategies help you identify patterns, recall prototypes or model examples, and devise and implement a strategy to solve problems.

- Going into retrieval mode, shifting your mind back and forth between the problem and memory searches, visualizing and reconstructing information, and moving to other problems are ways you can use your working memory effectively.

- Identifying ten common test-taking errors and conducting an error analysis on graded tests can help you improve your performance on math tests.

3 *Explain how to use essential strategies for answering essay test questions.*

- You can prepare for essay tests by identifying ways subjects are organized, creating summary notes, and predicting, writing, and answering practice test questions.
- Different strategies are used for tests in which topics or questions are announced in advance, the test is an open-book test, or it is a take-home test.
- Strategies for writing essay answers include identifying the direction word and key words in the question, writing a strong thesis sentence, creating an organizational plan, and using the five-paragraph format for composing an answer.

CHAPTER 13 REVIEW QUESTIONS

ANSWERS APPEAR ON PAGE A5

Fill-in-the-Blanks

Write one word on each line to correctly complete each sentence.

1. The three basic cognitive learning modalities are _____, _____, and _____.

2. _____ questions on tests are questions that require very specific answers, often in a specific order.

3. A _____ sentence states the writer's main point about an entire essay.

4. _____ are words used in objective tests that indicate how frequently or how completely something occurs. Examples are *sometimes, seldom, always,* and *never.*

5. The third step of the Cornell Notetaking System, called the _____ step, promotes talking out loud and in complete sentences.

6. _____ can be eliminated by using goal-setting and time-management techniques that encourage a person not to put things off for a later time.

7. _____-_____ memory and the central _____ are two parts of working memory in the Information Processing Model.

8. _____ is the process of understanding how your mind works, how different learning tasks require different strategies, and which strategies to use for different tasks.

Definition Questions

On separate paper, define two of the following terms. Include details.

1. The Brain Dominance Theory
2. Central Executive
3. The Loci Method
4. Self-Efficacy

Listing Questions

On separate paper, answer the following questions.

1. Name the eight intelligences as defined by Howard Gardner.
2. List four ways to deal with test anxiety.
3. List the steps involved in the SQ4R Reading System.
4. Name any six concentration strategies to deal with internal or external distractors.
5. List the Twelve Principles of Memory.

Short-Answer Questions

On separate paper, answer any *two* of the following questions.

1. Explain how to study from the highlighting done in your textbook.
2. Describe the benefits of using positive self-talk.
3. How do the discrepancies among the rate of speech, the rate of writing, and the rate of thinking affect a person's notetaking skills?
4. Discuss types of time-management schedules students can create to organize their time more effectively.

Essay Questions

On separate paper, answer *one* of the following essay questions. Include your organizational plan with your essay.

1. Describe three important strategies students can use to manage stress.
2. Compare and contrast the functions and capabilities of sensory memory, working memory, and long-term memory.
3. Summarize strategies to use for any three self-management skills.
4. Discuss different kinds of associations you can use when you are learning new information.

 **ACE the Test**
Four Online Practice Tests

 **Online Resources**

Appendixes

APPENDIX A: ANSWER KEYS

Master Profile Chart

	Learning Styles	Processing Memory	Twelve Memory Principles	Time Manager; Goal Setter	Self-Management	Test-Taking Skills	Reading Skills	College Textbooks	Notetaking Skills	Listening; Lecture Notes	Visual Notes	Objective Tests	Recall, Math, and Essay Tests
Chapter:	1	2	3	4	5	6	7	8	9	10	11	12	13
100%	10	10	10	10	10	10	10	10	10	10	10	10	10
90%	9	9	9	9	9	9	9	9	9	9	9	9	9
80%	8	8	8	8	8	8	8	8	8	8	8	8	8
70%	7	7	7	7	7	7	7	7	7	7	7	7	7
60%	6	6	6	6	6	6	6	6	6	6	6	6	6
50%	5	5	5	5	5	5	5	5	5	5	5	5	5
40%	4	4	4	4	4	4	4	4	4	4	4	4	4
30%	3	3	3	3	3	3	3	3	3	3	3	3	3
20%	2	2	2	2	2	2	2	2	2	2	2	2	2
10%	1	1	1	1	1	1	1	1	1	1	1	1	1
0%	0	0	0	0	0	0	0	0	0	0	0	0	0

Beginning-of-the-Term Profile

1. As you begin a new chapter, complete the chapter profile chart. If you prefer, you can complete the profile online and then record your score above.
2. Score your profile. (See Chapter 1, page 4.) Find the chapter number above. Circle your score to show the number of correct responses.
3. Connect the circles with lines to create a graph (your Master Profile Chart).

Profile Answer Keys

CHAPTER 1:
Learning Styles

1. Y	6. Y
2. Y	7. N
3. Y	8. Y
4. N	9. Y
5. Y	10. Y

CHAPTER 2:
Processing Memory

1. Y	6. Y
2. Y	7. Y
3. N	8. N
4. Y	9. Y
5. Y	10. Y

CHAPTER 3:
Twelve Memory Principles

1. Y	6. Y
2. N	7. Y
3. Y	8. Y
4. N	9. N
5. Y	10. Y

CHAPTER 4:
Time Manager; Goal Setter

1. Y	6. Y
2. Y	7. Y
3. N	8. Y
4. N	9. N
5. Y	10. Y

CHAPTER 5:
Self-Management

1. N	6. Y
2. N	7. N
3. Y	8. Y
4. Y	9. N
5. Y	10. Y

CHAPTER 6:
Test-Taking Skills

1. Y	6. N
2. N	7. N
3. Y	8. N
4. N	9. Y
5. Y	10. Y

CHAPTER 7:
Reading Skills

1. Y	6. Y
2. N	7. N
3. N	8. Y
4. Y	9. Y
5. Y	10. Y

CHAPTER 8:
College Textbooks

1. N	6. Y
2. Y	7. Y
3. Y	8. N
4. Y	9. Y
5. N	10. Y

CHAPTER 9:
Notetaking Skills

1. Y	6. Y
2. N	7. N
3. Y	8. Y
4. Y	9. N
5. N	10. Y

CHAPTER 10:
Listening; Lecture Notes

1. Y	6. N
2. N	7. Y
3. N	8. N
4. Y	9. Y
5. N	10. Y

CHAPTER 11:
Visual Notes

1. N	6. N
2. Y	7. Y
3. Y	8. N
4. Y	9. Y
5. Y	10. Y

CHAPTER 12:
Objective Tests

1. N	6. Y
2. Y	7. Y
3. Y	8. Y
4. Y	9. N
5. Y	10. Y

CHAPTER 13:
Recall, Math, and Essay Tests

1. N	6. Y
2. N	7. Y
3. N	8. Y
4. N	9. N
5. N	10. Y

End-of-the-Term Profile

1. Cut a two-inch-wide strip of paper to cover up the original answers on the profile questions at the beginning of each chapter (or complete the profiles on the website for this textbook). Redo all the profile questions so you can see the changes that you have made this term. Write Y or N *next to the number of each profile question.*
2. Score your profile answers using the answer key above.
3. Chart your scores on the Master Profile Chart. Use a different color ink so that you can compare these scores with your original scores.

Chapter Answer Keys

CHAPTER 1: Learning Styles

Check Point 1.1
1. F   2. F   3. T   4. F   5. T

Check Point 1.2
1. F   2. T   3. T   4. F   5. F

Check Point 1.3
1. T   2. F   3. F   4. T

Chapter 1 Review Questions

True or False?
1. F   2. T   3. T   4. T   5. T

Multiple Choice
1. c   2. d   3. b   4. d

Definitions
Answers will vary.*

Short-Answer Question
Answers will vary.*

CHAPTER 2: Processing Memory

Check Point 2.1
1. F   2. F   3. F   4. T   5. F

Check Point 2.2
1. d   2. a   3. d   4. b

Chapter 2 Review Questions
Matching
1. g   2. h   3. f   4. i   5. a
6. b   7. d   8. c   9. j   10. e

True or False?
1. F   2. T   3. T   4. T   5. T
6. F   7. T   8. T

Recall Question
Compare to Figure 2.1.

CHAPTER 3: Twelve Memory Principles

Check Point 3.1
1. T   2. T   3. F

Check Point 3.2
1. F   2. T   3. T   4. T   5. T

Check Point 3.3
1. d   2. d   3. b

Check Point 3.4
1. Feedback
2. goal
3. Organization or Elaboration
4. spaced
5. Review

Chapter 3 Review Questions
Matching
1. g   2. h   3. b   4. a   5. e
6. j   7. c   8. f   9. d   10. i

True or False?
1. F   2. F   3. T   4. T   5. F

Short-Answer Question
Answers will vary.*

CHAPTER 4: Time Manager; Goal Setter

Check Point 4.1
1. T   2. F   3. F   4. F   5. T

Check Point 4.2
1. g   2. i   3. d   4. b   5. j
6. a   7. h   8. c   9. e   10. f

Check Point 4.3
1. T   2. F   3. T   4. F   5. F

Check Point 4.4
1. F   2. F   3. T   4. T   5. T

Chapter 4 Review Questions

True or False?
1. T   2. T   3. T   4. T

Multiple Choice
1. b   2. b   3. b   4. b   5. a
6. d   7. d   8. b

Short-Answer Questions
Answers will vary.*

CHAPTER 5: Self-Management

Check Point 5.1
1. T   2. T   3. F   4. F

Check Point 5.2
1. F   2. F   3. T   4. T   5. T

Check Point 5.3
1. b   2. d   3. a

Check Point 5.4
1. T   2. T   3. T   4. T

Chapter 5 Review Questions

Fill-in-the-Blanks Questions
1. External
2. check mark
3. Incentive
4. Intrinsic
5. efficacy

6. stressors
7. perfect place
8. Procrastination

Multiple Choice
1. d   2. d   3. d   4. a   5. c
6. d

Short-Answer Questions
Answers will vary.*

CHAPTER 6: Test-Taking Skills

Check Point 6.1
1. T   2. F   3. F   4. T

Check Point 6.2
1. T   2. F   3. T   4. F

Check Point 6.3
1. a   2. d

Check Point 6.4
1. F   2. F   3. T   4. T

Chapter 6 Review Questions
Multiple Choice
1. a   2. a   3. c   4. d   5. d
6. b   7. a   8. d

Definitions
Answers will vary.*

Short-Answer Questions
Answers will vary.*

CHAPTER 7: Reading Skills

Check Point 7.1
1. d   2. d

Check Point 7.2
1. T   2. F   3. F   4. F

Check Point 7.3
1. T   2. F   3. F   4. T

Check Point 7.4
1. T   2. T   3. T   4. F

Chapter 7 Review Questions
True or False?
1. T   2. T   3. T   4. F   5. F
6. F   7. T   8. F

Locating Definitions
Discuss your answers with other students or your instructor.

Short-Answer Questions
Answers will vary.*

*Answers vary. Check your answers with another student or with your instructor.

CHAPTER 8: College Textbooks

Check Point 8.1
1. T   2. F   3. T   4. F

Check Point 8.2
1. T   2. F   3. T   4. T

Check Point 8.3
1. F   2. T   3. F

Check Point 8.4
1. T   2. T   3. F   4. T

Chapter 8 Review Questions

True or False?
1. T   2. F   3. T   4. F   5. T
6. T   7. F   8. T

Multiple Choice
1. b   2. d   3. a   4. c

Short-Answer Questions
Answers will vary.*

CHAPTER 9: Notetaking Skills

Check Point 9.1
1. F   2. T   3. T   4. T

Check Point 9.2
1. a   2. d

Check Point 9.3
1. F   2. T   3. T   4. T

Check Point 9.4
1. F   2. T   3. T   4. F

Check Point 9.5
1. T   2. F   3. T   4. F

Chapter 9 Review Questions

True or False?
1. F   2. T   3. F   4. F   5. T
6. T   7. T   8. T

Application
Answers will vary.*

CHAPTER 10: Listening; Lecture Notes

Check Point 10.1
1. F   2. T   3. T   4. F

Check Point 10.2
1. F   2. T   3. F   4. T

Check Point 10.3
1. F   2. T   3. T   4. T

Chapter 10 Review Questions

Multiple Choice
1. b   2. d   3. a   4. d   5. a
6. d   7. b   8. d

Short-Answer Questions
Answers will vary.*

CHAPTER 11: Visual Notes

Check Point 11.1
1. F   2. T   3. T   4. F

Check Point 11.2
1. a   2. d

Check Point 11.3
1. T   2. T   3. F   4. T

Check Point 11.4
1. T   2. F   3. F   4. T   5. T

Check Point 11.5
1. T   2. T   3. F   4. T

Chapter 11 Review Questions

Multiple Choice
1. d   2. d   3. a   4. b   5. c

Application
Answers will vary.*

CHAPTER 12: Objective Tests

Exercise 12.1
1. T   2. F   3. T   4. F   5. T
6. F   7. T   8. T   9. F   10. F

Exercise 12.2
1. T   2. F   3. F   4. T   5. T

Exercise 12.3
1. T   2. F   3. F   4. F   5. T
6. T   7. F   8. T   9. F   10. T

Check Point 12.1
1. T   2. F   3. F   4. T   5. F

Exercise 12.4
1. a   2. b   3. d   4. b   5. d

Check Point 12.2
1. d   2. a

Exercise 12.5
1. e   2. g   3. a   4. k   5. c
6. b   7. h   8. m   9. i   10. f
11. j   12. l   13. d

Check Point 12.3
1. T   2. F   3. T

Check Point 12.4
1. T   2. F   3. F   4. F   5. F

Chapter 12 Review Questions

True or False?
1. F   2. T   3. F   4. F   5. T
6. F   7. T   8. T

Multiple Choice
1. d   2. c   3. c   4. c   5. b

Matching
1. d   2. i   3. a   4. l   5. b
6. j   7. h   8. k   9. e   10. g

CHAPTER 13: Recall, Math, and Essay Tests

Check Point 13.1
1. T   2. F   3. F   4. F

Check Point 13.2
1. F   2. F   3. T   4. F   5. T

Check Point 13.3
1. T   2. F   3. F   4. T

Chapter 13 Review Questions

Fill-in-the-Blanks
1. visual, auditory, kinesthetic
2. Closed
3. thesis
4. Modifiers
5. Recite
6. Procrastination
7. Short-term; executive
8. Metacognition

Definition Questions
Answers will vary.*

Listing Questions
Answers will vary.*

Short-Answer Questions
Answers will vary.*

Essay Questions
Answers will vary.*

---

*Answers vary. Check your answers with another student or with your instructor.

APPENDIX B: EXERCISES, INVENTORIES, AND CHECKLISTS

EXERCISE 2.6

(CHAPTER 2, PAGE 53)

Working Memory Inventory

Think back to the last time you sat down to study. Answer the following questions.

Circle **1** if you did not use the working memory strategy during the study block.
Circle **2** if you used the working memory strategy occasionally during the study block.
Circle **3** if you used the working memory strategy consistently during the study block.

1. I was aware of the kinds of sensory stimuli from the physical world that I was receiving.	1	2	3
2. I used selective attention to focus on important stimuli and ignored the unimportant stimuli and distractions.	1	2	3
3. As I studied, I was aware of different ways I encoded the information.	1	2	3
4. I studied without the interference of visual or auditory stimuli from a television or background music.	1	2	3
5. To avoid information dropping out of my short-term memory, I started thinking about or working with information as soon as I read it.	1	2	3
6. I limited the number of items I studied at one time by working with no more than five chunks of information at one time.	1	2	3
7. I rehearsed or repeated the information in some form at least one time.	1	2	3
8. I worked slowly to give my working memory time to work effectively.	1	2	3
9. I broke large chunks of information in my notes or in the textbook into smaller units to study.	1	2	3
10. I freed up some working memory by removing intrusive thoughts.	1	2	3
11. I paid attention to categories of information or schemas connected to the new information I was studying.	1	2	3
12. I maintained a positive attitude toward studying and toward the subject matter and materials.	1	2	3
13. I was aware of using retrieval cues and conducting memory searches to locate information in my long-term memory.	1	2	3
14. I intentionally created new retrieval cues so I could recall the information more quickly at later times.	1	2	3
15. I spent extra time rehearsing the items in the middle of a list of items because I know the first items and the last items are often easier to recall.	1	2	3
16. I used some form of self-quizzing and "chatted my way" to answers.	1	2	3
17. I took time to connect different pieces of information to each other.	1	2	3
18. I either felt a natural excitement or created an interest in studying.	1	2	3
19. I set a learning goal when I studied so I knew what I wanted to accomplish.	1	2	3
20. I used multisensory strategies to work with the information.	1	2	3

TOTAL SCORE:

YOUR SCORE

20–35 You can make better use of your working memory. Look at all the items that received a "1." Strive to include these strategies when you study.

36–50 You are making average use of your working memory, but there is room to improve. Strive to include the strategies marked with a "1" or a "2" on a more consistent basis when you study.

51–60 You are using your working memory effectively. Continue to use all of the strategies consistently when you study.

EXERCISE 4.1   (CHAPTER 4, PAGE 94)

Three-Day Time Log

DAY 1

Time	Activity	Time	Activity
MIDNIGHT		NOON	
12:30 A.M.		12:30 P.M.	
1:00 A.M.		1:00 P.M.	
1:30 A.M.		1:30 P.M.	
2:00 A.M.		2:00 P.M.	
2:30 A.M.		2:30 P.M.	
3:00 A.M.		3:00 P.M.	
3:30 A.M.		3:30 P.M.	
4:00 A.M.		4:00 P.M.	
4:30 A.M.		4:30 P.M.	
5:00 A.M.		5:00 P.M.	
5:30 A.M.		5:30 P.M.	
6:00 A.M.		6:00 P.M.	
6:30 A.M.		6:30 P.M.	
7:00 A.M.		7:00 P.M.	
7:30 A.M.		7:30 P.M.	
8:00 A.M.		8:00 P.M.	
8:30 A.M.		8:30 P.M.	
9:00 A.M.		9:00 P.M.	
9:30 A.M.		9:30 P.M.	
10:00 A.M.		10:00 P.M.	
10:30 A.M.		10:30 P.M.	
11:00 A.M.		11:00 P.M.	
11:30 A.M.		11:30 P.M.	

DAY 2

Time	Activity	Time	Activity
MIDNIGHT		NOON	
12:30 A.M.		12:30 P.M.	
1:00 A.M.		1:00 P.M.	
1:30 A.M.		1:30 P.M.	
2:00 A.M.		2:00 P.M.	
2:30 A.M.		2:30 P.M.	
3:00 A.M.		3:00 P.M.	
3:30 A.M.		3:30 P.M.	
4:00 A.M.		4:00 P.M.	
4:30 A.M.		4:30 P.M.	
5:00 A.M.		5:00 P.M.	
5:30 A.M.		5:30 P.M.	
6:00 A.M.		6:00 P.M.	
6:30 A.M.		6:30 P.M.	
7:00 A.M.		7:00 P.M.	
7:30 A.M.		7:30 P.M.	
8:00 A.M.		8:00 P.M.	
8:30 A.M.		8:30 P.M.	
9:00 A.M.		9:00 P.M.	
9:30 A.M.		9:30 P.M.	
10:00 A.M.		10:00 P.M.	
10:30 A.M.		10:30 P.M.	
11:00 A.M.		11:00 P.M.	
11:30 A.M.		11:30 P.M.	

DAY 3

Time	Activity	Time	Activity
MIDNIGHT		NOON	
12:30 A.M.		12:30 P.M.	
1:00 A.M.		1:00 P.M.	
1:30 A.M.		1:30 P.M.	
2:00 A.M.		2:00 P.M.	
2:30 A.M.		2:30 P.M.	
3:00 A.M.		3:00 P.M.	
3:30 A.M.		3:30 P.M.	
4:00 A.M.		4:00 P.M.	
4:30 A.M.		4:30 P.M.	
5:00 A.M.		5:00 P.M.	
5:30 A.M.		5:30 P.M.	
6:00 A.M.		6:00 P.M.	
6:30 A.M.		6:30 P.M.	
7:00 A.M.		7:00 P.M.	
7:30 A.M.		7:30 P.M.	
8:00 A.M.		8:00 P.M.	
8:30 A.M.		8:30 P.M.	
9:00 A.M.		9:00 P.M.	
9:30 A.M.		9:30 P.M.	
10:00 A.M.		10:00 P.M.	
10:30 A.M.		10:30 P.M.	
11:00 A.M.		11:00 P.M.	
11:30 A.M.		11:30 P.M.	

THREE-DAY TIME LOG

Activity	Day 1	Day 2	Day 3
School: Classes, labs, studying, test preparation			
School: Meetings, practices			
Work: Job			
Work: Parenting, chores, other work			
Leisure: Family			
Leisure: Friends			
Leisure: Personal time; recreation			
Naps, Sleep			
Snacks, Meals			
Other/Unaccounted for Hours			
TOTAL HOURS (Should be 24)	**TOTAL HOURS:**	**TOTAL HOURS:**	**TOTAL HOURS:**

Exercise 4.4

(Chapter 4, page 104)

Weekly Time-Management Schedule

Time	Monday	Tuesday	Wednesday	Thursday	Friday	Saturday	Sunday
FOR THE WEEK OF			**NAME**				
12–6 A.M.							
6–7:00							
7–8:00							
8–9:00							
9–10:00							
10–11:00							
11–12 NOON							
12–1:00 P.M.							
1–2:00							
2–3:00							
3–4:00							
4–5:00							
5–6:00							
6–7:00							
7–8:00							
8–9:00							
9–10:00							
10–11:00							
11–12 A.M.							

EXERCISE 4.4   (CHAPTER 4, PAGE 104)

Time-Management Self-Assessment Checklist

Name _____   Date _____

Check only the statements that are true for your weekly time-management schedule.

STUDY BLOCKS

My schedule shows:

_____ Sufficient study blocks set aside for *each* class using the 2:1 ratio.

_____ Each study block labeled with the subject to be studied at that time.

_____ Study blocks spread throughout the week (spaced practice).

_____ Two or more study blocks scheduled on the weekend.

_____ No marathon studying (no more than 3 study hours in a row).

_____ The majority of study hours are during the day or early evening hours.

_____ Two or more FLEX blocks scheduled throughout the week.

_____ Study times for most difficult classes scheduled earlier in the day.

_____ Study blocks for lecture and math classes scheduled shortly after class.

FIXED ACTIVITIES

My schedule shows:

_____ Sufficient hours of sleep each night.

_____ A fairly regular sleep schedule throughout the week.

_____ Time set aside for three meals a day.

_____ My work schedule.

_____ Specific meetings or appointments that occur on a weekly basis.

BALANCING YOUR LIFE

My schedule shows:

_____ Time set aside to spend with family and friends.

_____ Time set aside for exercise, hobbies, or recreation.

_____ Time set aside for necessary errands, chores, or personal responsibilities.

_____ Time set aside to work on specific goals.

GENERAL GUIDELINES

Check only the statements that apply to you or your schedule.

_____ I walked through each day in my mind and believe it is realistic.

_____ As much as is possible, I used my peak energy times during the day to study.

_____ I color-coded my schedule so different activities are easier to identify.

_____ Using a schedule will help me have a more organized week.

_____ Using a schedule will help me achieve more tasks during the week.

_____ I will strive to follow this schedule to my greatest abilities this week.

_____ I will note problem areas on the schedule and use this information to adjust next week's schedule.

_____ I will use a "star system" to track the blocks of time I follow successfully.

QUESTIONS/COMMENTS/EXPLANATIONS

EXERCISE 5.3

(CHAPTER 5, PAGE 140)

Stress Test

PURPOSE: Good and bad events in one's life can increase stress levels. Knowing how to manage stress reduces the chances that stress will take a negative toll on your health and emotional well-being. In 1967, Dr. Thomas H. Holmes and Dr. Richard H. Rahe developed the following "stress test" to help individuals identify their stress levels. By knowing stress levels, people can make an even greater asserted effort to use strategies to manage stress effectively.

DIRECTIONS:

1. In the following list of events, circle every experience that you have had in the *last twelve months.*

2. Total the point values next to each of the experiences you circled. Use that total to find your stress level in the scoring section that follows.

Event	Point Value
Death of a Spouse	100
Divorce	73
Marital Separation	65
Jail Term	63
Death of a Close Family Member	63
Personal Injury or Illness	53
Marriage	50
Fired at Work	47
Marital Reconciliation	45
Retirement	45
Change in Health of a Family Member	44
Pregnancy	40
Sex Difficulties	39
Gain of a New Family Member	39
Business Readjustments	39
Change in Financial State	38
Death of a Close Friend	37
Change to a Different Line of Work	36
Change in Number of Arguments with Spouse	35
Mortgage over $50,000	31
Foreclosure of Mortgage	30

Event	Point Value
Change in Responsibilities at Work	29
Son or Daughter Leaving Home	29
Trouble with In-Laws	29
Outstanding Personal Achievements	28
Partner Begins/Stops Work	28
Begin or End School	26
Change in Living Conditions	25
Revision of Personal Habits	24
Trouble with Boss	23
Change in Work Hours or Conditions	20
Change in Residence	20
Change in School	20
Change in Recreation	19
Change in Religious Activities	19
Change in Social Activities	18
Loan Less than $50,000	17
Change in Sleeping Habits	16
Change in Number of Family Gatherings	15
Change in Eating Habits	15
Vacation	13
Holidays	12
Minor Violation of Laws	11
TOTAL SCORE:	

SCORING

Low Stress Level	<149
Mild Stress Level	150–200
Moderate Stress Level	200–299
Major Stress Level	>300

Source: Holmes, T. H. & Rahe, R. H. (1967). The social readjustment rating scale. *Journal of Psychosomatic Research,* 11, 213–218. Publisher: Pergamon Press. Source of article: http://okvoices.org/stress.html.

EXERCISE 6.1

(CHAPTER 6, PAGE 161)

Assessing Your Strategies Inventory

DIRECTIONS: To assess how you are preparing for any test, check the Memory Principles that you are currently using.

_____ 1. **Selectivity:** I carefully select the main ideas and the important details to learn.

_____ 2. **Association:** I link new information to previously learned information, and I create and practice paired associations and chained associations.

_____ 3. **Visualization:** I create and picture images and movies in my mind of information from my textbook and my notes.

_____ 4. **Elaboration:** I encode information in new ways and use elaboration by asking and answering *Why* and *How* questions.

_____ 5. **Concentration:** I use strategies to keep my mind focused on studying.

_____ 6. **Recitation:** I recite information without looking at printed materials.

_____ 7. **Intention:** I create learning goals and plans of action each time I study.

_____ 8. **Big and Little Pictures:** I create study tools that show the relationship between big pictures (concepts) and little pictures (details).

_____ 9. **Feedback:** I use self-quizzing strategies and respond to the feedback that I receive.

_____ 10. **Organization:** I personalize the learning process by rearranging or reorganizing the information into meaningful groups or clusters of related information.

_____ 11. **Time on Task:** I schedule ample time to study, rehearse, and review; I spread studying over different periods of time.

_____ 12. **Ongoing Review:** I practice retrieving and reviewing information on an ongoing basis.

EXERCISE 6.3

Academic Preparation Inventory

DIRECTIONS: After identifying a specific class and the most recent test grade you received in that class, think back to the days prior to that test. Check **YES** or **NO** for each statement.

What is the specific class you are using for this inventory? _____

What was the last test grade you received in this class? _____

		YES	NO
1.	I had all the reading assignments and homework assignments done on time.	____	____
2.	I attended class regularly and was prepared for each class.	____	____
3.	I reviewed comments and my responses on my homework assignments when they were returned.	____	____
4.	I asked questions about information I did not understand.	____	____
5.	I worked with a tutor, with a study partner, or in a review group to prepare for the test.	____	____
6.	I participated in class discussions, asked questions, and responded to questions during class.	____	____
7.	I followed my time-management schedule and used the 2:1 ratio.	____	____
8.	I was an active learner and created a variety of study tools to rehearse and review information.	____	____
9.	I spent time each week reviewing information that I had previously studied.	____	____
10.	I knew the definitions for all the textbook terminology.	____	____
11.	I used study techniques that gave me feedback; I used both positive and negative feedback constructively.	____	____
12.	I read my textbook carefully and took notes on important textbook information.	____	____
13.	I was able to stay fairly motivated about the class and the work.	____	____
14.	I was organized, understood assignments, and had the materials necessary to study and review.	____	____
15.	I created a specific plan of action to prepare for the test.	____	____
16.	I avoided cramming the night before the test.	____	____
17.	I felt confident that I was prepared for the test.	____	____
18.	I can honestly say that I gave it my best.	____	____

All the **YES** responses for the above strategies indicate you are using those strategies effectively.

All the **NO** responses indicate strategies that you could use more effectively to achieve better test results.

EXERCISE 6.4   (CHAPTER 6, PAGE 170)

Test Anxiety Inventory

DIRECTIONS: Check the response that seems to best describe you this term.

	NEVER	SOMETIMES	ALWAYS
1. I have trouble sleeping the night before a test.	___	___	___
2. I can feel a lot of tension in my shoulders, arms, or face on the day of a test.	___	___	___
3. My heart beats fast during a test, and I feel hot, clammy, or downright sick during a test.	___	___	___
4. I am irritable, snappy, impatient, and sometimes even rude right before a test.	___	___	___
5. I try to find excuses not to go to school on the day of a test.	___	___	___
6. I prepare for tests by cramming the day or the night before the test.	___	___	___
7. I read my textbook, but when I start to review for tests, I get worried about how much I do not remember.	___	___	___
8. I procrastinate so much about studying that I am always behind in my assignments.	___	___	___
9. I find myself blaming the teacher, my family, or my friends for the fact that I am not prepared for tests.	___	___	___
10. I run short on time to study and do not make summary notes or review effectively.	___	___	___
11. My negative voice is quick to remind me that I never do well on tests.	___	___	___
12. I cannot seem to forget how disappointed I was with my last grade on a test; I really blew it.	___	___	___
13. It is difficult for me to get motivated to study for tests because the results are always discouraging.	___	___	___
14. I fear the consequences of failing a test because so much is riding on getting good grades.	___	___	___
15. I get so nervous about tests because anything less than my personal standards deflates my self-esteem.	___	___	___
16. I get stuck on one question and do not want to move on until I remember the answer.	___	___	___
17. I get distracted and annoyed by the littlest things others do in class during a test.	___	___	___
18. I am so anxious to get out of the classroom, that I seldom check my answers or proofread.	___	___	___
19. I turn in tests that are incomplete even when I have more time.	___	___	___
20. Without knowing why, I panic and start changing answers right before I turn the test in.	___	___	___
21. I make careless mistakes on the test. Sometimes I can't believe the answers that I marked.	___	___	___
22. My mind goes blank, but as soon as I leave the classroom after taking a test, I remember the answers.	___	___	___

Answers in the **NEVER** column   = Not major indicators of test anxiety.
Answers in the **SOMETIMES** column = Possible indicators; seek ways to alter your approach.
Answers in the **ALWAYS** column   = Strong indicators of test anxiety; use strategies to reduce test anxiety.

| EXERCISE 8.15 | (CHAPTER 8, PAGE 241) |

Textbook Reading Inventory

DIRECTIONS: Complete the following Reading Inventory for different textbooks. Check each reading strategy *that you currently use* for each type of textbook. Continue to use these effective textbook reading strategies. Strategies that you *do not check* are strategies you will want to learn to use on a regular basis to increase your textbook reading performance.

COMPOSITION TEXTBOOKS

_____ 1. I read all explanations and examples carefully.

_____ 2. I highlight key points, jot notes in the margins, or take notes.

_____ 3. I analyze and relate individual parts of the examples to the skills emphasized in that section of the chapter.

_____ 4. I ask myself questions about the examples and explain to myself the structure, details, and processes used.

_____ 5. I create notes or index cards for definitions. I learn the terminology.

_____ 6. I learn the recommended writing steps—even if they are different from my way of writing.

_____ 7. I practice, practice, practice so the writing skills become more automatic.

_____ 8. I work with other students or tutors to get feedback on my writing skills.

_____ 9. I use spaced practice. I allow ample time to work on writing assignments because I know that polished writing is not a process that can be rushed.

_____ 10. I use available writing resources, such as tutorials, videos, and tutors.

LITERATURE TEXTBOOKS

_____ 1. I identify the theme, setting, characters, plot, point of view, author's purpose, and the author's tone (such as serious, humorous, satirical, or sarcastic).

_____ 2. I look for figurative language and special images created through words.

_____ 3. I analyze the author's style by identifying techniques used to unfold events, develop characters, and weave details into the plot.

_____ 4. I look for writing patterns, such as the use of description, narration, and the seven organizational patterns.

_____ 5. I see the big and the little pictures. I identify the most important details or parts of the writing and determine how they blend into the whole picture to develop a theme, purpose, or specific point of view.

_____ 6. I create a visual image or a movie in my mind of the setting, characters, and the action in the plot from the beginning to the conclusion.

_____ 7. I compare elements. I look for similarities and differences among characters, plots, settings, or writing styles between authors or different titles.

_____ 8. I identify relationships. I pose questions about cause-effect relationships, such as: *What caused the character to think or react a specific way? What effect does the setting have on the plot? What would have happened if . . . ?*

_____ 9. I create time lines in my notes to "map out" the main actions in the plot or the storyline.

_____ 10. I read to critique. I form an opinion about the selection and then support my opinion with specific examples, details, or direct quotations.

SOCIAL SCIENCE TEXTBOOKS

_____ 1. I select and use an appropriate reading system to use: SQ4R, Triple Q, Customized, or another system. The system begins with surveying and ends with review.

_____ 2. I learn the terminology. I memorize the definitions for course-specific terminology and include examples and applications with the definitions.

_____ 3. I identify major concepts, patterns, models, and trends.

_____ 4. I look for cause-effect relationships, specific details that support or form a concept, relationships among different groups or categories of information, and specific data or evidence that supports concepts, theories, and models.

_____ 5. I examine and interpret visual materials. I study the data presented in charts, graphs, diagrams, and illustrations and relate the data to the text.

_____ 6. I convert visual materials into verbal explanations.

_____ 7. I visualize and verbalize the information. I create clear visual images of concepts, terms, or processes, and I pose questions, explain information verbally, and recite frequently.

_____ 8. I personalize the information. I attach personal experiences or applications of the information to an event, situation, or person in my life.

_____ 9. I take notes. I use annotations (highlighting, marking, and making marginal notes) and use a notetaking system appropriate for the material.

_____ 10. I use available resources to increase my comprehension and reinforce concepts and details: study guides, lecture outlines, lab lessons, video materials, tutorials, and online resources. I participate in study groups and use tutoring services.

SCIENCE TEXTBOOKS

_____ 1. I look for common patterns, such as cause-effect, process, definition, examples, and whole-and-parts patterns. I also watch for the patterns that classify and list details and the theory-evidence/argument-solution pattern.

_____ 2. I carefully read, examine, and interpret graphic materials.

_____ 3. I examine examples carefully, break them into smaller parts, understand each part, and then explain the relationship of the example to the concept, theory, or principle I am studying.

_____ 4. I create notes or study tools to use to practice reciting and explaining definitions for all the terminology, symbols, and formulas.

_____ 5. I create associations by linking pictures, familiar situations, visual images, or mnemonics to important concepts or charts. I practice the associations so they become retrieval cues for memory.

_____ 6. I create visual materials to show schemas. I draw visual mappings, diagrams, or charts to show relationship among key concepts. I rehearse, recite, and review my drawings.

_____ 7. I think out loud. I verbally explain information, processes, or scientific reasoning to myself, my lab partner, or my study partner. I check my accuracy and use feedback.

_____ 8. I visualize. I create strong visual impressions of processes, charts, or diagrams. I practice looking away from the material and recalling the images from memory.

_____ 9. I use elaborative rehearsal strategies for factual information. I use repetition for procedural knowledge.

_____ 10. I realize that understanding processes occurs in stages and that each time I rework problem sets, lab procedures, or steps to solve a problem, my comprehension deepens. Each time I rework problems, I compare the steps I use and my solution to the original problem and answer.

MATH TEXTBOOKS

_____ 1. I recognize which information is factual and which is procedural. I use appropriate strategies to read and study the two different kinds of knowledge.

_____ 2. I carefully read examples and create prototypes (models) that I memorize and use to recall characteristics of a specific type of problem as well as the steps to use to solve that type of problem.

_____ 3. I translate verbal information into visual forms. As I read word or story problems, I create pictures or charts to show the known information and information I need to find.

_____ 4. I translate visual information into verbal forms. I explain to myself what charts or diagrams represent and how they can be used.

_____ 5. I use math symbols and equations to form sentences. I practice converting numbers and symbols into verbal sentences.

_____ 6. I create strong visual images of equations, formulas, and charts that I can use as retrieval cues.

_____ 7. I practice visualizing and reconstructing images of problem prototypes, patterns, formulas, steps, illustrations, or diagrams.

_____ 8. I rework textbook examples, lecture problems, and homework problem sets and then compare my work to the original problems.

_____ 9. I use repetition, repetition, and repetition to increase my speed and accuracy and understand processes sufficiently that I am able to form generalizations and apply the skills to new problems.

_____ 10. I recognize different forms of the same information. I understand that math concepts may appear as verbal explanations, symbols and formulas, tables and graphs, or real world story problems. Instead of seeing chunks of information as isolated and unrelated, I identify similarities and group or cluster them into related schemas.

EXERCISE 9.1   (CHAPTER 9, PAGE 170)

Annotation Checklist

DIRECTIONS: After annotating a passage, use the following checklist to assess your work.

	NO	SOMEWHAT	YES
1. I completely highlighted only one sentence, the topic sentence, in every paragraph.	___	___	___
2. I selectively highlighted key words or phrases to show details that support the topic sentence.	___	___	___
3. I circled all terminology.	___	___	___
4. I highlighted key words or phrase that define terminology.	___	___	___
5. I numbered details in the paragraphs that appear with ordinals.	___	___	___
6. The notes I wrote in the margins are brief.	___	___	___
7. I used abbreviations for some of the information that I wrote in the margins.	___	___	___
8. To avoid highlighting too much, I used brackets to remind me about larger blocks of important text.	___	___	___
9. For important graphic materials, I marked them and their captions in some meaningful way.	___	___	___
10. At a glance, I can quickly pick out the important points when I review each paragraph.	___	___	___
11. I used colors effectively.	___	___	___
12. I was selective and did not over-mark the paragraphs.	___	___	___

EXERCISE 9.3 (Chapter 9, page 266)

Cornell Notetaking Self-Assessment Checklist

Name _____ Date _____

Topic of Notes _____ Assignment _____

RECORD STEP YES NO

1. Did you clearly show headings in your notes so you can see the main topics? ____ ____
2. Did you underline the headings and avoid putting numbers or letters in front of the headings? ____ ____
3. Did you leave a space between headings or larger groups of information so that your notes are not cluttered or crowded? ____ ____
4. Did you include sufficient details so that you do not need to return to the textbook to study this information? ____ ____
5. Did you use numbering between the different details under the headings? ____ ____
6. Did you indent and uses dashes or other symbols to show supporting details? ____ ____
7. Did you use meaningful phrases or shortened or complete sentences so that the information will be clear at a later time? ____ ____
8. Did you paraphrase or shorten the information so that your notes are not too lengthy? ____ ____
9. Did your notes refer to important charts, diagrams, or visual materials in the chapter, or did you make reference to the textbook pages in your notes? ____ ____
10. Did you write on only one side of the paper, leaving the back side blank? ____ ____
11. Did you label the first page of your notes (course, chapter number, and date) and use page numbers on the other pages? ____ ____
12. Did you write your notes so that they are neat and easy to read? ____ ____

RECALL COLUMN (REDUCE STEP) YES NO

1. Did you move each heading into the recall column and underline it? ____ ____
2. Did you use a two-and-one-half-inch margin on the left for the recall column? ____ ____
3. Did you include study questions in the recall column for the key points in your notes? ____ ____
4. Did you include enough information in the recall column to guide you when you recite your notes? ____ ____
5. Did you include in the recall column some key words that you need to define or explain? ____ ____
6. Did you write the questions and the key words directly across from the corresponding information in your notes column? ____ ____
7. Did you avoid writing too much information or giving yourself all of the information in the recall column, thus leaving you with little to recite from memory? ____ ____
8. Did you try using the recall column? ____ ____
9. Did you add or delete information in the recall column after you tried using that column for reciting? ____ ____

EXERCISE 9.3   (CHAPTER 9, PAGE 266)

Cornell Notetaking Instructor Assessment Form

Name _____   Date _____

Notes for _____

Check the statements that apply to a specific set of Cornell notes.

YOUR NOTES COLUMN

_____ You clearly showed and underlined the headings.

_____ Your notes will be easier to study because you left a space between new headings or sections of information.

_____ Your notes show accurate and sufficient details.

_____ You used meaningful phrases or shortened sentences effectively so that the information is clear and understandable.

_____ You shortened information effectively and captured the important ideas.

_____ Your notes are well organized. You effectively used numbering and indentations for supporting details.

_____ You included important visual graphics from the textbook.

_____ Your notes are neat and easy to read.

_____ You used notetaking standards effectively: you wrote on one side of the paper, you included a heading, and you numbered pages.

YOUR RECALL COLUMN

_____ You used a 2½-inch column.

_____ You placed your headings, questions, and key words directly across from the information in your notes.

_____ Your questions and key words are effective.

_____ Use the recall column to check its effectiveness. Add more self-quizzing questions, visual cues, or hints to guide reciting if necessary.

_____ Use a 2½-inch column on the left.

_____ Place the headings, questions, and key words directly across from the information in your notes.

_____ You need more meaningful questions and key words in the recall column.

_____ You are giving yourself too much information in the recall column; use questions without answers so that you will have more to recite.

AREAS FOR IMPROVEMENT IN YOUR NOTES

_____ Strive to identify and underline headings.

_____ Leave a space before you begin a new heading or section of information so your notes will be less crowded or cluttered.

_____ Include more information in your notes. Your notes lack some important details.

_____ Short phrases or isolated words lose meaning over time. Use more sentences or more detailed phrases to capture important ideas.

_____ Use shortened sentences to capture the important ideas. Your notes are unnecessarily lengthy.

_____ Strive for clearer organization. Number and indent supporting details.

_____ Include graphic information in your notes.

_____ Strive for neater penmanship and readability.

_____ Write on one side of the paper. Include a heading on the first page. Number all the pages of your notes.

OTHER COMMENTS

Photocopy this form before you use it.

(CHAPTER 10, PAGE 304)

EXERCISE 10.4

Lecture Notetaking Checklist

DIRECTIONS: Select any set of lecture notes you have for any one of your courses. Rank the quality of each of the following items in your notes, with **3** representing the highest quality.

	1	2	3
1. The notetaking system I used was effective for the lecture.	1	2	3
2. The headings or main ideas are clear in my notes.	1	2	3
3. I paraphrased the instructor's words.	1	2	3
4. I used shortened sentences but did not lose the meaning.	1	2	3
5. I used abbreviations and/or symbols in my notes.	1	2	3
6. I used a combination of printing and cursive writing.	1	2	3
7. I left a gap or shifted to paragraph form when I started falling behind taking notes.	1	2	3
8. My notes include definitions for important terminology.	1	2	3
9. My notes include supporting details: dates, names, facts, or statistics.	1	2	3
10. My notes summarize examples without including every detail.	1	2	3
11. I numbered individual details so they are easy to identify.	1	2	3
12. I used the instructor's verbal, visual, and nonverbal clues to help identify important information for my notes.	1	2	3
13. My notes include explanations for details or for steps in a process.	1	2	3
14. My notes either include visual materials or references to textbook pages that have those visual materials.	1	2	3
15. My notes are well-organized and have sufficient details so I will be able to use them for studying and review.	1	2	3

TOTAL SCORE:

SCORING YOUR RESPONSES: Total all the circled numbers for your final score.

15–20 Strive to use more effective strategies; your notes may lack sufficient information to be effective as a study tool to review lecture content.

21–40 Continue developing your notetaking skills for the areas ranked 1 and 2; your notes include adequate information for studying, but they could be stronger.

41–45 Continue using your notetaking skills; you have quality notes that you can use to study and review.

EXERCISE 10.6

(CHAPTER 10, PAGE 305)

Instructor Questionnaire

DIRECTIONS TO THE INSTRUCTOR:

In the _____ course, students are developing their lecture notetaking skills. One of your students, _____, chose to use your lecture class to practice notetaking skills. Your feedback on the student's notes would be greatly appreciated. Please take a few minutes to review the student's notes and answer the following questions. Students are asked to turn in this questionnaire with their practice notes.

Instructor Name _____

Class _____

1. Do the notes appear to include the important information presented in the lecture?

    _____ Yes   _____ No   _____ Somewhat

    Comments:

2. Do the notes also show information that was presented on the overhead projector, blackboard, or other form of visual presentation?

    _____ Yes   _____ No   _____ Somewhat

    Comments:

3. In what way could this student improve his or her notes for your lecture?

EXERCISE 11.6

Visual Notes Checklist

Name _____   Date _____

Topic _____   Check one: ____ Visual mapping ____ Hierarchy

	YES	NO
ORGANIZATION		
1. The skeleton with level-one and level-two information is clear and easy to identify.	____	____
2. Connectors or lines clearly connect levels of information.	____	____
3. The visual notes are uncluttered and easy to read.	____	____
4. Headings and supporting details are well spaced.	____	____
5. I was selective and only used key words or short phrases.	____	____

	YES	NO
VISUAL EFFECTS		
1. I used colors or color-coding to emphasize different information or levels of information.	____	____
2. I used borders, shapes, or pictures for some information.	____	____
3. All of the writing is on a horizontal plane.	____	____

	YES	NO
STUDYING FROM THE VISUAL NOTES		
1. I have mentally imprinted the image of the skeleton.	____	____
2. I can visualize the skeleton without looking at the notes.	____	____
3. I have practiced reciting level-three and level-four information without referring to my notes.	____	____
4. I have completed at least one reflect activity with my notes.	____	____
5. I have reviewed my notes at least one additional time.	____	____

Appendix C: Textbook Exercises

NOTE: *You can use Appendix C excerpts to practice any reading or notetaking skills.*

EXERCISE 1.2	(CHAPTER 1, PAGE 15)

Using Cognitive Modalities

SKILL: *Applying Cognitive Modalities*

DIRECTIONS: Work by yourself, with a partner, or in a small group. Follow the directions.

PART 1: Read each statement below. Circle **V** (visual), **A** (auditory), or **K** (kinesthetic) to indicate the modality or modalities used by each student.

V   A   K   1. To review sections of a chapter, Mark looks at the ceiling, mentally recalls pictures and graphs in the textbook, and then recites information about each one.

V   A   K   2. Within the first week of every class, Sharon finds a "study buddy"—someone who wants to meet on a regular basis to discuss class work and topics.

V   A   K   3. After each class, Cindy uses three different colors to highlight main ideas in her notes. She then makes flashcards for the terminology so she can recite the definitions and sort the cards into meaningful categories.

V   A   K   4. Mark loves history and enjoys discovering relationships among different events. He tacked a long piece of paper across his bedroom wall so he can chart all kinds of events on a continuous time line.

V   A   K   5. Liz types all her papers on a computer and then asks a tutor or a friend to read each paper out loud so she can listen to the way she expressed her ideas.

PART 2: Solve the following problem. Pay attention to the approach you use to find the answer.

A parent and a child are standing together on the sidewalk. They both start walking at the same time. Each person begins the first step with the right foot. The child must take three steps for every two steps the parent takes. How many steps must the child take until they both land again on the same foot?

1. How many steps did the child need to take? _____

2. Did they both land on the right foot or the left foot? _____

3. How did you solve this problem?

EXERCISE 3.5

Working with the Twelve Principles of Memory

SKILL: *Create a Visual Mapping*

DIRECTIONS:

1. Expand the following visual mapping for the Twelve Principles of Memory. Add *level-three information.* Be selective. Use any of the other strategies from the chapter for creating visual mappings.

2. Practice visualizing the skeleton and reciting the level-three details for each memory principle.

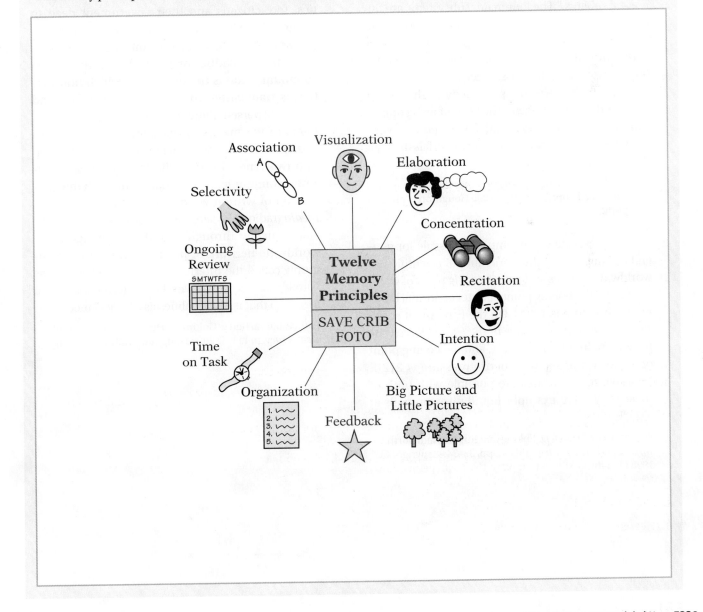

EXERCISE 8.1   (CHAPTER 8, PAGE 216)

Converting Words to Pictures

SKILL: *Draw to Improve Comprehension*

DIRECTIONS: With a partner or on your own, highlight the main idea and the important details in each paragraph. Then, on separate paper, convert the information in the following paragraphs into pictures.

1. The earth system contains a number of interconnected subsystems, often described as "environmental spheres." The four major subsystems are the *atmosphere,* or the ocean of air that overlies the entire earth's surface; the *hydrosphere,* or the water of the surface and near-surface regions of the earth; the *lithosphere,* or the massive accumulation of rock and metal that form the solid body of the planet itself; and the *biosphere,* or the layer of living organisms of which we are a part. All four respond in various ways to the flow of energy and materials through the earth system.

   Source: Holt Atkinson, *Reading Enhancement and Development,* 5th ed., pp. 218–219. © 1995 Houghton Mifflin Company.

2. The Celsius scale is the temperature scale for general use in much of the world and for scientific use worldwide. On this scale, the freezing point of water is 0°C, and the boiling point of water at normal barometric pressure is 100°C. On the Fahrenheit scale, *the scale in common usage in the United States,* the freezing point of water is 32°F, and the boiling point of water at normal barometric pressure is 212°F. Negative temperatures are possible with both of these scales. For example, liquid nitrogen boils at –321°F and –196°C.

   Source: From Darryll D. Ebbing and Rupert Wentworth, *Introductory Chemistry,* 2nd ed., pp. 33–34. Copyright © 1998 Houghton Mifflin Company. Used with permission.

3. "We never talk anymore" is a common lament of couples who are not getting along very well. In politics, too, citizens and their government need to communicate in order to get along well. *Communication* is the process of transmitting information from one individual or group to another. *Mass communication* is the process by which information is transmitted to large, heterogeneous, and widely dispersed audiences. The term **mass media** refers to the means for communication to these audiences. The mass media are commonly divided into two types. *Print* media (newspapers, magazines) communicate information through the publication of written words and pictures. *Broadcast media* (radio, television) communicate information electronically through sounds and images. The worldwide network of personal computers, commonly called the Internet, can also be classified as "broadcast" technology, and the Internet has grown in size so that it also qualifies as a "mass" media.

   Source: Janda/Berry/Goldman/Hula. *The Challenge of Democracy,* p. 111. © 2008 Houghton Mifflin Company.

EXERCISE 11.2

(CHAPTER 11, PAGE 320)

Other Solar System Objects

SKILL: *Using an Excerpt to Create Visual Notes or Study Tools*

OTHER SOLAR SYSTEM OBJECTS

Background

The *solar system* is a complex system of moving masses held together by gravitational forces. At the center of this system is a star called the Sun. Revolving around the Sun are nine rotating planets and over 70 satellites (moons). In addition to the planets and the satellites, the solar system consists of thousands of asteroids, vast numbers of comets, meteoroids, and other solar objects such as interplanetary dust particles, gases, and a solar wind.

Asteroids

Ceres, the first of many planetary bodies between the orbits of Mars and Jupiter, was discovered by an Italian astronomer in 1801. Ceres is the largest of more than 2000 solar objects named and numbered that orbit the Sun between Mars and Jupiter. These objects are called **asteroids**, or *minor planets.*

The diameters of the known asteroids range from that of Ceres (940 kilometers) down to only a few kilometers, but most asteroids are probably less than a few kilometers in diameter. There are perhaps thousands the size of boulders, marbles, and grains of sand.

Asteroids are believed to be early solar-system material that never collected into a single planet. One piece of evidence supporting this view is that there seem to be several different kinds of asteroids. Those at the inner edge of the belt appear to be stony, whereas those farther out are darker, indicating more carbon content. A third group may be composed mostly of iron and nickel.

Like the planets, asteroids revolve counterclockwise around the Sun. More than 26,000 have been cataloged. Although most asteroids move in a orbit between Mars and Jupiter, some have orbits that range beyond Saturn or inside the orbit of Mercury.

Meteoroids

Meteoroids are interplanetary metallic and stony objects that range in size from a fraction of a millimeter to a few hundred meters. They are probably the remains of comets and fragments of shattered asteroids. They circle the Sun in elliptical orbits and strike the Earth from all directions at very high speeds.

A meteoroid is called a **meteor**, or "shooting star," when it enters the Earth's atmosphere and becomes luminous because of the tremendous heat generated by friction with the air. Most meteoroids are vaporized in the atmosphere, but some larger ones survive the flight through the atmosphere and strike the Earth's surface, in which case they become known as **meteorites**. When a large meteorite strikes the Earth's surface, a large crater is formed.

Comets

Comets are named from the Latin words *aster kometes,* which mean "long-haired stars." They are the solar system members that periodically appear in our sky [for] a few weeks or months and then disappear. A **comet** is a reasonably small object composed of dust and ice and revolves about the Sun in a highly elliptical orbit. As it comes near the Sun, some of the surface vaporizes to form a gaseous head and a long tail.

Halley's comet, named after the British astronomer Edmond Halley (1656–1742), is one of the brightest and best-known comets. Halley was the first to suggest and predict the periodic appearance of the same comet (he did not discover it). Halley observed the comet that bears his name in 1682, and correctly predicted its return in 76 years. Halley's comet has appeared every 76 years, including 1910 and 1986.

Source: Adapted from Shipman, Wilson, and Todd, *An Introduction to Physical Science,* 10th ed. (Boston: Houghton Mifflin Company, 2003), p. 381, pp. 404–408. Copyright © 2003. Reprinted by permission of Houghton Mifflin Co.

EXERCISE 11.9

(CHAPTER 11, PAGE 331)

Industries That Attract Small Businesses

SKILL: *Highlight and Create a Comparison Chart*

DIRECTIONS: Read and highlight the following excerpt. Then convert the information into a comparison chart. You will need to identify categories to label the columns.

INDUSTRIES THAT ATTRACT SMALL BUSINESSES

The various kinds of businesses generally fall into three broad categories of industry: distribution, service, and production. Within these categories, small businesses tend to cluster in service and retailing.

Distribution Industries

This category includes retailing, wholesaling, transportation, and communications—industries concerned with the movement of goods from producers to consumers. Distribution industries account for approximately 33 percent of all small businesses. Of these, almost three-quarters are involved in retailing, that is, the sale of goods directly to consumers. Clothing and jewelry stores, pet shops, bookstores, and grocery stores, for example, are all retailing firms. Slightly less than one-quarter of the small distribution firms are wholesalers. Wholesalers purchase products in quantity from manufacturers and then resell them to retailers.

Service Industries

This category accounts for over 48 percent of all small businesses. Of these, about three-quarters provide such nonfinancial services as medical and dental care; watch, shoe, and TV repairs; hair-cutting and styling; restaurant meals; and dry cleaning. About 8 percent of the small service firms offer financial services, such as accounting, insurance, real estate, and investment counseling. An increasing number of self-employed Americans are running service businesses from home.

Production Industries

This last category includes the construction, mining, and manufacturing industries. Only about 19 percent of all small businesses are in this group, mainly because these industries require relatively large initial investments. Small firms that do venture into production generally make parts and subassemblies for larger manufacturing firms or supply special skills to larger construction firms.

Source: From Pride, Hughes, and Kapoor, *Business,* 7th ed. (Boston: Houghton Mifflin Co., 2000), pp. 158–159. Copyright © 2002. Reprinted by permission of Houghton Mifflin Co.

Exercise 11.10   (Chapter 11, page 334)

Kinds of Managers

SKILL: *Highlight and Create Index Card Notes*

DIRECTIONS: Read the following excerpt carefully. Highlight or annotate the information if you wish. Then create a comprehensive set of index card notes. Include at least one question card, two category cards, and as many definition cards as you think are important.

KINDS OF MANAGERS

Managers can be classified two ways: according to their level within the organization and according to their area of management. In this section we use both perspectives to explore the various types of managers.

Levels of Management

For the moment, think of an organization as a three-story structure. Each story corresponds to one of the three general levels of management: top managers, middle managers, and first-line managers.

Top Managers   A **top manager** is an upper-level executive who guides and controls the overall fortunes of the organization. Top managers constitute a small group. In terms of planning, they are generally responsible for developing the organization's mission. They also determine the firm's strategy. It takes years of hard work, long hours, and perseverance, as well as talent and no small share of good luck, to reach the ranks of top management in large companies. Common job titles associated with top managers are president, vice president, chief executive officer (CEO), and chief operating officer (COO).

Middle Managers   Middle management probably comprises the largest group of managers in most organizations. A **middle manager** is a manager who implements the strategy developed by top managers. Middle managers develop tactical plans and operational plans, and they coordinate and supervise the activities of first-line managers. Titles at the middle-management level include division manager, department head, plant manager, and operations manager.

First-Line Managers   A **first-line manager** is a manager who coordinates and supervises the activities of operating employees. First-line managers spend most of their time working with and motivating their employ-

ees, answering questions, and solving day-to-day problems. Most first-line managers are former operating employees who, owing to their hard work and potential, were promoted into management. Many of today's middle and top managers began their careers on this first management level. Common titles for first-line managers include office manager, supervisor, and foreman.

Areas of Management

Organizational structure can also be divided into areas of management specialization. The most common areas are finance, operations, marketing, human resources, and administration. Depending on its mission, goals, and objectives, an organization may include other areas as well—research and development, for example.

Financial Managers   A **financial manager** is primarily responsible for the organization's financial resources. Accounting and investment are specialized areas within financial management. Because financing affects the operation of the entire firm, many of the CEOs and presidents of this country's largest companies are people who got their "basic training" as financial managers.

Operations Managers   An **operations manager** manages the systems that convert resources into goods and services. Traditionally, operations management has been equated with manufacturing—the production of goods. However, in recent years many of the techniques and procedures of operations management have been applied to the production of services and to a variety of nonbusiness activities. Like financial management, operations management has produced a large percentage of today's company CEOs and presidents.

Marketing Managers   A **marketing manager** is responsible for facilitating the exchange of products between the organization and its customers or clients. Specific areas within marketing are marketing research, advertising, promotion, sales, and distribution. A sizable number of today's company presidents have risen from the ranks of marketing management

Human Resources Managers A **human resources manager** is charged with managing the organization's human resources programs. He or she engages in human resources planning; designs systems for hiring, training, and evaluating the performance of employees; and ensures that the organization follows government regulations concerning employment practices. Because human resources management is a relatively new area of specialization in many organizations, few top managers have this kind of background. However, this situation should change with the passage of time.

Administrative Managers An **administrative manager** (also called a *general manager*) is not associated with any specific functional area but provides overall administrative guidance and leadership. A hospital administrator is a good example of an administrative manager. He or she does not specialize in operations, finance, marketing, or human resources management but instead coordinates the activities of specialized managers in all these areas. In many respects, most top managers are really administrative managers.

Whatever their level in the organization and whatever area they specialize in, successful managers generally exhibit certain key skills and are able to play certain managerial roles. But, as we shall see, some skills are likely to be more critical at one level of management than at another.

Source: Pride, William M., Robert J. Hughes, and Jagdish R. Kapoor, *Business,* 5th ed., ©1996, Houghton Mifflin Co., pp. 180–182.

Photo Credits

Chapter 1   p. 2: © Royalty-Free, Flying Colours Ltd/Getty Images; p. 24: © Royalty-Free, Image Source/Getty Images.

Chapter 2   p. 34: © Paul Cooklin/Brand X/Corbis; p. 51: © Royalty-Free, Stockbyte/Getty Images.

Chapter 3   p. 60: © Royalty-Free, Corbis; p. 77: © Royalty-Free, Purestock/Getty Images.

Chapter 4   p. 90: © Royalty-Free, Digital Vision/Getty Images; p. 111: © Royalty-Free, Janis Christie/Getty Images.

Chapter 5   p. 122: © Royalty-Free, Jacobs Stock Photography/Getty Images; p. 145: © Royalty-Free, College Education/Getty Images.

Chapter 6   p. 154: © Royalty-Free, Image Source/Getty Images; p. 170: © Royalty-Free, Adam Crowley/Getty Images.

Chapter 7   p. 182: © Royalty-Free, Stockbyte/Getty Images; p. 195: © Royalty-Free, Digital Vision/Getty Images.

Chapter 8   p. 210: © Royalty-Free, Flying Colours Ltd/Getty Images; p. 230: © Royalty-Free, Leukos/Getty Images.

Chapter 9   p. 250: © Royalty-Free, Digital Vision/Getty Images; p. 275: © Royalty-Free, Corbis.

Chapter 10   p. 282: © Royalty-Free, Stockbyte/Getty Images; p. 297: © image100/Corbis.

Chapter 11   p. 310: © Royalty-Free, Stockbyte/Getty Images; p. 327: © Mark Karrass/Corbis.

Chapter 12   p. 338: © image100/Corbis; p. 360: © Royalty-Free, Digital Vision/Getty Images.

Chapter 13   p. 364: © Royalty-Free, Digital Vision/Getty Images; p. 380: © Royalty-Free, Digital Vision/Getty Images.

INDEX

Page numbers followed by "f" refer to figures; those followed by "t" refer to tables.